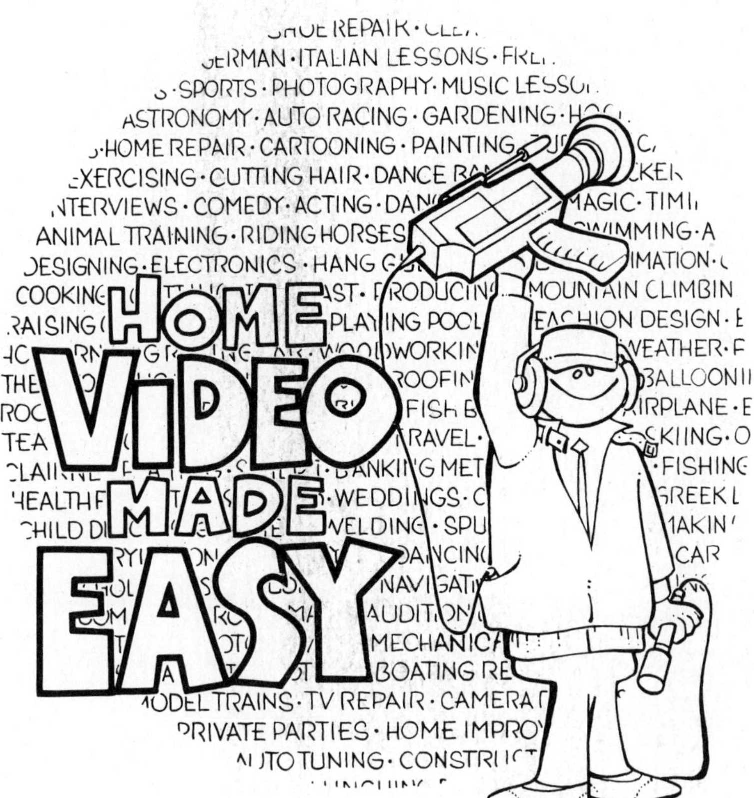
SHOE REPAIR · CLE...
GERMAN · ITALIAN LESSONS · FRE...
SPORTS · PHOTOGRAPHY · MUSIC LESSO...
ASTRONOMY · AUTO RACING · GARDENING · HO...
HOME REPAIR · CARTOONING · PAINTING...
EXERCISING · CUTTING HAIR · DANCE...
INTERVIEWS · COMEDY · ACTING · DAN... MAGIC · TIM...
ANIMAL TRAINING · RIDING HORSES... SWIMMING · A
DESIGNING · ELECTRONICS · HANG G... IMATION
COOKING... PRODUCING... MOUNTAIN CLIMBIN
RAISING... PLAYING POOL... FASHION DESIGN ·
WOODWORKIN... WEATHER ·
THE... ROOFIN... BALLOON
ROC... FISH... AIRPLANE ·
TEA... TRAVEL... SKIING · O
CLAIM... BANKING MET... FISHING
HEALTH... WEDDINGS... GREEK
CHILD... WELDING · SP... MAKIN
DANCING... CAR
NAVIGATI
AUDITION
MECHANIC
BOATING RE
MODEL TRAINS · TV REPAIR · CAMERA
PRIVATE PARTIES · HOME IMPRO
AUTO TUNING · CONSTRUCT
HOME
VIDEO
MADE
EASY

AF478104

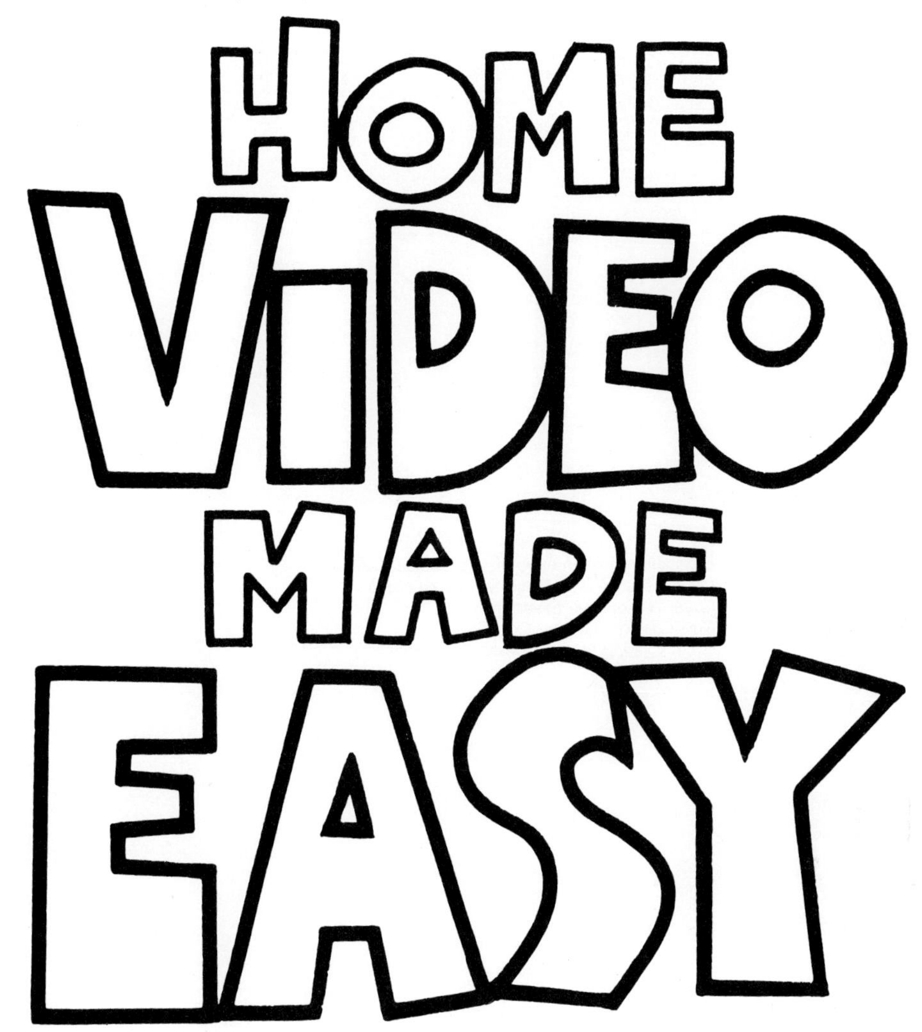

KEN MUSE & DAVE MUSE

PRENTICE-HALL, ENGLEWOOD CLIFFS, N.J. 07632

Library of Congress Cataloging-in-Publication Data

MUSE, KEN, (date)
    Home video made easy.

    Includes index.
    1. Video tape recorders and recording—Amateurs'
manuals.   2. Television—Production and direction—
Amateurs' manuals.   I. Muse, David,   II. Title.
TK9961.M87   1986   778.59′9   85-24439
ISBN 0-13-393042-4

Editorial/production supervision: Denise Gannon
Interior design: Ken Muse and David Muse
Cover photo: Paul Silverman
Cover design: George Cornell
Manufacturing buyer: Gordon Osbourne

Printed in the United States of America

10 9 8 7 6 5 4 3 2 1

ISBN 0-13-393042-4 025

PRENTICE-HALL INTERNATIONAL (UK) LIMITED, *London*
PRENTICE-HALL OF AUSTRALIA PTY. LIMITED, *Sydney*
PRENTICE-HALL CANADA INC., *Toronto*
PRENTICE-HALL HISPANOAMERICANA, S.A., *Mexico*
PRENTICE-HALL OF INDIA PRIVATE LIMITED, *New Delhi*
PRENTICE-HALL OF JAPAN, INC., *Tokyo*
PRENTICE-HALL OF SOUTHEAST ASIA PTE. LTD., *Singapore*
EDITORA PRENTICE-HALL DO BRASIL, LTDA., *Rio de Janeiro*
WHITEHALL BOOKS LIMITED, *Wellington, New Zealand*

DOING WHAT EVERYBODY ELSE CAN DO
IS NO ACCOMPLISHMENT.
BUYING VIDEO EQUIPMENT AND PUSHING
BUTTONS IS NO SUBSTITUTE FOR
ORIGINALITY.

HOPEFULLY, THIS WILL BE YOUR
IDEA BOOK—
NOT YOUR EQUIPMENT BOOK.

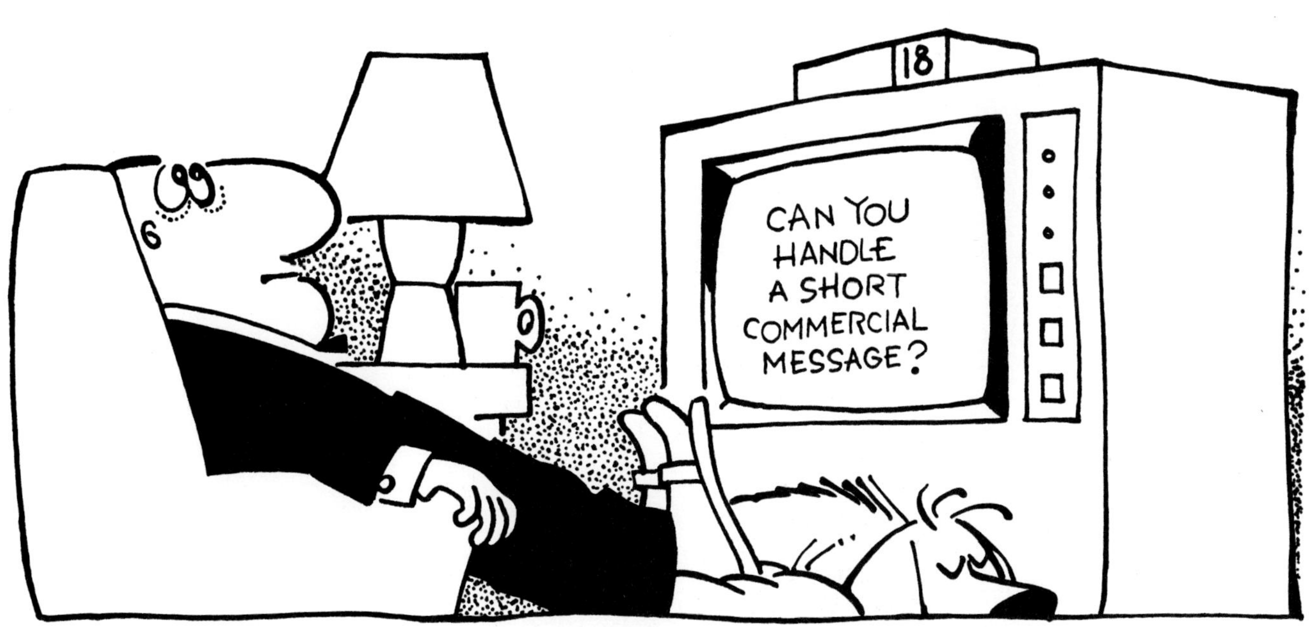

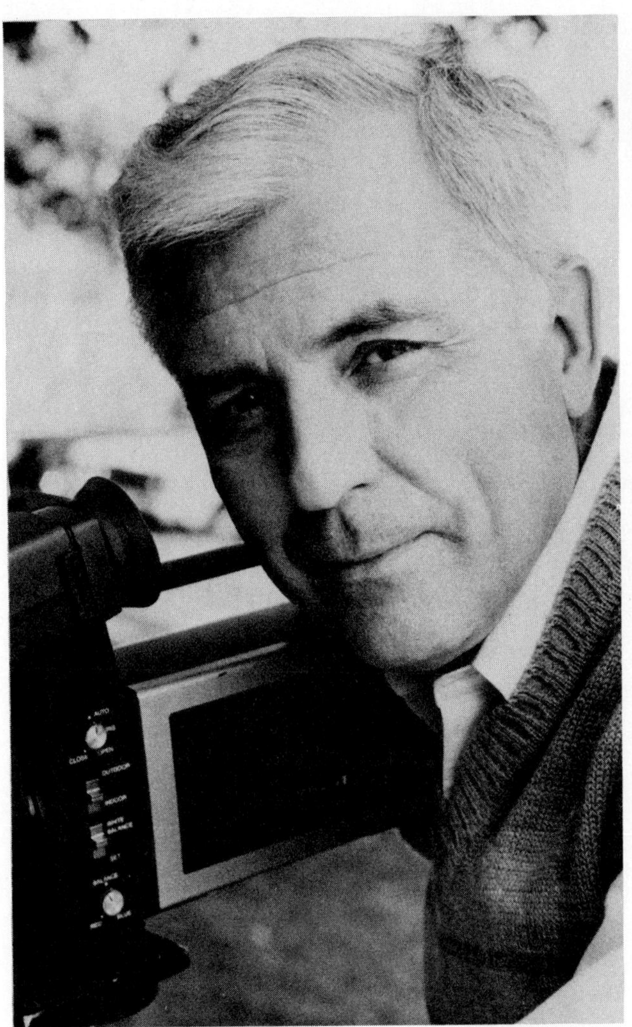

KEN MUSE HAS AN EXTENSIVE CAREER IN COMMERCIAL ART AND PHOTOGRAPHY, ART DIRECTING, ANIMATION, TECHNICAL ART, TV, ADVERTISING, AND A NATIONALLY SYNDICATED COMIC STRIP. FOR OVER 17 YEARS, KEN HAS BEEN TEACHING COMMERCIAL ART AND PHOTOGRAPHY AT MACOMB COMMUNITY COLLEGE IN WARREN, MICHIGAN. THIS IS KEN'S FIFTH BOOK WITH PRENTICE-HALL-THIS ONE IN COLLABORATION WITH HIS SON, DAVID.

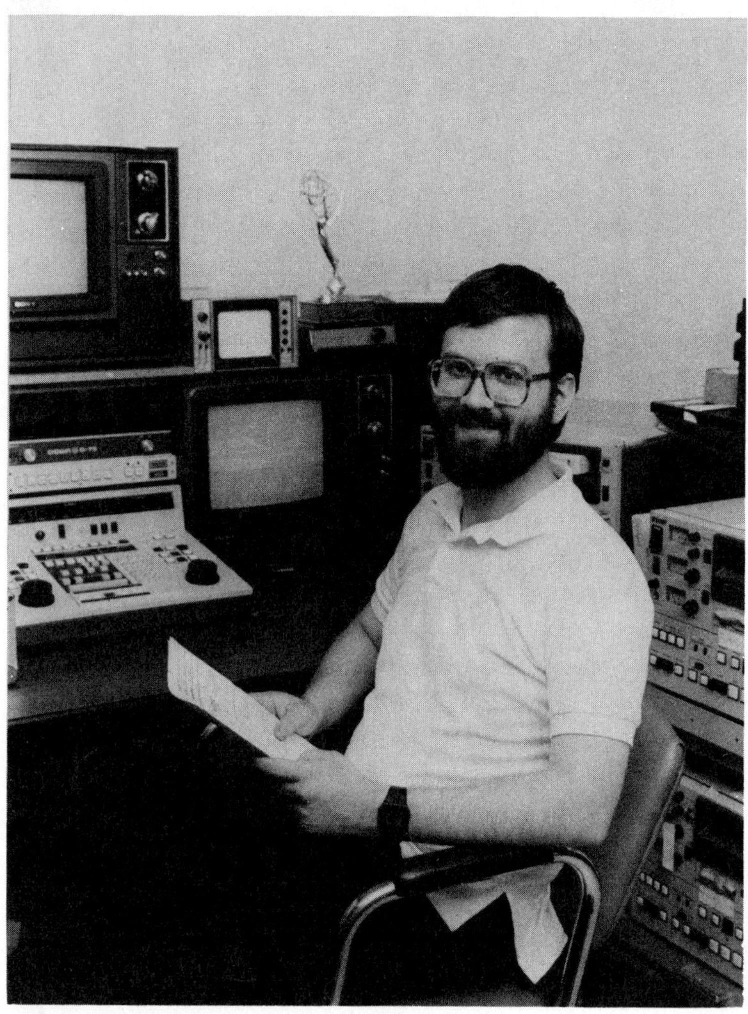

DAVE MUSE IS CURRENTLY TECHNICAL
DIRECTOR FOR THE "PM MAGAZINE
DETROIT" TV SHOW AT WJBK-TV WHERE
HE HAS SPENT HALF OF HIS 15 YEARS IN
BROADCASTING. A VIDEO ADDICT, DAVE
HAS WON AREA EMMY AWARDS FOR
DIRECTING, PHOTOGRAPHY, VIDEOTAPE
EDITING, AND SOUND RECORDING. AT
HOME, DAVE ENJOYS PLAYING WITH HIS
HOME COMPUTER, HIS VIDEO EQUIPMENT,
AND HIS WIFE, KAREN.
(NOT NECESSARILY IN THAT ORDER.)

(ALL PHOTOGRAPHS IN THIS BOOK BY KAREN MUSE UNLESS OTHERWISE INDICATED)

TABLE of CONTENTS

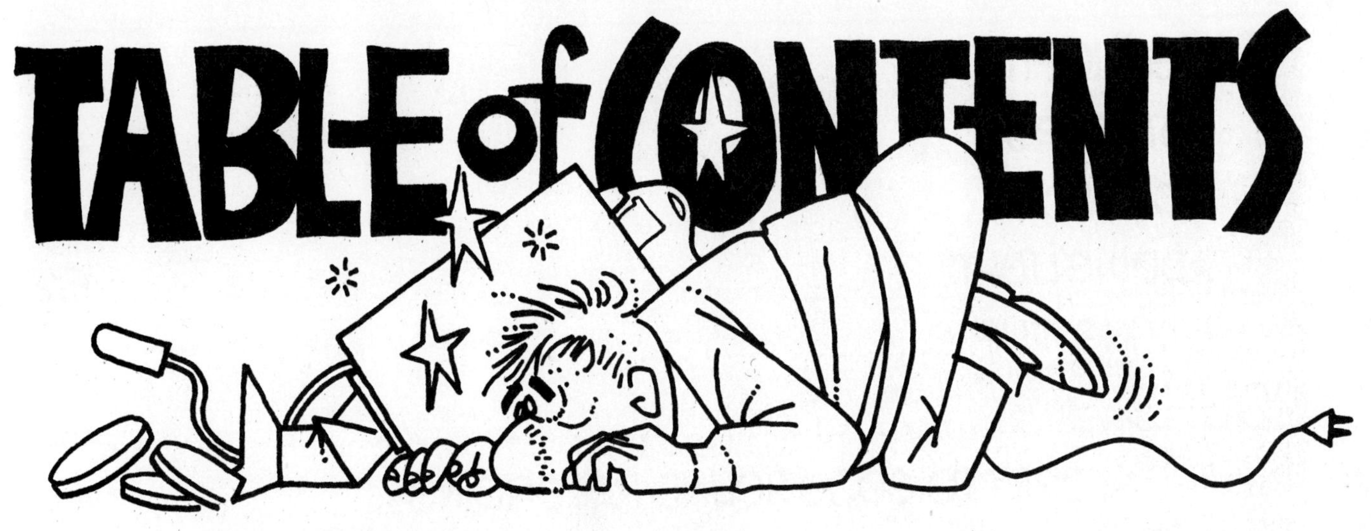

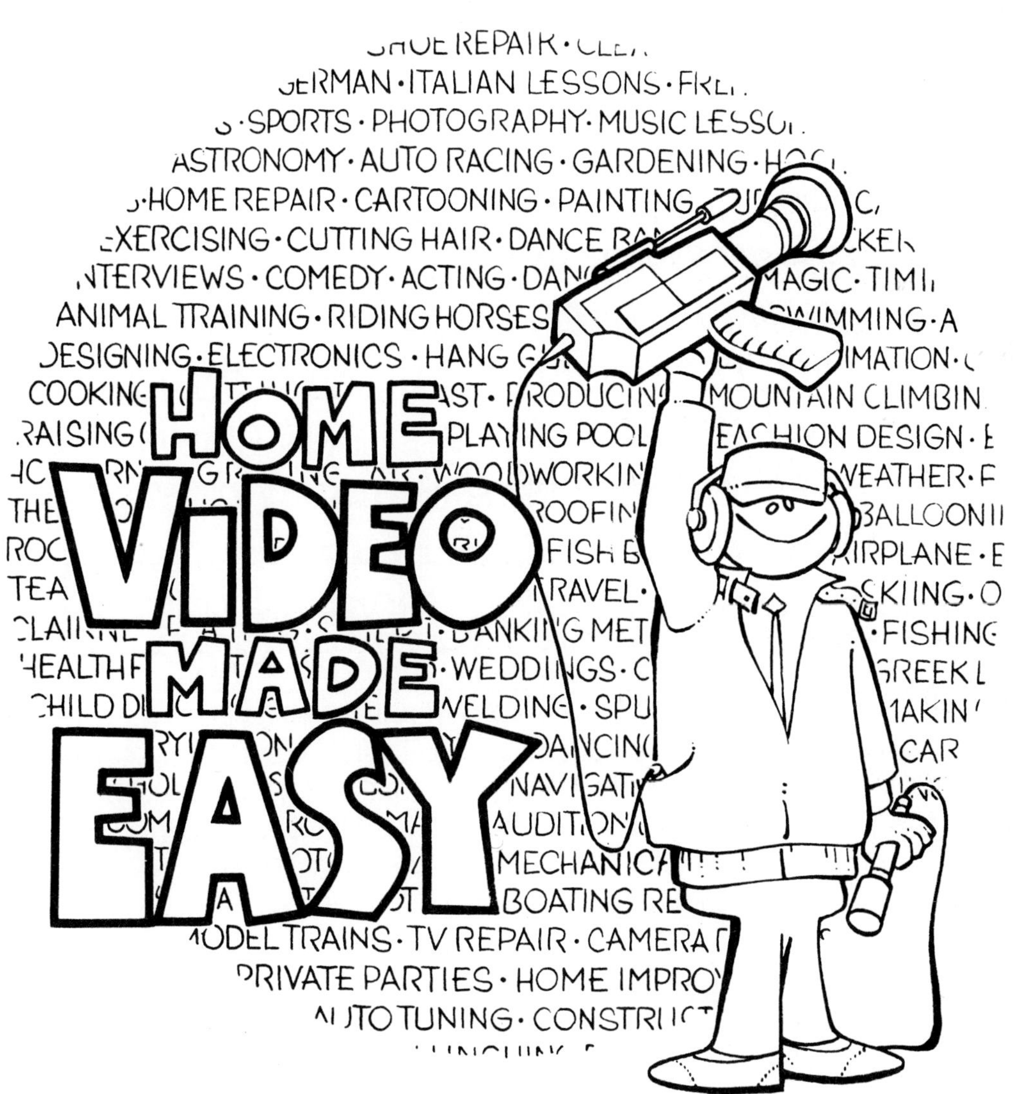

SHOE REPAIR · CLEA
GERMAN · ITALIAN LESSONS · FRE
S · SPORTS · PHOTOGRAPHY · MUSIC LESSO
ASTRONOMY · AUTO RACING · GARDENING · HO
HOME REPAIR · CARTOONING · PAINTING
EXERCISING · CUTTING HAIR · DANCE
INTERVIEWS · COMEDY · ACTING · DAN
ANIMAL TRAINING · RIDING HORSES
DESIGNING · ELECTRONICS · HANG G
COOKING
RAISING
THE
ROC
TEA
CLAI
HEALTH
CHILD D
MAGIC · TIM
SWIMMING · A
IMATION ·
ST · PRODUCIN
PLAYING POOL
WOODWORKIN
ROOFIN
FISH B
RAVEL
BANKING MET
WEDDINGS · C
WELDING · SPU
DANCING
NAVIGATI
AUDITION
MECHANICA
BOATING RE
MOUNTAIN CLIMBIN
FASHION DESIGN · E
WEATHER · F
BALLOON I
AIRPLANE · E
SKIING · O
FISHING
GREEK L
MAKIN
CAR
MODEL TRAINS · TV REPAIR · CAMERA
PRIVATE PARTIES · HOME IMPRO
AUTO TUNING · CONSTRUC
HOME
VIDEO
MADE
EASY

PREFACE

MY
CHANCE TO BE "ON TV" HAPPENED
IN 1967 WHILE I WAS IN THE 9th GRADE AT
KENNEDY JR. HIGH SCHOOL IN ST. CLAIR SHORES,
MICHIGAN. OUR SPEECH TEACHER, MISS MALCHESKI,
WHEELED HER CONTRAPTIONS INTO OUR CLASSROOM ONE
AFTERNOON, ANNOUNCING THAT SHE HAD THE MEANS TO LET US
"CRITIQUE OURSELVES" AFTER WE GAVE OUR SPEECHES TO OUR CLASS.
THE VIDEO TAPE RECORDER WAS A LARGE, FRIGHTENING APPARATUS,
WITH ITS LANDSCAPE OF KNOBS, METERS, AND MEANDERING TAPE
PATH. THE CAMERA, BY CONTRAST, WAS SMALL, AND MADE A DULL BLACK-
AND-WHITE IMAGE THAT ALWAYS LOOKED A LITTLE FUZZY NO MATTER HOW
THE LENS WAS TWISTED. DESPITE ITS LIMITATIONS, IT BOTH ENTERTAINED
AND HORRIFIED US WITH PICTURES OF EACH STUDENT STAMMERING FORTH
HIS ASSIGNMENT. AFTER RECOVERING FROM THE SHOCK OF SEEING HOW
I *REALLY* LOOKED, I WAS HOOKED. I WAS A KID WHO LOVED
MYSTIFYING FRIENDS WITH MAGIC TRICKS, AND THE TV CAMERA
LOOKED TO ME LIKE THE ULTIMATE MAGIC TRICK.
TODAY'S VIDEO EQUIPMENT IS A VAST IMPROVEMENT OVER THE BARELY
ADEQUATE CAMERAS AND BULKY REEL-TO-REEL DECKS OF THAT
FORMER AGE. TO THE POTENTIAL VIDEO MAGICIAN WHO WANTS
TO CREATE TELEVISION... AND NOT SPEND HIS LIFE'S FORTUNE
FOR THE EQUIPMENT, OR BECOME AN ELECTRONIC
ENGINEER TO UNDERSTAND IT... YOUR DAY
IS FINALLY HERE!
I HOPE I CAN HELP YOU WITH YOUR BAG OF TRICKS.

DAVE MUSE

IS THIS BOOK GOING TO BE HARD?

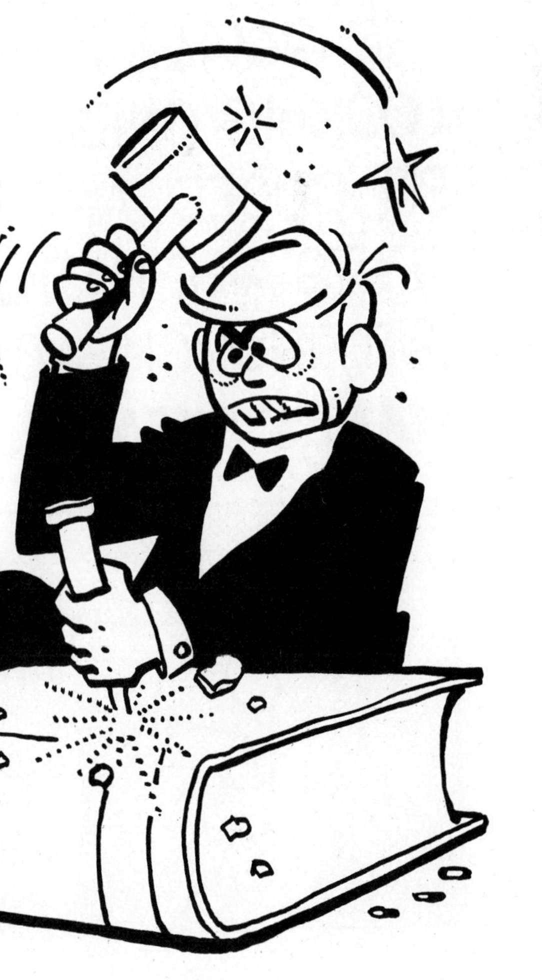

MOST PEOPLE WHO WATCH TELEVISION COULD RIGHTLY CALL THEMSELVES EXPERTS ON TELEVISION COMMERCIALS

WHO HASN'T SAT THROUGH HUNDREDS OF THEM IN A WEEK'S WORTH OF TELEVISION WATCHING? BESIDES BEING ABLE TO RECITE SLOGANS AND JINGLES BY THE **DOZEN**, YOU HAVE PROBABLY NOTICED A FEW FINER POINTS TOO.

HAVE YOU EVER COMMENTED TO A FRIEND ABOUT THE **QUALITY** OF A COMMERCIAL? THE *"CHEAP"* LOOKING ONES ALWAYS SEEM TO BE LOCALLY PRODUCED, AND THE REALLY *"SLICK"* LOOKING SPOTS ARE NATIONAL CONCERNS. WHAT EXACTLY IS IT, THOUGH, ABOUT LOCAL COMMERCIALS THAT **MAKES THEM LOOK CHEAP?**

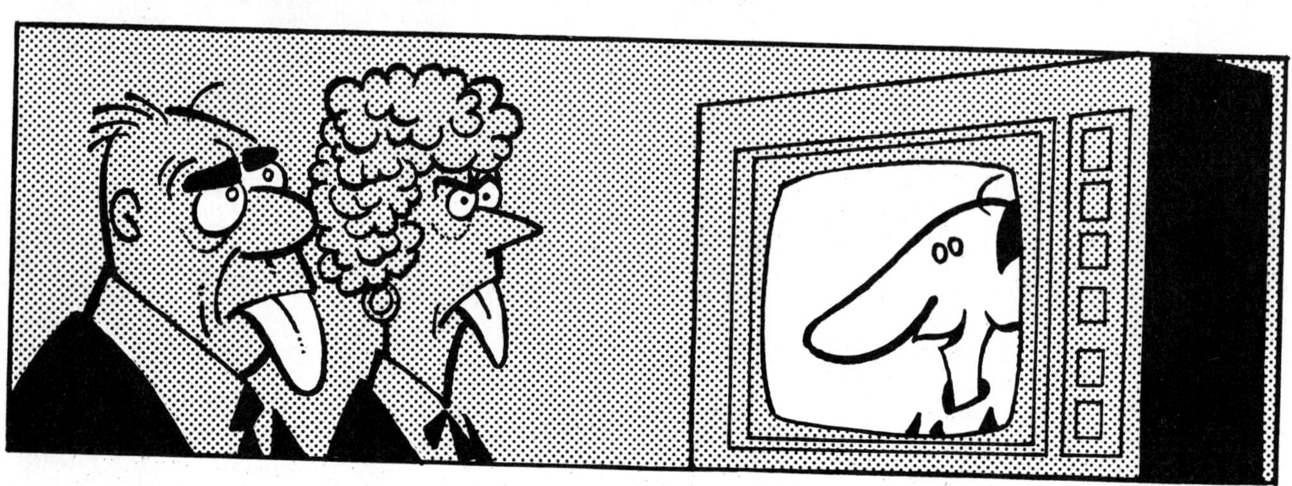

GENERALLY SPEAKING THOUGH, IT'S NOT SIMPLY ONE FACTOR THAT SETS THE LOCAL COMMERCIALS APART FROM THE NATIONAL ONES. LIKE A RECIPE FOR AN **EXQUISITE DISH,** ALL THE INGREDIENTS MUST BE PRESENT IN THEIR PROPER PROPORTIONS FOR IT TO WORK. *THE QUALITY OF THE PERFORMER, LIGHTING, CAMERA WORK, SOUND RECORDINGS, EDITING, WRITING, DIRECTION—* AND A DOZEN OTHER FACTORS ALL CONTRIBUTE TO THE OVER-ALL IMPRESSION THE COMMERCIAL GIVES YOU.

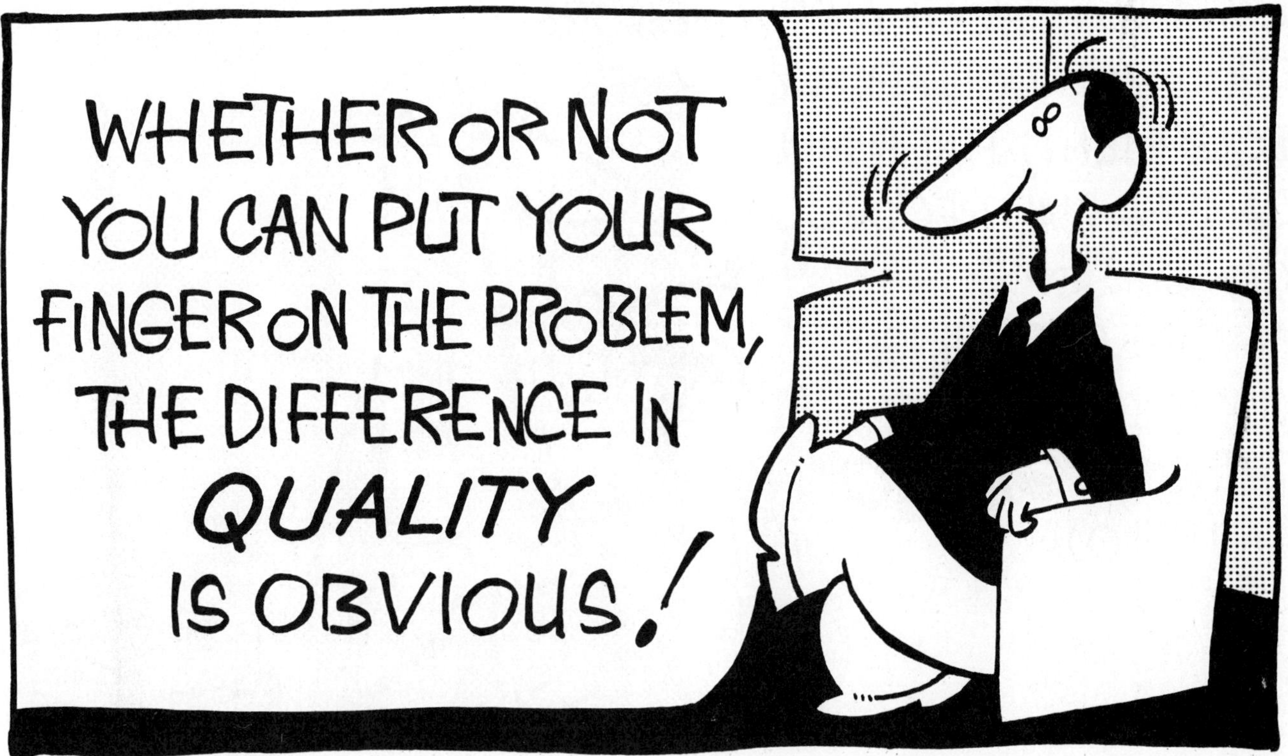

THIS BOOK WILL TEACH YOU
EXACTLY WHAT THE DIFFERENCE IS.
IT WILL SHOW YOU HOW THE
PROFESSIONALS PRODUCE TELEVISION.
IT WILL ALSO SHOW YOU HOW –
AS AN AMATEUR – TO PRODUCE
QUALITY TELEVISION WITH INEX-
PENSIVE EQUIPMENT.

YOU PROBABLY DON'T HAVE A
MILLION-DOLLAR TELEVISION STUDIO
AT YOUR DISPOSAL. IN FACT, THE
ONLY PIECES OF TELEVISION
EQUIPMENT YOU MAY OWN ARE A
CAMERA AND RECORDER. WHILE
THERE ARE SOME THINGS YOU JUST
CAN'T DO WITHOUT A FEW HUNDRED
THOUSAND DOLLARS WORTH OF
EQUIPMENT, THAT SIMPLE
CAMERA AND RECORDER
CAN DO SOME
MARVELOUS THINGS
(INCLUDING A FEW
THINGS A *STUDIO*
CAN'T DO).

YOU MAY NOT BE
ABLE TO PRODUCE
NATIONAL COMMERCIALS
BY THE END OF THIS BOOK.
(THOUGH YOU COULD
PERHAPS CHALLENGE
SOME OF THE LOCAL ONES.)
YOU MAY NOT BE ABLE TO TAKE YOUR
CAMERA APART AND PUT IT TOGETHER
AGAIN (NO, YOU DON'T NEED TO KNOW HOW.)

YOU MIGHT, HOWEVER,
BE SURPRISED HOW
EASY IT IS TO CREATE
HOURS OF ENTERTAINING
TELEVISION.. WHETHER
IT'S COUSIN CINDY'S
WEDDING OR YOUR OWN
ROCK VIDEO!

YOUR VIDEO CAMERA

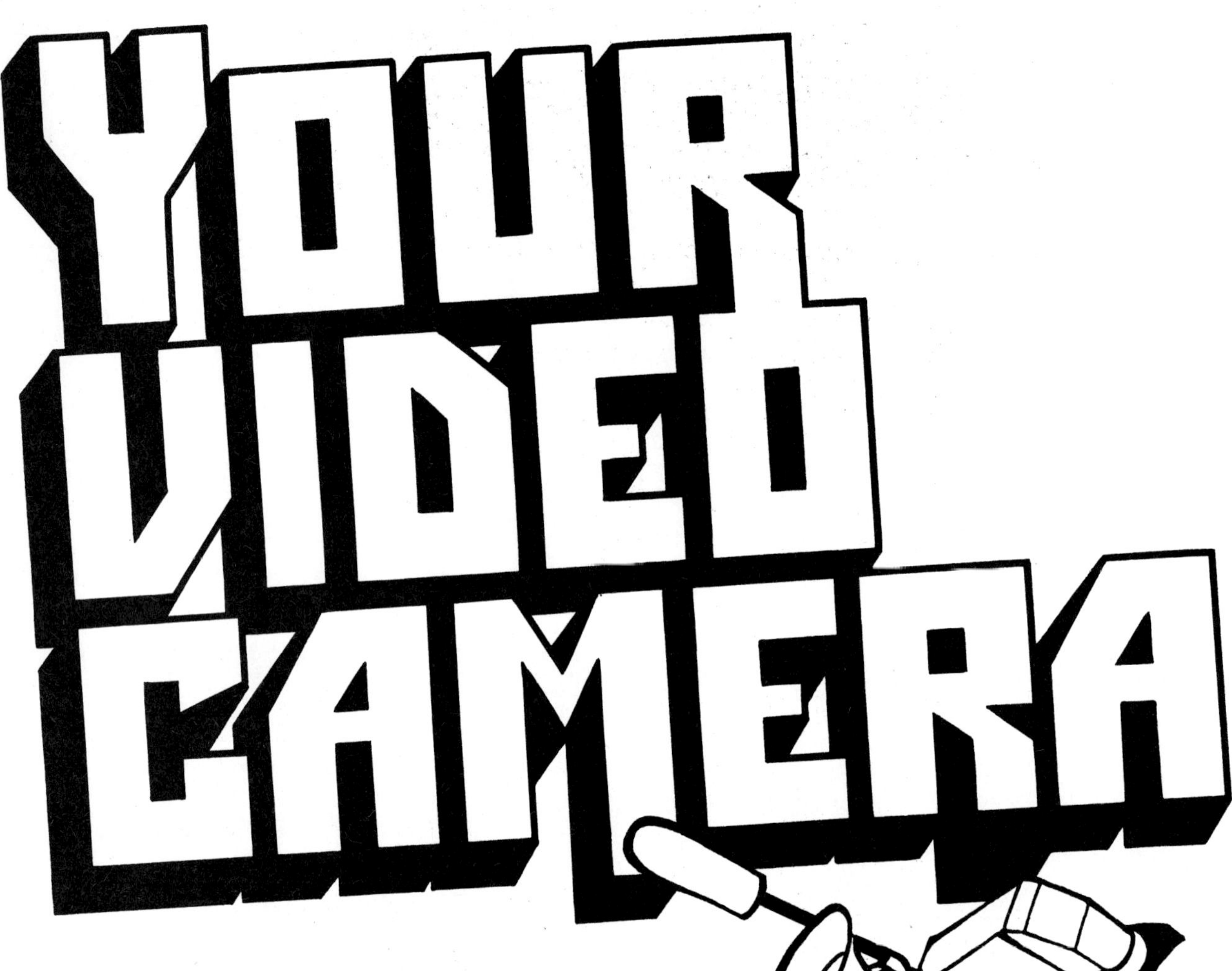

IF YOU HAD TRIED TO BUY A COLOR TV CAMERA 25 YEARS AGO, YOUR PURCHASE WOULD NOT ONLY HAVE RUN YOU HUNDREDS OF THOUSANDS OF DOLLARS, BUT YOU WOULD BE FACED WITH LUGGING HOME A CAMERA THE SIZE OF A REFRIGERATOR!

THE TECHNOLOGY THAT BROUGHT THAT EARLY MONSTER (WITH THE TWO INCH THICK CABLES) DOWN TO A FEW OUNCES AND A COUPLE OF WEEKS' EARNINGS, HAS ALSO ADDED MANY FEATURES NOT FOUND ON THE PROFESSIONAL CAMERAS OF THE PAST. A CUMBERSOME LENS TURRET, WHICH WAS ROTATED TO PUT THE APPROPRIATE LENS ON THE CAMERA, HAS BEEN REPLACED BY A COMPACT ZOOM LENS. COLOR BALANCING ONCE TOOK A TEAM OF TECHNICIANS AND A BANK OF SPECIAL EQUIPMENT. ON YOUR CAMERA, YOU NEED ONLY PUSH A BUTTON . . . . EARLY CAMERAS ALSO REQUIRED DAILY ADJUSTMENT AND REPAIR, WHEREAS YOUR CAMERA IS ALMOST MAINTENANCE-FREE — *AND PROBABLY NEARLY ADJUSTMENT-FREE AS WELL!*

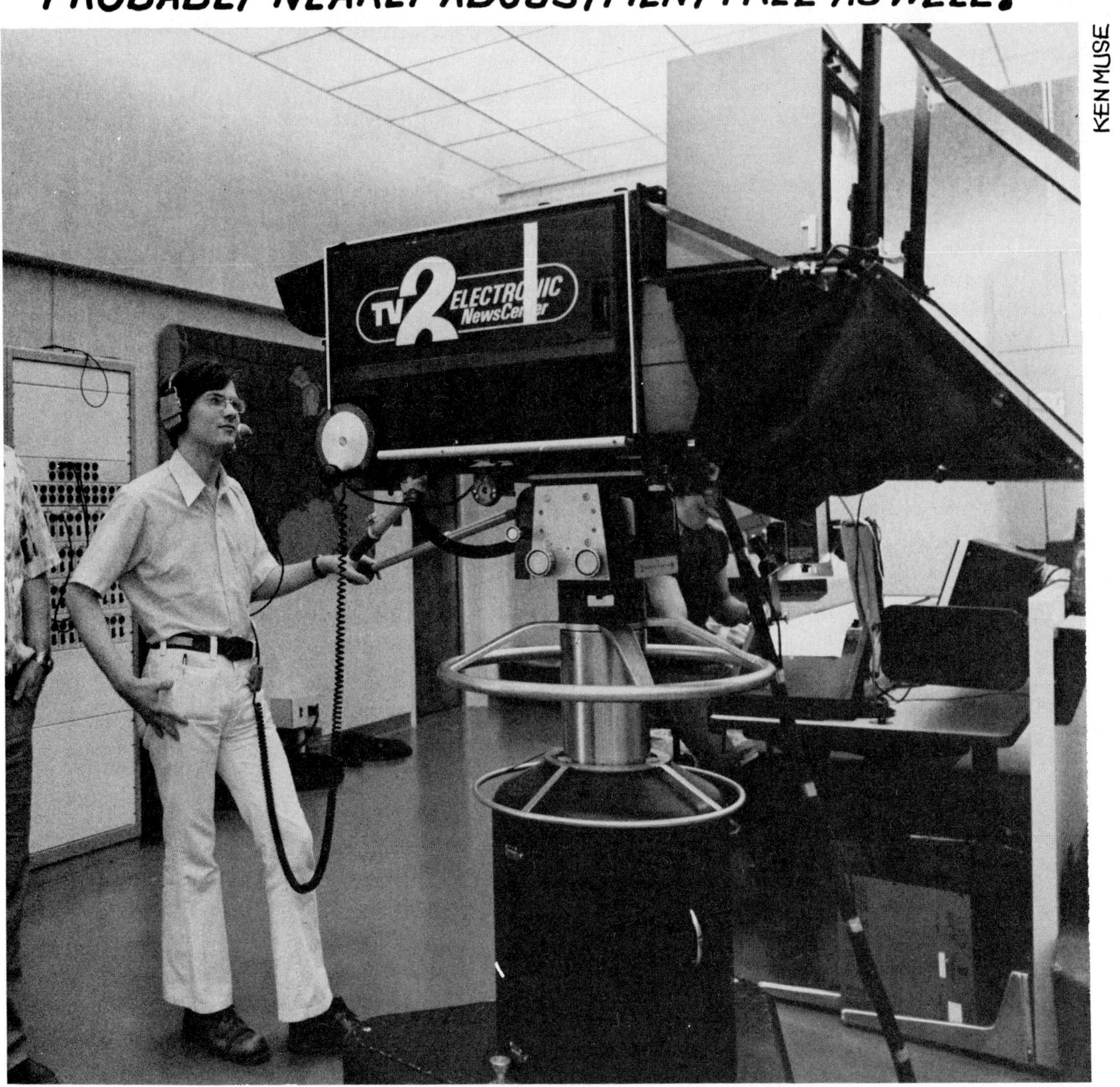

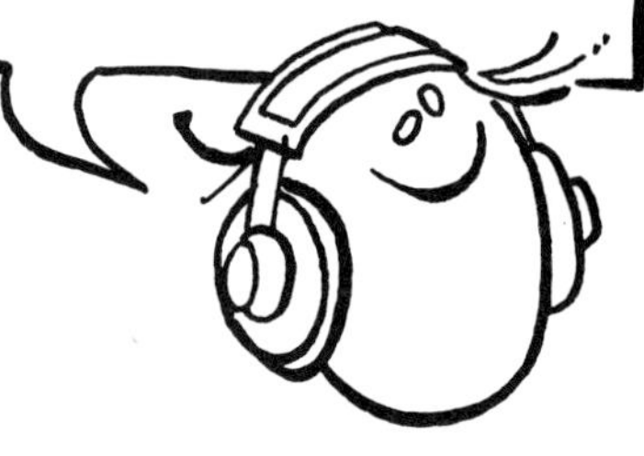

A CAMERA THAT EXPOSES AND FOCUSES ITSELF IS PERFECT FOR THE *NEOPHYTE* VIDEOGRAPHER WHO WANTS *GOOD RESULTS RIGHT AWAY!*

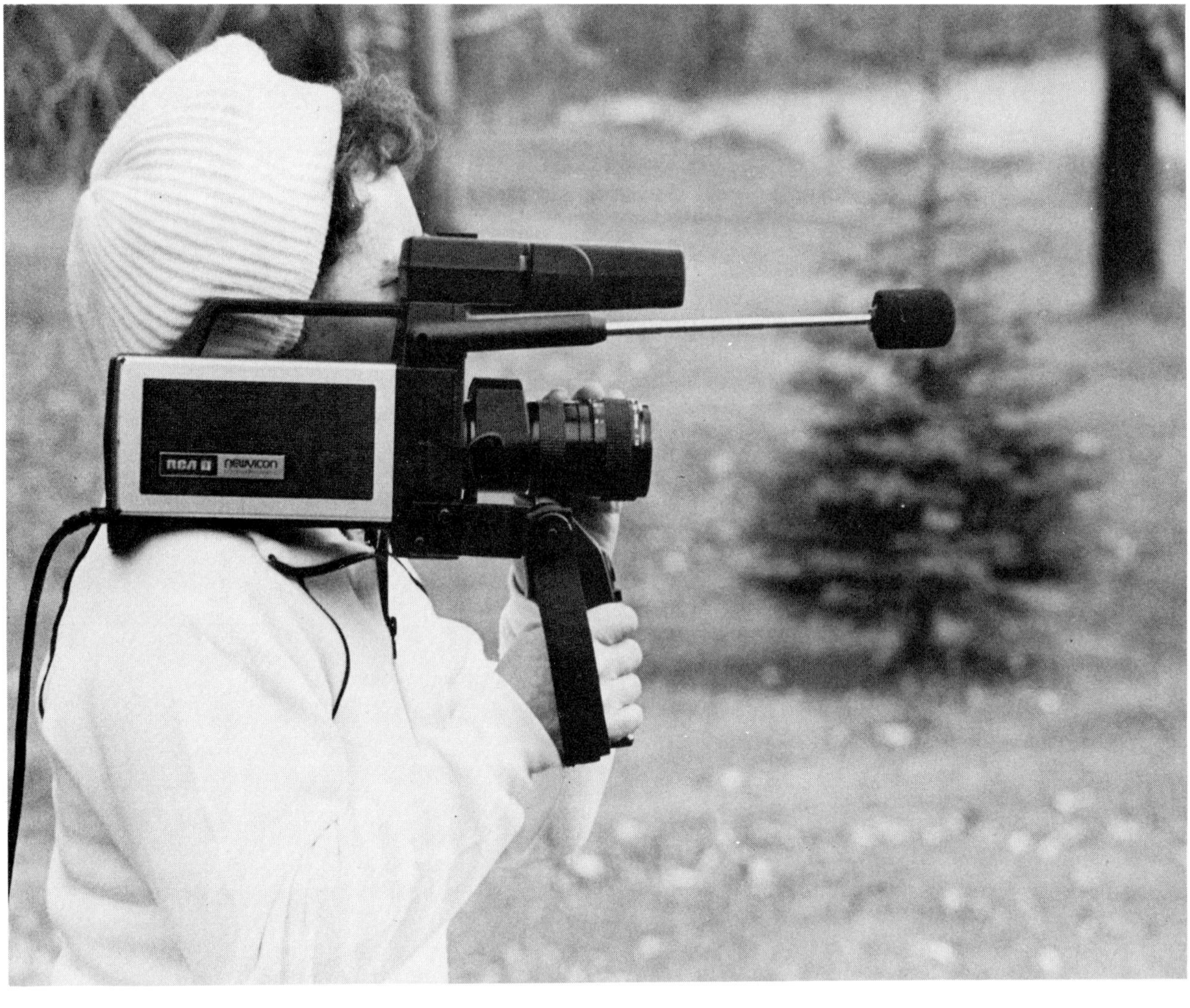

ONCE YOU'VE LEARNED HOW TO EXPOSE AND FOCUS FOR YOURSELF, HOWEVER, YOU'LL SEE HOW YOU CAN OFTEN DO A BETTER JOB THAN YOUR CAMERA CAN.

NO CAMERA CAN THINK LIKE A PHOTOGRAPHER!

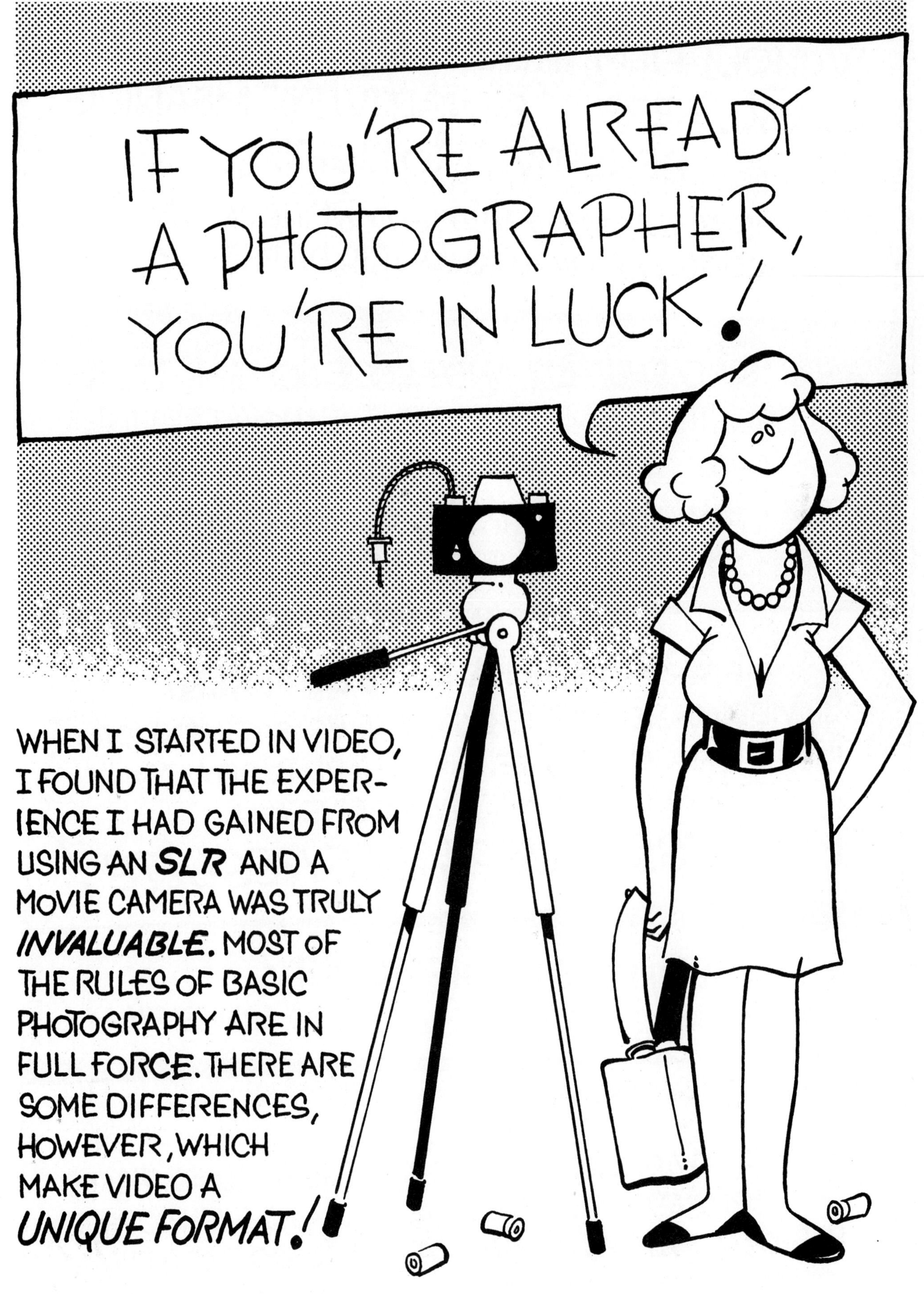

IF YOU'RE ALREADY A PHOTOGRAPHER, YOU'RE IN LUCK!
WHEN I STARTED IN VIDEO, I FOUND THAT THE EXPERIENCE I HAD GAINED FROM USING AN SLR AND A MOVIE CAMERA WAS TRULY INVALUABLE. MOST OF THE RULES OF BASIC PHOTOGRAPHY ARE IN FULL FORCE. THERE ARE SOME DIFFERENCES, HOWEVER, WHICH MAKE VIDEO A UNIQUE FORMAT!

WITHOUT FILM, THERE IS NO *FILM SPEED.* INSTEAD, THERE IS "SENSITIVITY," MEANING SENSITIVITY TO LIGHT.

SOME CAMERAS VARY THE **SENSITIVITY** OF THE CAMERA TUBE IN ADDITION TO PROVIDING AN IRIS DIAPHRAGM.!

THERE IS NO *SHUTTER* AND HENCE NO "SHUTTER SPEED." THE CAMERA TUBE IS EXPOSED TO THE IMAGE AT ALL TIMES.

THERE IS A **FRAME RATE** WHICH IS 30 FRAMES PER SECOND. UNLIKE MOVIE CAMERAS, THERE IS NO WAY TO VARY THIS.!

THE CONTRAST RANGE IS DIFFERENT

YOUR VIDEO CAMERA CAN'T EXPOSE A **BRIGHT** AND A **DIM** OBJECT IN THE **SAME FRAME.** THIS IS HARD TO DO ANYWAY, BUT THE VIDEO CAMERA WILL GIVE YOU *EVEN LESS ACCEPTABLE RESULTS!*

EDITING IS DIFFICULT!

YOU CAN'T CUT AND SPLICE TAPE THE WAY YOU DO **MOVIE FILM!**

TAPE IS CHEAP!

UNLIKE FILM, WITH ITS EXPENSIVE PROCESSING COSTS, *TAPE* CAN BE PLAYED IMMEDIATELY, REUSED, AND EVEN COPIED *WITHOUT PAYING A LABORATORY TO DO THE WORK!*

OPERATING THE CAMERA

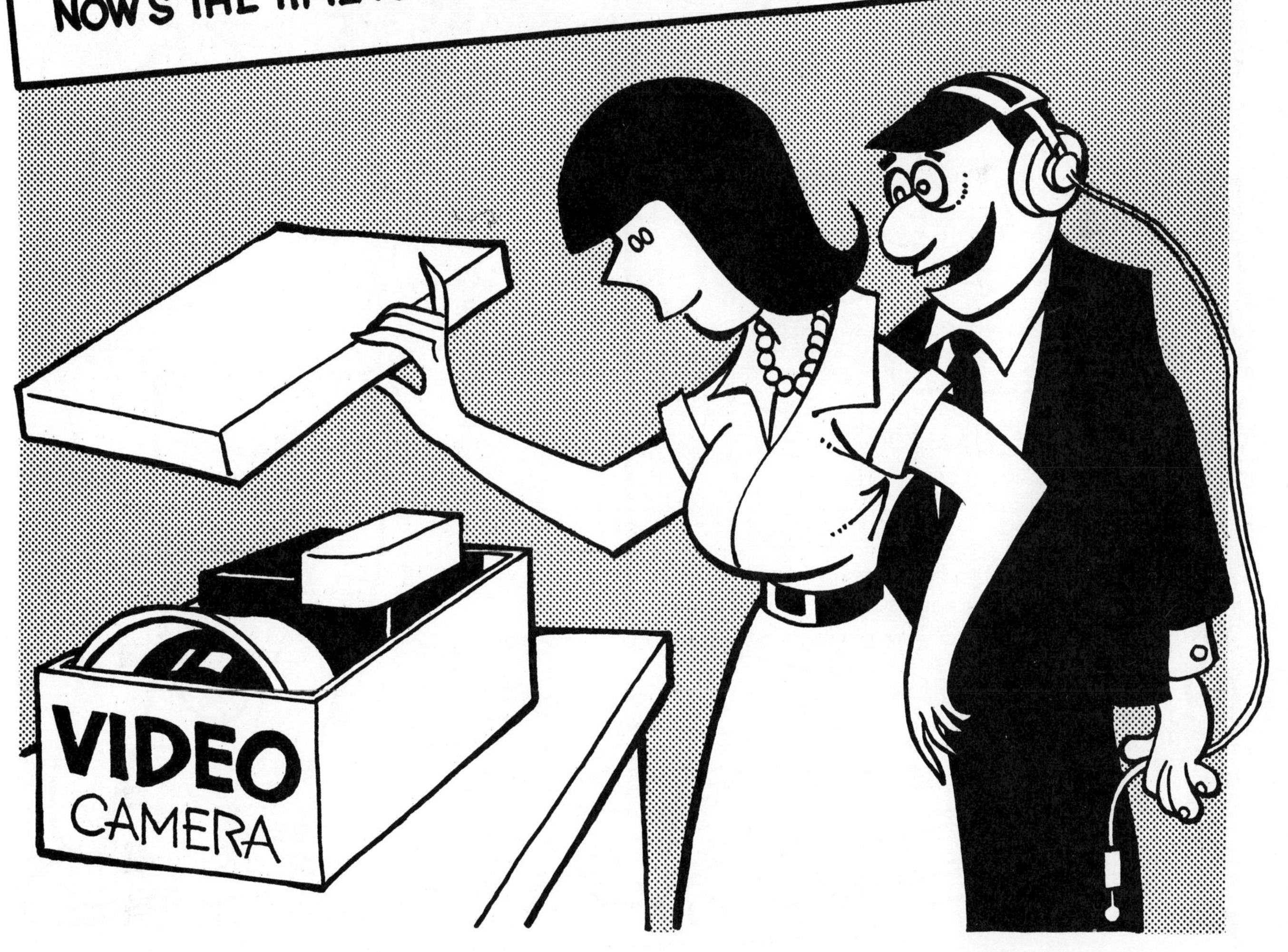

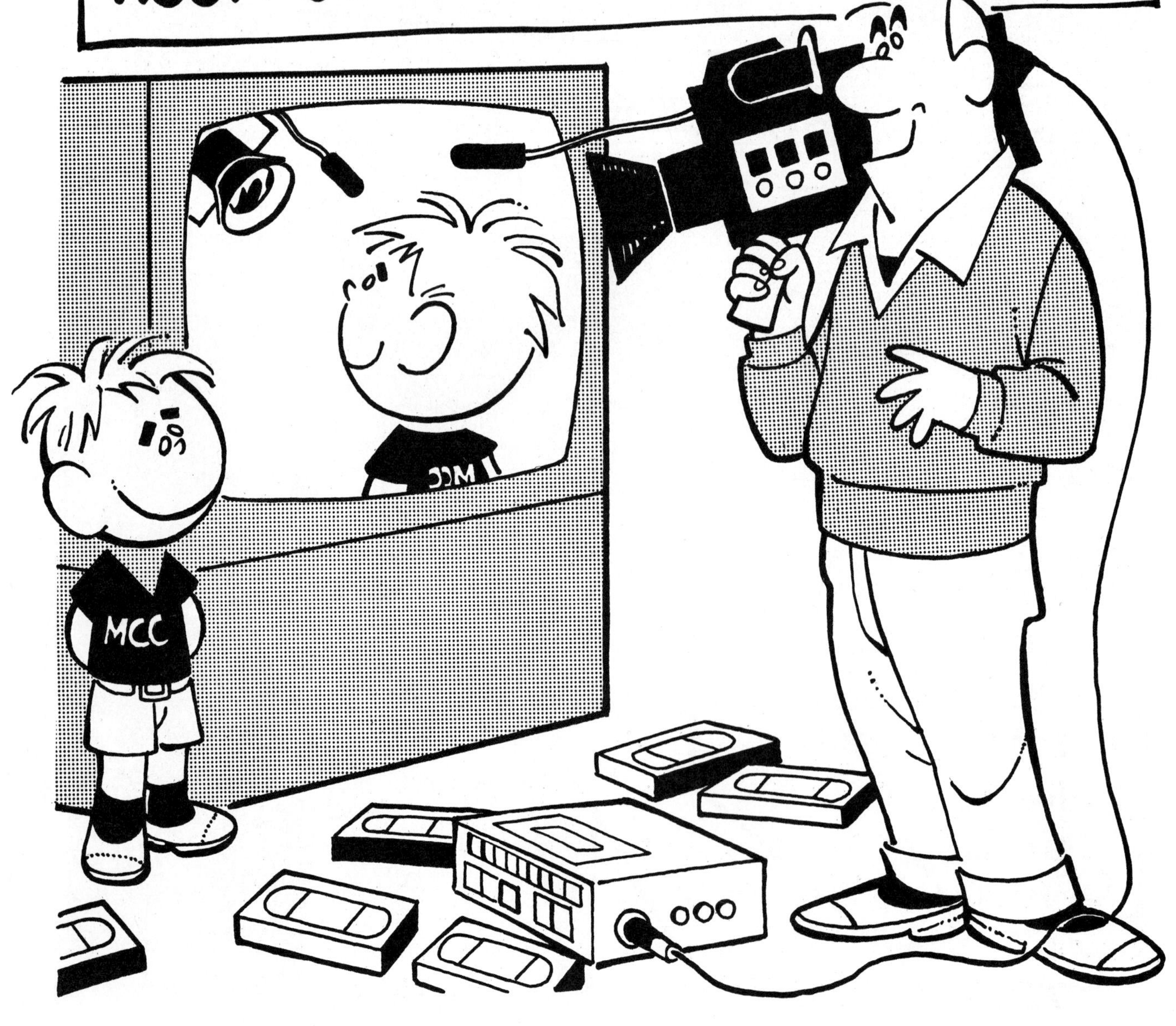

REFER TO YOUR MANUAL AND CONNECT IT TO YOUR RECORDER AND TV SET SO YOU CAN SEE THE PICTURE FROM THE CAMERA. SET YOUR ZOOM LENS ON *WIDE* (PUSH THE ZOOM CONTROL AND HOLD IT UNTIL THE RING ON THE LENS STOPS MOVING).

TURN ON ALL THE LIGHTS IN THE ROOM SO YOU CAN GET A PICTURE!

MCC
MCC

COLOR BALANCING

WHAT'S THE MATTER WITH THE COLOR IN YOUR PICTURE? THERE MIGHT BE TOO MUCH RED, OR TOO MUCH BLUE, OR GREEN... THIS IS BECAUSE

YOU HAVEN'T COLOR BALANCED YET!!!

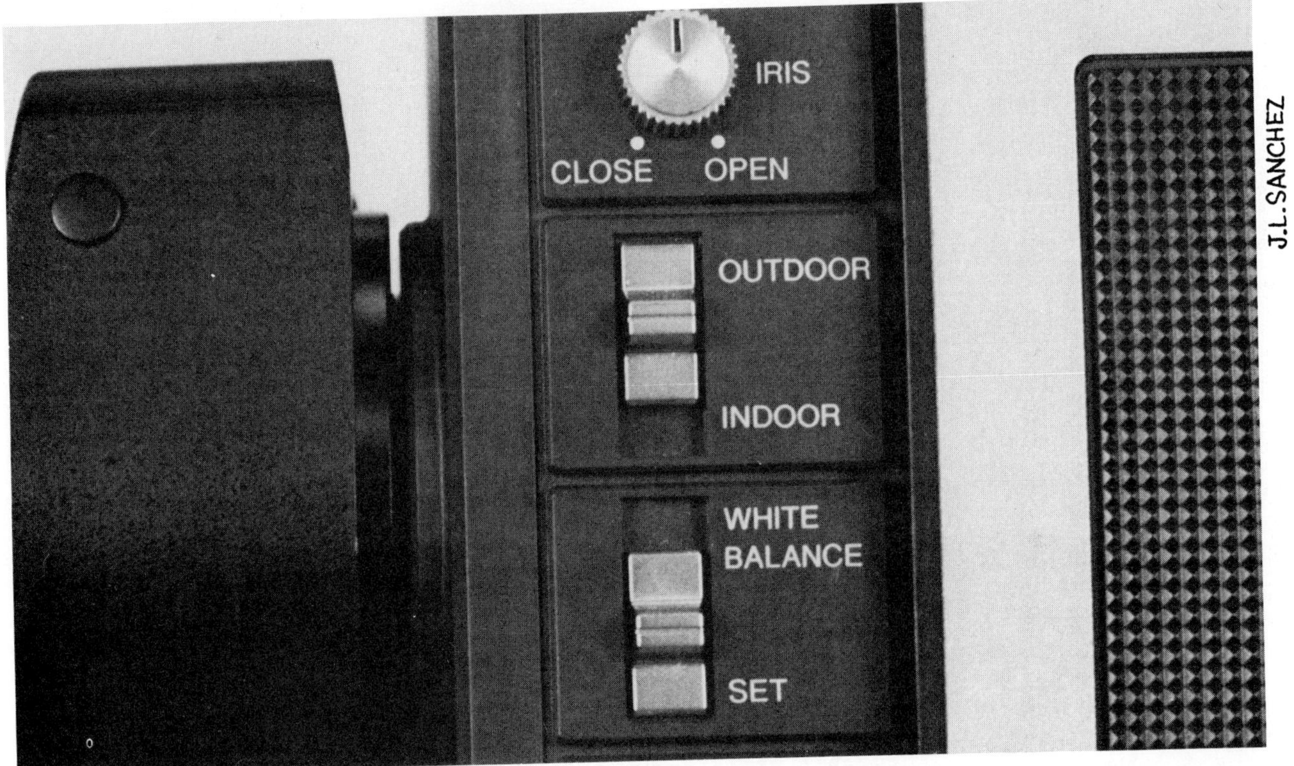

COLOR BALANCING (OR WHITE BALANCING) IS NECESSARY BECAUSE **LIGHT ISN'T REALLY WHITE.** OUR EYES COMPENSATE FOR DIFFERENT KINDS OF LIGHT **AUTOMATICALLY.** A WHITE OBJECT LOOKS WHITE INDOORS OR OUTDOORS. A TV CAMERA, HOWEVER, NEEDS TO BE **TOLD** WHEN THE LIGHT CHANGES. EVERY TIME YOU TAKE YOUR TV CAMERA FROM ONE TYPE OF LIGHT TO ANOTHER TYPE (FROM OUTDOORS TO INDOORS, OR FROM INCANDESCENT TO FLUORESCENT LIGHT) OR THE CAMERA IS TURNED OFF AND ON, YOU WILL HAVE TO COLOR BALANCE AGAIN. THIS IS IMPORTANT TO REMEMBER. **REFER TO YOUR CAMERA MANUAL FOR COLOR BALANCING!**

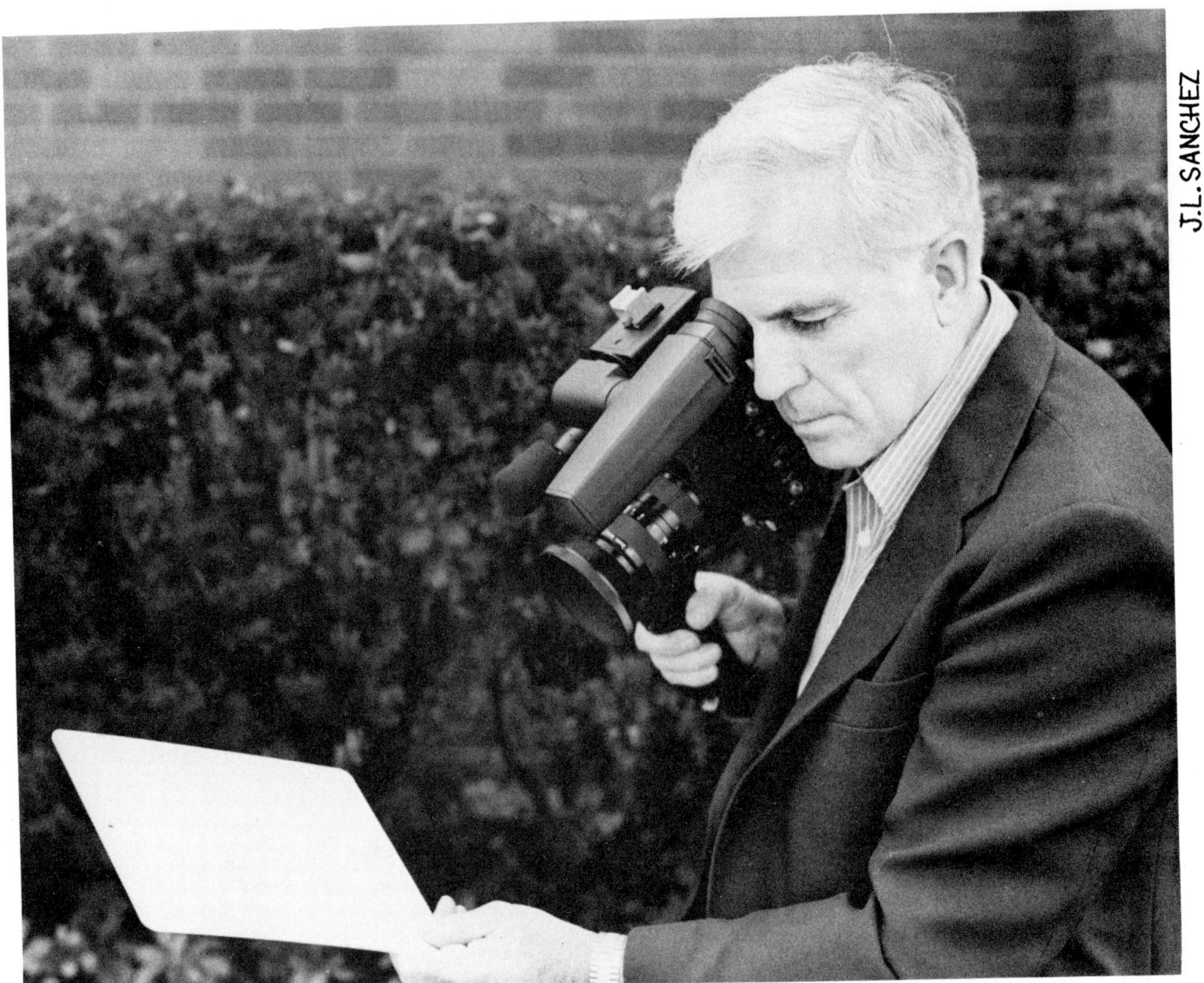

FOR THE BEST RESULTS, HOLD A PIECE OF WHITE PAPER IN FRONT OF YOUR LENS (ANGLE IT SO LIGHT FROM THE ROOM HITS IT) WHEN YOU PUSH THE BUTTON!

IMPORTANT: DO NOT USE AN 18% GREY CARD

EXPOSURE

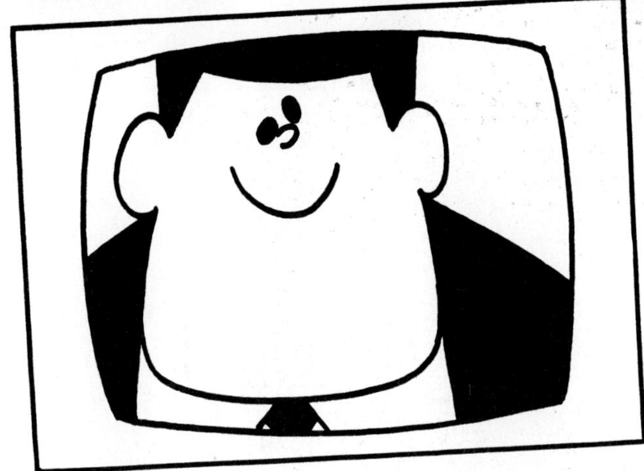
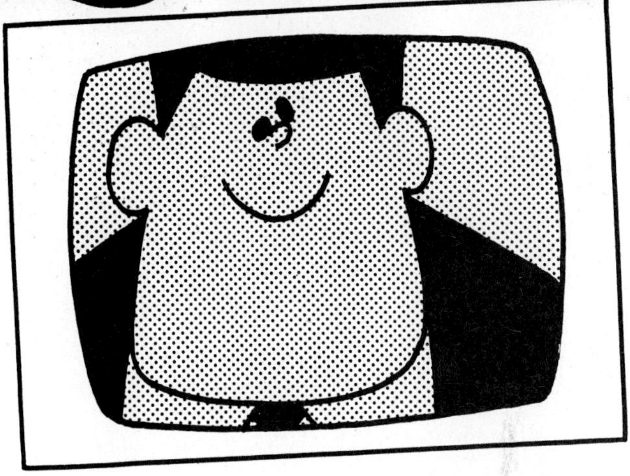

NEARLY EVERY VIDEO CAMERA SOLD HAS AN AUTOMATIC EXPOSURE FEATURE. IF THE CAMERA HAS AN IRIS DIAPHRAGM, THEN THE SIZE OF THE DIAPHRAGM (THE F-STOP) IS CONTROLLED ELECTRONICALLY BY THE CAMERA TO KEEP THE PICTURE FROM BEING TOO LIGHT OR TOO DARK.

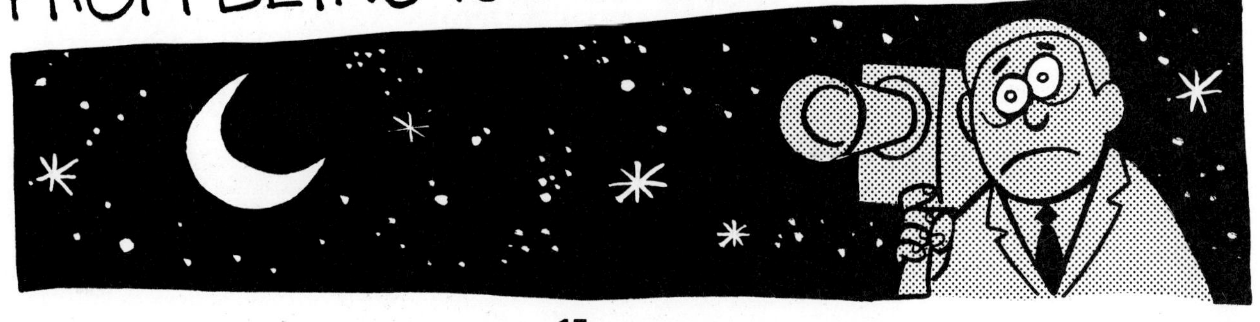

VIDEO CAMERA EXPOSURE RING WITH F-STOPS!

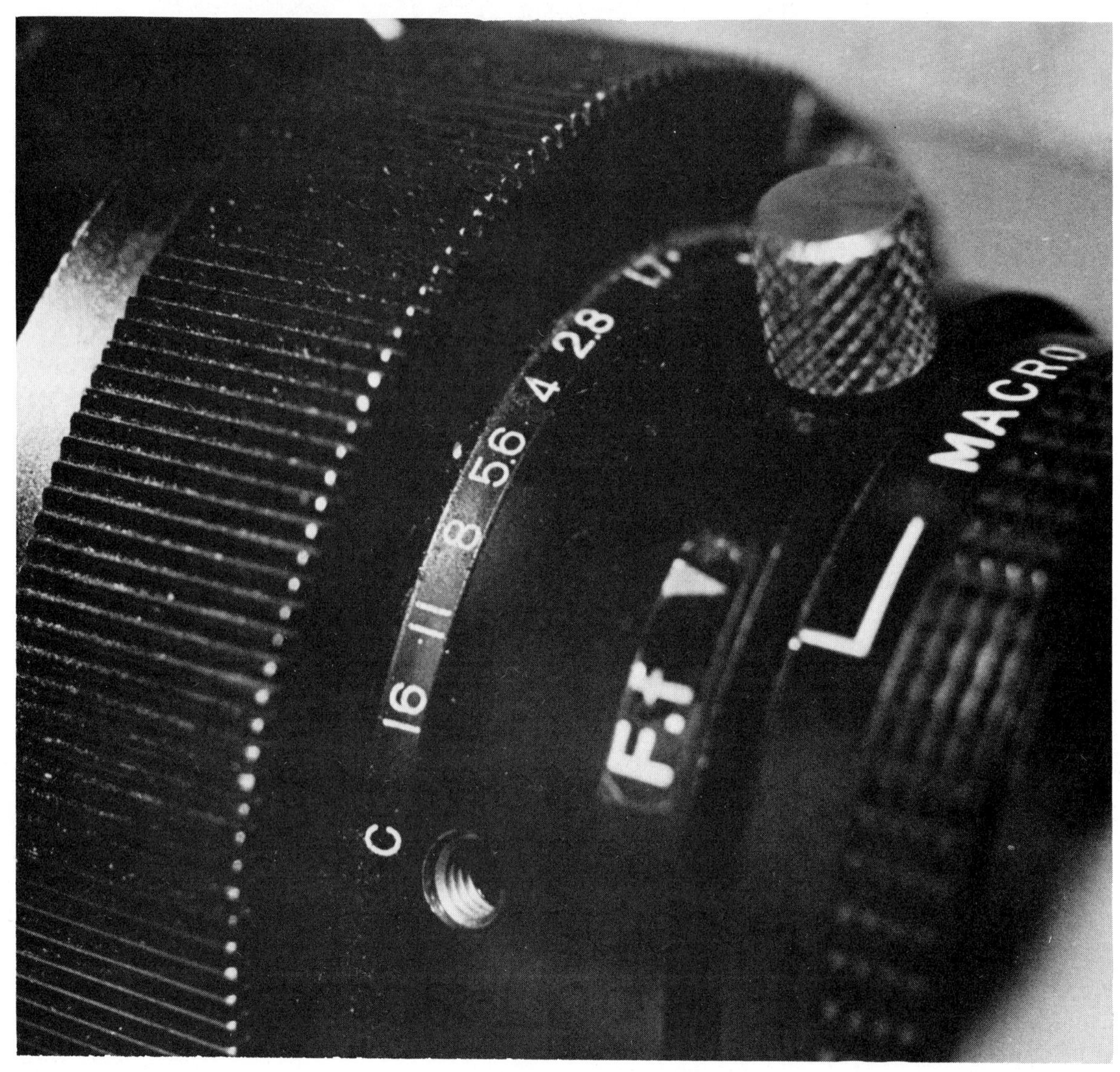

IF YOU HAVE A "STILL CAMERA", YOU'LL NOTICE THE
SAME NUMBERS APPEAR ON THE F-STOP RING.!.!!
THE F-STOPS FUNCTION THE SAME WAY ON A VIDEO
CAMERA — *THEY CONTROL THE AMOUNT OF LIGHT
ENTERING THE CAMERA, AND THE DEPTH OF FIELD!*

IN ADDITION TO THE DIAPHRAGM, SOMETIMES THE **_ACTUAL SENSITIVITY_** OF THE PICKUP TUBE IS CONTROLLED — UNFORTUNATELY, THERE'S A PROBLEM WITH THE AUTOMATIC EXPOSURE!

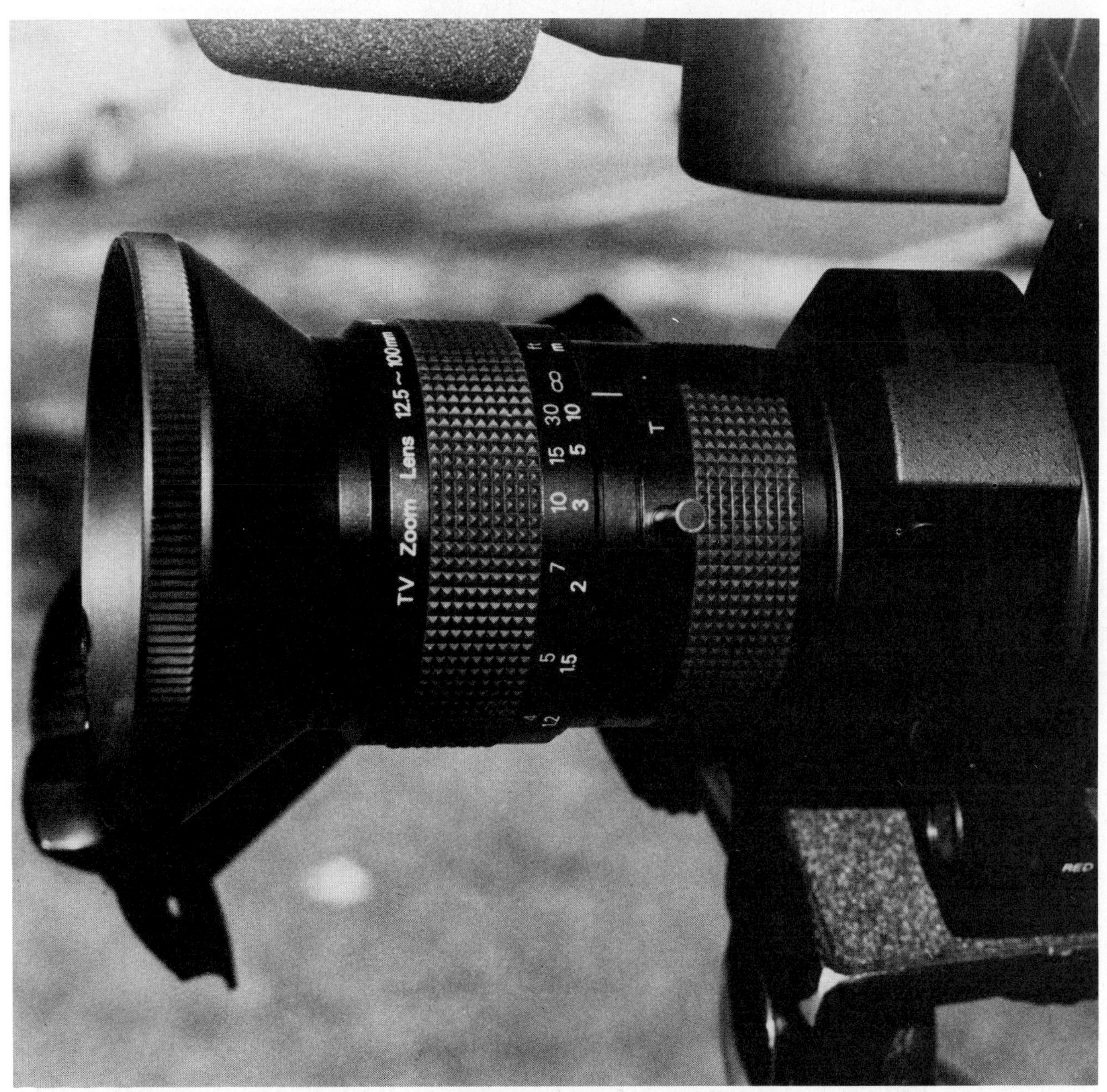

HERE'S A VIDEO CAMERA WITHOUT AN IRIS RING.

AS YOU CAN SEE, THERE IS ONLY A FOOTAGE SCALE! (THIS COULD BE AN IMPORTANT CONSIDERATION.)

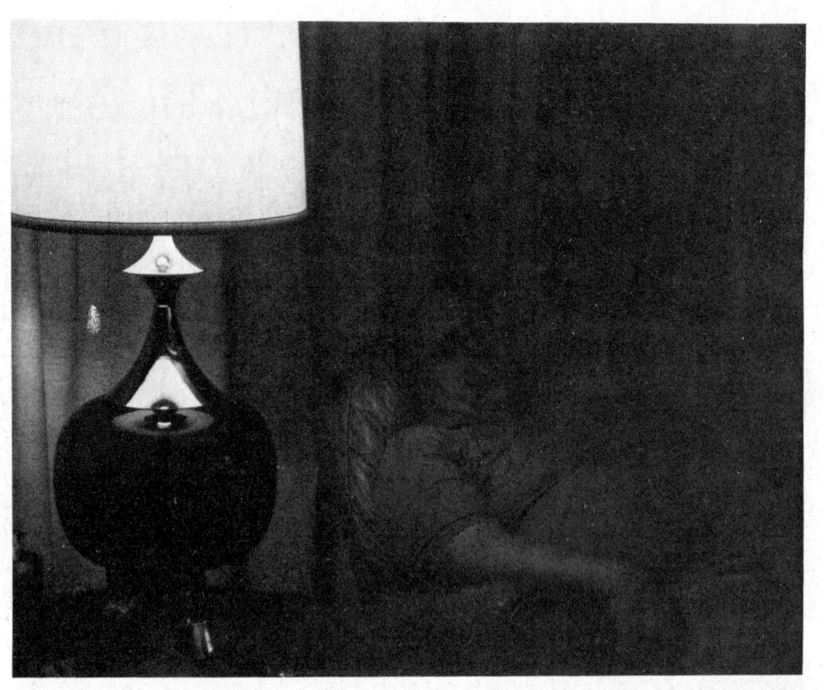

WHAT'S THE PROBLEM HERE? THE AUTOMATIC EXPOSURE CIRCUIT WILL ALWAYS ADJUST FOR THE BRIGHTEST OBJECT IN THE FRAME, WHETHER YOU WANT TO OR NOT. OTHER PARTS OF YOUR PICTURE MAY COME OUT TOO DARK TO SEE. IF YOU CAN DIS-ABLE OR OVERRIDE THE AUTOMATIC EXPOSURE, THIS IS THE TIME TO DO IT. IT MAY ONLY BE POSSIBLE TO **PARTIALLY** OVERRIDE IT. THIS PICTURE IS IMPROPERLY EXPOSED BECAUSE THE BRIGHT LAMP CLOSED DOWN THE IRIS!

THIS CONTROL MIGHT BE LABELLED *LIGHT/DARK OR BACKLIGHT!!* OPEN THE LENS UP A STOP OR TWO, OR ADJUST THE CONTROL TOWARD THE *LIGHT—* AND LOOK AT YOUR FRIEND ON THE SCREEN!

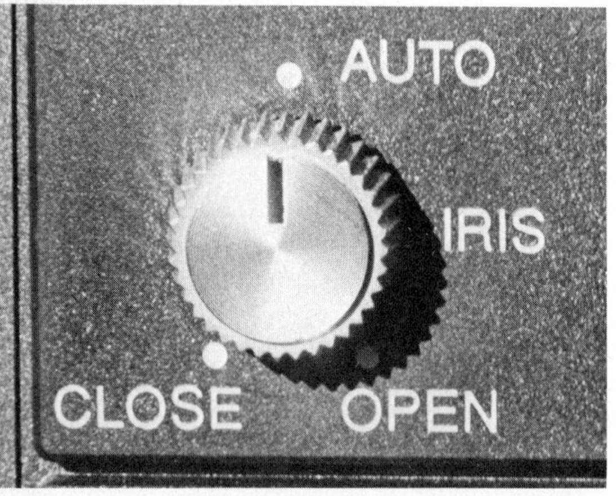

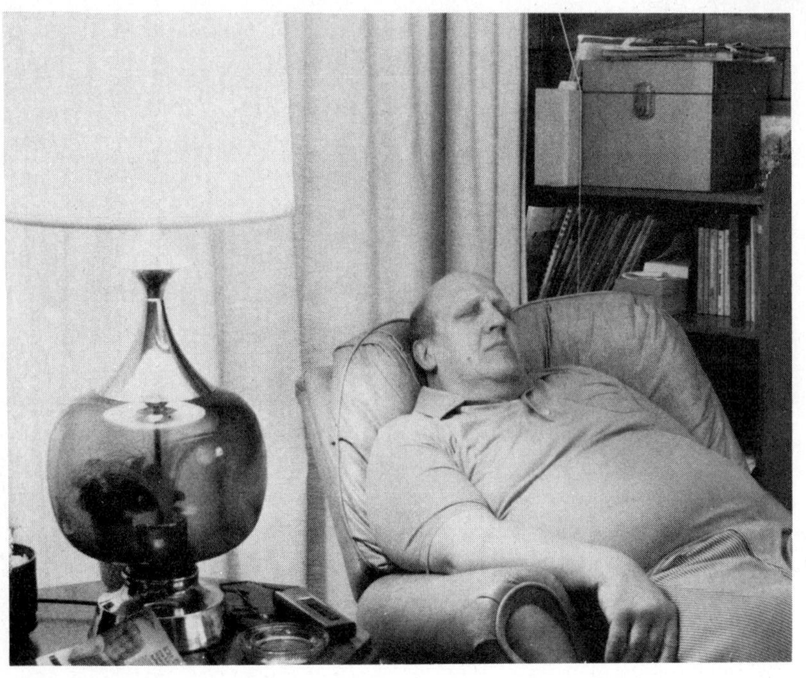

THIS IS WHAT YOU HAVE TO DO WHEN SHOOTING A SCENE WITH A BRIGHT LIGHT IN IT — OR WHEN THE SUN, OR A BRIGHT WINDOW IS IN THE BACKGROUND!

THIS PICTURE IS PROPERLY EXPOSED BY OVERRIDING THE AUTOMATIC EXPOSURE.

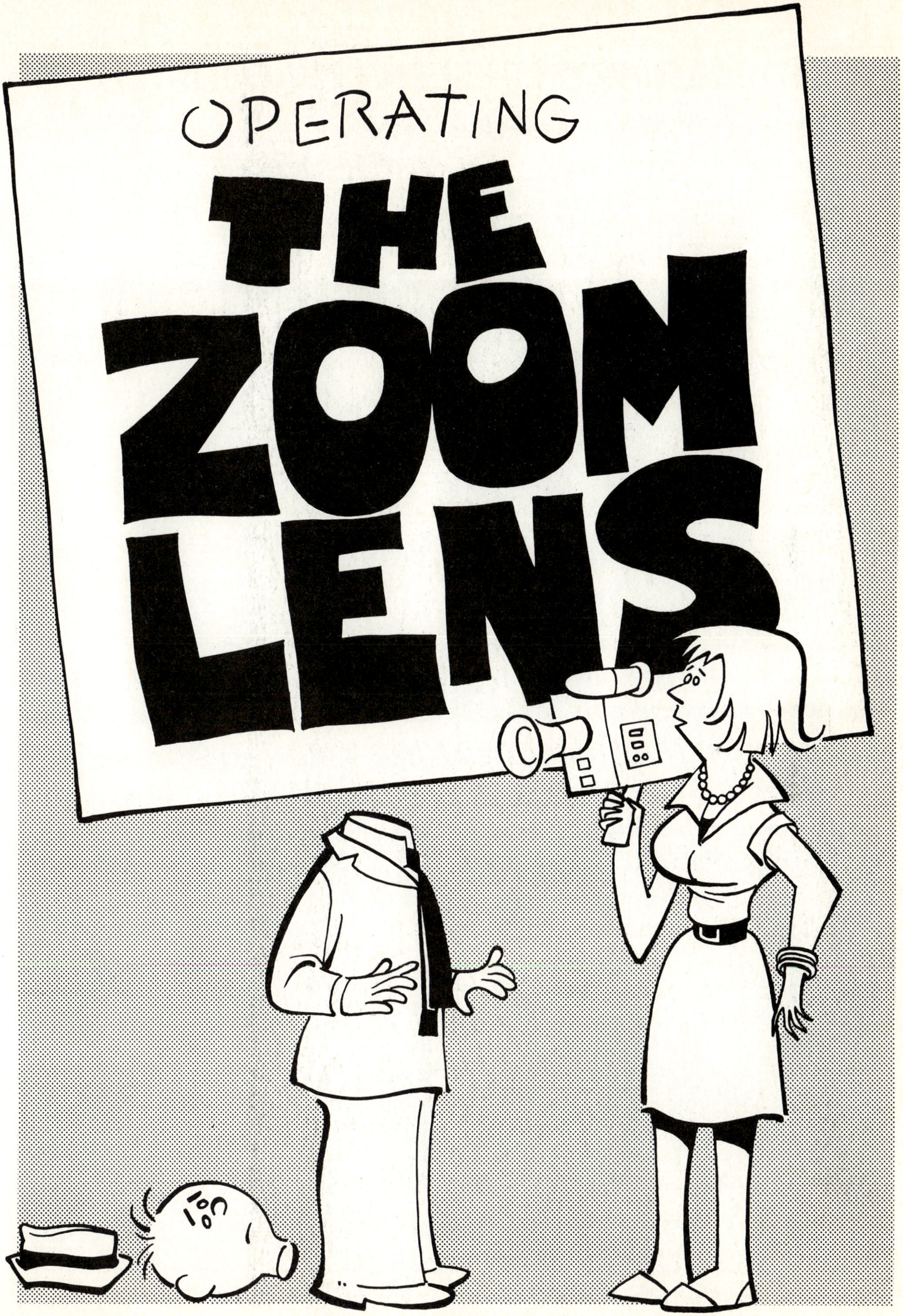

OPERATING
THE
ZOOM
LENS

THE FOCUS RING ON THE LENS IS ADJUSTED SO THAT THE IMAGE IS SHARP AND CLEAR. THE ZOOM RING ADJUSTS THE EFFECTIVE *FOCAL LENGTH* OF THE LENS !

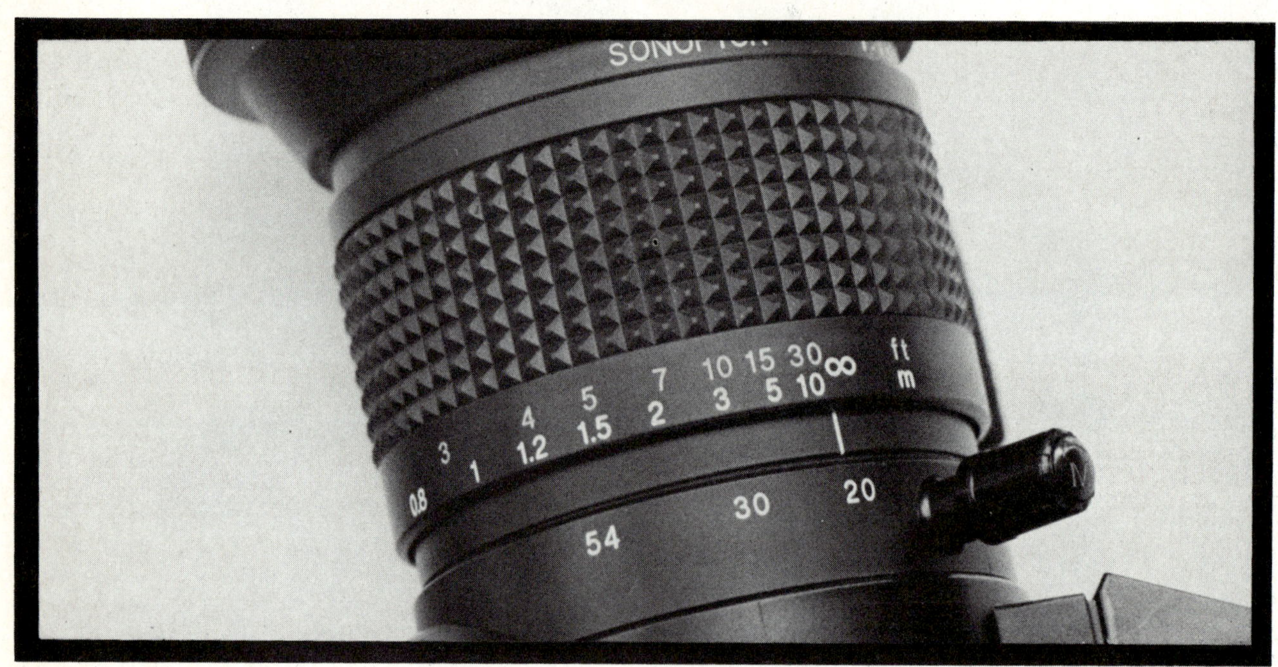

AT ITS *SHORTEST SETTING* IT IS A *WIDE ANGLE* LENS.... IN OTHER WORDS, IT IS TAKING IN A WIDE ANGLE OF VIEW.

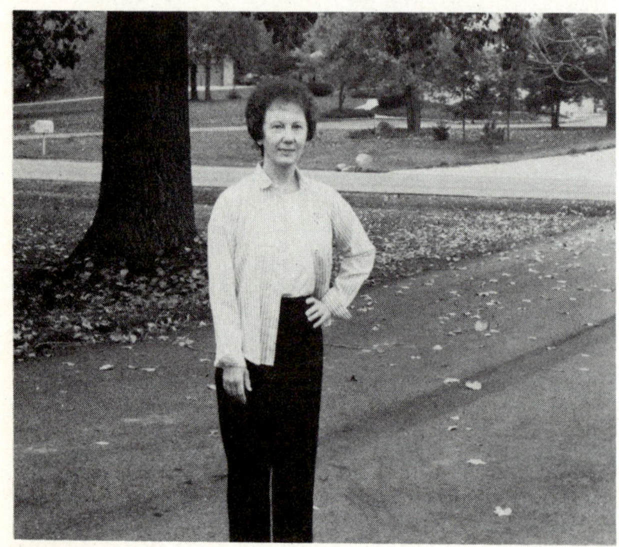

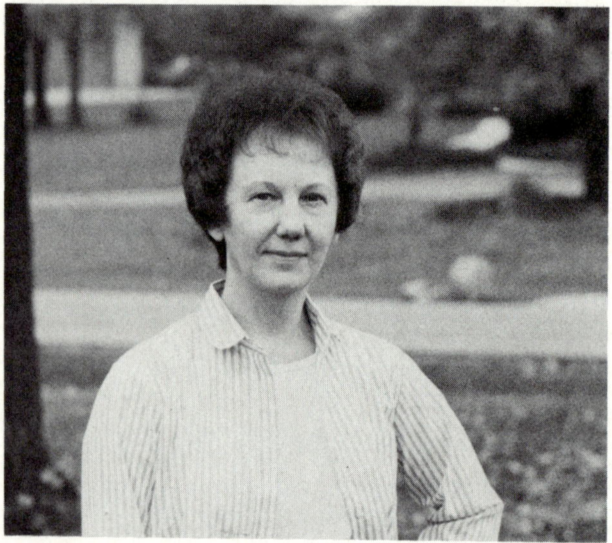

AS YOU OPERATE THE ZOOM TOWARD THE *LONGEST* FOCAL LENGTH (CALLED THE TELEPHOTO SETTING), YOUR SUBJECT *INCREASES* IN SIZE AS THE ANGLE OF VIEW *GETS NARROWER* !

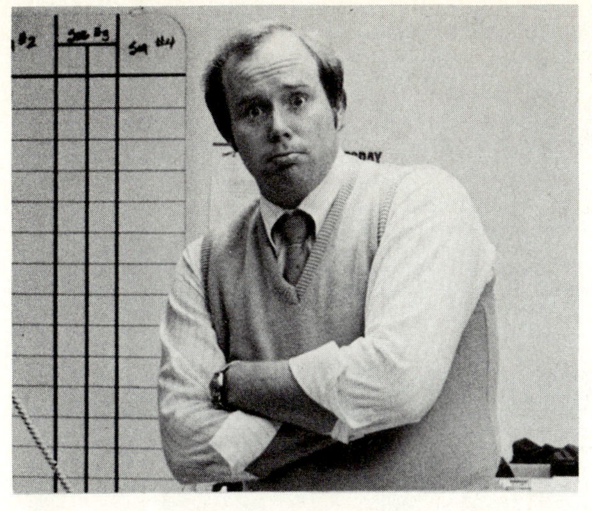

NOTICE ALSO HOW THE PICTURE IS GOING OUT OF FOCUS AS YOU ZOOM IN. THIS IS BECAUSE OF A RELATIONSHIP BETWEEN THE FOCAL LENGTH OF THE LENS AND ITS *DEPTH OF FIELD!* AT ITS WIDEST SETTING, THE LENS SEEMS FOCUSED ALL THE TIME. THE MORE YOU ZOOM IN, HOWEVER, THE MORE CRITICAL THE FOCUS BECOMES.

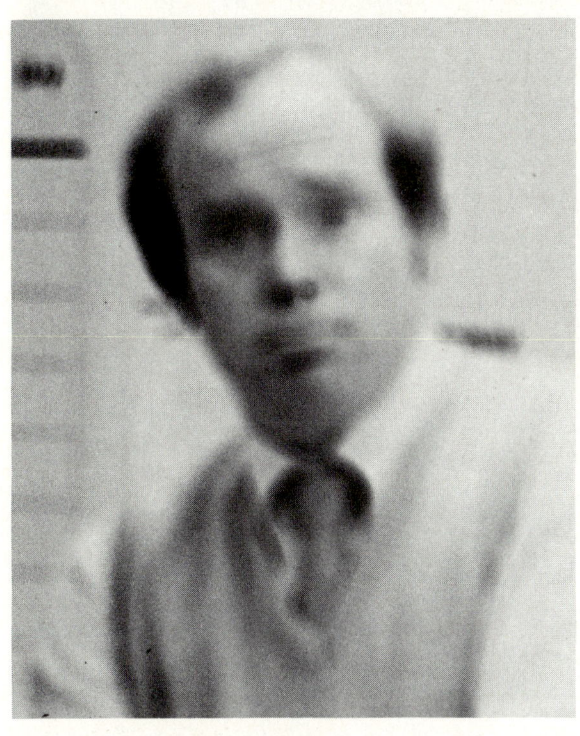

THE ONLY SOLUTION TO THIS MOST IRRITATING RELATIONSHIP (WHICH WILL CAUSE YOU TO LOSE FOCUS WHEN EVER YOU ZOOM IN) IS TO ALWAYS ZOOM YOUR LENS ALL THE WAY IN (SET IT AT ITS LONGEST FOCAL LENGTH), FOCUS, AND THEN SET THE LENS WHERE YOU WANT IT. *MAKE THIS A HABIT!*

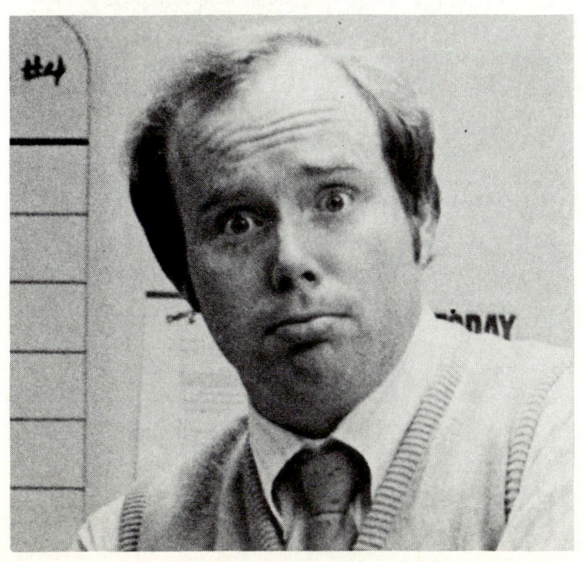

FOCUS THIS WAY BEFORE YOU START TO SHOOT, AND THE LENS WILL BE IN FOCUS THROUGH THE ENTIRE RANGE OF THE ZOOM LENS. OF COURSE, IF EITHER THE CAMERA OR THE SUBJECT IS MOVING, THE FOCUS WILL CHANGE. THEN YOU FOCUS WHILE SHOOTING. *A GOOD RULE WHEN SHOOTING MOVEMENT IS TO KEEP THE CAMERA IN CLOSE SO YOU WON'T HAVE TO ZOOM!*

KEEPING THE LENS SET "WIDE" (SHORTEST FOCAL LENGTH) MAKES IT EASIER TO FOLLOW FOCUS

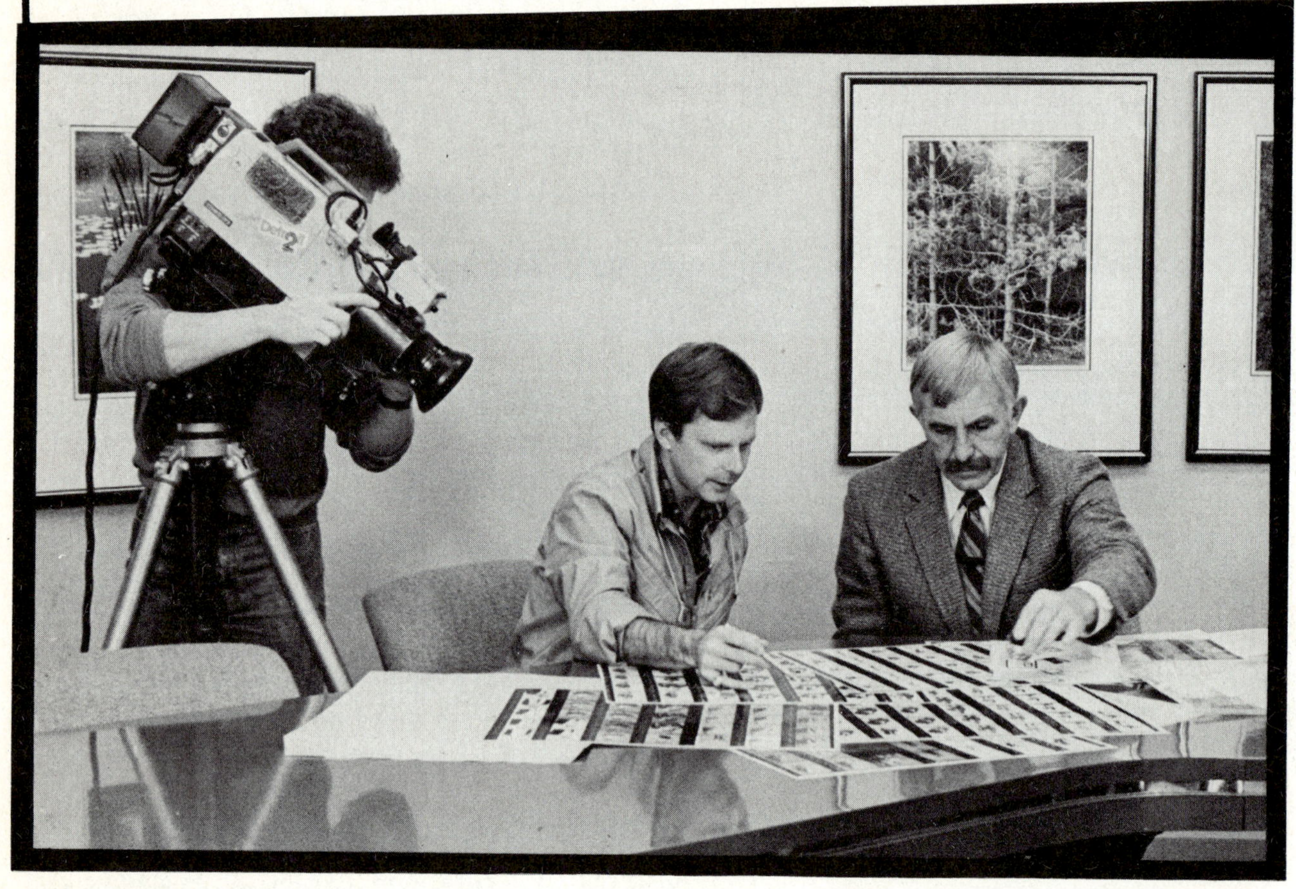

CONTROLLING DEPTH OF FIELD AND PERSPECTIVE

IT'S A PAIN TO HAVE TO FOCUS ALL THE TIME, BUT YOU CAN CONTROL THE *DEPTH OF FIELD* OF THE LENS TO YOUR ADVANTAGE. WHAT DEPTH OF FIELD REFERS TO IS THAT PORTION OF THE PICTURE IN FRONT AND BACK OF YOUR SUBJECT THAT IS ALSO IN ACCEPTABLE FOCUS. BESIDES ITS RELATIONSHIP TO FOCAL LENGTH, THE DEPTH OF FIELD IS DETERMINED BY THE *APERTURE* OF THE LENS. THE SMALLER THE APERTURE (THE LARGER THE F-STOP NUMBER), THE GREATER THE DEPTH OF FIELD!

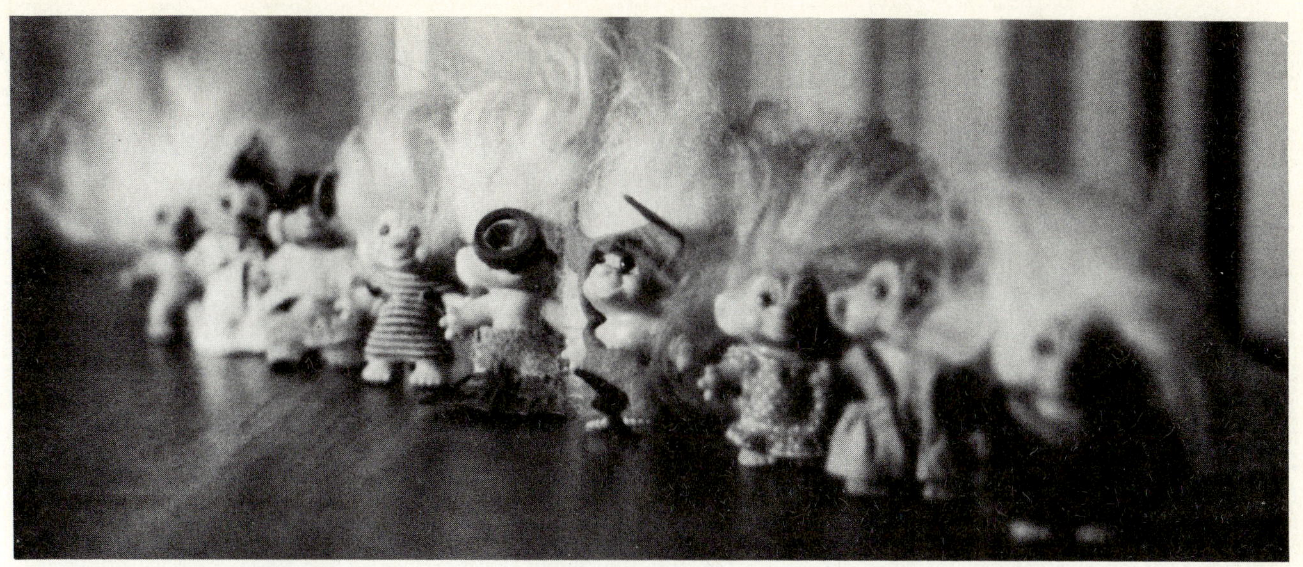

THIS PICTURE WAS TAKEN WITH AN F-STOP OF **F2.8!**
ONLY THE CENTER, OR THE EXACT POINT OF FOCUS IS SHARP

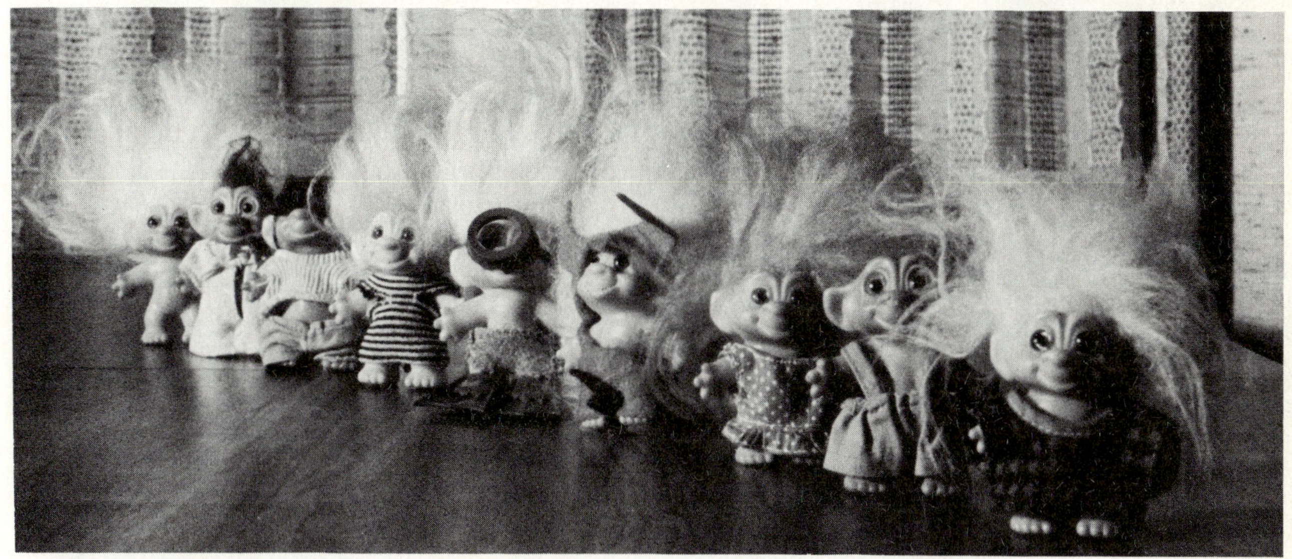

IN THIS PHOTO, THE F-STOP WAS CHANGED TO **F16!**

THE DIFFERENCE IN THE SHARPNESS IS **AMAZING!** SINCE THE APERTURE SETTING AFFECTS YOUR VIDEO LEVEL (THE BRIGHTNESS OF THE IMAGE), REMEMBER TO ADD MORE LIGHT TO YOUR SCENE WHEN YOU USE HIGHER F-STOPS OR INCREASE THE SENSITIVITY OF THE PICKUP TUBE, IF YOUR CAMERA LETS YOU DO THIS.!! IF YOUR CAMERA HAS NO IRIS **ADJUSTMENT—** **FORGET IT!** YOU CAN'T CONTROL DEPTH OF FIELD THIS WAY.

HERE'S A DIFFERENT WAY TO DO THE SAME THING!

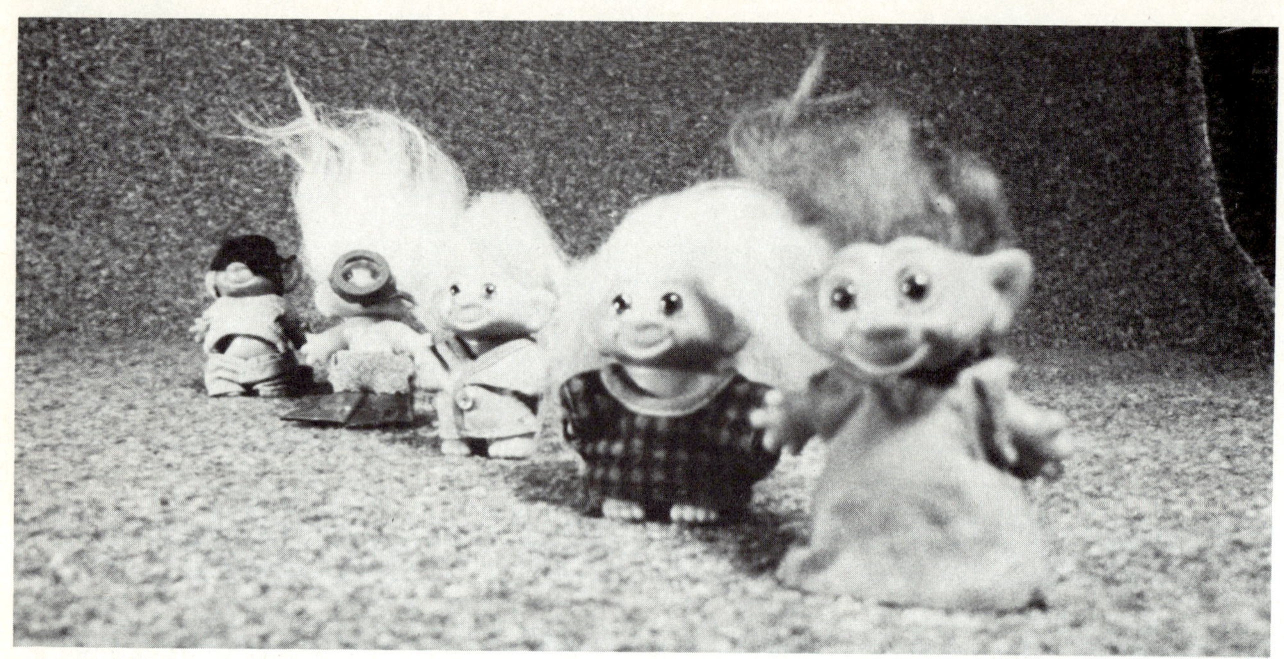

THIS PICTURE WAS MADE USING THE WIDE ANGLE SETTING OF THE ZOOM LENS. THE FOCUS IS SHARP THROUGHOUT THE PHOTO.!!

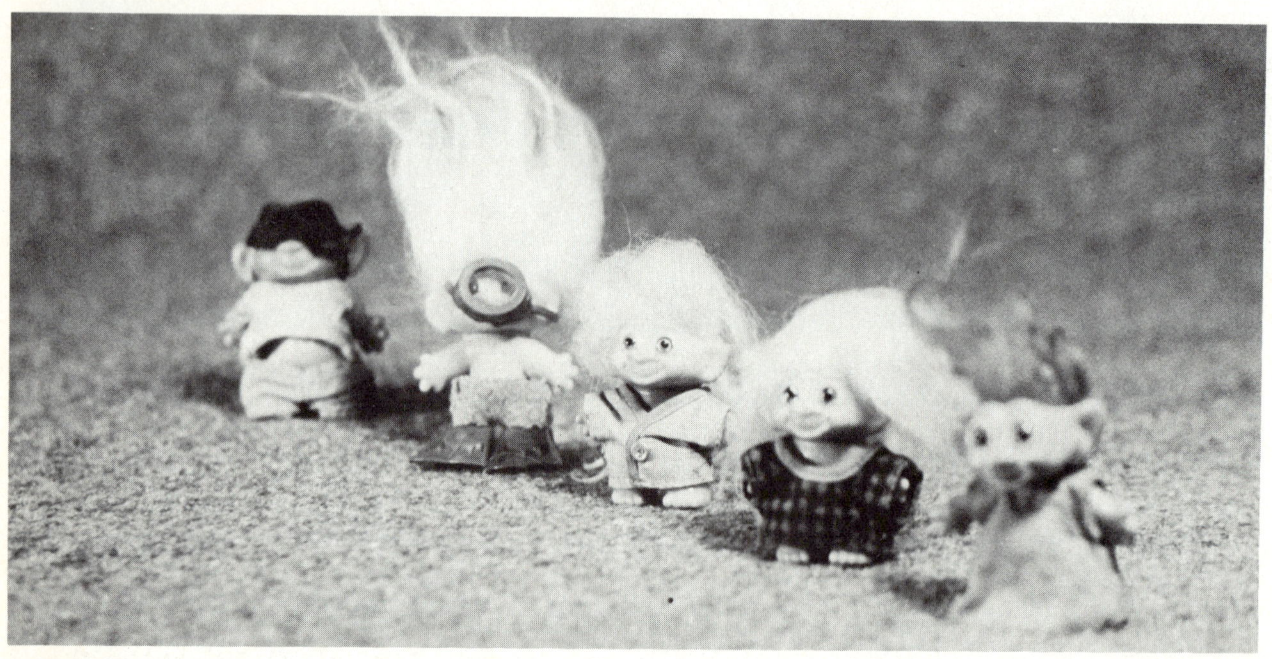

WHEN THE TELEPHOTO SETTING IS USED, LOOK WHAT HAPPENS.! *NOT ONLY IS THE DEPTH OF FIELD REDUCED* (ONLY ONE PART OF THE PICTURE IS IN FOCUS) *BUT THE WHOLE PERSPECTIVE OF THE PICTURE HAS CHANGED.!* TELEPHOTO LENSES TEND TO COMPRESS PERSPECTIVE, WHEREAS WIDE ANGLE LENSES **STRETCH IT.!**

THESE PHOTOS SHOW A SITUATION WHERE YOU WOULD WANT TO CONTROL YOUR DEPTH OF FIELD!

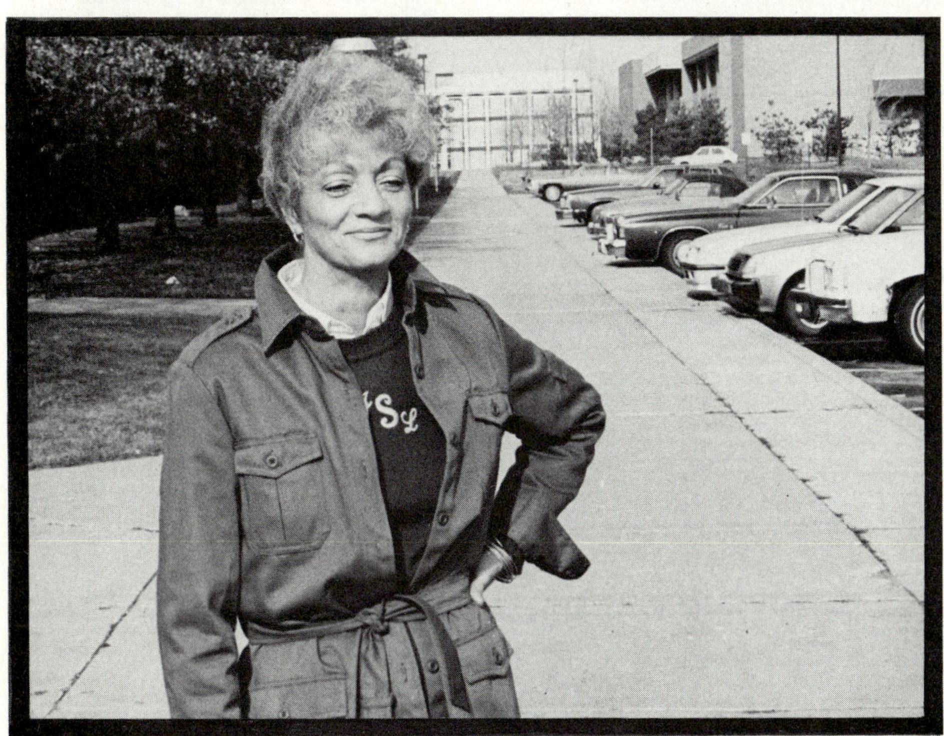

THE BACKGROUND BEHIND JOYCE IS UNPLEASANT AND DISTRACTING. BY BACKING THE CAMERA UP SEVERAL FEET, A LONGER SETTING OF THE ZOOM LENS CAN BE USED.

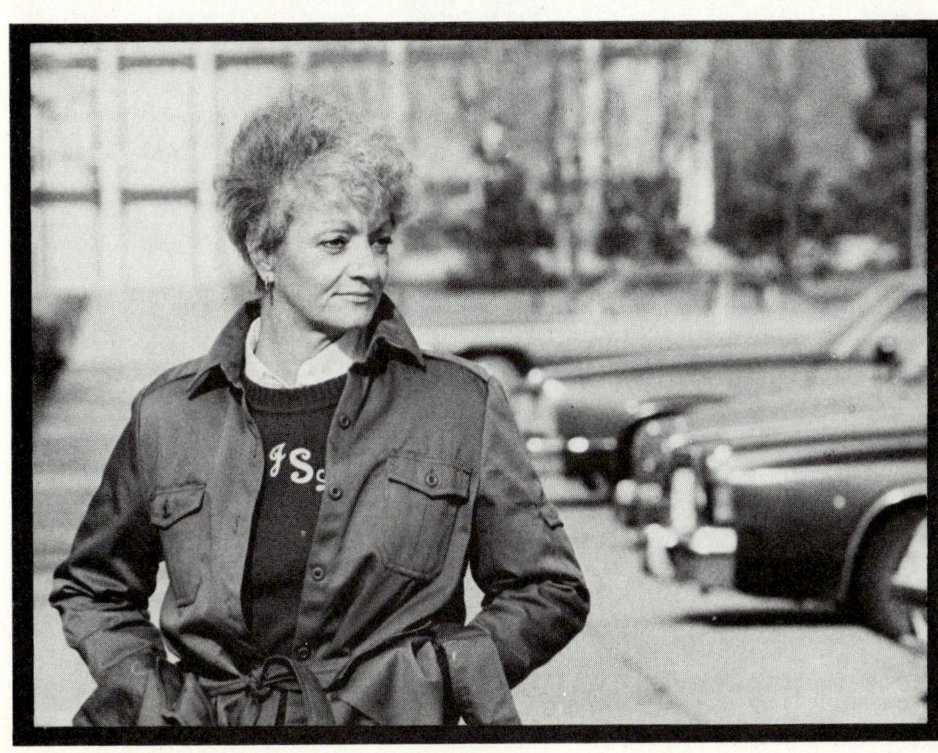

NOTICE HOW THE UGLY BACKGROUND BECOMES INVISIBLE!

IN THE NEXT SITUATION, WE NEED TO CONTROL THE PERSPECTIVE OF THE PICTURE.

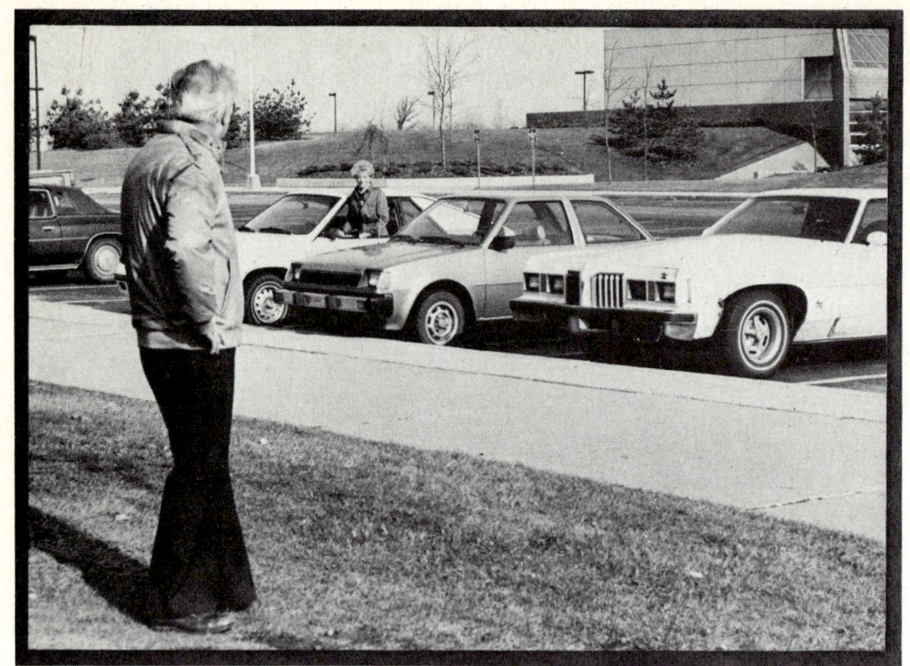

KEN IS TALKING TO JOYCE, BUT SHE'S TOO SMALL TO BE SEEN WELL !

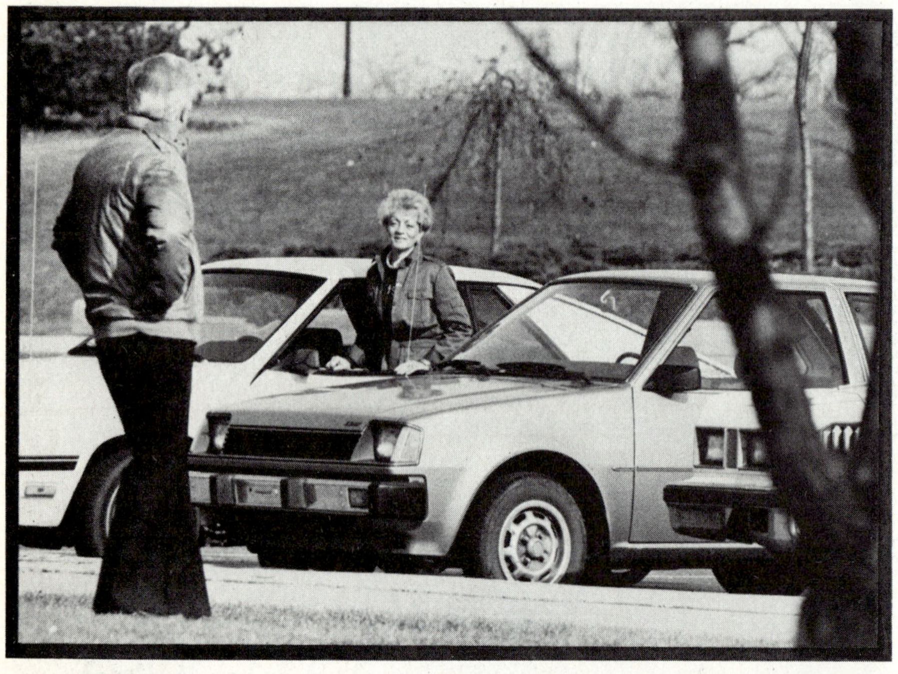

BY BACKING THE CAMERA UP AND USING A LONG LENS SETTING, THE TWO SUBJECTS BECOME CLOSER IN SIZE TO EACH OTHER.
THE DEPTH OF FIELD IS BETTER IN THIS TELE-PHOTO SHOT BECAUSE THE LENS WAS FOCUSED CLOSE TO ITS INFINITY SETTING.

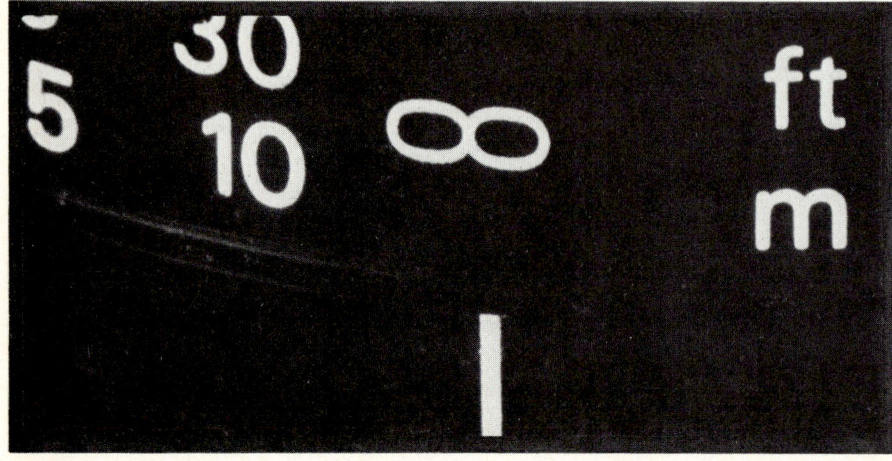

THE DEPTH OF FIELD OF ANY LENS *INCREASES* AS IT IS USED TOWARD ITS MOST *DISTANT* FOCUS SETTING.

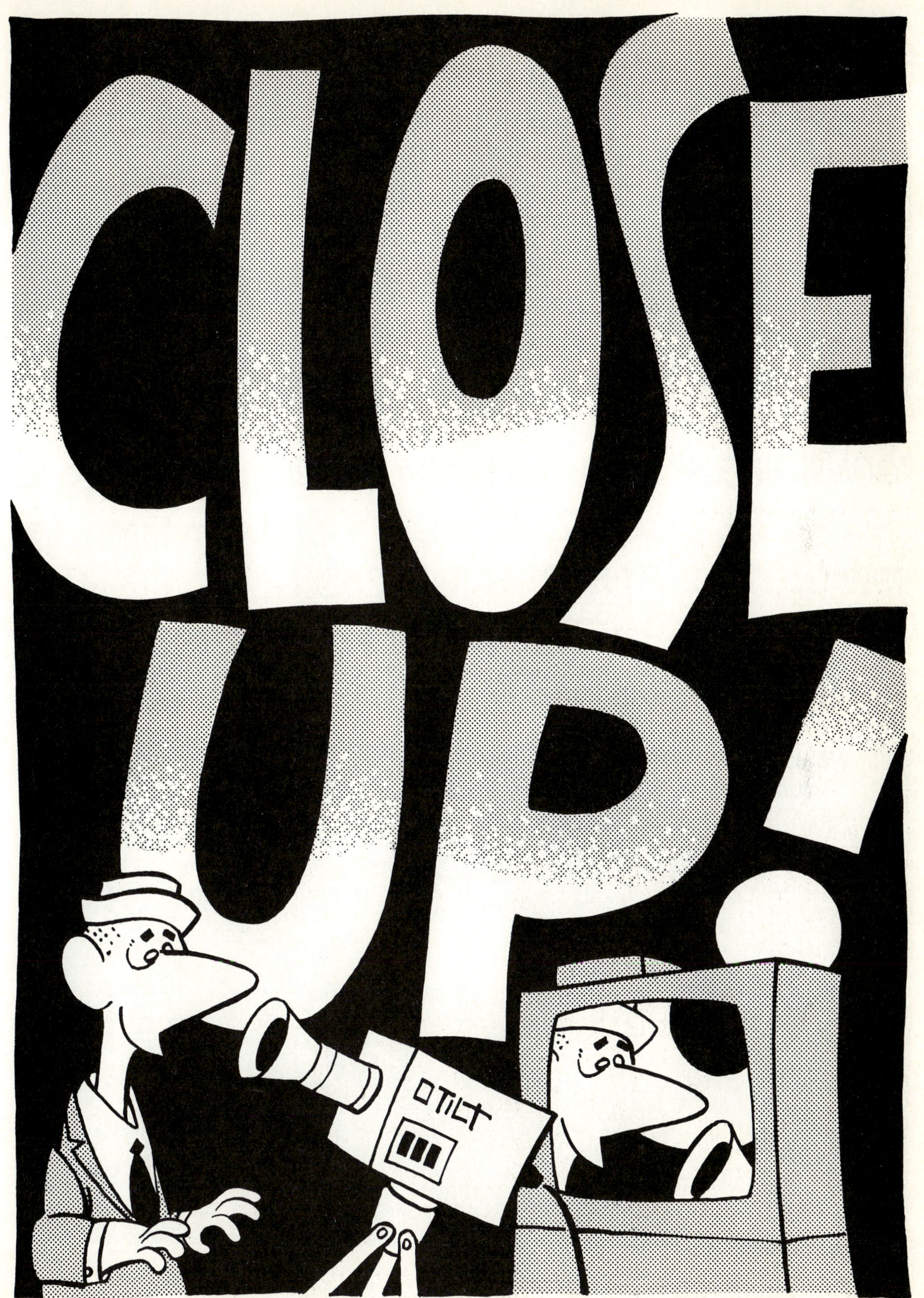

CLOSE
UP!
TILT

FOCUS BECOMES MORE CRITICAL WHEN THE LENS IS USED AT ITS **CLOSER** SETTINGS. THERE IS A LIMIT TO HOW CLOSE THE LENS WILL FOCUS, HOWEVER. MANY ZOOM LENSES HAVE A **MACRO** ADJUSTMENT FOR FOCUSING CLOSER THAN THE NORMAL 3 OR 4 FOOT LIMIT.

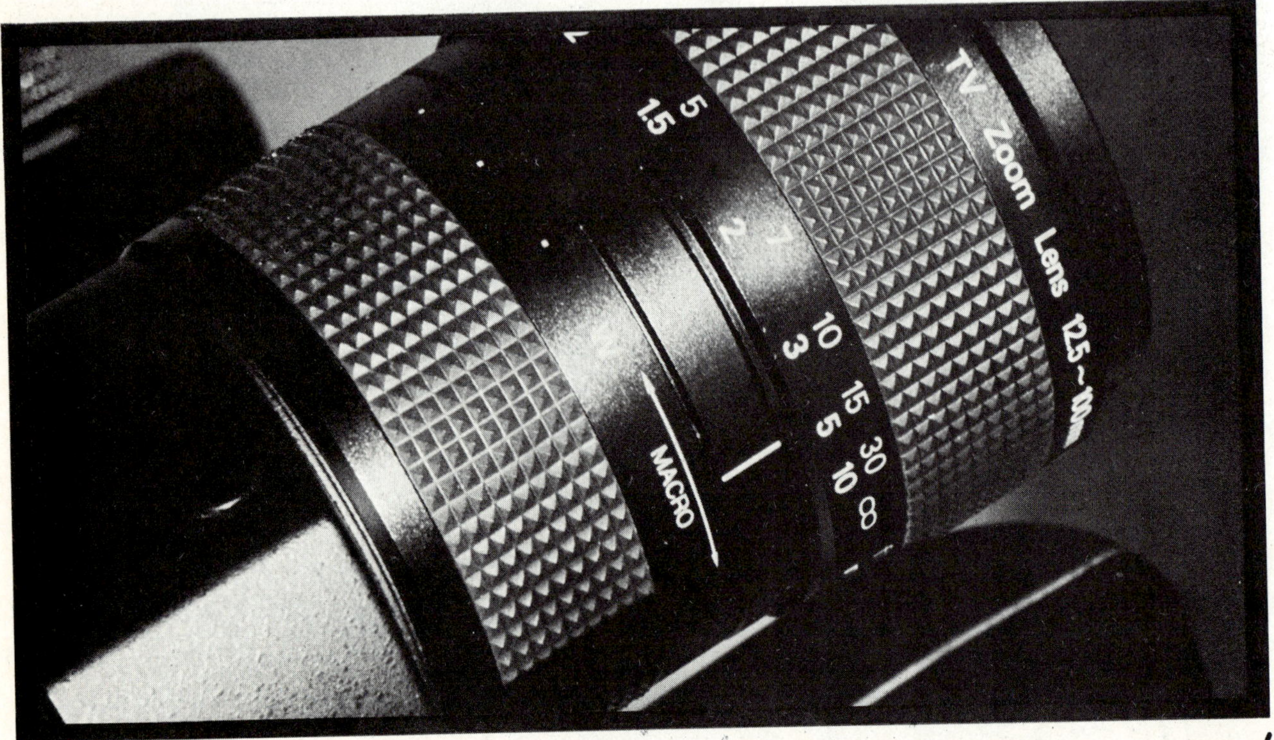

NOTICE THE ARROW SHOWING THE MACRO'S FOCUSING RANGE!

THE MACRO LENS IS ADJUSTED UNTIL THE PICTURE IS IN FOCUS. OBJECTS AS CLOSE AS A FEW INCHES FROM THE LENS CAN THEN BE VIDEOTAPED !

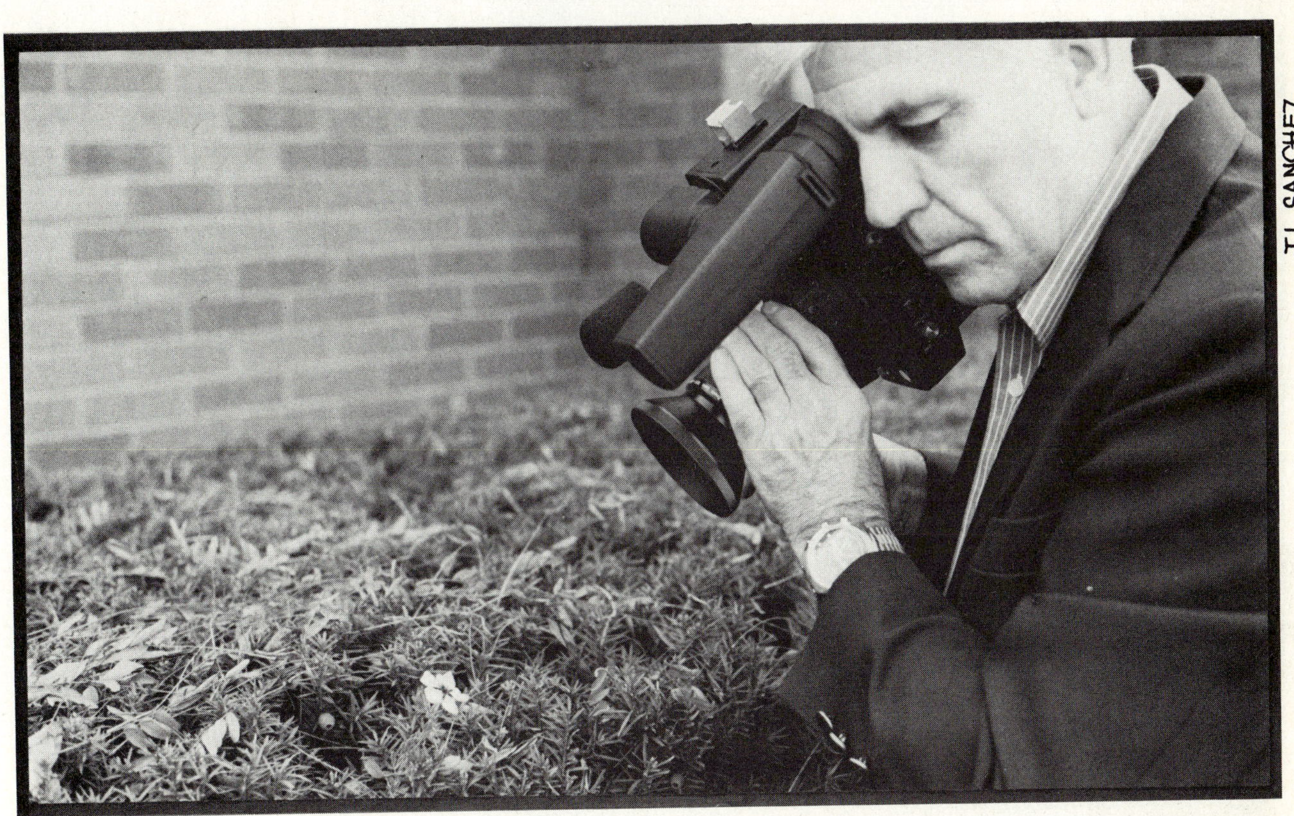

EXPERIMENT WITH THE SETTING OF THE ZOOM LENS FOR THE RESULT YOU WANT. LEAVING THE LENS SET TO **WIDE** WILL LET YOU FOCUS THE CLOSEST TO THE CAMERA, BUT A LARGER MAGNIFICATION MAY ACTUALLY BE POSSIBLE ON **TELEPHOTO** (EVEN THOUGH YOU'LL HAVE TO POSITION THE CAMERA FARTHER AWAY).

UNFORTUNATELY, THE NORMAL CHARACTERISTICS OF THE ZOOM ARE SACRIFICED WHILE USING THE MACRO.

IF THE ZOOM IS OPERATED DURING THE SHOT,
THE FOCUS WILL BE LOST !

USING THE MACRO SETTING TO PHOTOGRAPH A FLOWER OR AN APPLE CLOSE-UP SHOULD GIVE PRETTY GOOD SCREEN-FILLING RESULTS!

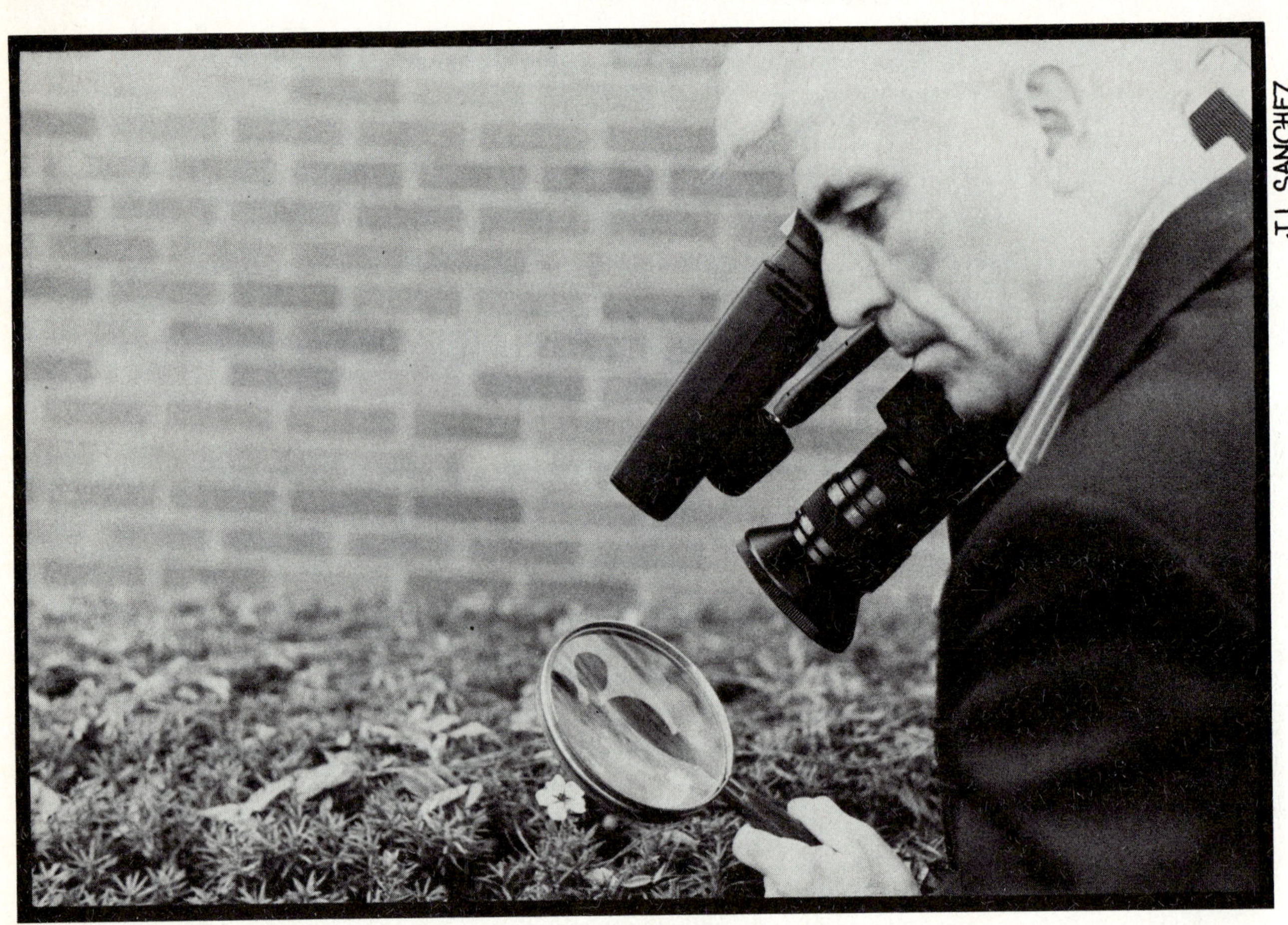

TRYING TO PHOTOGRAPH AN INSECT WOULD BE ANOTHER MATTER. A **CLOSE-UP** ATTACHMENT (THE EQUIVALENT OF USING A MAGNIFYING LENS) WILL PROVIDE A MUCH BETTER MAGNIFICATION WHEN VIDEOTAPING VERY SMALL OBJECTS. (IF YOU DON'T HAVE ONE, YOU CAN **ACTUALLY** HOLD A MAGNIFYING LENS IN FRONT OF YOUR CAMERA AND FOCUS THROUGH IT.)

YOU CAN EVEN USE **TWO** MAGNIFYING GLASSES!

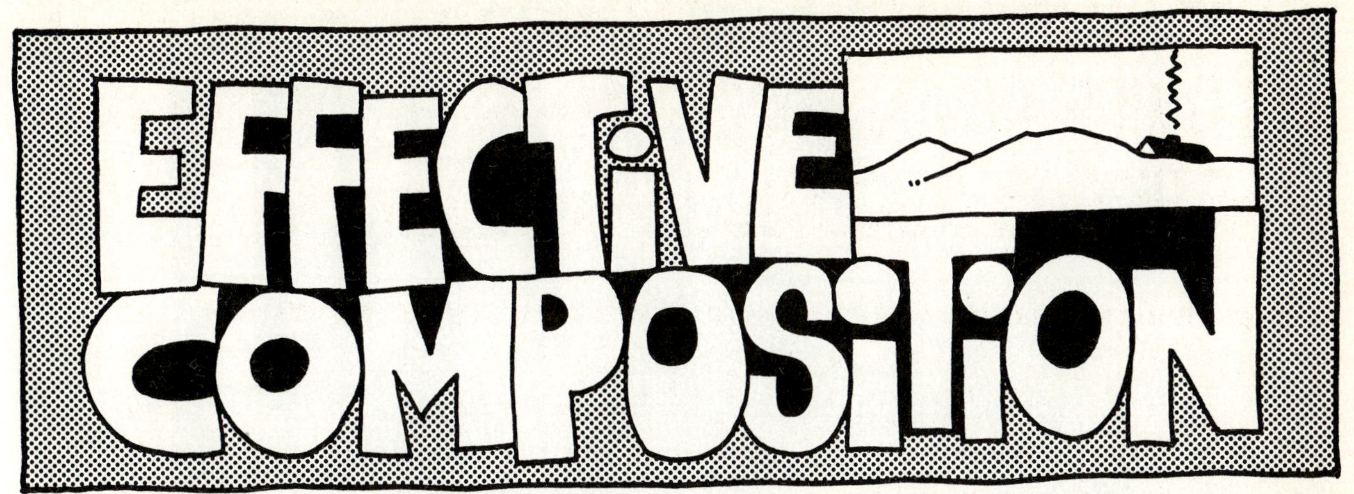

EFFECTIVE COMPOSITION

COMPOSITION IN THIS CASE DOESN'T REFER TO WRITING BUT TO THE ARRANGEMENT OF OBJECTS IN YOUR VIDEO FRAME. THIS IS ANOTHER AREA WHERE ANY EXPERIENCE IN STILL PHOTOGRAPHY WILL HELP YOU. HERE ARE SOME EXAMPLES OF *BAD,* IN FACT, *HORRENDOUS COMPOSITION!*

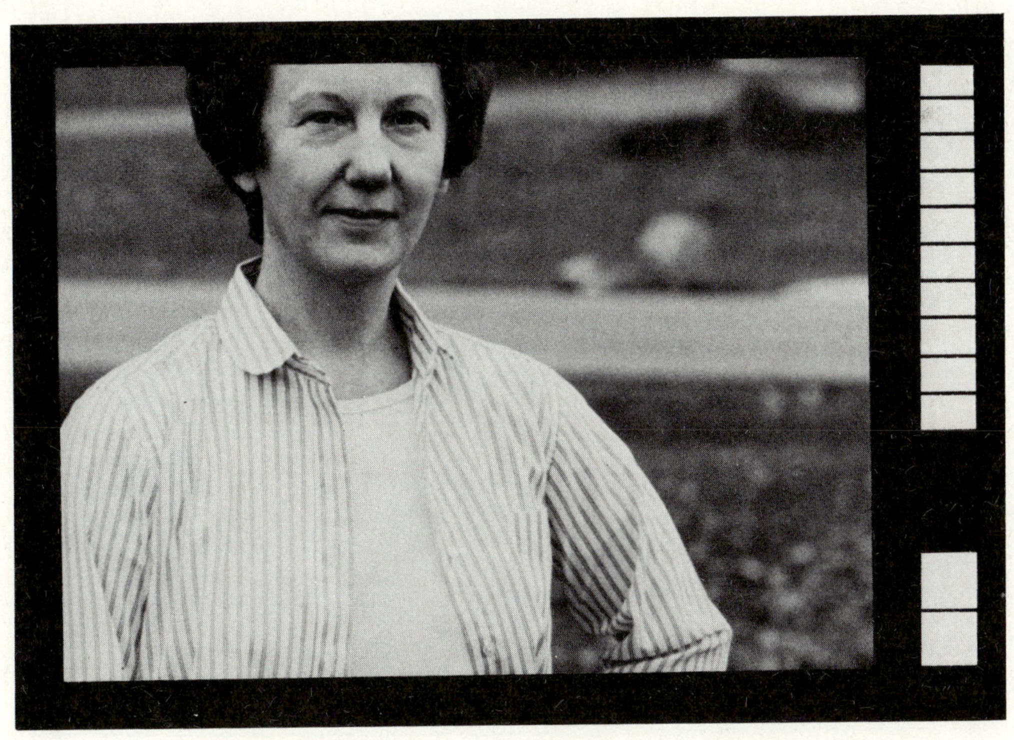

WHAT'S THE MATTER HERE?
THE TOP OF THE SUBJECT'S HEAD IS CUT OFF!

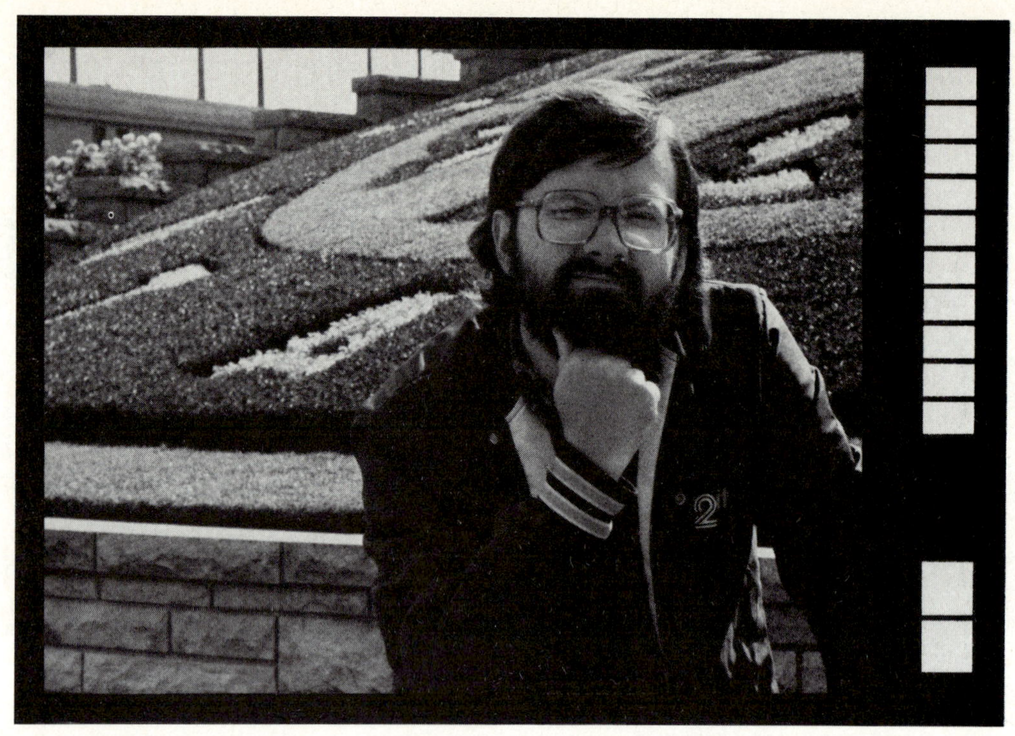

THE PROBLEM HERE IS THAT THERE IS TOO MUCH EMPTY SPACE WHERE WE DON'T NEED IT.

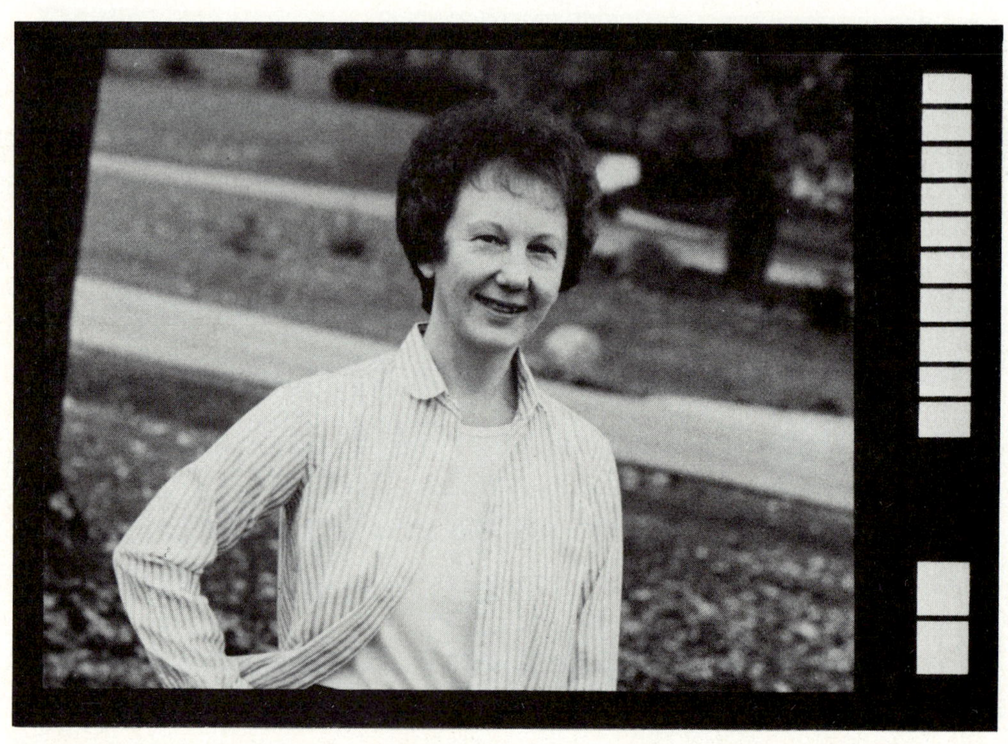

THE SUBJECT SEEMS TO BE ABOUT TO FALL OVER IN THIS ONE.

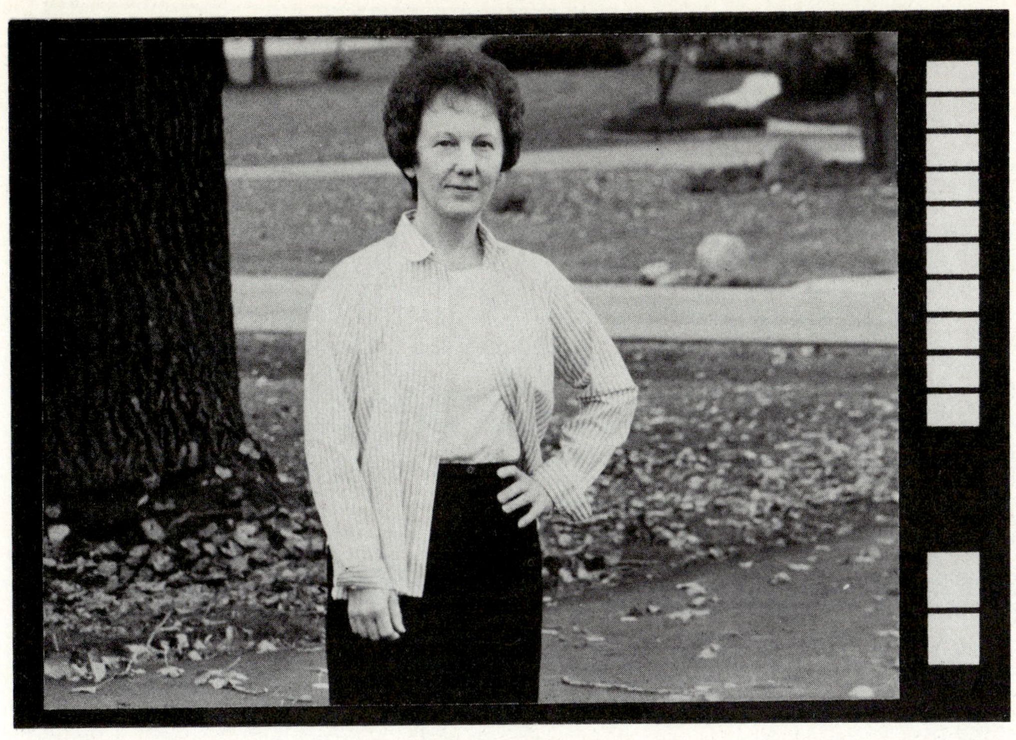

HAVE YOU FOUND THAT THESE PICTURES BOTHER YOU?... *WELL,* THEY SHOULD. LOOKING AT A POORLY COMPOSED PICTURE CAN BE A REAL STRAIN ON YOUR SANITY. BELOW IS A **WELL** COMPOSED SHOT!

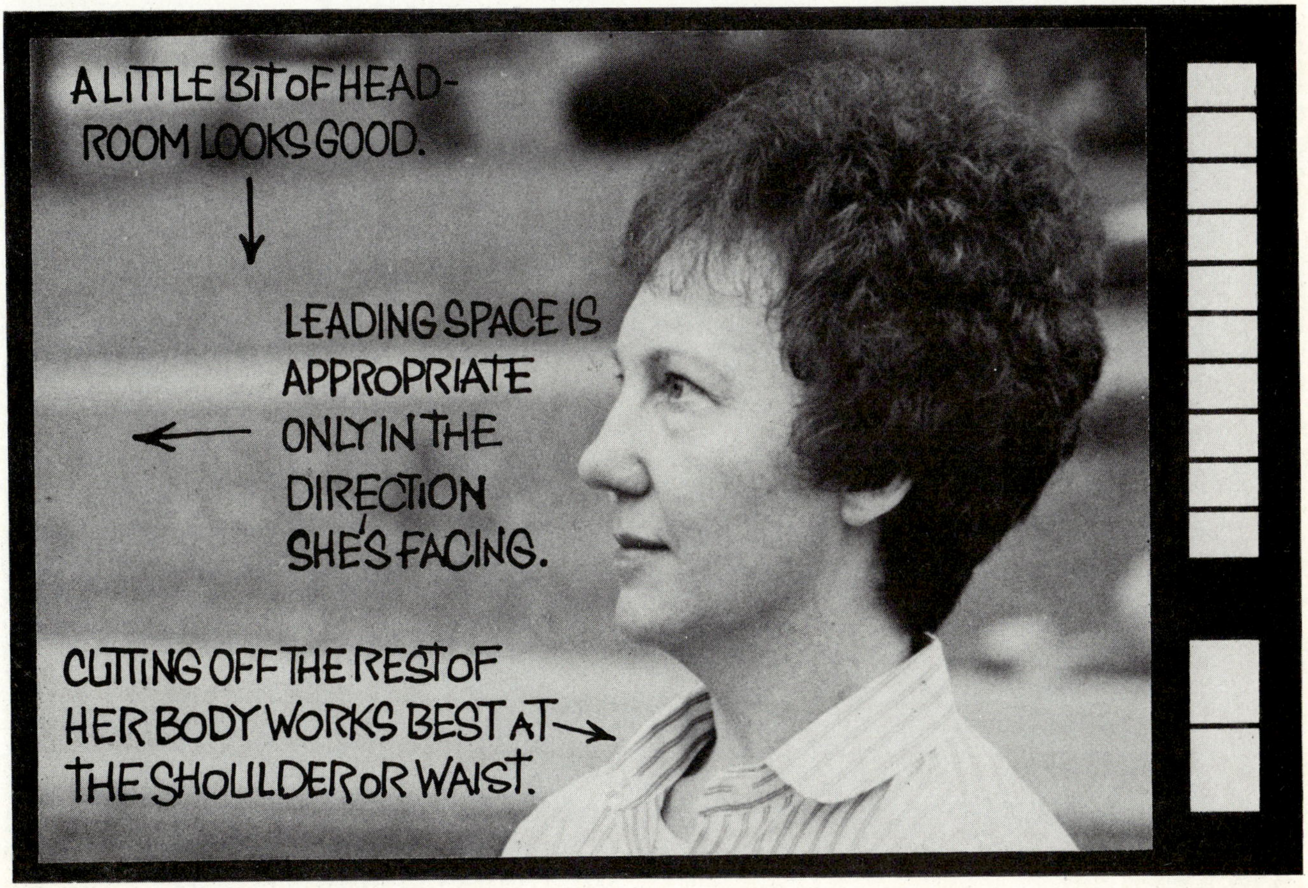

NOTICE THAT THE CAMERAPERSON KEPT THE CAMERA LEVEL

IN THE LINGO OF THE SCRIPT WRITER, THE COMPOSITION OF THE PREVIOUS PHOTO WOULD BE KNOWN AS A **CLOSE-UP** OR **CU** FOR SHORT. HERE ARE SOME OTHER COMPOSITIONS:

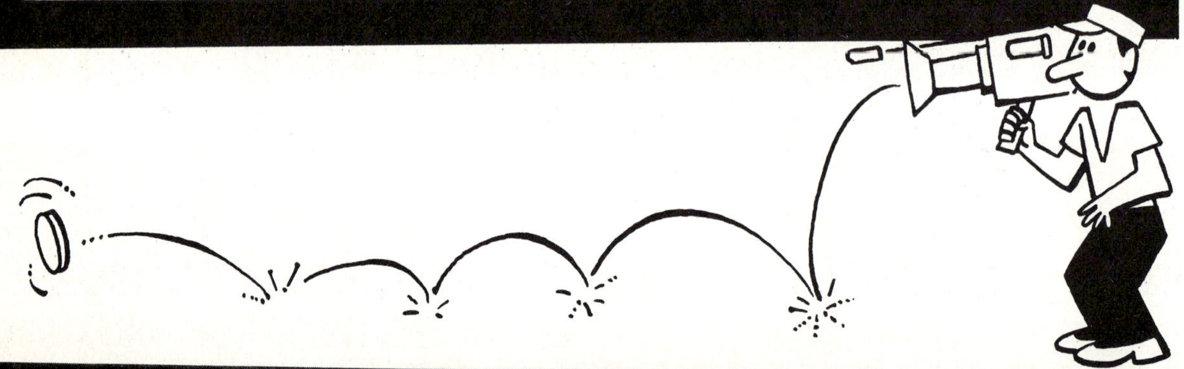

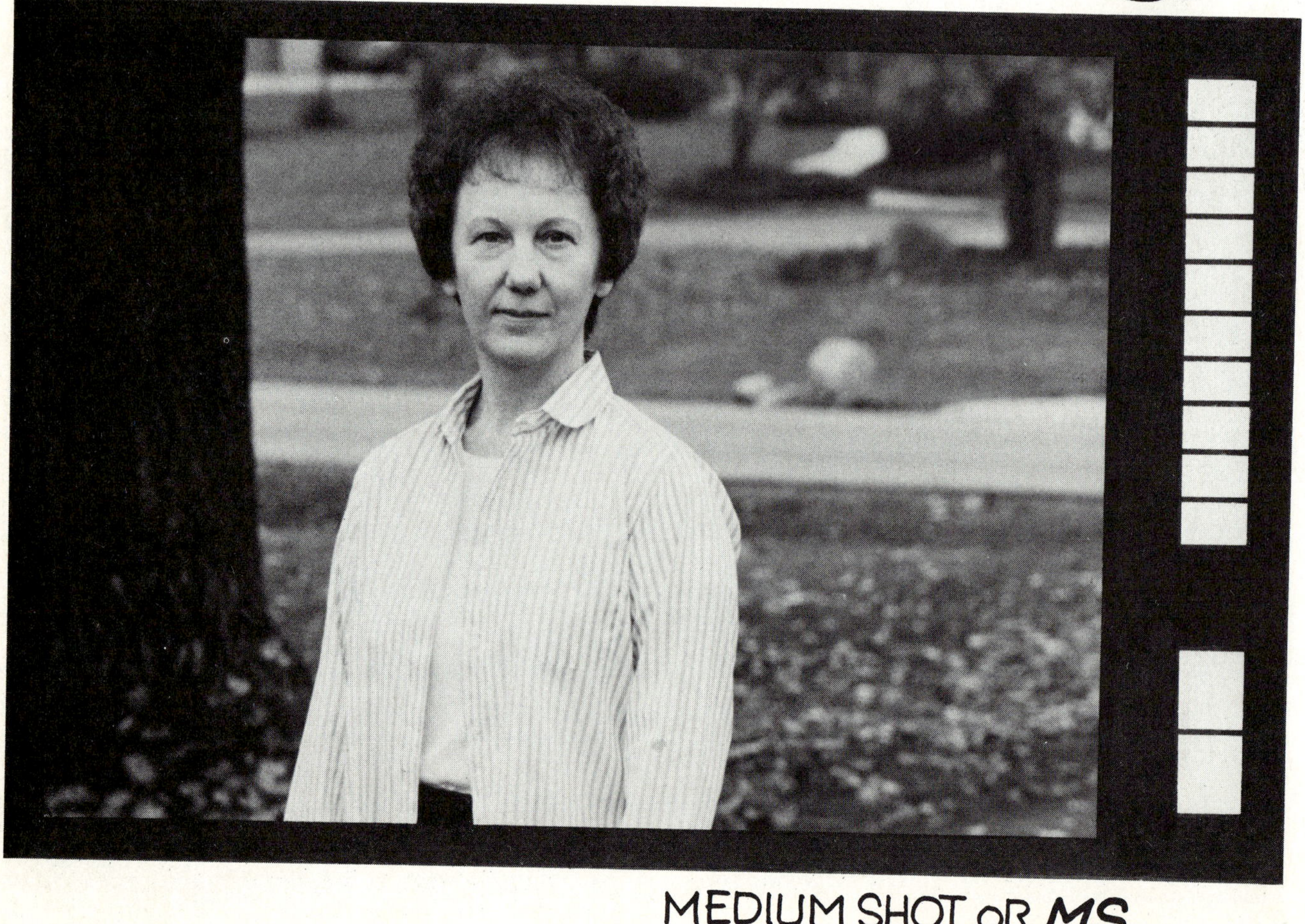

MEDIUM SHOT OR **MS**

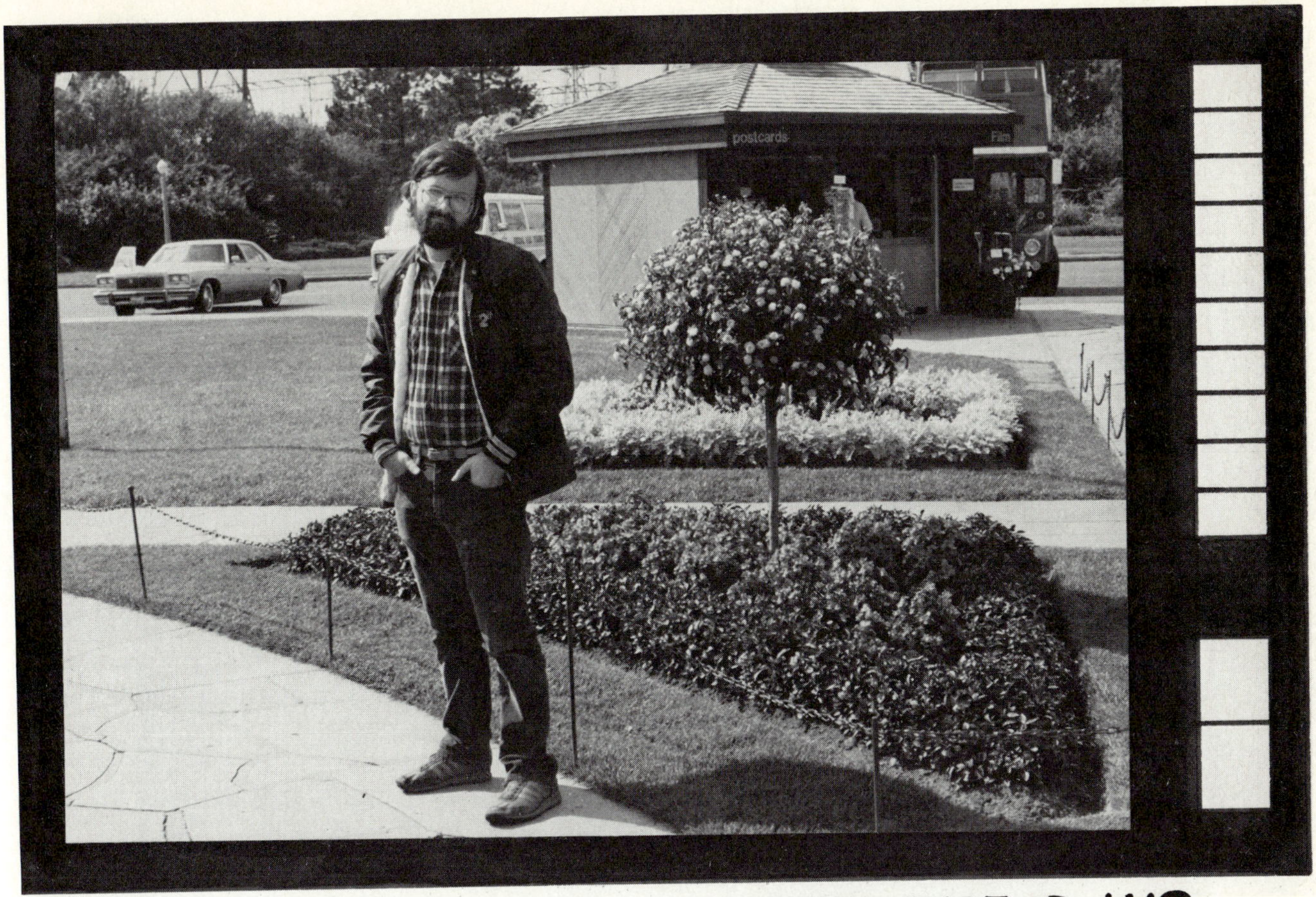

WIDE SHOT OR **WS**

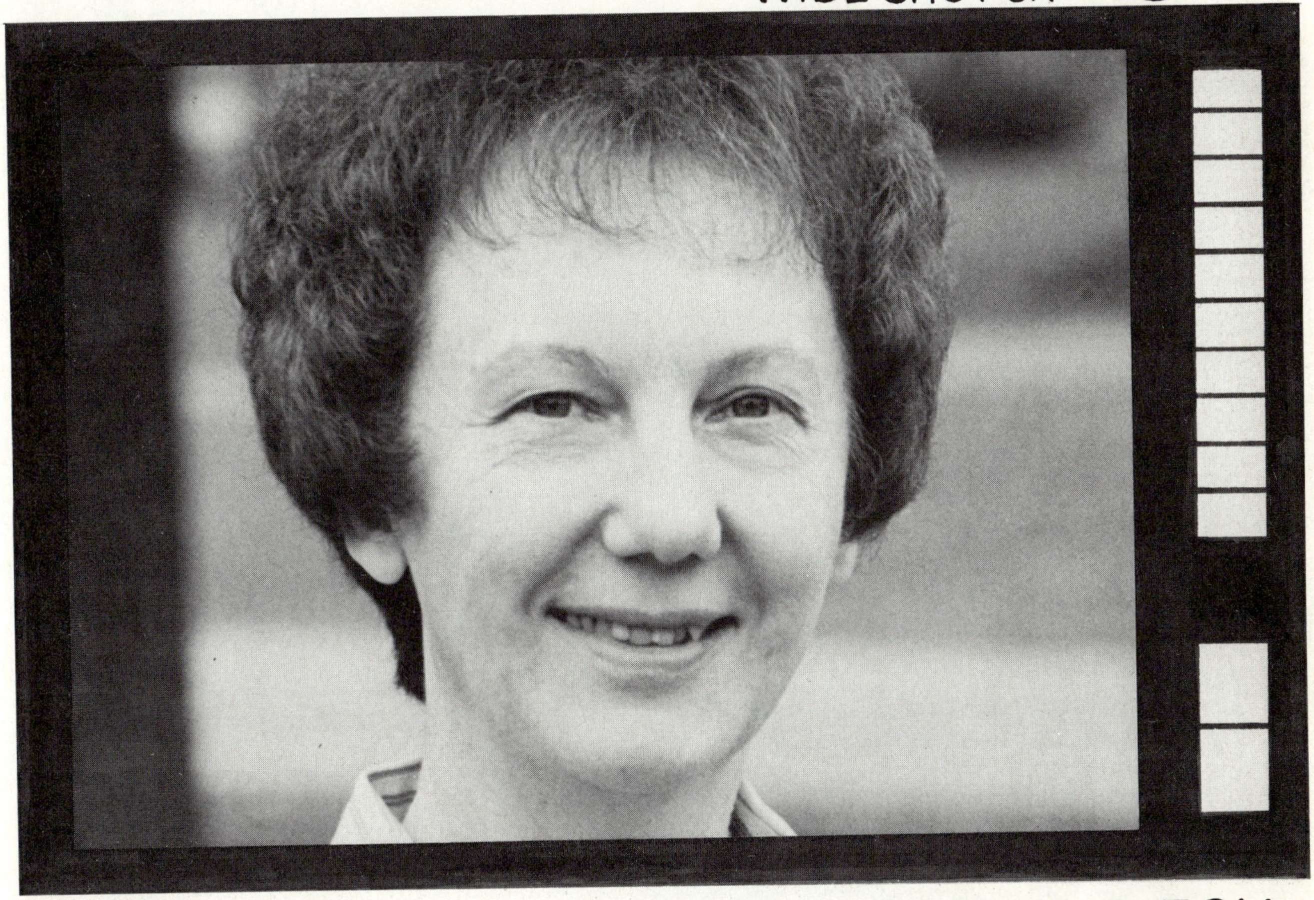

EXTREME CLOSE UP OR **ECU**

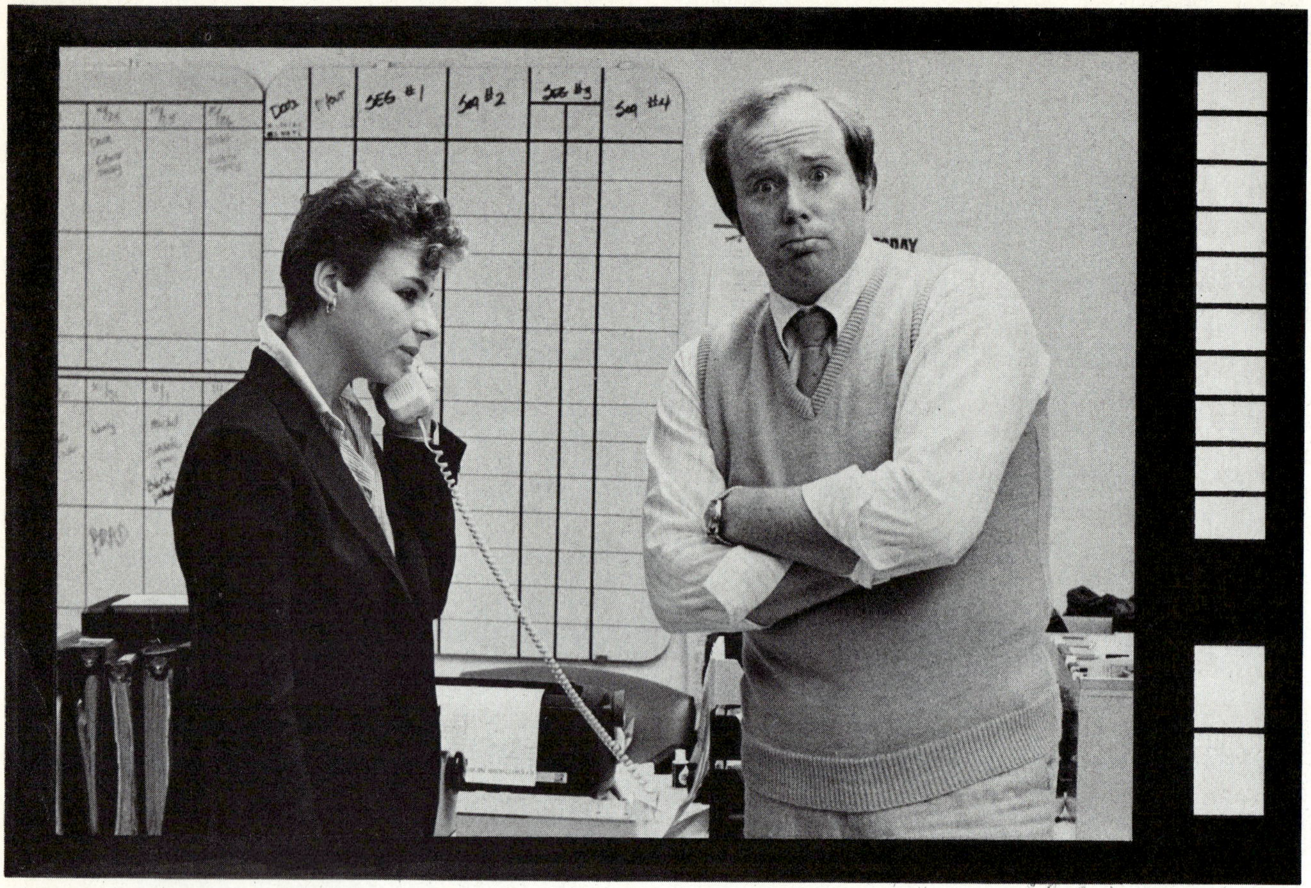

TWO SHOT

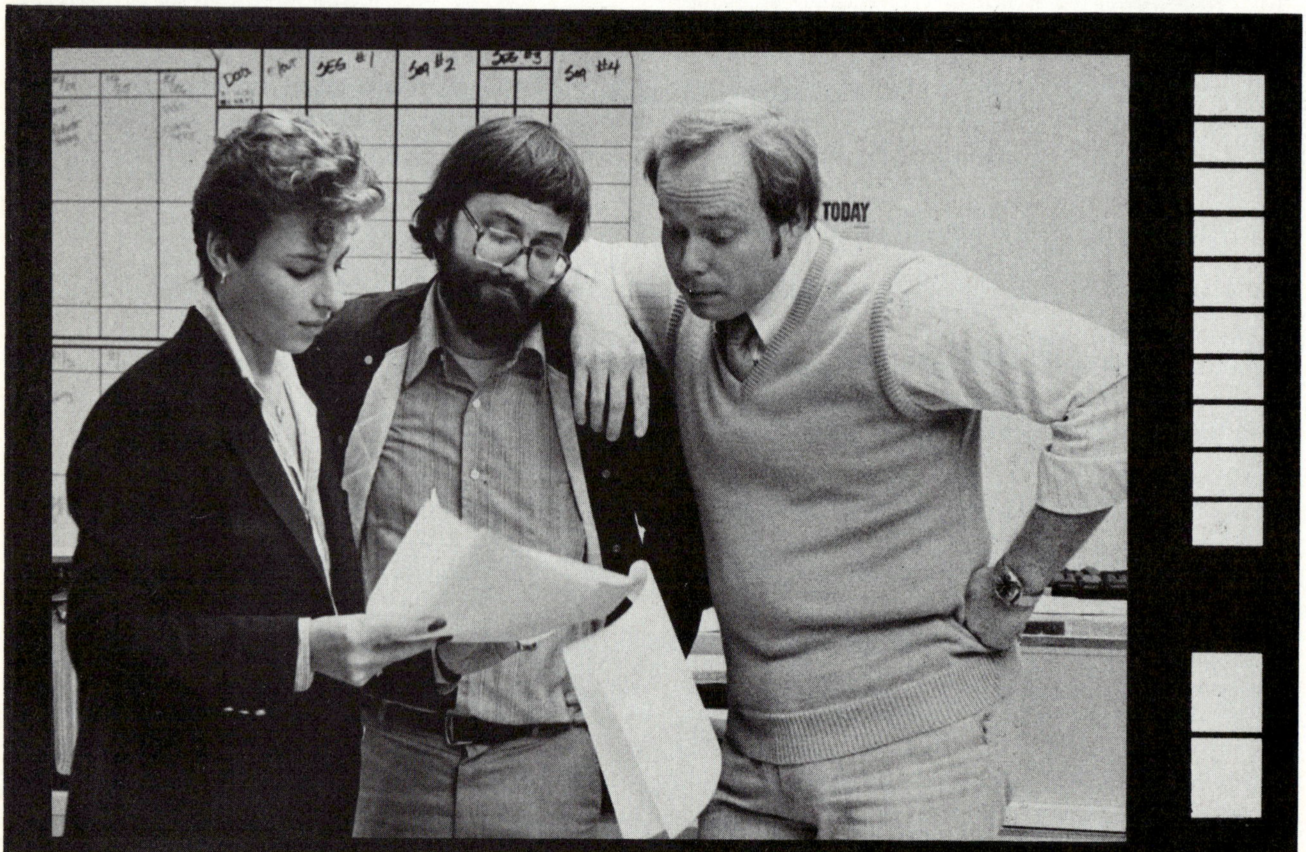

THREE SHOT

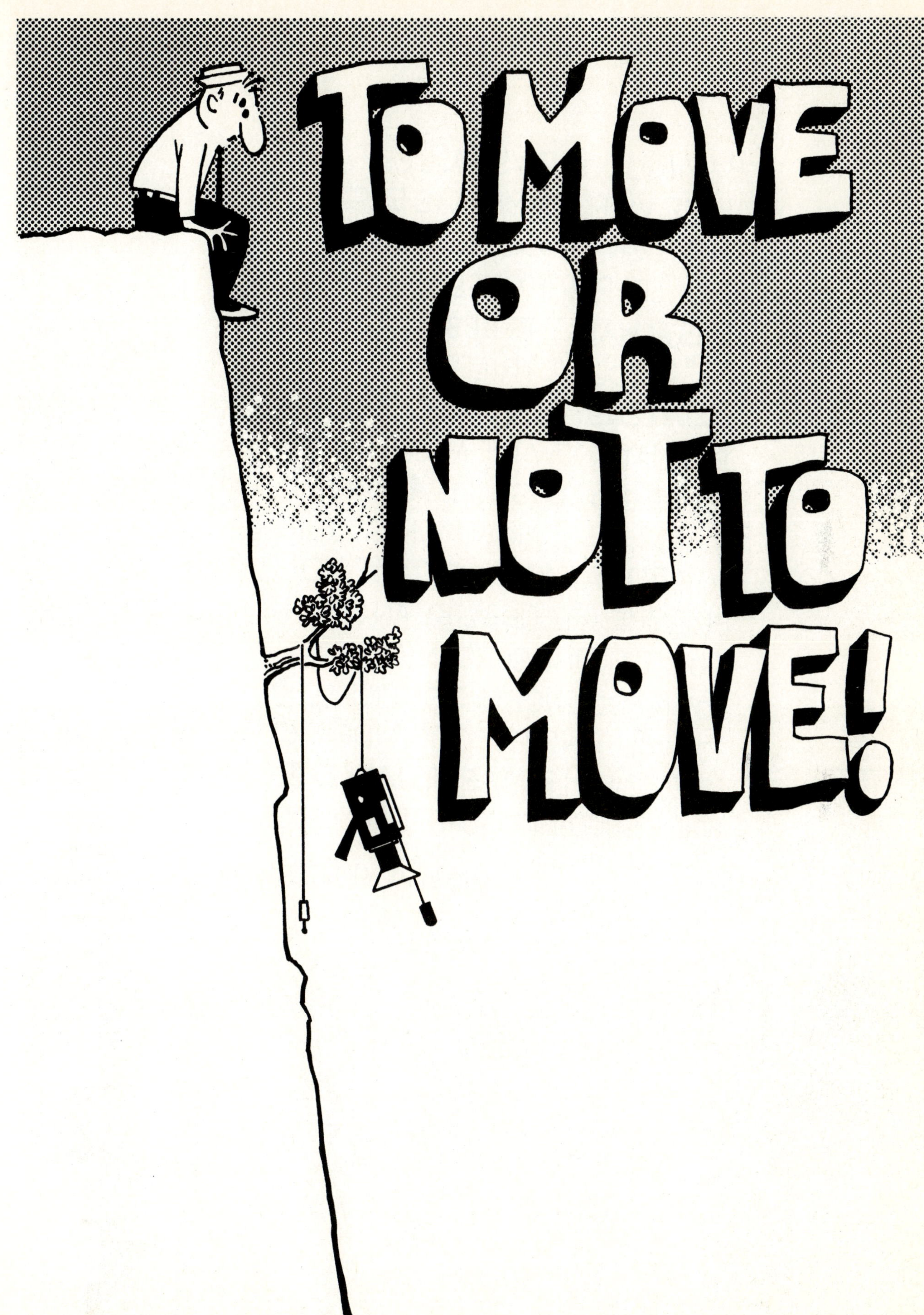

TO MOVE
OR
NOT TO
MOVE!

BY VIRTUE OF ITS SMALL SIZE, THE HOME VIDEO CAMERA IS EASY TO CARRY ON THE CAMERAPERSON'S SHOULDER. THE QUESTION IS: **"IS THIS ALWAYS THE BEST PLACE FOR IT?"** IF YOU'VE TRIED TO USE THE ZOOM LENS FROM YOUR SHOULDER, YOU MAY KNOW THE ANSWER. THE TELEPHOTO LENS WILL **AMPLIFY** YOUR TINIEST MOVEMENTS TO THE POINT THAT **EVERY TIME** YOU BREATHE, IT LOOKS LIKE AN EARTH-QUAKE ON THE SCREEN! TO SAVE YOUR AUDIENCE MOTION SICKNESS, YOU WILL FIND IT A GOOD IDEA TO KEEP YOUR LENS SET TO **WIDE** WHILE SHOOTING FROM THE SHOULDER.

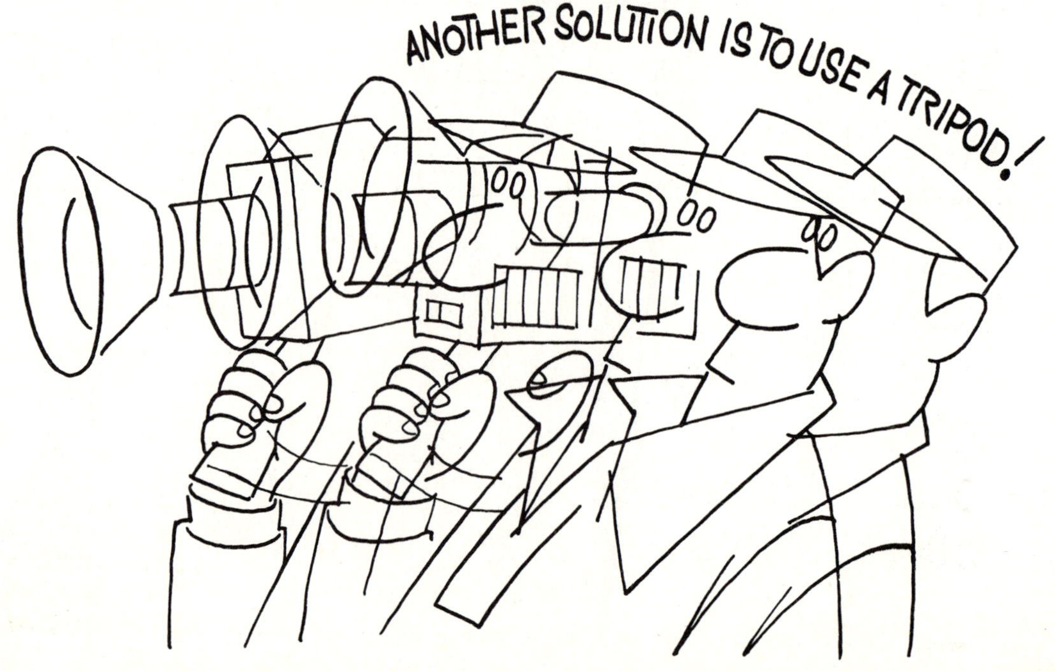

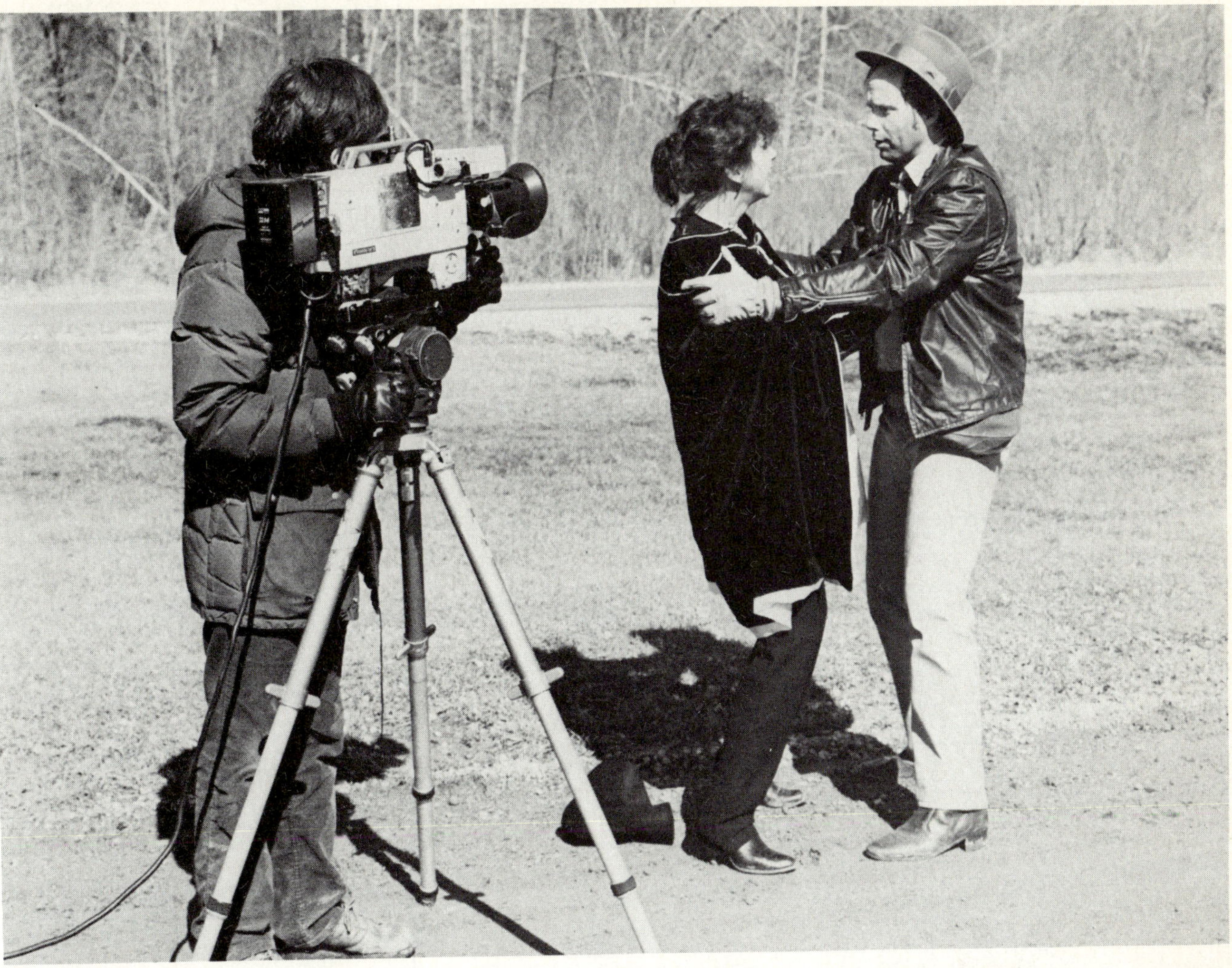

A CAMERA ON A TRIPOD WILL GIVE YOU A ROCK-STEADY VIDEO, EVEN AT THE *LONGEST* TELEPHOTO SETTING. USING A TRIPOD HAS THE ADDITIONAL ADVANTAGE of MAKING CERTAIN TYPES of CAMERA MoVEMENTS MUCH *SMOOTHER AND NEATER.!!*

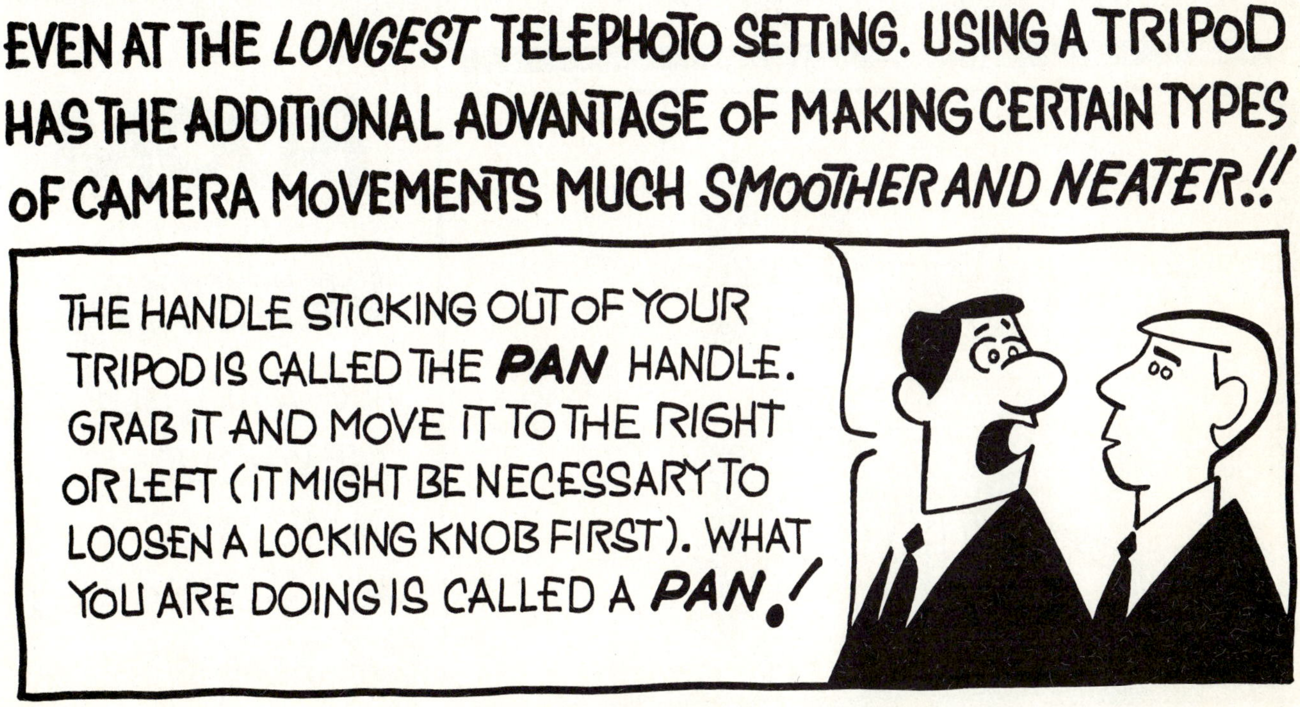

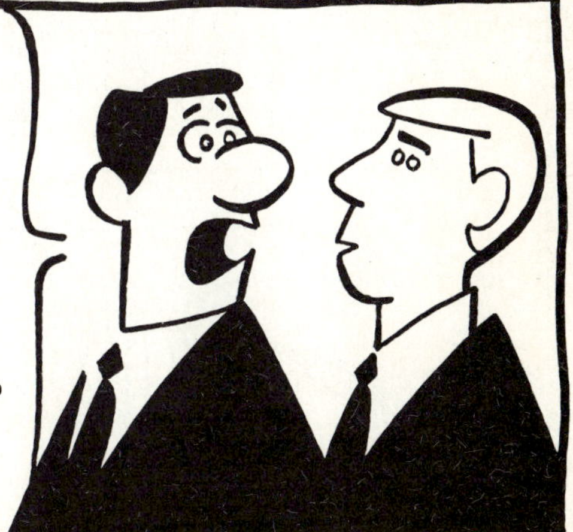

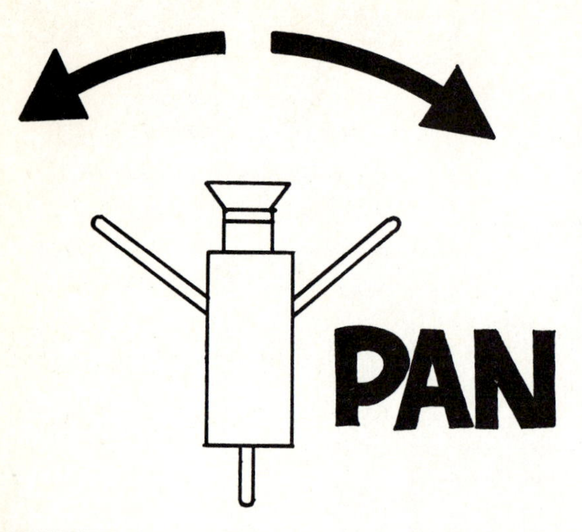

A PAN IS USEFUL WHEN YOU WANT TO SHIFT EMPHASIS FROM ONE SUBJECT TO ANOTHER IN THE SAME GENERAL PLACE, FOR INSTANCE PANNING BACK AND FORTH BETWEEN TWO PEOPLE TALKING. IT WILL TAKE SOME PRACTICE TO DO IT SMOOTHLY, ESPECIALLY WITH AN INEXPENSIVE TRIPOD. A BETTER TRIPOD WILL HAVE A **FLUID HEAD**, WHICH SERVES TO DAMPEN AND SMOOTH THE MOTION.

HERE ARE SOME OTHER "SCRIPTWRITER" TERMS FOR CAMERA MOTIONS:

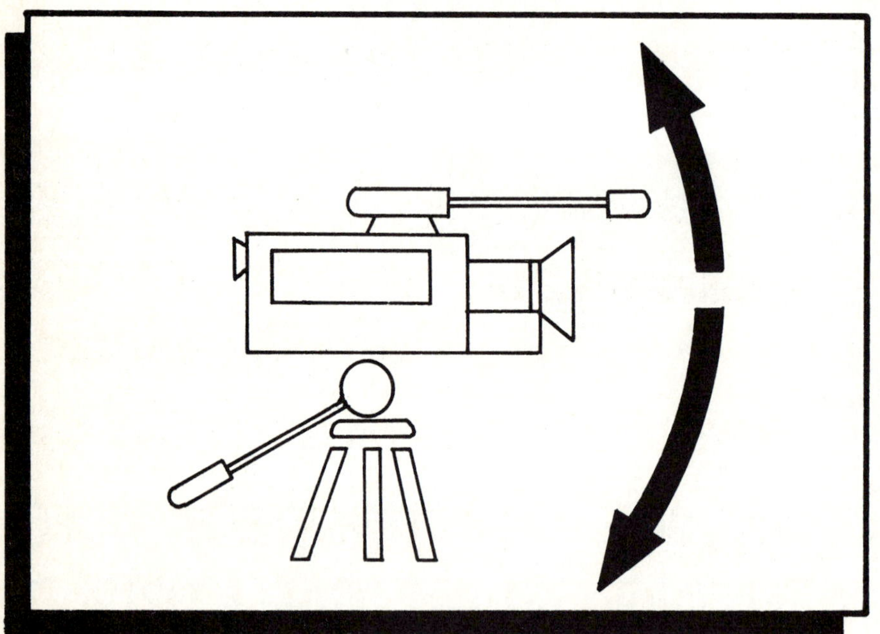

TILT

LIKE A PAN, BUT UP OR DOWN INSTEAD OF LEFT OR RIGHT!

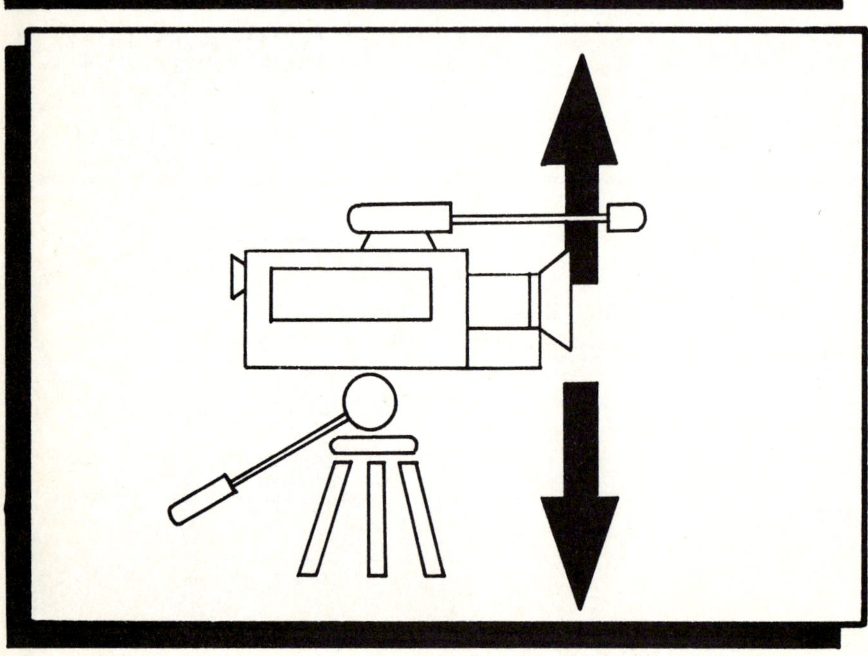

BOOM
OR
PEDESTAL

LIKE A TILT, BUT THE WHOLE CAMERA IS ACTUALLY MOVED UP OR DOWN!

ZOOM

AN OPERATION OF THE ZOOM LENS DURING THE SHOT, MAKING THE PICTURE GROW OR SHRINK IN SIZE.

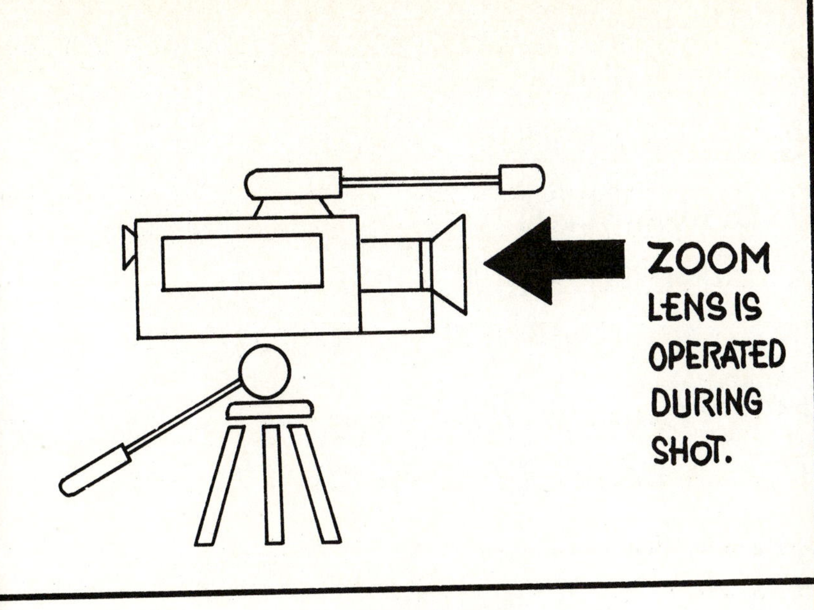

DOLLY

LIKE A ZOOM, BUT THE WHOLE CAMERA IS MOVED TOWARD OR AWAY FROM THE SUBJECT.

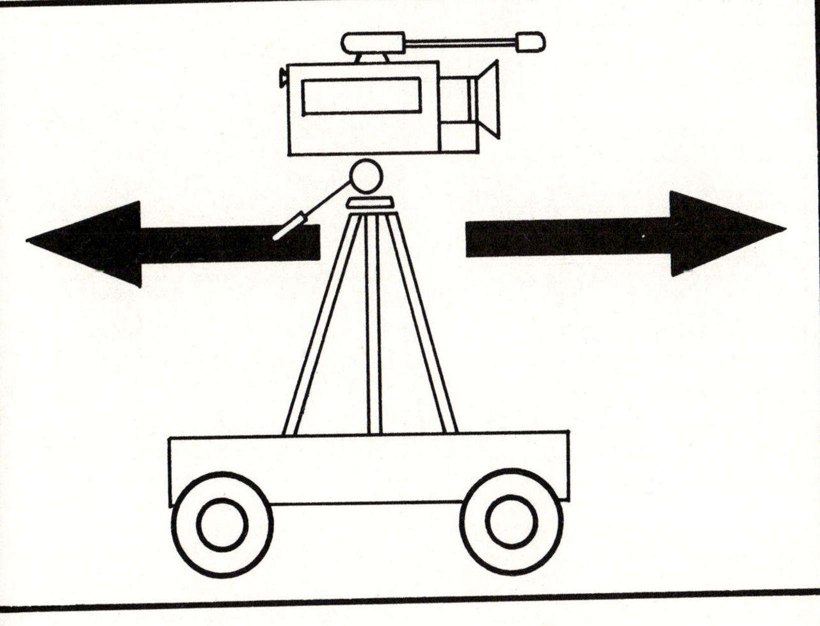

TRUCK

THE CAMERA IS MOVED SIDEWAYS OR PERPENDICULAR TO THE SUBJECT.

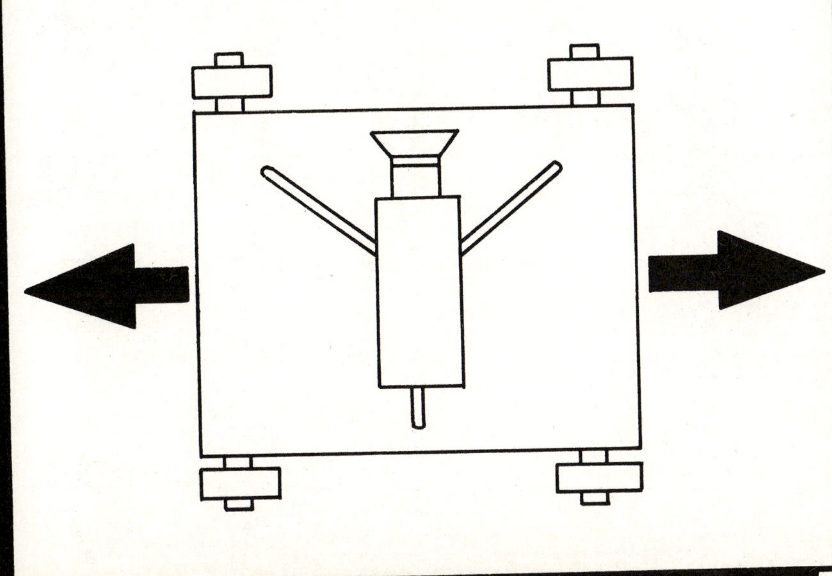

WHAT, YOU MAY WONDER, IS THE
REAL DIFFERENCE BETWEEN A
TILT AND A BOOM? DOES A DOLLY
REALLY LOOK DIFFERENT FROM
A ZOOM? GENERALLY, THE RESULT
OF AN ACTUAL CAMERA MOVEMENT
(DOLLY, TRUCK, BOOM) WILL LOOK
MORE DRAMATIC THAN A TRIPOD
MOVEMENT (ZOOM, PAN, TILT).
THE REASON IS THAT A CHANGE IN
PERSPECTIVE TAKES PLACE DURING
A REAL CAMERA MOVEMENT.
OBJECTS CHANGE THEIR SIZE AND
PLACEMENT RELATIVE TO EACH
OTHER. ZOOMS, PANS, AND TILTS
DON'T HAVE THIS EFFECT. ALL THIS
IS CONTINGENT, OF COURSE, ON
YOUR ABILITY TO PERFORM MOVES
SMOOTHLY, WHICH IS NO SMALL
TASK! EXECUTING A NEAT SIDE-
WAYS OR BACKWARD MOVEMENT
WITH THE CAMERA ON YOUR
SHOULDER IS APT TO BE SO
DIFFICULT THAT YOU'RE BETTER
OFF STICKING TO THE TRIPOD!

ADD SOME WHEELS!

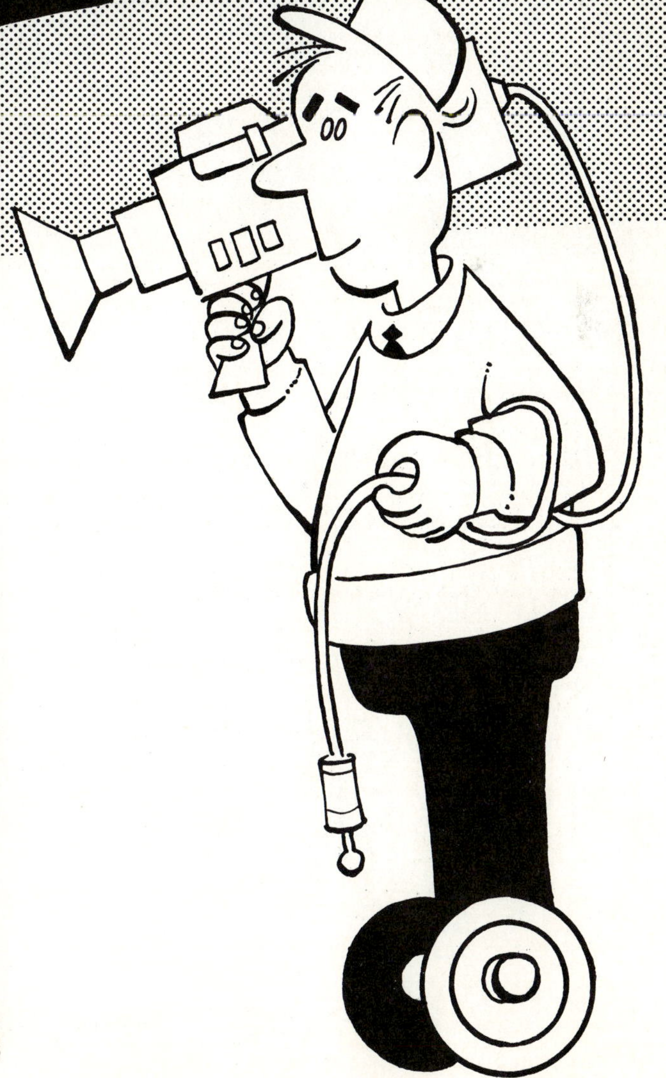

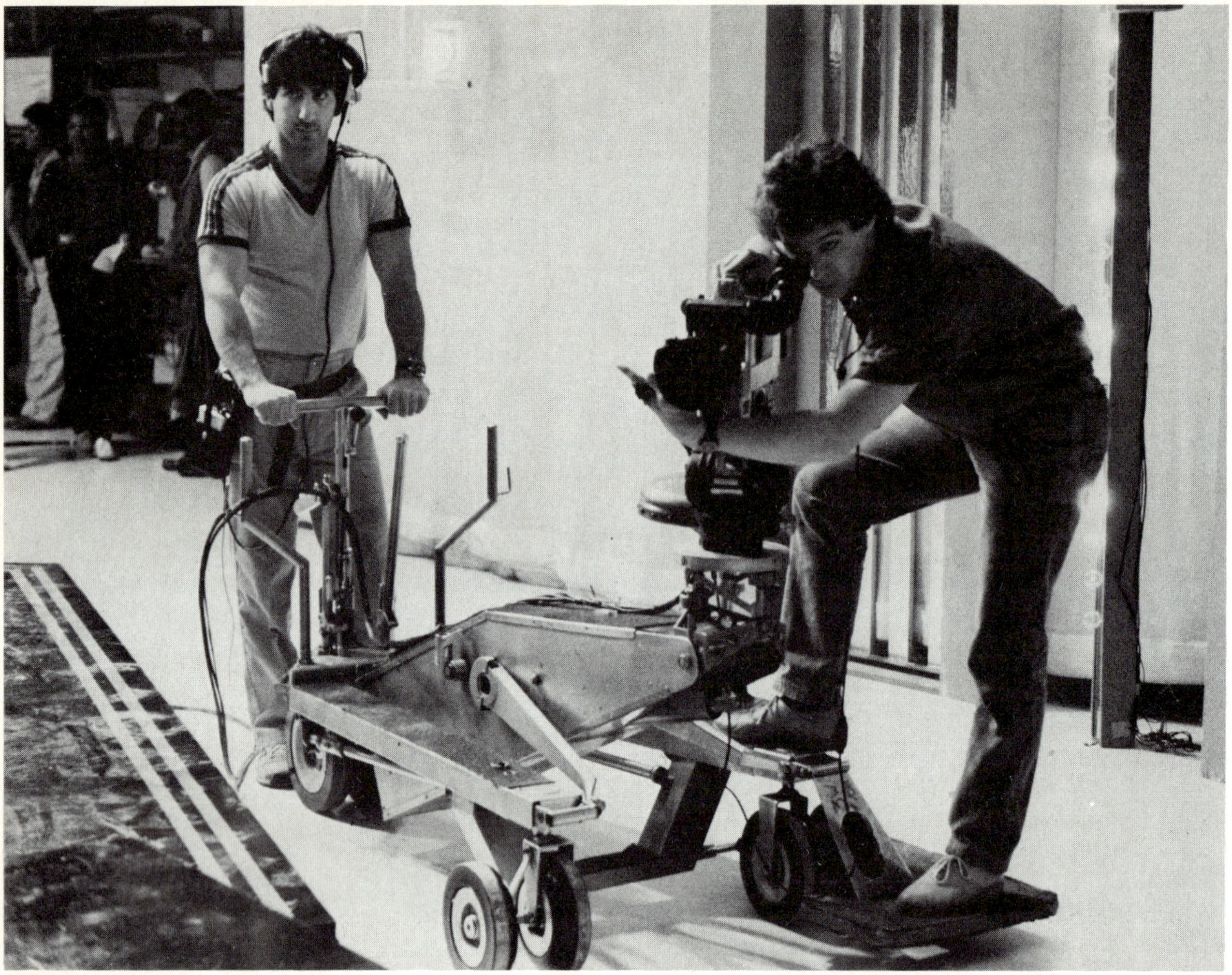

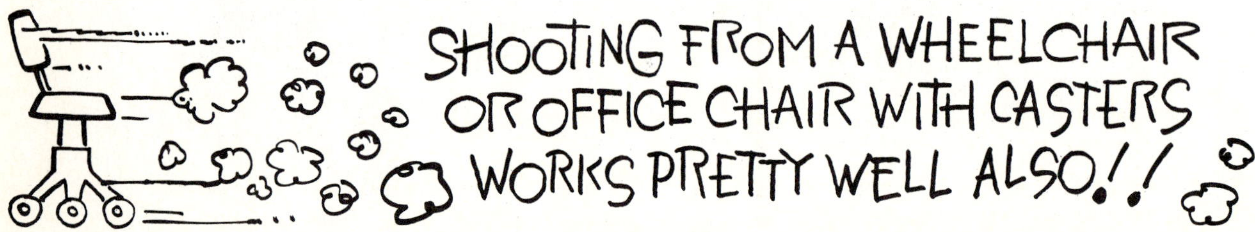

THE BASIC DOLLY IS A PLATFORM WITH **WHEELS** WHERE THE CAMERA AND OPERATOR CAN RIDE. DOLLY TRACKS (THINK OF RAILROAD TRACKS) ARE SOMETIMES USED WHEN THE CAMERA HAS TO MOVE OVER BUMPY GROUND. A **BOOM** GIVES THE CAMERA (AND SOMETIMES THE OPERATOR TOO) A SMOOTH UP-AND-DOWN RIDE! FOR SMALLER BUDGETS, A **TRIPOD** WITH WHEELS WILL GIVE PRETTY GOOD RESULTS WHEN USED ON A SMOOTH SURFACE, LIKE A DANCE FLOOR OR GYMNASIUM!!

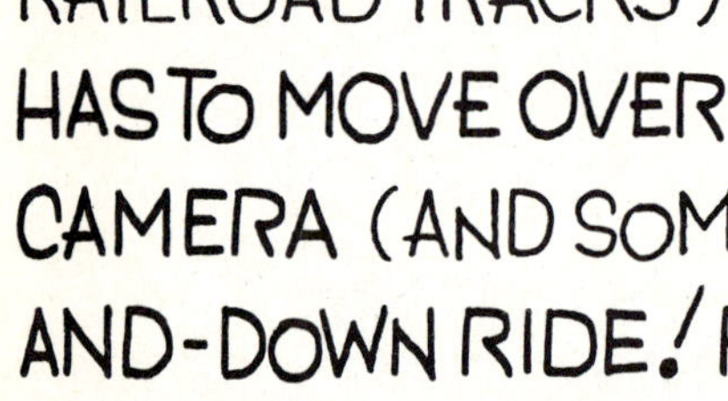

SHOOTING FROM A WHEELCHAIR OR OFFICE CHAIR WITH CASTERS WORKS PRETTY WELL ALSO!!

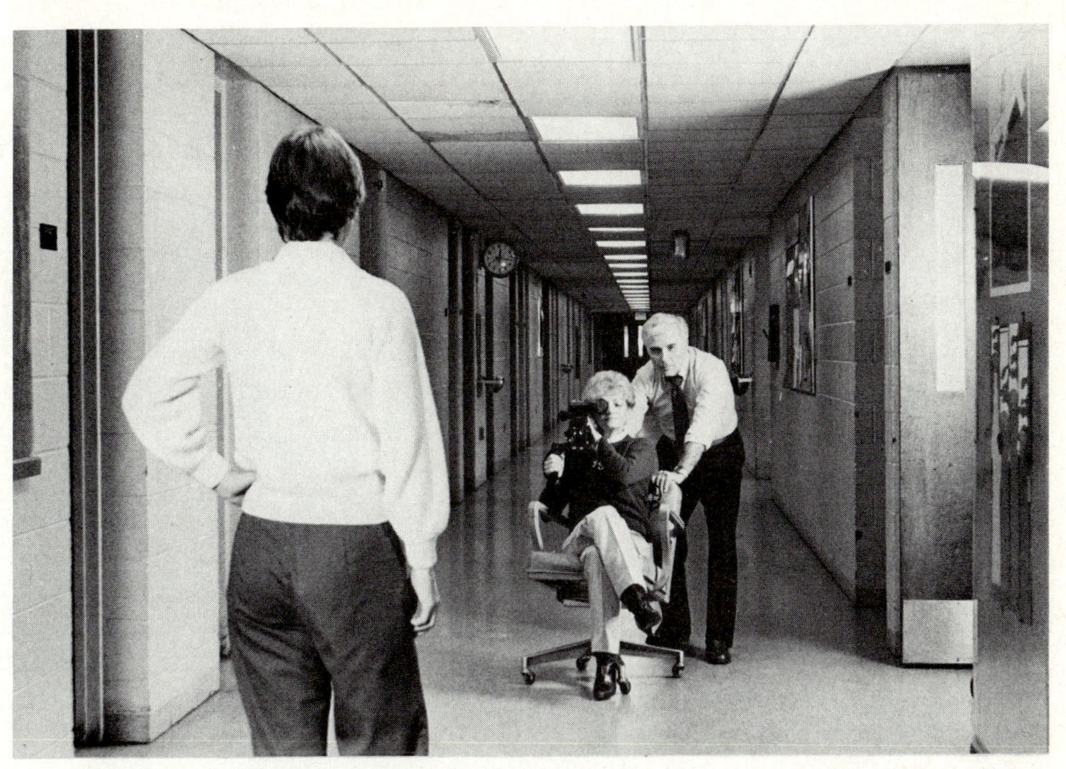

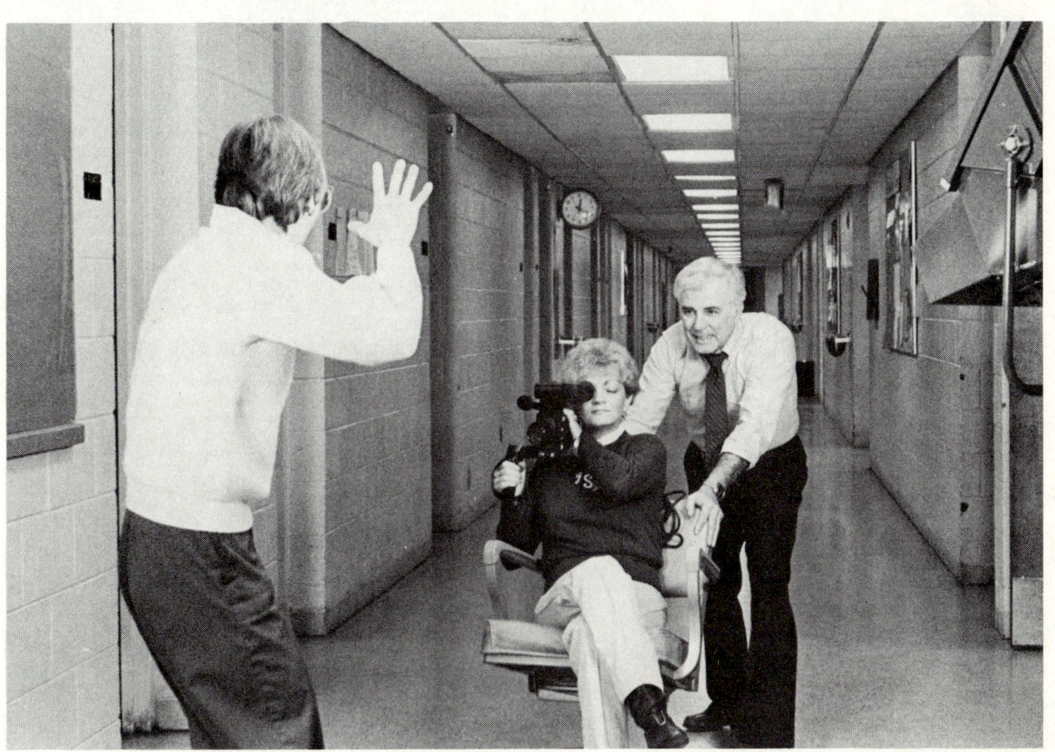

THE CAMERAPERSON SITS IN THE CHAIR WITH THE CAMERA WHILE AN ACCOMPLICE PUSHES AND STEERS TO *FOLLOW THE ACTION!*

THE CAMERAPERSON'S BODY ACTUALLY AB-
SORBS SOME OF THE VIBRATIONS COMING
FROM A ROUGH GROUND SURFACE, MAKING

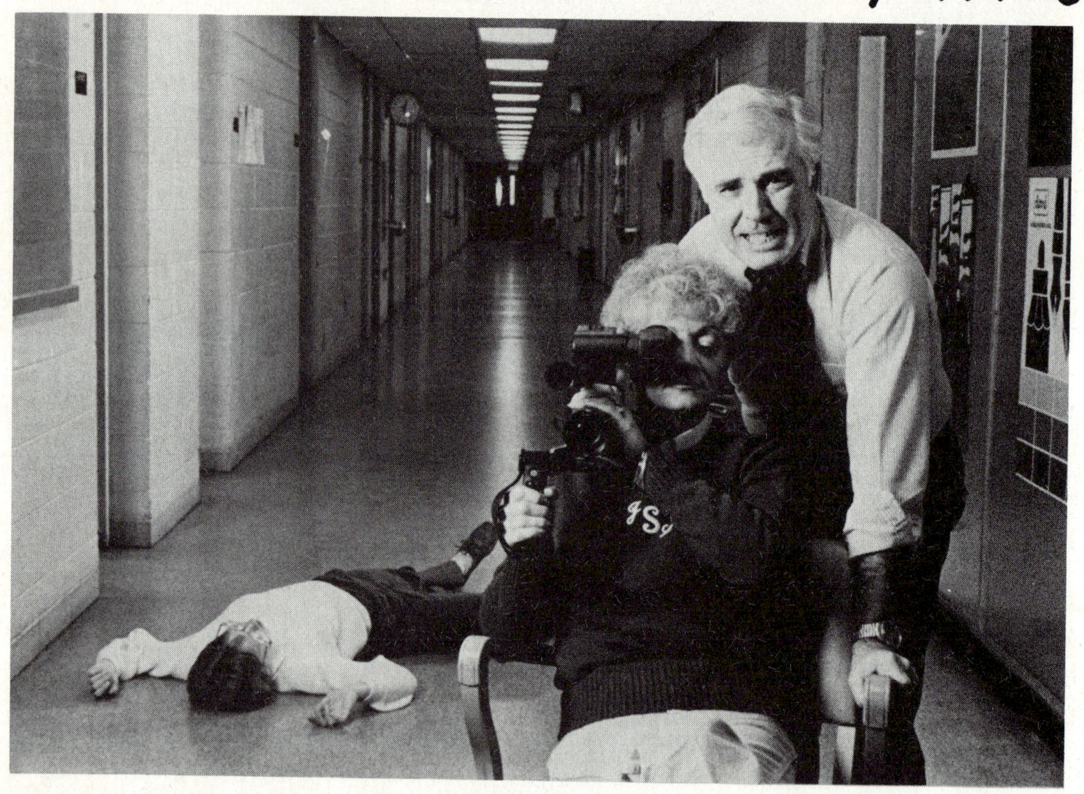

FOR A RELATIVELY STABLE PICTURE. WITH
ANY MOVING CAMERA PICTURE, KEEP THE
CAMERA LENS SET PRETTY *WIDE* AND
YOUR VIDEO WILL STAY STEADY.

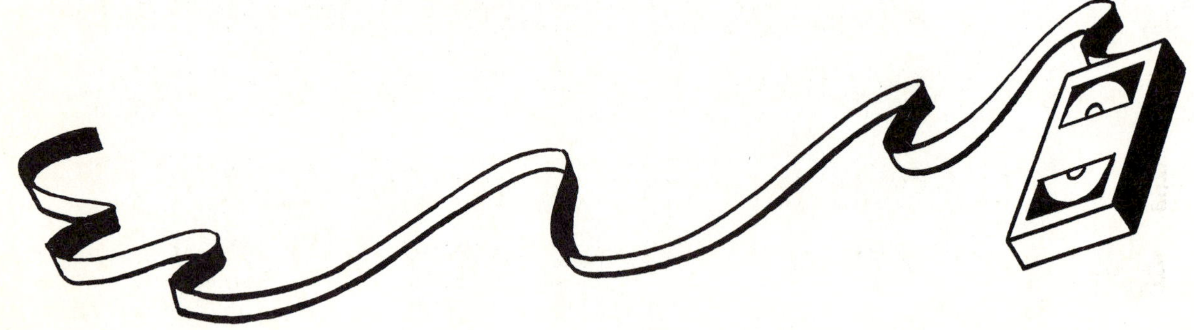

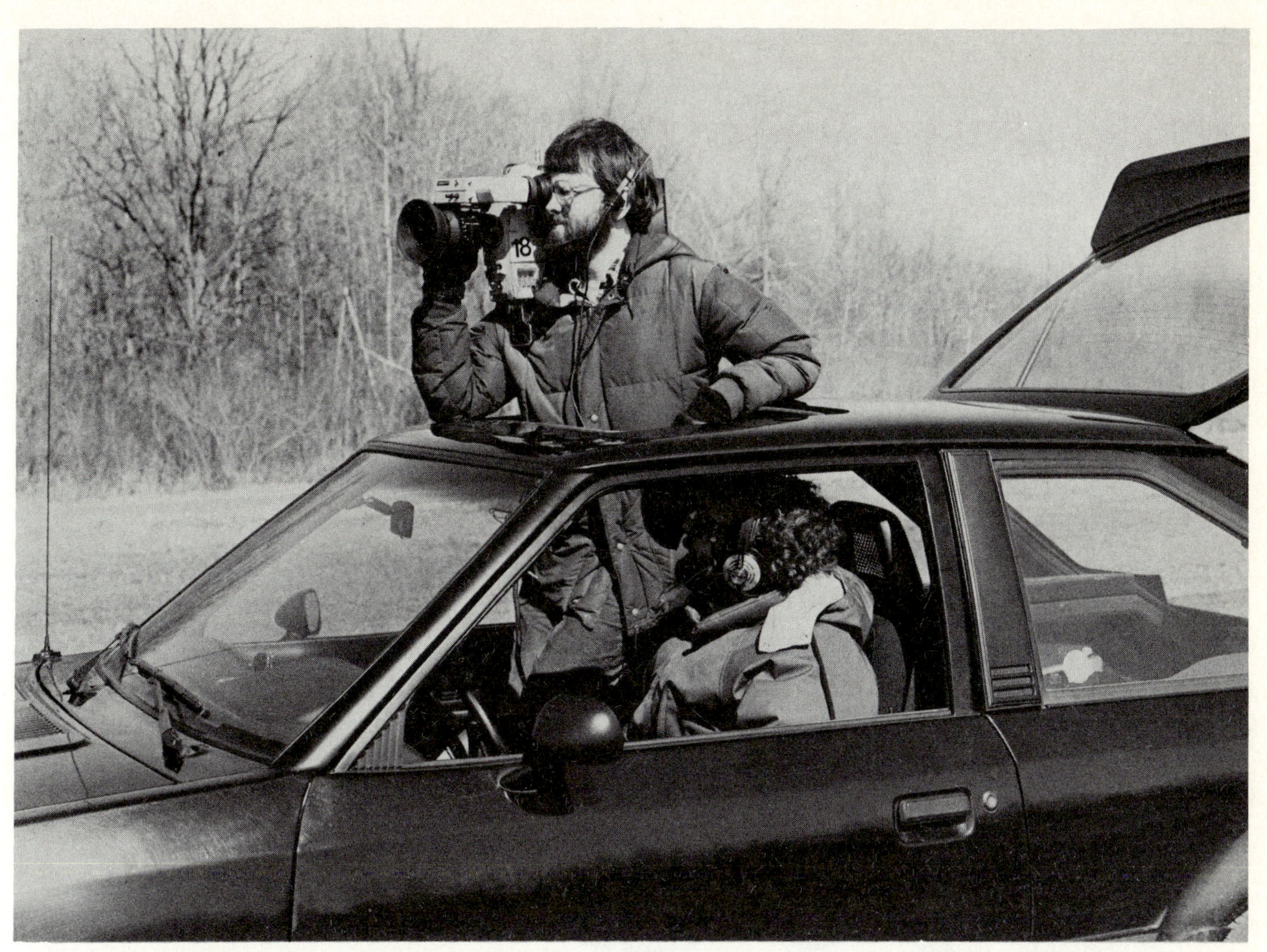

SHOOTING FROM AN AUTOMOBILE OR OTHER VEHICLE IS ANOTHER SPECIAL SITUATION. AIMING THE CAMERA THROUGH THE FRONT WINDSHIELD MIGHT WORK OK IF THE GLASS IS CLEAN .. BUT FOR BETTER VIDEO, SHOOT THROUGH A ROLLED DOWN SIDE WINDOW OR POKE YOUR CAMERA THROUGH AN OPEN SUN ROOF. CAR MOUNTS ARE AVAILABLE THAT WILL ALLOW YOU TO CLAMP THE CAMERA TO A SIDE WINDOW OR *"SUCTION CUP"* IT TO THE HOOD!

ONCE AGAIN — TRY TO PICK SMOOTH DRIVING TERRAIN, AND KEEP LENS <u>WIDE</u>!

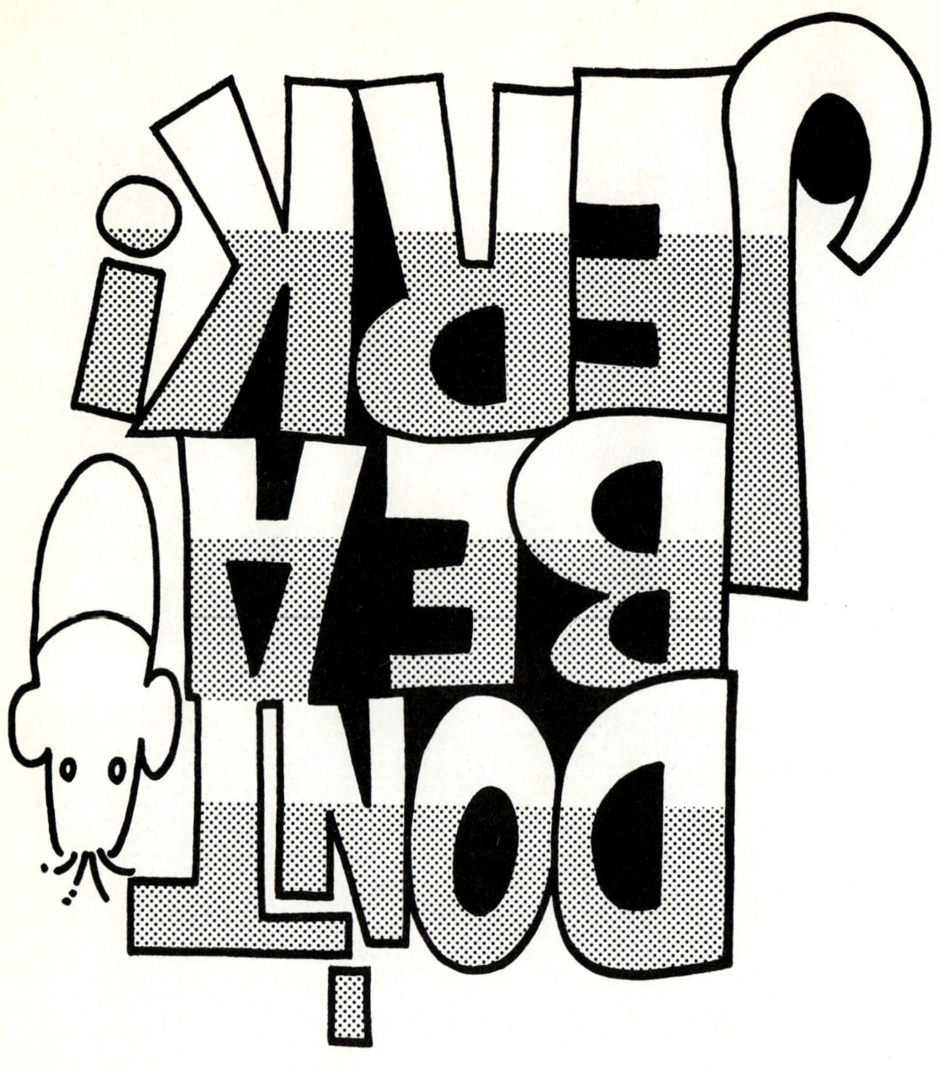

THINK ABOUT WHAT YOUR FINISHED PRODUCTION WILL LOOK LIKE. HAVE YOU BEEN DOING YOUR CAMERA MOVES SMOOTHLY? *JERKY* OR HAPHAZARD CAMERA MOVEMENTS ARE ESPECIALLY UNCOMFORTABLE TO WATCH. HAVE YOU BEEN MOVING YOUR CAMERA TOO MUCH? IT IS INAPPROPRIATE FOR *EVERY* CAMERA SHOT TO CONTAIN PANS, ZOOMS, AND DOLLIES. VARY THE CAMERA MOVES FROM SHOT TO SHOT, AND DON'T BE AFRAID TO BE STATIONARY WHEN APPROPRIATE. IF THE SUBJECT IS COMPELLING, FANCY CAMERA WORK MAY ONLY *DETRACT* FROM IT. ANOTHER WAY TO CREATE *MOVEMENT* IS THROUGH *EDITING*. EVEN IF EDITING FACILITIES ARE BEYOND YOUR MEANS, READ THE CHAPTER ON EDITING FOR IDEAS ON PLANNING AND PACING YOUR CAMERA SHOTS!

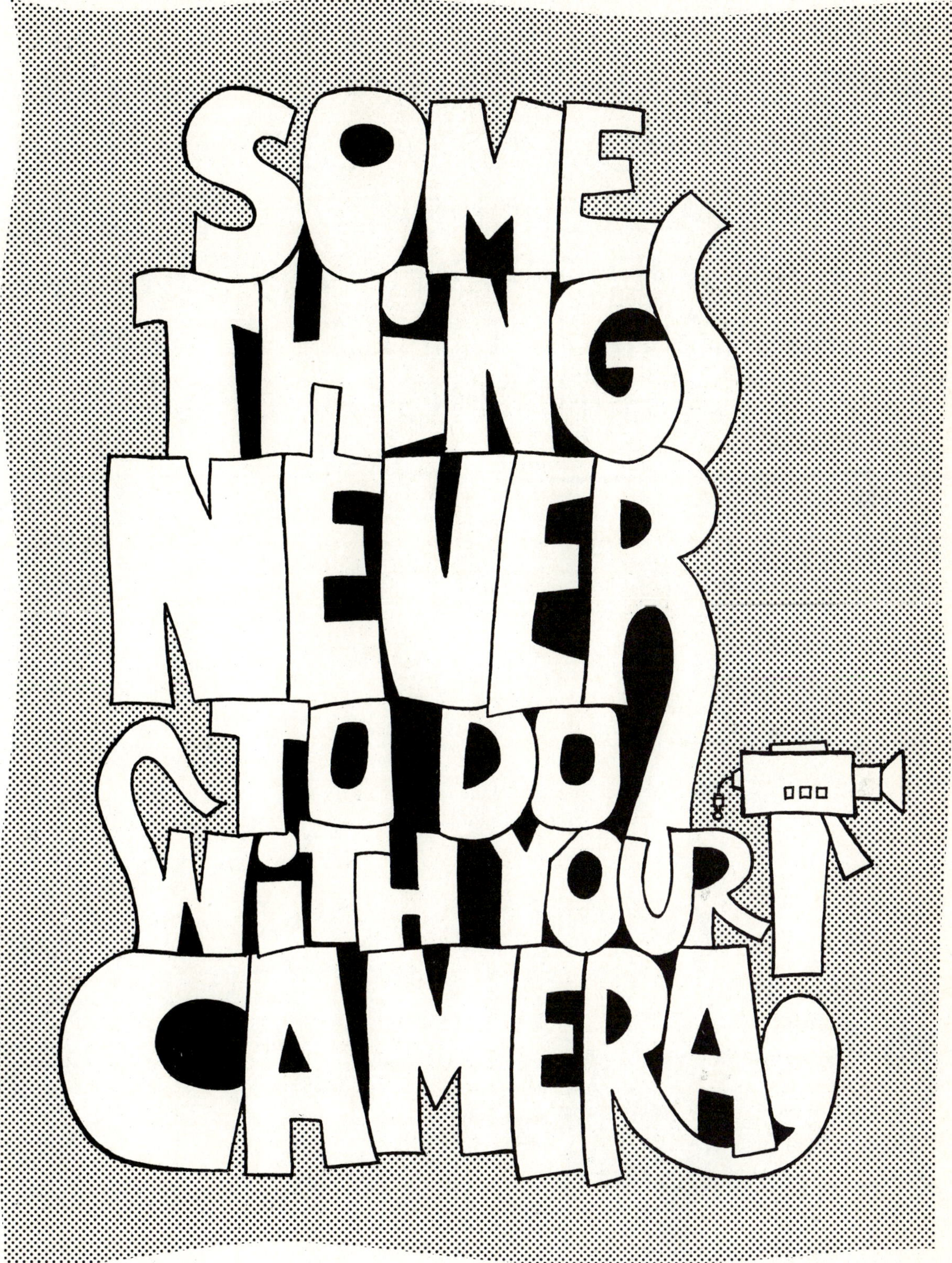
SOMETHING NEVER TO DO WITH YOUR CAMERA

DON'T POINT IT AT THE SUN!

THINK WHAT WOULD HAPPEN TO YOUR EYES IF YOU STARED AT THE SUN! YOUR CAMERA IS JUST AS SENSITIVE AND CAN BE RUINED BY AIMING IT AT THE SUN OR A BRIGHT LIGHT FOR VERY LONG. BE SURE EVEN WHEN THE CAMERA IS **OFF** THAT YOU DON'T ACCIDENTALLY POINT IT THE WRONG WAY WITH THE LENS CAP OFF!

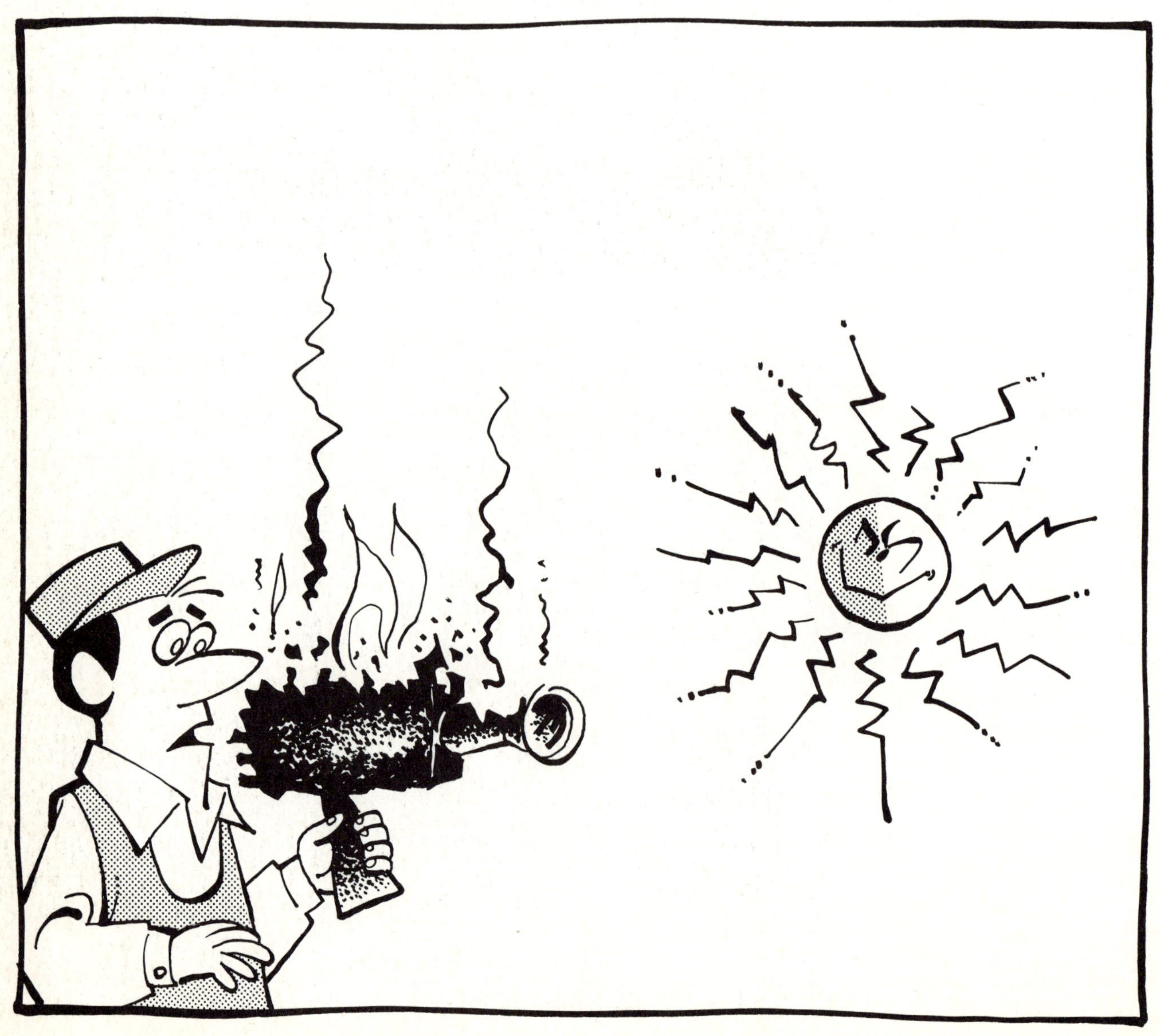

DON'T GET IT WET!

JACQUES COUSTEAU CAN AFFORD TO REPLACE HIS CAMERA. YOU CAN'T! YOUR VIDEO EQUIPMENT IS PACKED FULL OF MOISTURE-SENSITIVE ELECTRONIC PARTS. CHANCES ARE THAT IT CAN SURVIVE A LIGHT RAIN FOR A WHILE, BUT DON'T TAKE IT SURFING! UNDERWATER CASES ARE MADE FOR SOME VIDEO CAMERAS.
IF YOU USE ONE, MAKE SURE IT'S WATERTIGHT!

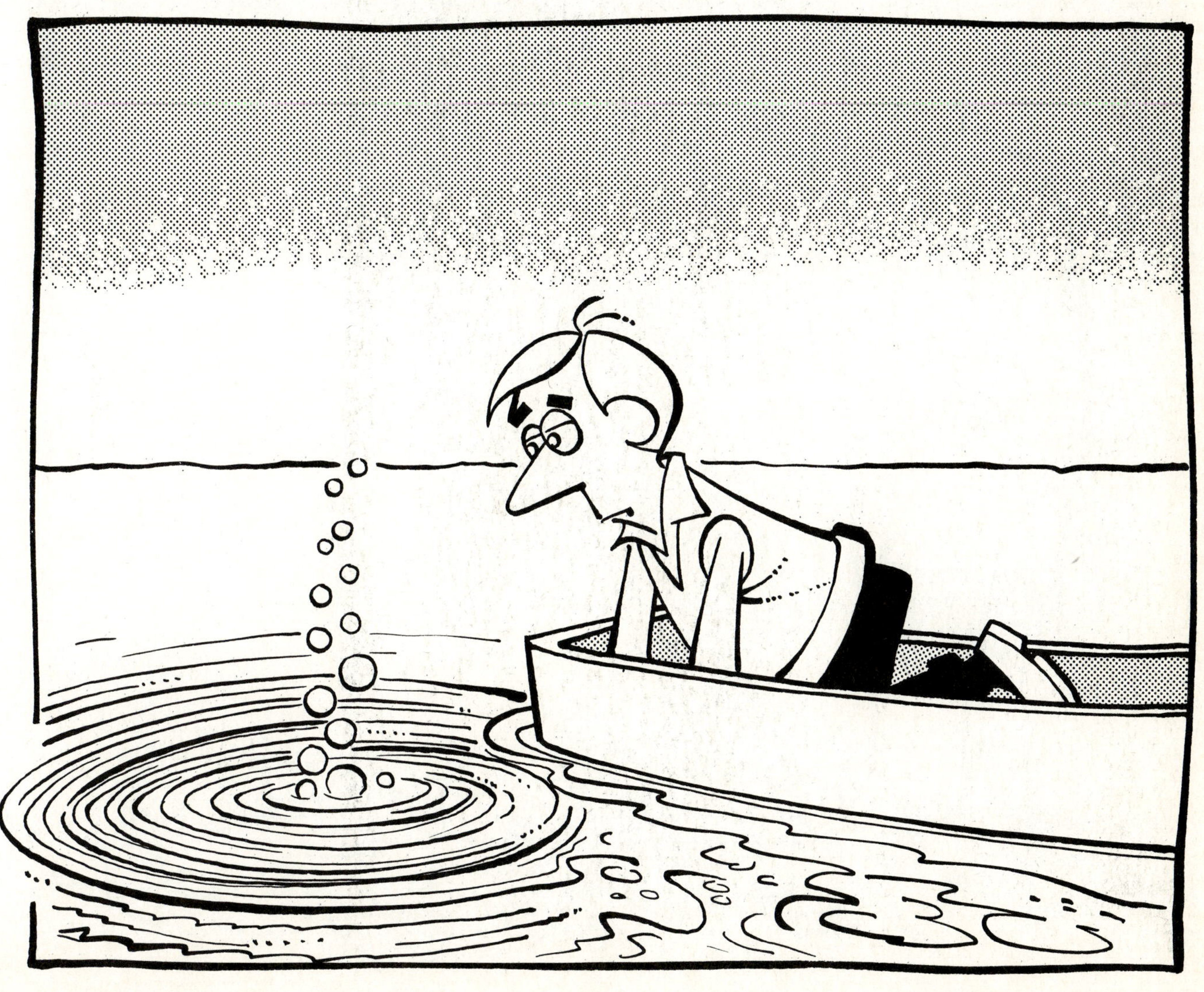

DON'T DROP IT!

THE CAMERA MAY SURVIVE HITTING THE GROUND ONCE OR TWICE, BUT REPEATED DROPPING OR KNOCKING AROUND CAN JAR DELICATE PARTS OUT OF ALIGNMENT. WORSE YET, YOU COULD CRACK YOUR LENS OR CAMERA TUBE! ALWAYS PACK THE CAMERA CAREFULLY WHEN TRAVELING (OR BETTER YET, CARRY IT ON YOUR LAP).

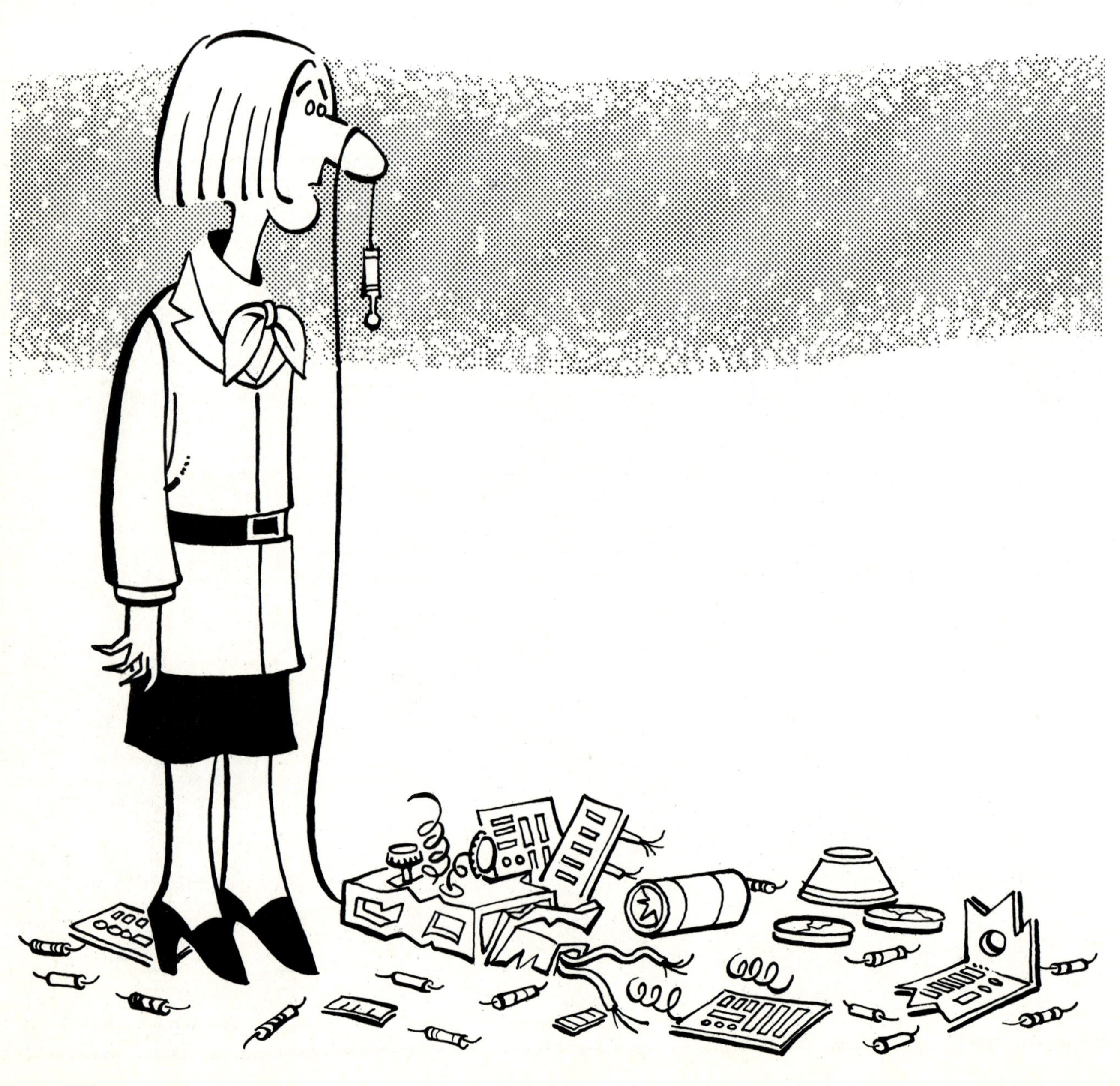

DON'T TOUCH THE LENS!

YOUR FINGERS HAVE OILS AND DIRT THAT WILL CONTAMINATE THE SPECIAL COATING OF THE LENS. USE A DRY TISSUE OR LENS CLEANING FLUID ON THE LENS. NO WATER, PLEASE!

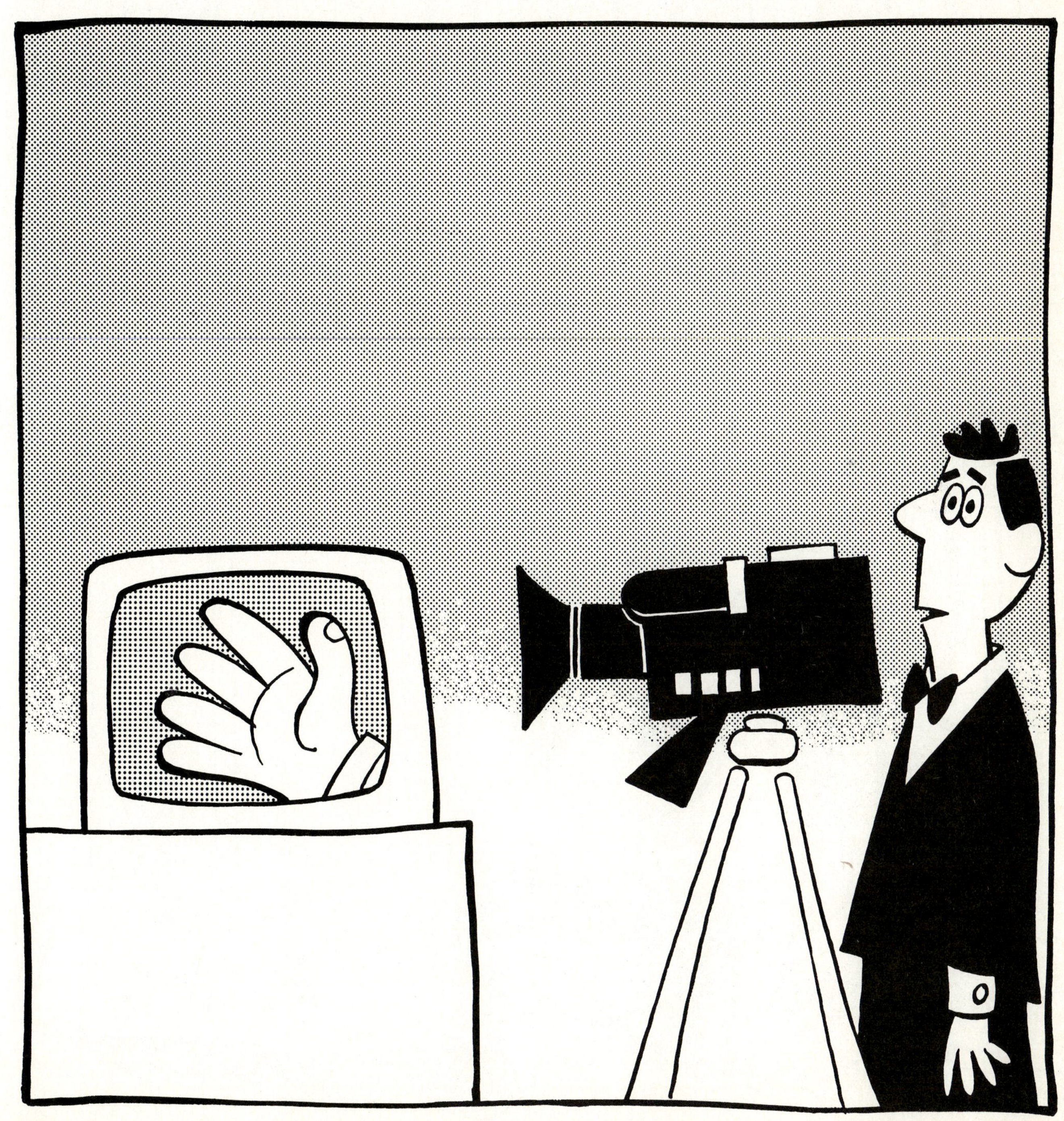

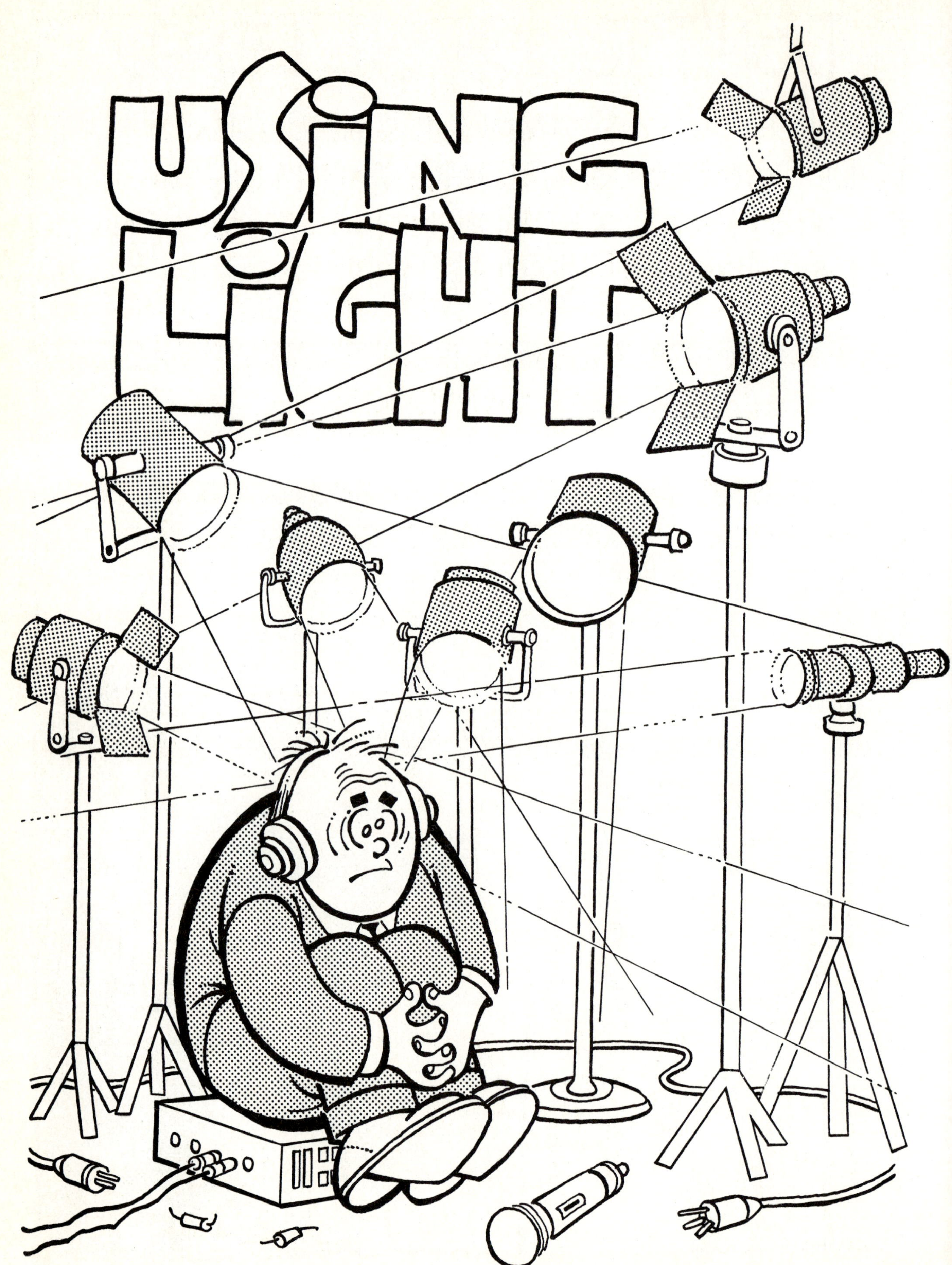

USING
LIGHT

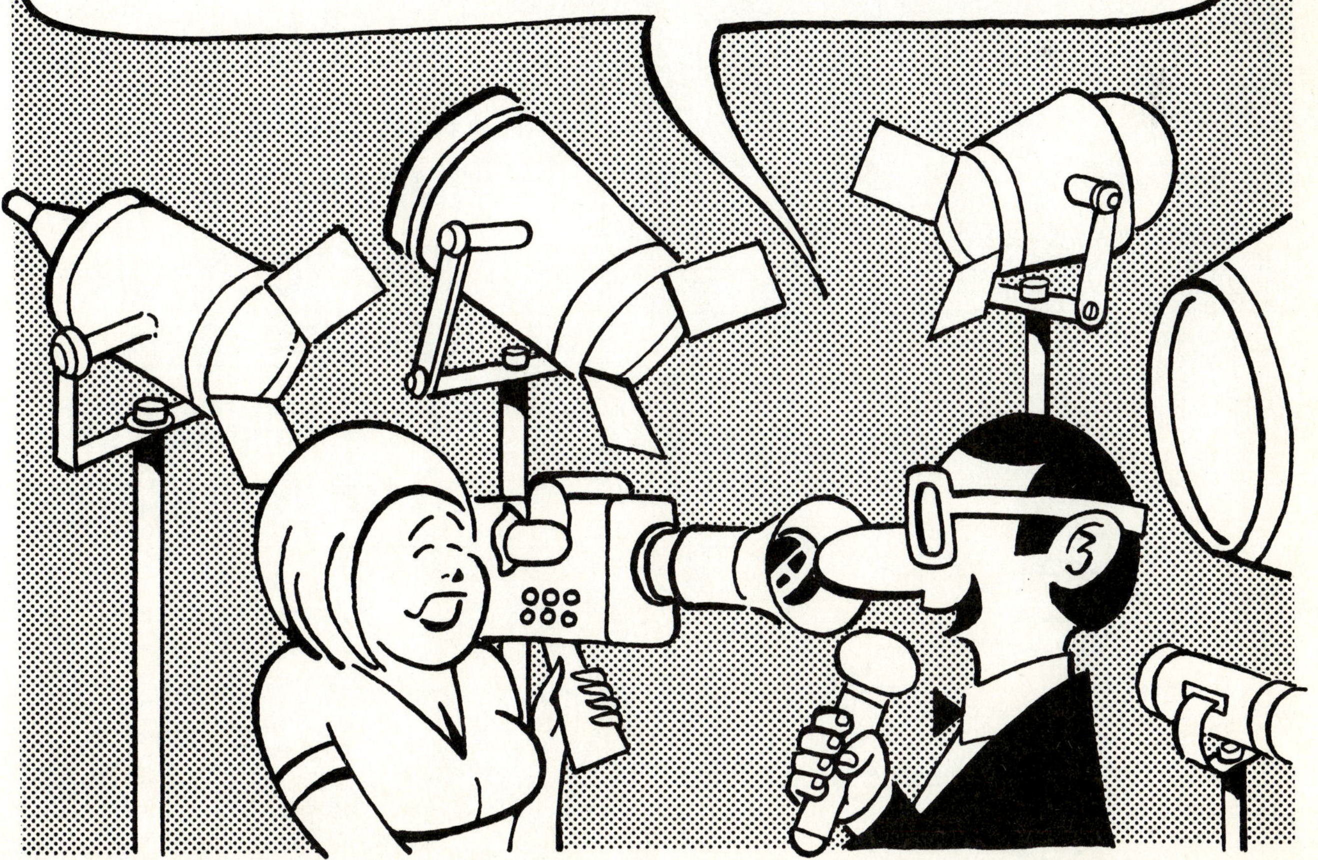
PROBABLY THE BEST THING ABOUT THE NEW GENERATION OF TV CAMERAS IS THEIR ENHANCED SENSITIVITY TO LIGHT. THE VIDEOGRAPHER CAN NOW AFFORD TO SHOOT TAPE UNDER NATURAL LIGHTING CONDITIONS, SOMETHING THAT I RECOMMEND DOING FOR A COUPLE OF REASONS. FIRST OF ALL, THE LIGHT EXISTING AT YOUR LOCATION IS UNDENIABLY *REAL* AND WILL TYPICALLY LOOK MORE AUTHENTIC THAN IT WOULD WITH ARTIFICIAL LIGHTING. SECONDLY, THE PEOPLE WHOSE LIVES YOU ARE TRYING TO CAPTURE ON TAPE WILL BEHAVE FAR MORE COMFORTABLY AND NATURALLY IF THEY DON'T HAVE TO CONTEND WITH A BANK OF HOT ELECTRIC BULBS!

VIDEO DOES HAVE ITS LIMITATIONS, HOWEVER. REMEMBER, YOUR CAMERA HAS A LIMITED CONTRAST RANGE, AND IT DOESN'T LIKE DEEP SHADOWS OR OTHER GREAT VARIATIONS IN BRIGHTNESS. SOMETIMES YOU'LL JUST HAVE TO ADD A LIGHT TO DRIVE AWAY THE SHADOWS!

OTHER TIMES, THE DIFFERENCE BETWEEN A SHOT THAT'S OKAY AND ONE THAT'S DOWNRIGHT GLAMOROUS WILL BE THE ADDITION OF A LIGHT OR TWO. THERE'S REALLY A LOT TO LIGHTING, WHICH IS AN ART IN ITSELF. HERE ARE JUST A FEW POINTERS:

OUTDOORS

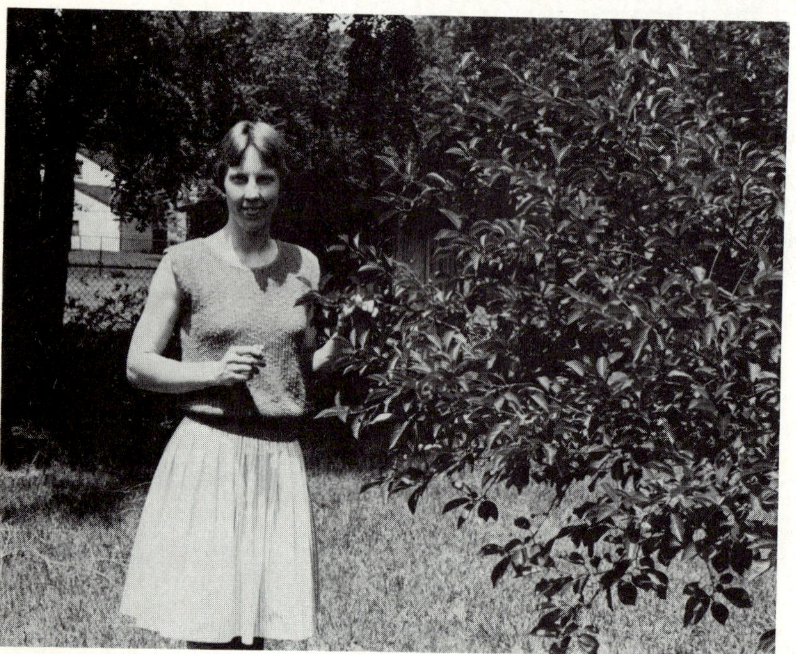

RULE NUMBER ONE:

YOU CAN'T MOVE THE SUN! THE ONLY WAY TO CONTROL YOUR RESULTS IS TO MOVE YOURSELF OR YOUR SUBJECT.

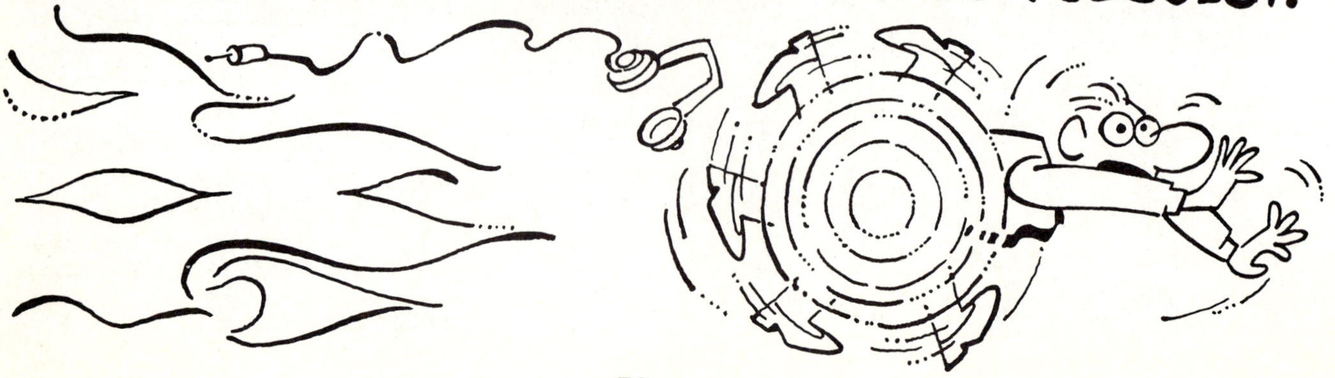

WHEN THE CAMERA IS ON THE SAME SIDE OF THE SUBJECT AS THE SUN IS, THE SHADOWS TEND TO FALL AWAY FROM THE CAMERA, WHERE THEY *WON'T MAKE MUCH TROUBLE!*

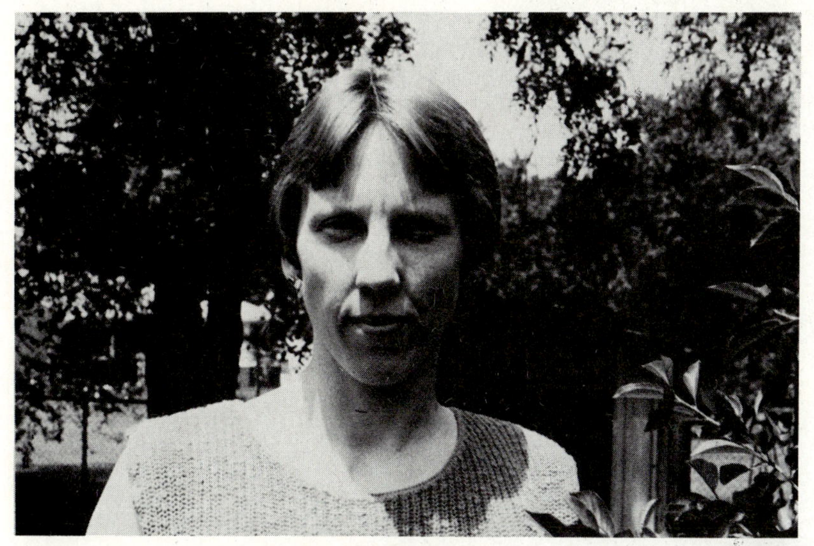

ALL IS WELL UNTIL THE CAMERA COMES IN CLOSE.... AND THE SHADOWS HIDE MUCH OF THE DETAIL IN KAREN'S FACE. THE SUN'S HARD, DIRECT LIGHT MAKES DEEP, SHARP SHADOWS THAT THE CAMERA CANNOT SEE INTO.

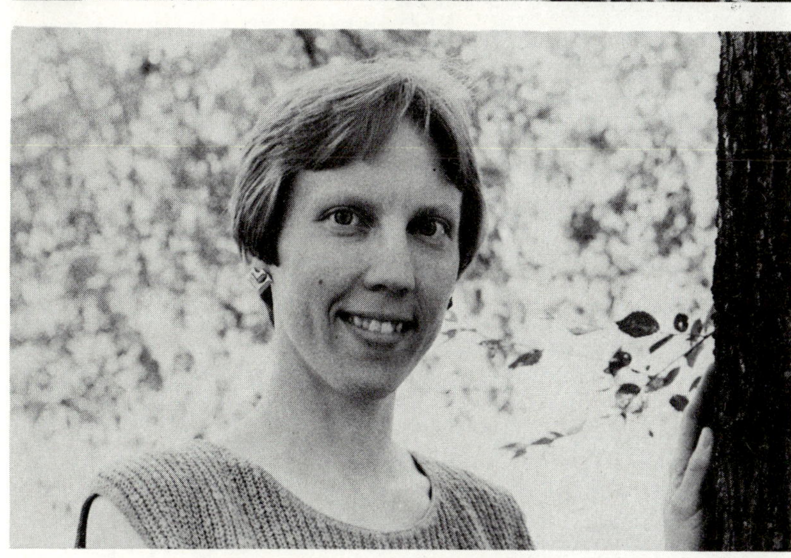

ONE SUPERB SOLUTION IS TO MOVE EVERYONE INTO THE SHADE. THE SOFT, DIFFUSE LIGHT FALLING ON KAREN NOW HAS NO SPECIFIC SOURCE, BUT ARRIVES FROM MANY DIRECTIONS, HENCE IT CASTS NO SHADOWS.

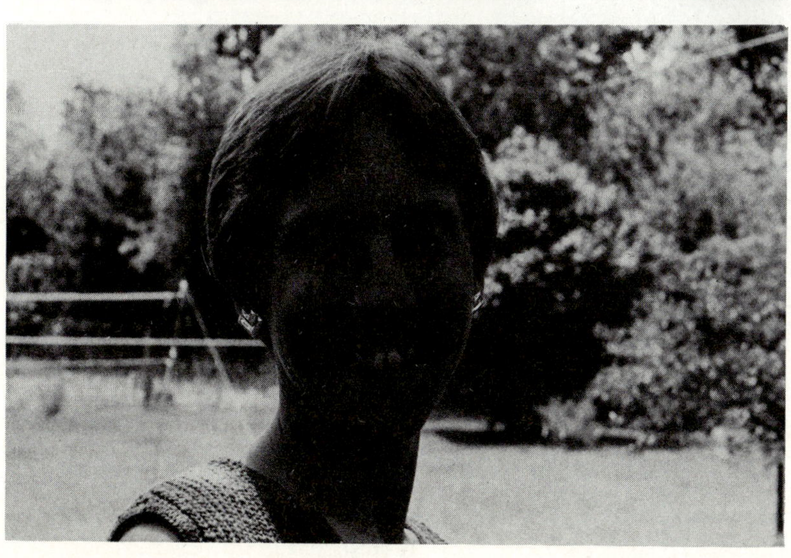

THIS ONE DOESN'T WORK SO WELL BE-CAUSE THE *BACK-GROUND* IS BRIGHTLY LIT WHILE KAREN IS IN THE SHADE. YOUR CAMERA DOESN'T KNOW HOW TO EXPOSE THIS.

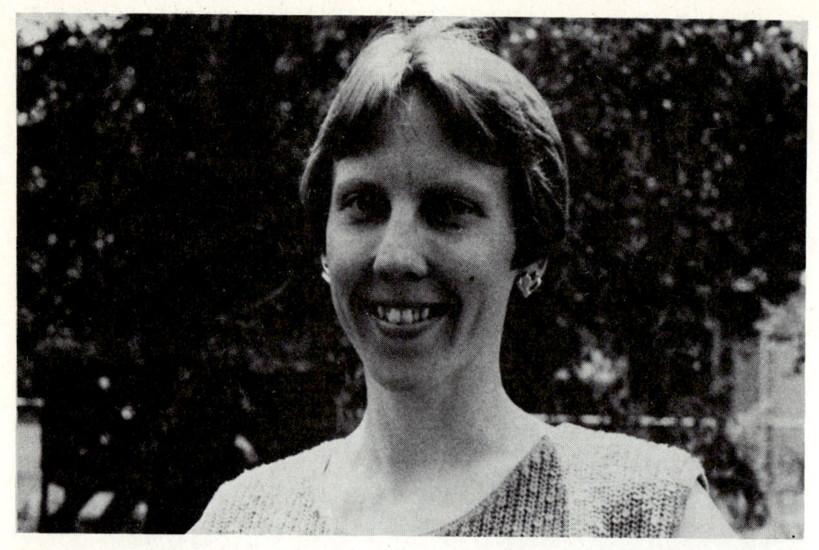

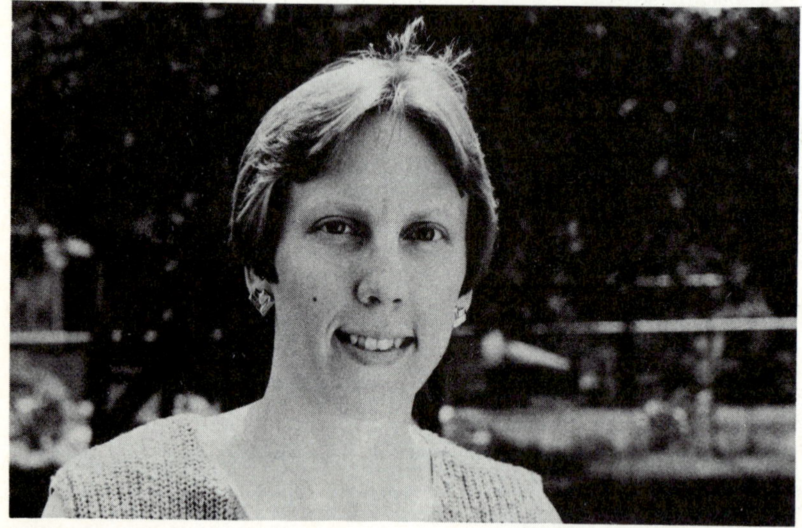

HERE'S THE SAME SHOT WITH A REFLECTOR.

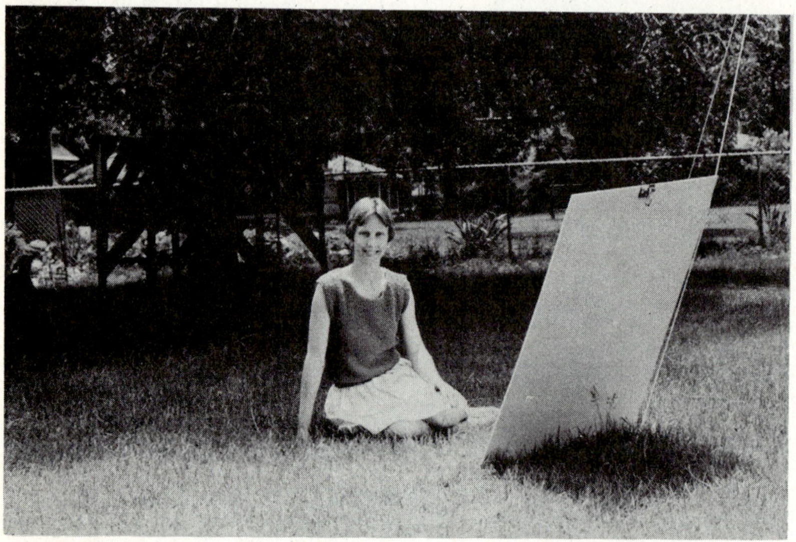

AND HERE'S THE WIDE SHOT WITH THE REFLECTOR BEING USED.

A SMALL REFLECTOR TO ADD A LITTLE SUNLIGHT TO KAREN'S FACE MAKES THIS SHOT NICER STILL. MY REFLECTOR IS SIMPLY CARDBOARD COVERED WITH ALUMINUM FOIL (DULL SIDE OUT).

INDOORS

CONSIDER THESE THREE QUESTIONS WHEN TAPING INDOORS. FIRST: IS THERE ENOUGH LIGHT? CHANCES ARE THAT YOUR CAMERA CAN DELIVER PICTURES WITH VERY LITTLE LIGHT. TOO LITTLE LIGHT, HOWEVER, AND THE IMAGES BEGIN TO LOOK BAD. AS THE GAIN OF THE CAMERA TUBE INCREASES (ONE OF THE WAYS IT COMPENSATES FOR LOW LIGHT) **THE *NOISE* IN THE PICTURE** (IT LOOKS LIKE SNOW, OR GRAIN, IF YOU'RE A FILM PHOTOGRAPHER) WILL INCREASE CONSIDERABLY!

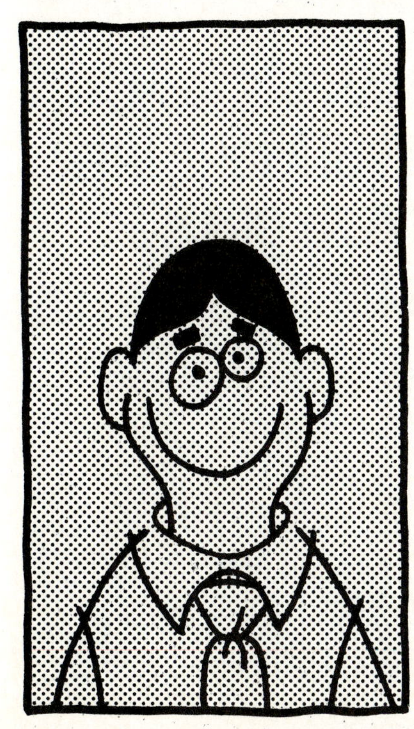 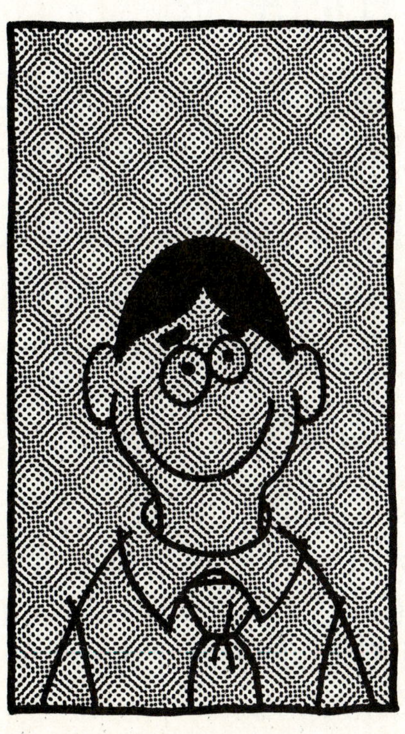 

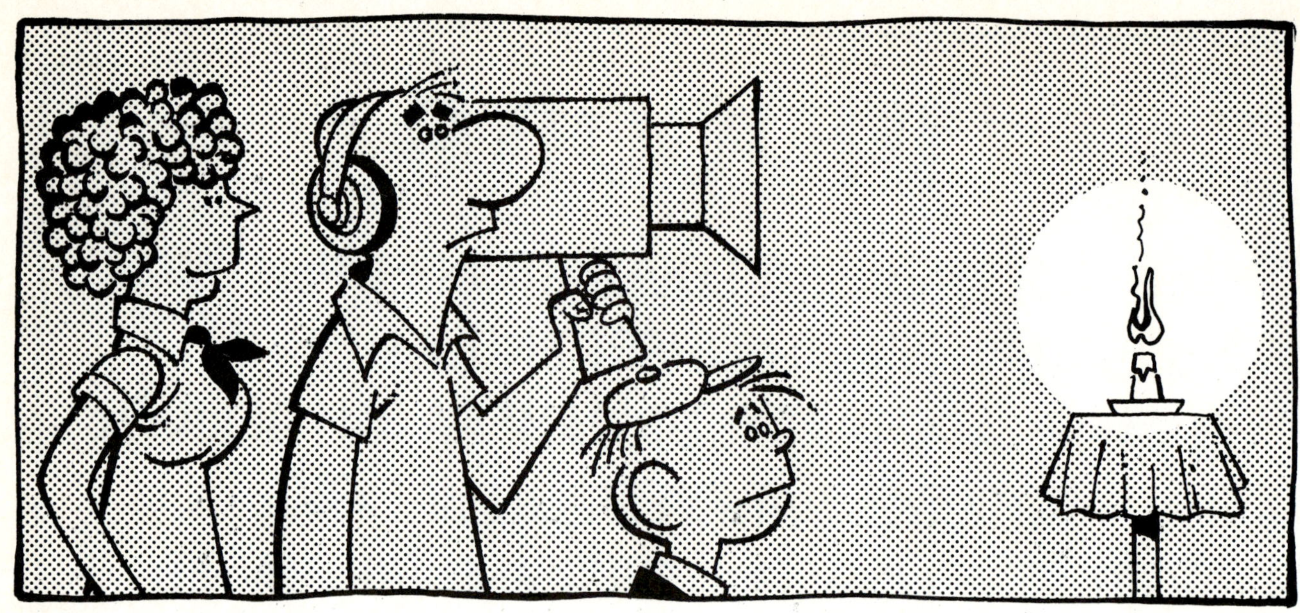

SECOND, WHAT *KIND* OF LIGHT IS AVAILABLE? REMEMBER, ALL LIGHT IS NOT CREATED EQUAL AS FAR AS YOUR CAMERA IS CONCERNED. A SOURCE OF LIGHT THAT APPEARS WHITE TO THE EYE IS ACTUALLY A MIXTURE OF MANY DIFFERENT *WAVE LENGTHS* (COLORS) OF LIGHT. THE VIDEO CAMERA BREAKS THIS LIGHT DOWN INTO THE THREE *PRIMARIES*: RED, BLUE, AND GREEN. ANY SHADE OF COLOR CAN BE REPRESENTED BY THE APPROPRIATE BLEND OF THESE THREE COLORS.

THE PROBLEM ARISES FROM THE FACT THAT EACH LIGHT SOURCE EMITS A SLIGHTLY DIFFERENT MIXTURE OF THE PRIMARIES. TUNGSTEN LIGHT (FROM A LIGHT BULB) HAS A HIGHER PROPORTION OF THE COLOR RED THAN THE SUN. IF YOU'VE COLOR BALANCED THE CAMERA IN SUNLIGHT, THEN BRING IT INDOORS, THE VIDEO WILL HAVE A VERY ORANGE CAST TO IT UNLESS YOU COLOR BALANCE AGAIN. CONVERSELY, THE SUN HAS MORE BLUE AND LESS RED THAN THE BULB AND WILL PRODUCE BLUE LOOKING VIDEO.

THE RATIO OF BLUE TO RED IN A LIGHT SOURCE IS DETERMINED BY THE LIGHT'S *COLOR TEMPERATURE*. WHEN YOU OPERATE THE COLOR BALANCE KNOB OR BUTTON ON THE CAMERA, IT IS ADJUSTING THE GAIN (THE STRENGTH) OF THE PRIMARY COLORS BLUE AND RED TO COMPENSATE FOR THE COLOR TEMPERATURE OF THE LIGHT WHERE YOU'RE SHOOTING!

THERE'S ONLY ONE BUG IN ALL THIS. SOME KINDS OF LIGHT (FLUORESCENT, MERCURY VAPOR AND OTHER GAS DISCHARGE LAMPS) DON'T FIT NEATLY INTO THE "COLOR TEMPERATURE" CONCEPT. IN THESE LIGHT SOURCES, THE RELATIVE STRENGTH OF THE THIRD PRIMARY, GREEN, VARIES ALSO. YOUR VIDEO CAMERA MAY OR MAY NOT BE ABLE TO COMPENSATE, DE- PENDING ON ITS DESIGN. IF FLUORESCENTS GIVE YOU "GREEN" VIDEO, YOU SHOULD AVOID THEM.

FINALLY, CONSIDER THE POSITION OF THE LIGHT SOURCES! JUST LIKE SHOOTING OUTDOORS, YOU MAY NEED TO POSITION YOURSELF OR YOUR SUBJECT TO TAKE THE BEST ADVANTAGE OF WINDOWS OR OVERHEAD LIGHTS.

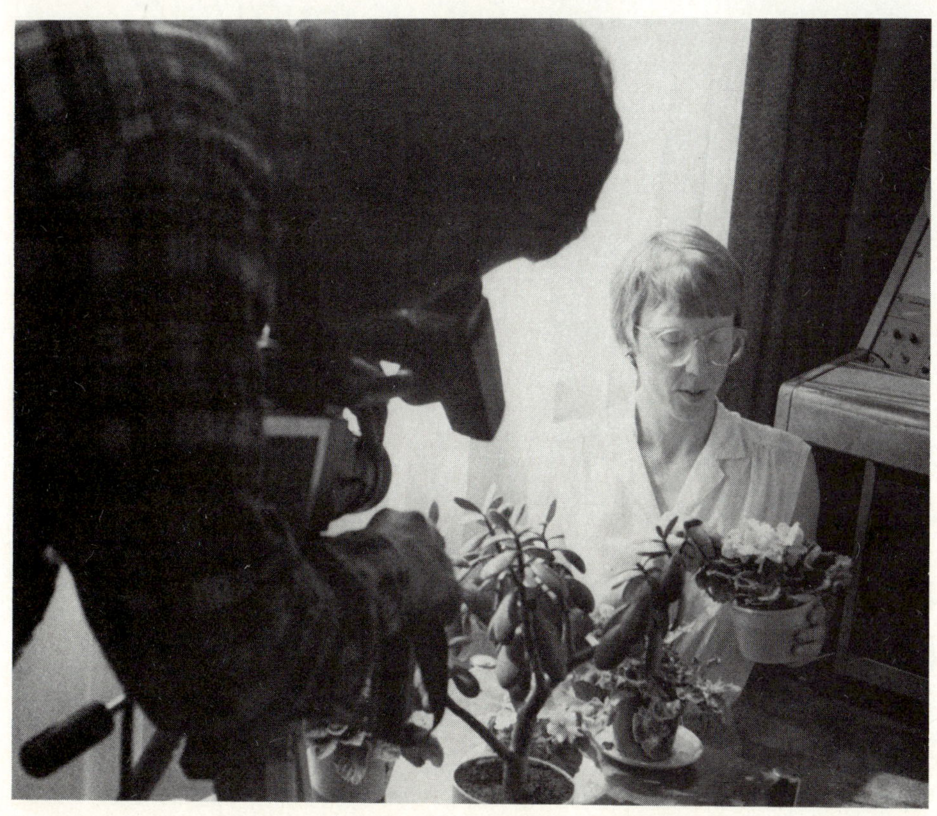

HOW A CAMERAMAN SELECTS THE BEST LOCATION TO TAKE ADVANTAGE OF WINDOW LIGHT!

ADDING LIGHT

WHEN THERE'S NOT ENOUGH LIGHT, OR THE EXISTING LIGHT IS THE WRONG KIND OR IN THE WRONG PLACE, YOU'LL HAVE TO ADD SOME OF YOUR OWN.

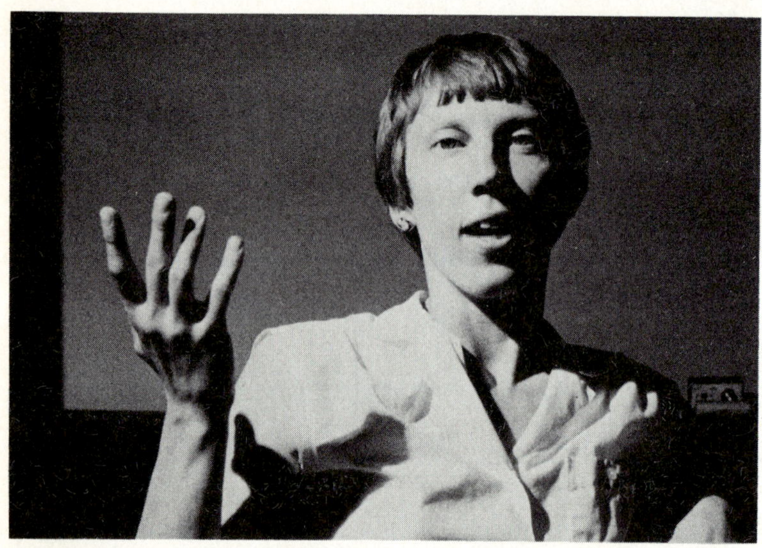

THIS PHOTO WAS TAKEN WITH A SINGLE QUARTZ LAMP ON A LIGHT STAND. VERY DRAMATIC LIGHTING, BUT THE VIDEO CAMERA HAS TROUBLE WITH THE DARK, DISTINCT SHADOWS.

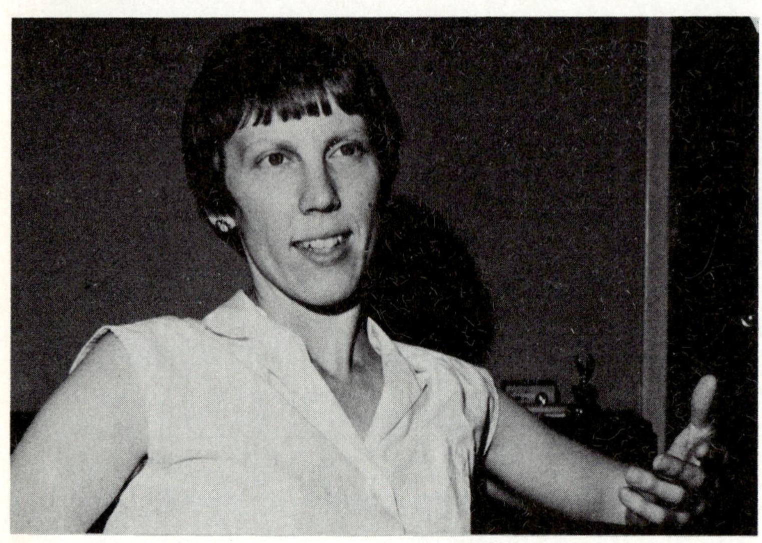

PUTTING YOUR LIGHT RIGHT NEXT TO THE CAMERA SOLVES THE PROBLEM BY CAUSING ALL THE SHADOWS TO FALL AWAY FROM THE CAMERA.

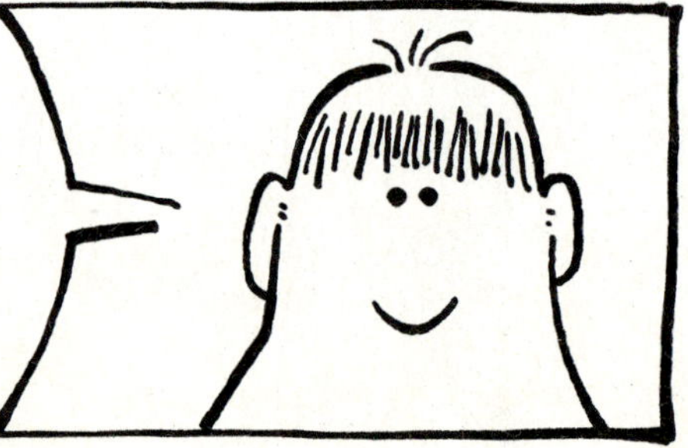

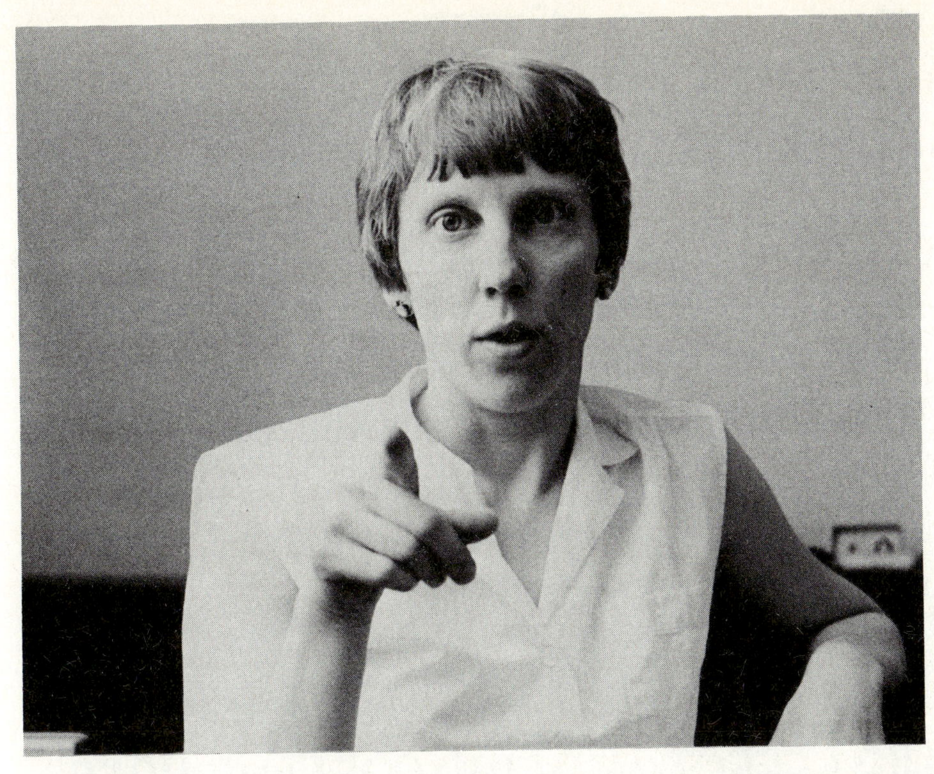

THIS COMPROMISE WAS ACHIEVED BY BOUNCING OUR LIGHT OFF A NEARBY WHITE WALL. BOUNCING LIGHT FROM A WHITE WALL OR CEILING WILL CAUSE IT TO DIFFUSE, OR SPREAD OUT. DIFFUSED LIGHT MAKES SOFTER, LIGHTER SHADOWS!

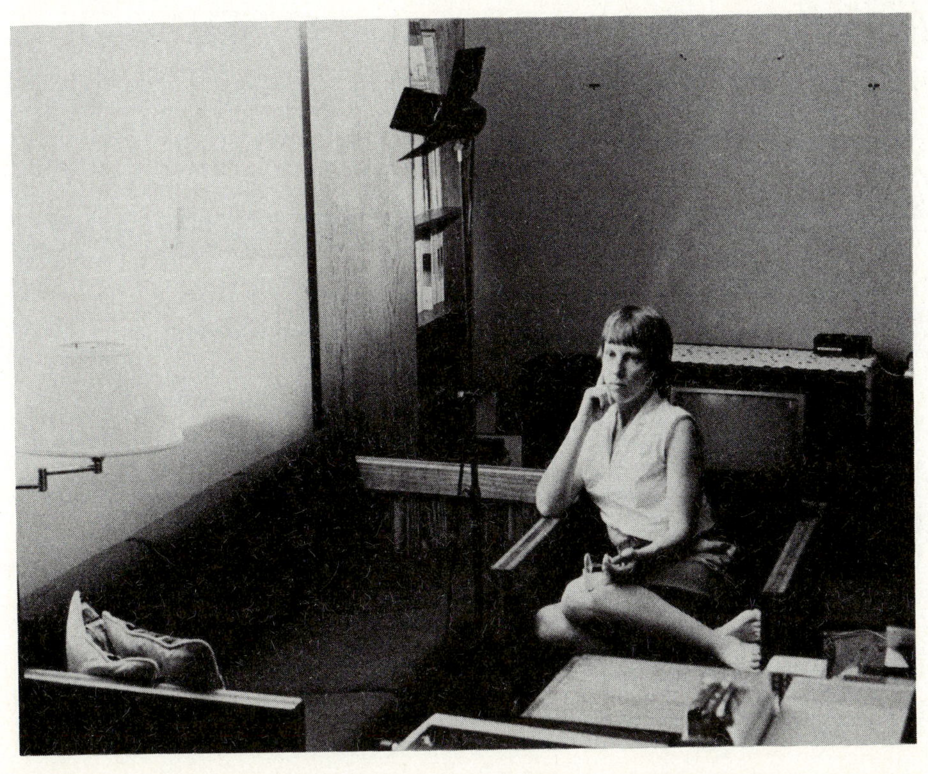

MIXING IT UP

WHENEVER POSSIBLE, I LIKE TO COMPLEMENT THIS EXISTING LIGHT RATHER THAN REPLACE IT WITH MY OWN. THERE'S JUST ONE IMPORTANT QUESTION TO KEEP IN MIND WHEN YOU DO THIS: IS YOUR LIGHT ABOUT THE SAME COLOR TEMPERATURE AS THE EXISTING LIGHT? WHEN TWO DIFFERENT *TYPES* OF LIGHT ILLUMINATE A SCENE FROM TWO DIFFERENT DIRECTIONS, SOME ODD COLORS ARE GOING TO CREEP INTO THE VIDEO.

THE CAMERA, AFTER ALL, CAN ONLY BE COLOR BALANCED FOR ONE KIND OF LIGHT AT A TIME. (NOTE…SOME PHOTOGRAPHERS *LIKE* THIS EFFECT, AND FIND CREATIVE USES FOR IT.) THERE ARE TWO WAYS AROUND THE PROBLEM!

THE FIRST IS TO USE A FILTER ON YOUR LIGHT. BLUE FILTERS ARE AVAILABLE FOR YOUR LIGHT THAT WILL MATCH ITS COLOR TEMPERATURE TO THAT OF DAYLIGHT. I HAVE ALSO SUCCESSFULLY MATCHED MY LIGHT TO DAYLIGHT BY BOUNCING IT OFF A LIGHT BLUE WALL. THE SECOND WAY TO DEAL WITH DIVERSE LIGHT SOURCES IS SIMPLY TO POSITION THE LAMP SO THAT ITS LIGHT STRIKES THE SCENE FROM THE *SAME DIRECTION* AS THE EXISTING LIGHT.

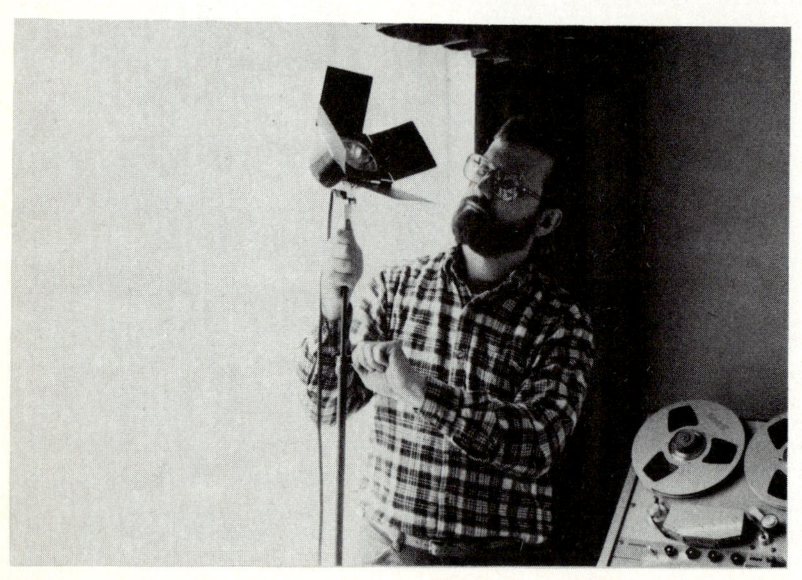

THE VIDEO CAMERA CAN USUALLY COLOR BALANCE SUCCESSFULLY ON AN *EVEN* MIXTURE OF LIGHT.

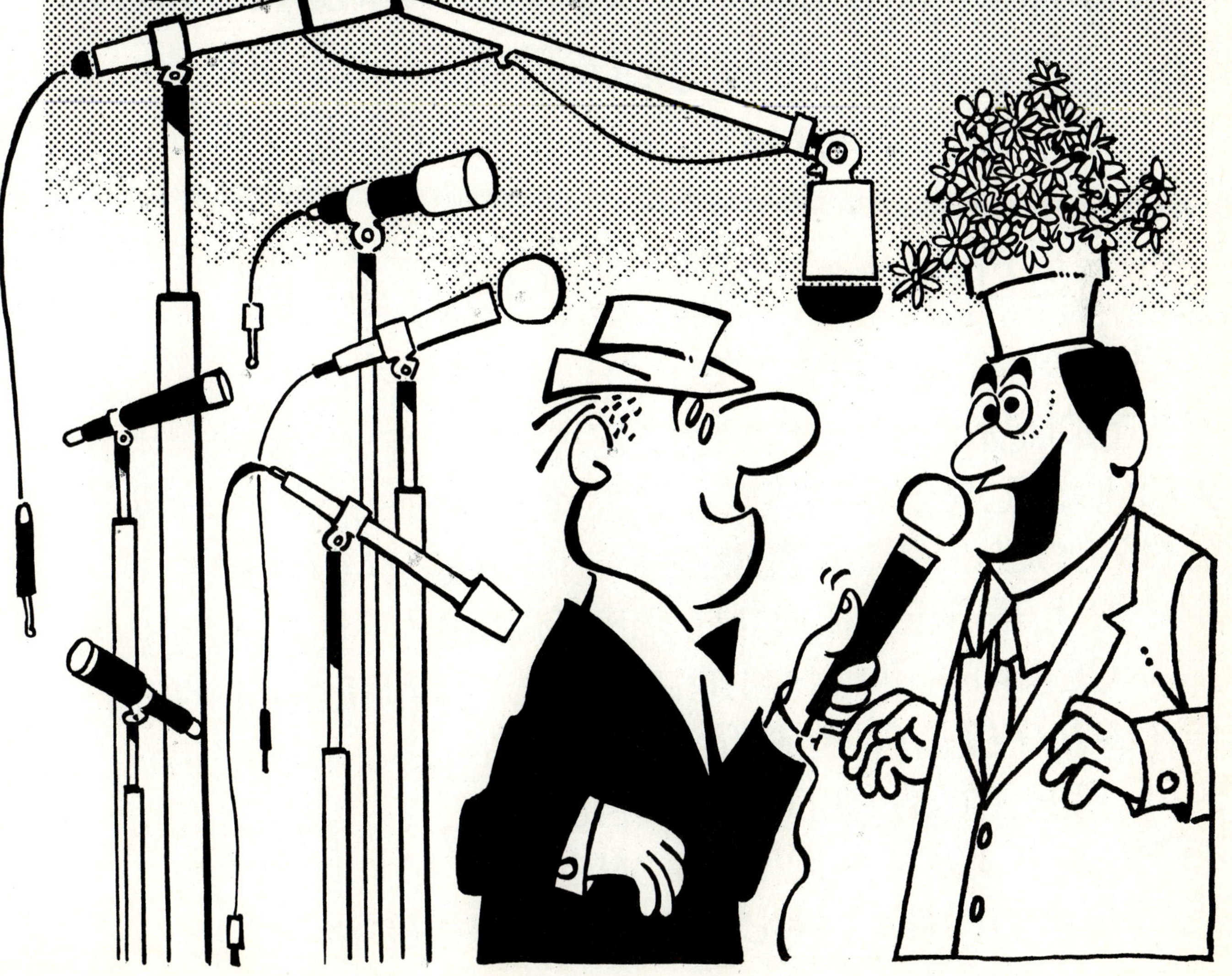
SOUND

ONE OF THE BIGGEST DIFFERENCES BETWEEN THE OLD HOME MOVIE FORMATS AND YOUR VIDEO SYSTEM IS THE ABILITY TO RECORD SOUND. SOUND, IF RECORDED AND MIXED WELL, CAN TRANSFORM A **RUN-OF-THE-MILL** PRESENTATION INTO A REAL ATTEN-TION *GETTER*. WHAT IMPACT WOULD **STAR WARS** HAVE MADE WITHOUT THE MUSIC SCORE? WITHOUT THE SOUND EFFECTS?

AS YOU CAN SEE, WE'RE TALKING ABOUT MORE THAN JUST THE MICROPHONE MOUNTED ON TOP OF YOUR CAMERA-EVEN IF THAT MICROPHONE IS ALL YOU HAVE, READ ON- RECORDING STUDIOS ARE NICE, BUT WE'LL HAVE TO MAKE DO WITHOUT ONE.

THE SECRET TO GOOD SOUND RECORDING

IN A WORD, THE SECRET IS: **CLOSE!** GETTING THE MICROPHONE CLOSER TO THE SOURCE MEANS BETTER SOUND. FOR EXAMPLE, SAY YOU'RE VIDEO TAPING YOUR COUSIN'S WEDDING FROM THE BACK OF THE CHURCH. IF THE MICROPHONE IS BACK THERE TOO, CHANCES ARE THE MARRIAGE VOWS ARE GOING TO BE **UNINTELLIGIBLE** (OR NEARLY SO) WHEN THE TAPE IS PLAYED BACK. AT THE OTHER EXTREME, PUTTING HIDDEN MICROPHONES ON THE GROOM, BRIDE, MINISTER, AND ORGANIST WILL GIVE YOU

AUDIO TO RIVAL ANY HOLLYWOOD PRODUCTION—THE LATTER IS, UNFORTUNATELY, GOING TO BE IMPRACTICAL FOR MOST WEDDINGS.

THE WAY TO MIKE ANY GIVEN SITUATION WILL BE A COMPROMISE BETWEEN SETTING YOUR MIKE IN CLOSE AND WHAT'S PRACTICAL (AND WHAT EQUIPMENT YOU CAN AFFORD).

CONNECTING a MIKE

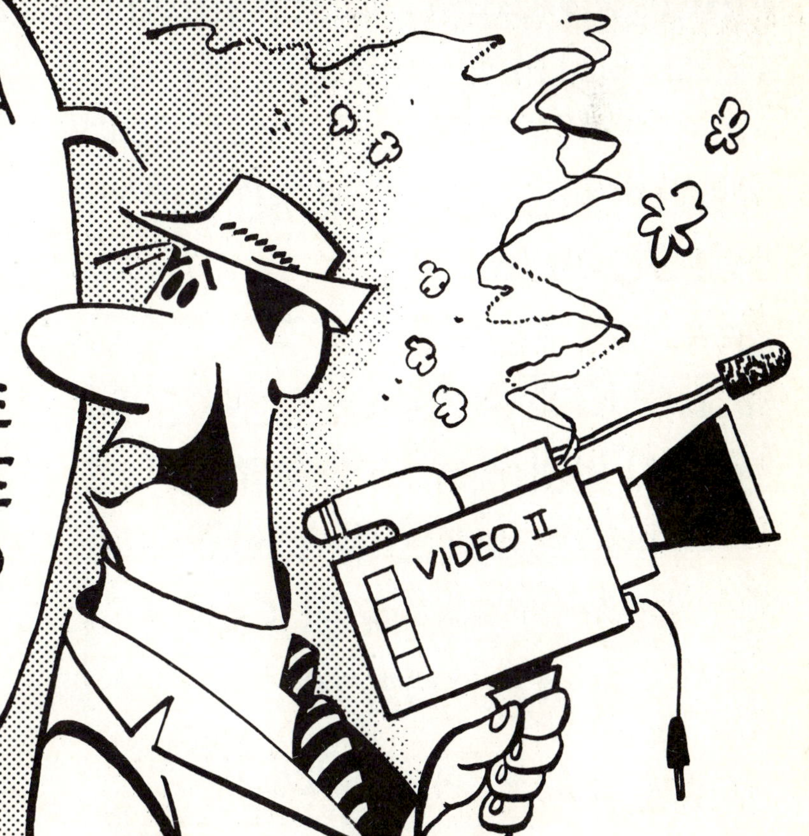

IF YOUR CAMERA HAS A BUILT-IN MIKE, YOU PROBABLY NEED DO NOTHING MORE THAN CONNECT THE CAMERA CABLE TO THE RECORDER TO USE IT!

IF YOUR MIKE HAS A PLUG
THAT DOESN'T FIT THE ONE
ON THE RECORDER, YOU'LL
HAVE TO USE AN ADAPTOR
TO MAKE IT FIT (SEE THE
CHAPTER "CONNECTING ANY-
THING TO ANYTHING").

THE MICROPHONE INPUT IS
PROBABLY DESIGNED FOR A *LOW*
IMPEDANCE" MICROPHONE (SEE
YOUR MANUAL). WHAT THIS MEANS
TO YOU IS THAT A *HIGH* IMPEDANCE"
MIKE, IF YOU TRY TO USE IT,
MAY NOT WORK. THE SENSITIVITY
(VOLUME) MAY BE POOR OR THE
FREQUENCY RESPONSE (ALL THE
HIGHS AND LOWS IN THE SOUND)
MAY SUFFER!

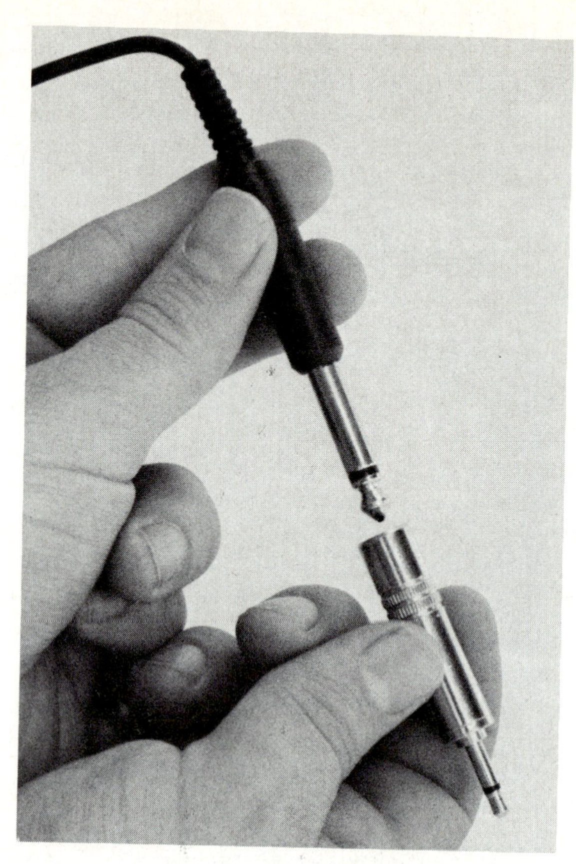

TRY TO BUY MICROPHONES
THAT WORK WITH THE INPUT
IMPEDANCE OF YOUR
RECORDER, OR BUY AN
ADAPTOR
TO CHANGE THE IMPEDANCE

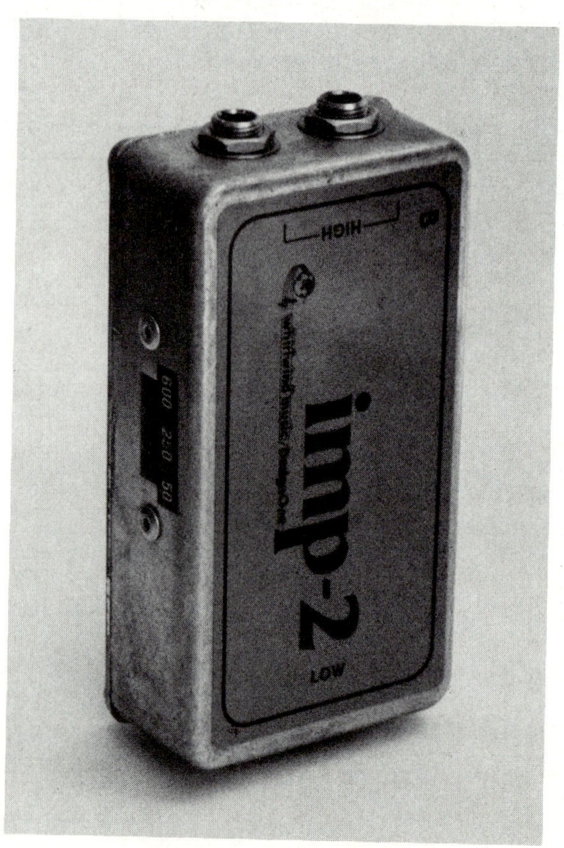

Setting Audio Level

Most ½ inch recorders sold these days have no adjustment for control of audio level. The level (volume of the sound recorded into the tape) is controlled automatically by an electronic circuit. If your machine has this adjustment, there will probably be a knob next to a meter labeled **"AUDIO"** or **"DB"** or **"VU."**

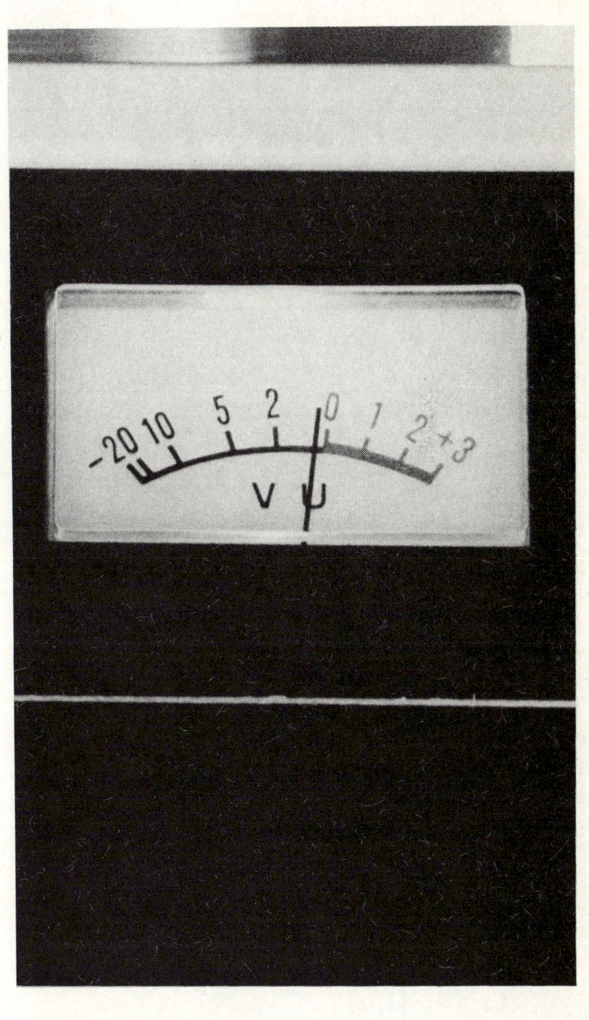

The knob is adjusted during recording so that the sound causes the meter to move as far up the scale as possible without going into the **RED PART.** Level control, whether manual or automatic, is necessary because the tape can only record sound well at a **CERTAIN LEVEL.**

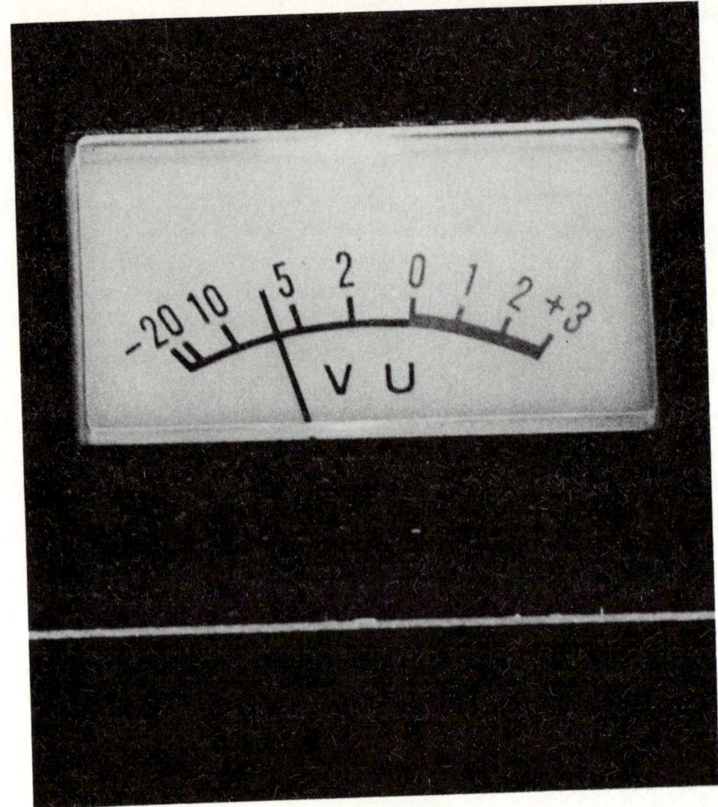

HERE'S WHAT A "VU" METER LOOKS LIKE SET TOO LOW!
-20 10 5 2 0 1 2 +3
VU

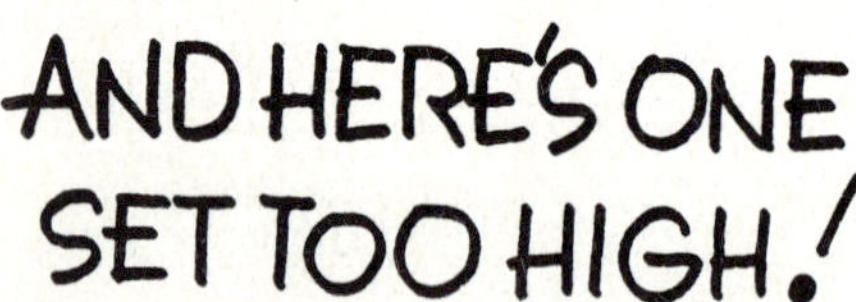

AND HERE'S ONE SET TOO HIGH!

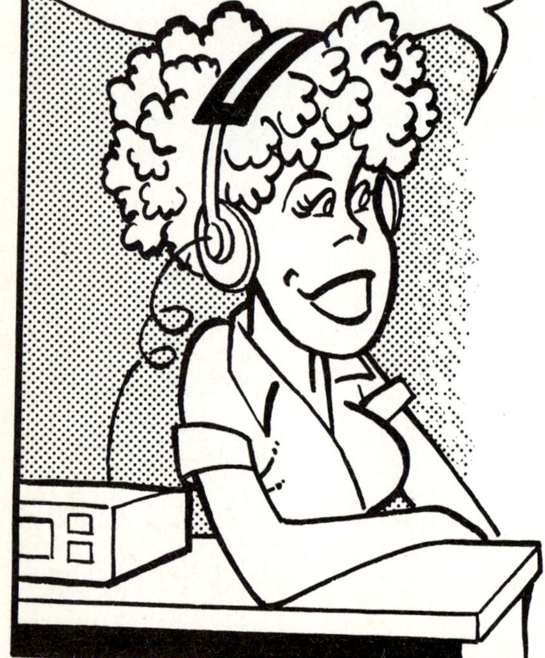

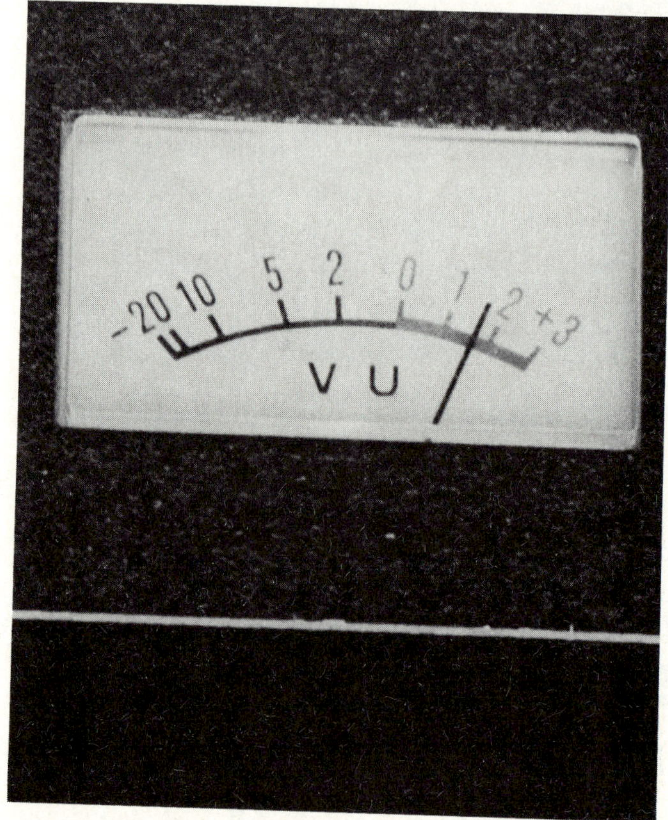

-20 10 5 2 0 1 2 +3
VU

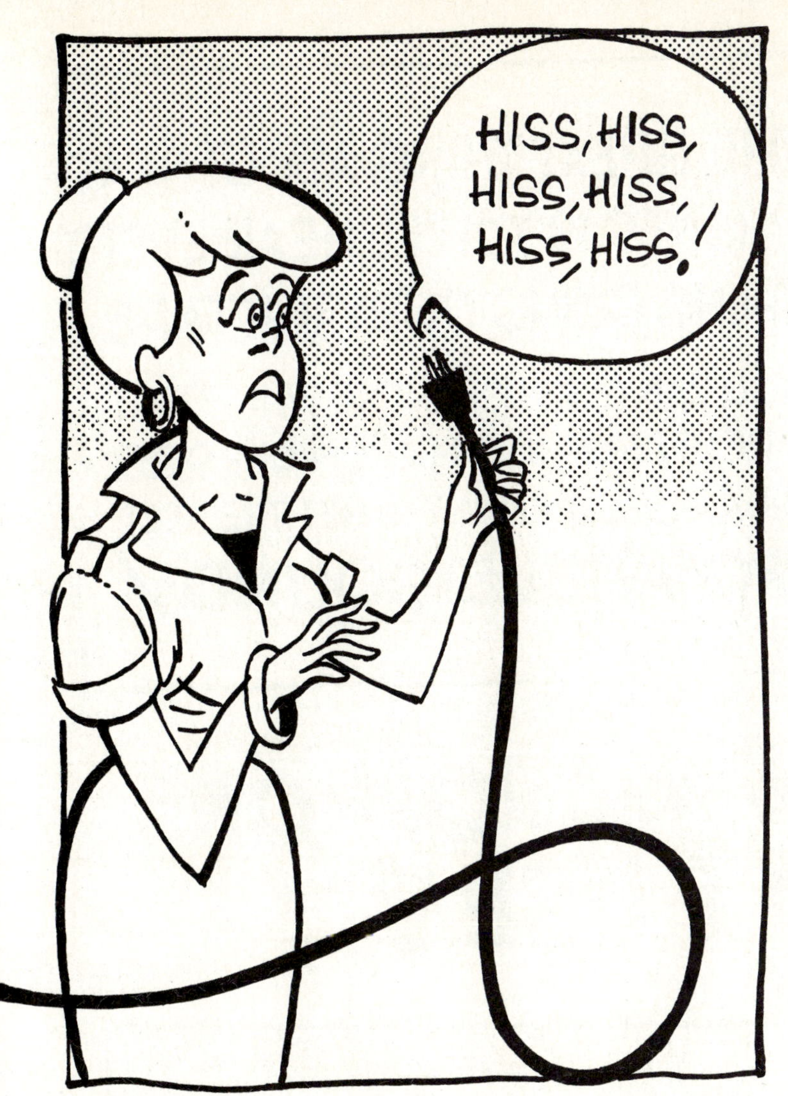

RECORDING AT TOO LOW A LEVEL WILL PRODUCE SOUND THAT HAS A LOT OF "HISS" IN IT DURING PLAYBACK.

RECORDING AT TOO HIGH A LEVEL WILL GIVE YOU SOUND WITH "DISTORTION" IN IT.

DISTORTED SOUND IS TO NORMAL SOUND WHAT AN *ELECTRIC* GUITAR IS TO AN *ACOUSTIC* GUITAR!

MONITOR YOUR SOUND

IT'S IMPORTANT TO KNOW WHAT'S COMING THROUGH YOUR MICROPHONE. IF YOU WIND UP WITH A LOT OF DIFFERENT MICROPHONES AND OTHER AUDIO EQUIPMENT, SOME OF THE PROBLEMS OF IMPROPER AUDIO LEVEL, POOR MIKE PLACEMENT, ETC., MAY PLAGUE YOU. A SMALL PAIR OF EARPHONES OR HEADPHONES IS AN EXCELLENT INVESTMENT IN THIS REGARD. THEY CAN BE PLUGGED INTO THE JACK MARKED **"EAR"** IN YOUR CAMERA OR RECORDER—AND WORN WHILE YOU'RE SHOOTING!

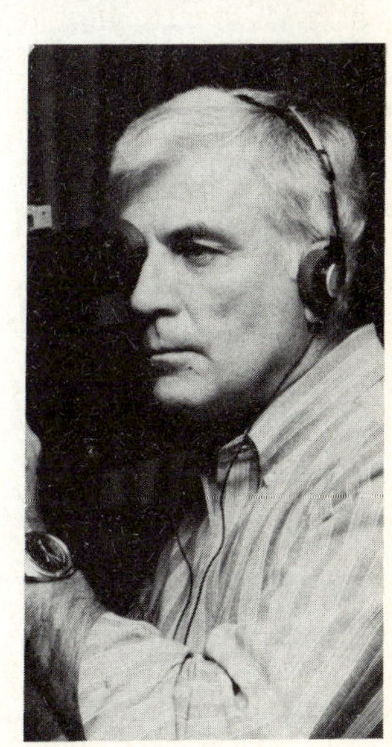

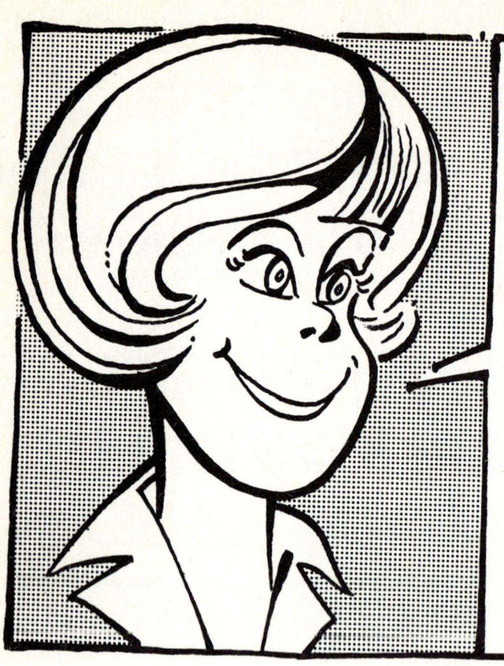

WHAT KIND OF MICROPHONE SHOULD I USE?

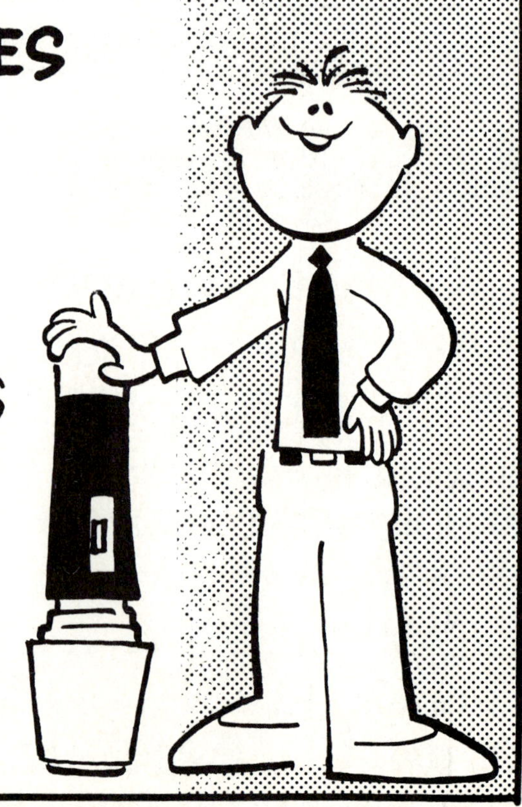

PICKUP PATTERN

THE PICKUP PATTERN REFERS TO THE DIRECTION FROM WHICH THE MIKE CAN HEAR SOUND!

AN OMNIDIRECTIONAL

MIKE HEARS SOUNDS FROM ALL SIDES. YOU WOULD USE A MIKE LIKE THIS WHEN THERE ARE MANY SOUNDS OR VOICES TO BE PICKED UP BY THE SAME MIKE.
THE DISADVANTAGE TO THIS PICKUP PATTERN IS THAT ALL THE NOISE YOU DON'T WANT IS GOING TO BE RE-CORDED TOO!

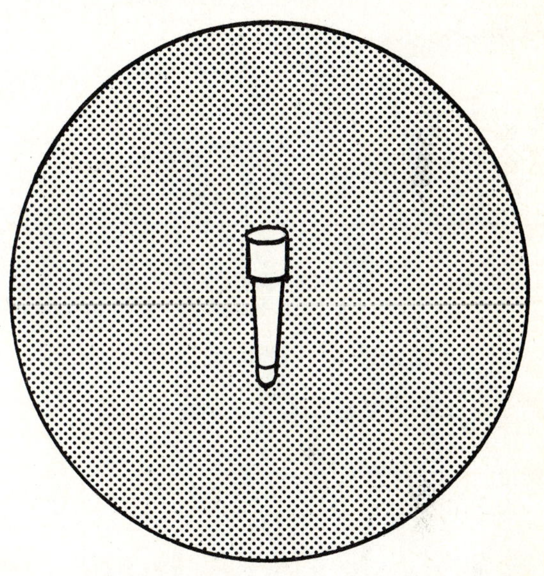

A UNIDIRECTIONAL

MIKE ONLY HEARS SOUND FROM ONE DIRECTION (*RIGHT IN FRONT OF THE MIKE*). THIS PICKUP PATTERN IS USEFUL FOR PICKING A SINGLE SOUND OUT OF A NOISY BACKGROUND. THIS MIKE CAN BE AIMED TOWARD THE SOUND, AND CAN DELIVER GOOD QUALITY SOUND EVEN AT A REASONABLE DISTANCE.
A DISADVANTAGE IS THAT CARE HAS TO BE TAKEN TO POINT THE MIKE AT THE SUBJECT, OR THEY MAY SOUND "OFF-MIKE."

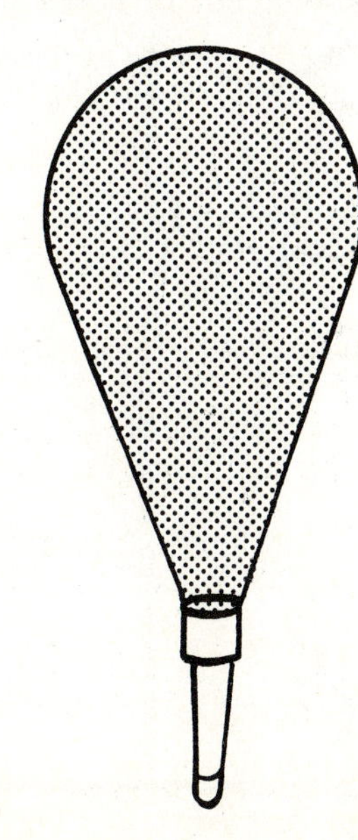

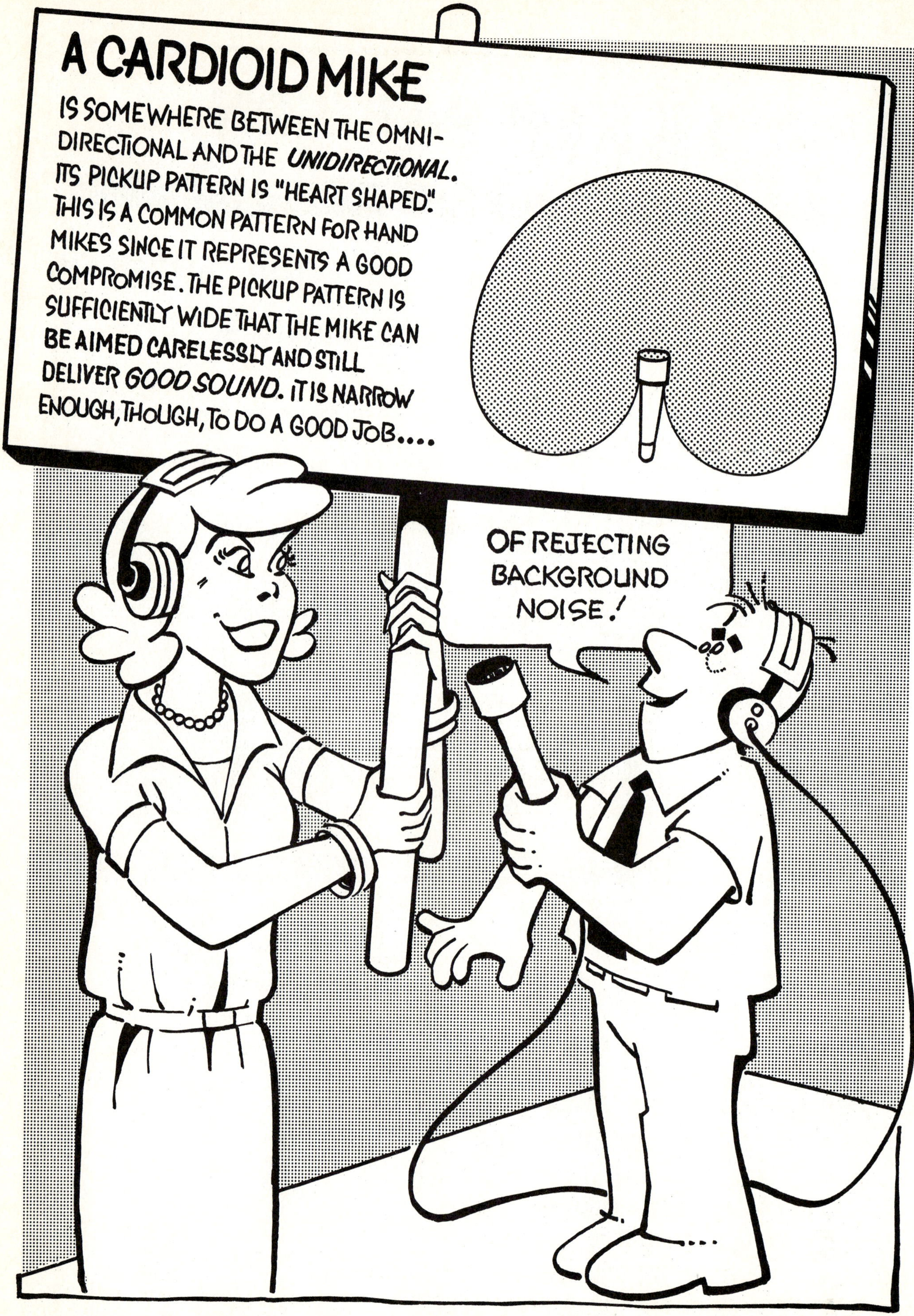

A CARDIOID MIKE

IS SOMEWHERE BETWEEN THE OMNI-DIRECTIONAL AND THE *UNIDIRECTIONAL.* ITS PICKUP PATTERN IS "HEART SHAPED." THIS IS A COMMON PATTERN FOR HAND MIKES SINCE IT REPRESENTS A GOOD COMPROMISE. THE PICKUP PATTERN IS SUFFICIENTLY WIDE THAT THE MIKE CAN BE AIMED CARELESSLY AND STILL DELIVER *GOOD SOUND.* IT IS NARROW ENOUGH, THOUGH, TO DO A GOOD JOB....

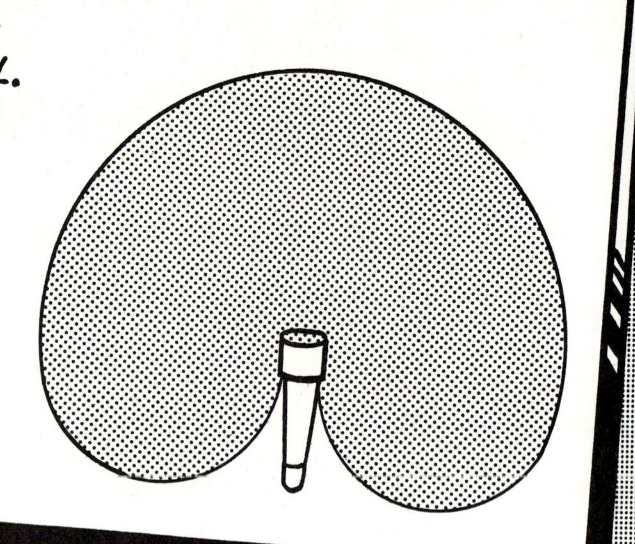

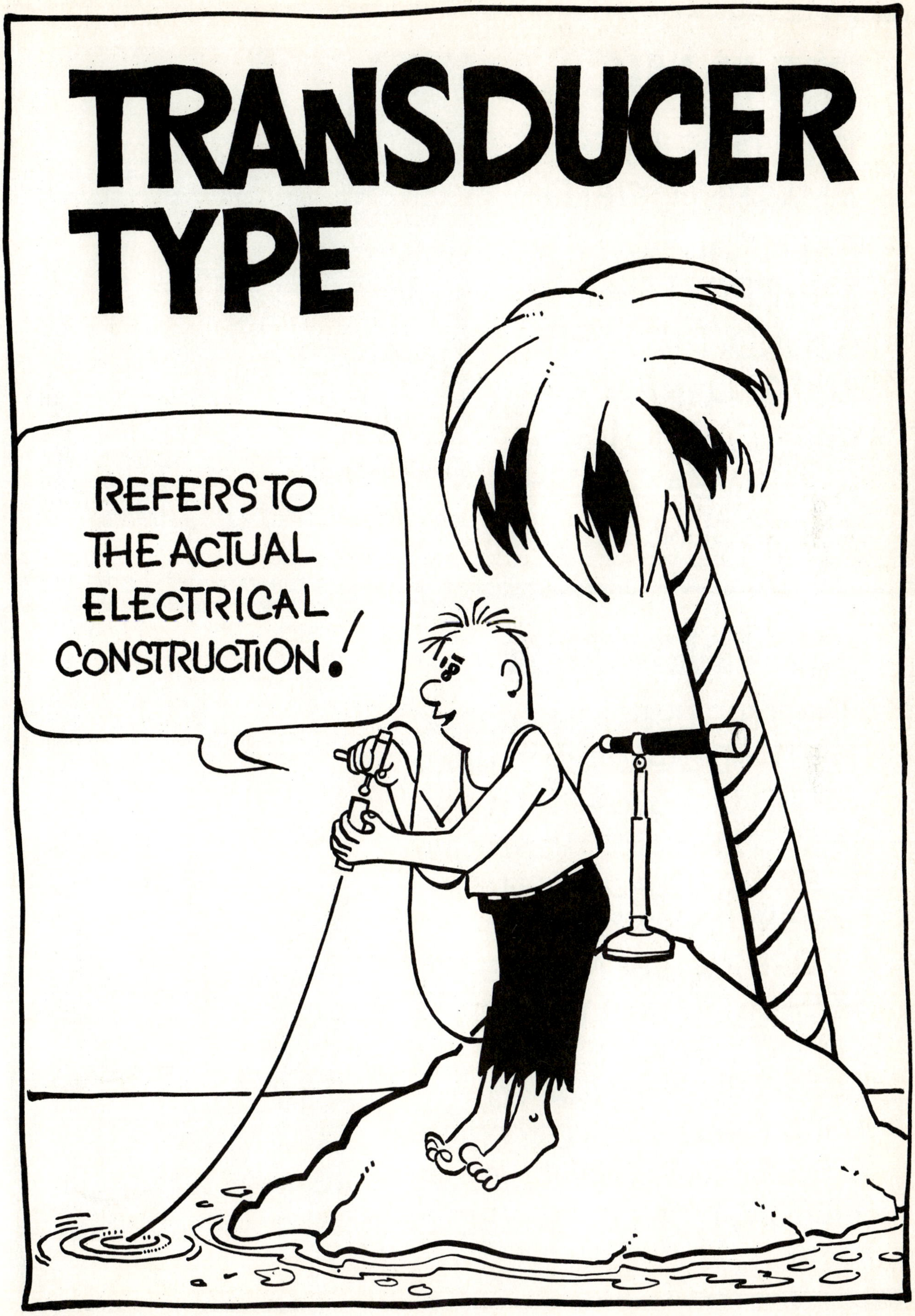

TRANSDUCER TYPE

DYNAMIC

THIS TYPE USES A MAGNETIC FIELD AND COIL TO INTERPRET THE SOUND. THEY ARE RUGGED, INEXPENSIVE, EASY TO USE, AND HAVE A SMOOTH SOFT SOUND!

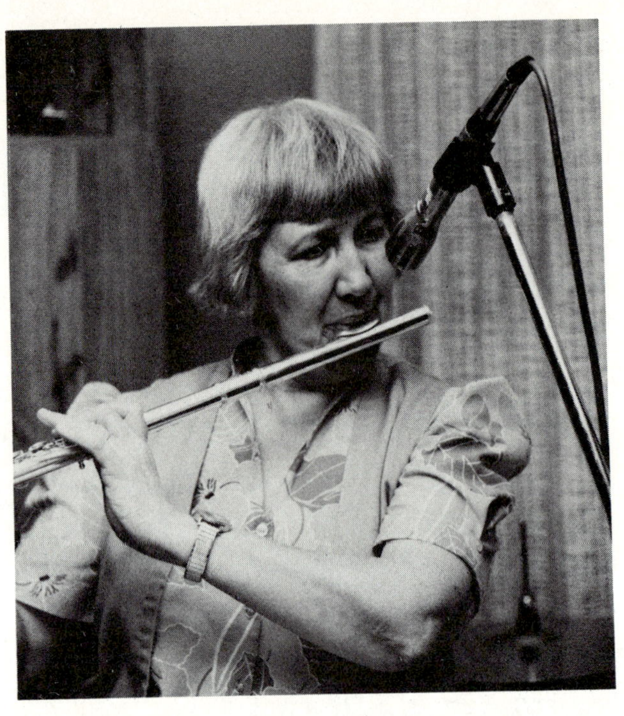

CONDENSER

THIS TYPE USES AN ELECTRIC FIELD AND CAPACITOR TO HEAR SOUND. UNLIKE OTHER TYPES, THESE MIKES NEED POWER TO OPERATE. USUALLY A SMALL BATTERY GOES INTO THE MIKE, OR ELSE IT WILL BE DESIGNED TO USE POWER FROM YOUR RECORDER. IT WILL BE LESS RUGGED THAN A DYNAMIC, BUT THE SOUND IS VERY CRISP, CLEAR, AND HAS AN ABUNDANCE OF THE QUALITY CALLED "PRESENCE".

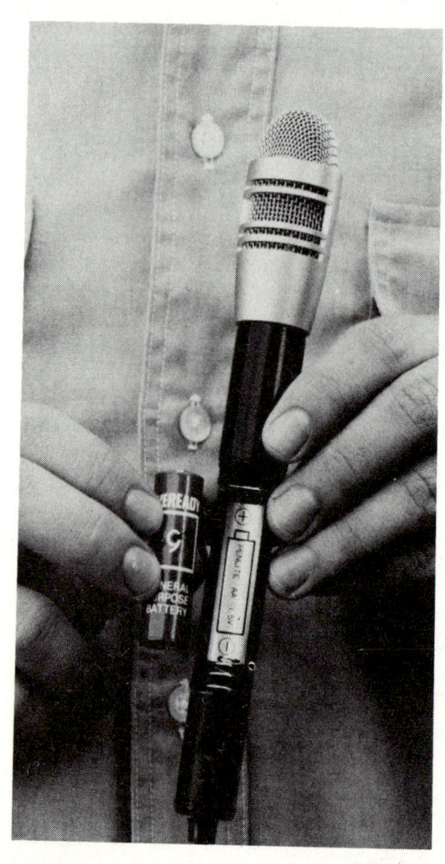

CERAMIC CRYSTAL

THIS MICROPHONE USES SOMETHING CALLED A "PIEZOELECTRIC CRYSTAL." THESE MIKES ARE CHEAP, BUT DON'T HAVE *MUCH ELSE* GOING FOR THEM. THE SOUND IS TYPICALLY *TINNY, HISSY,* AND LACKING IN BASS RESPONSE!

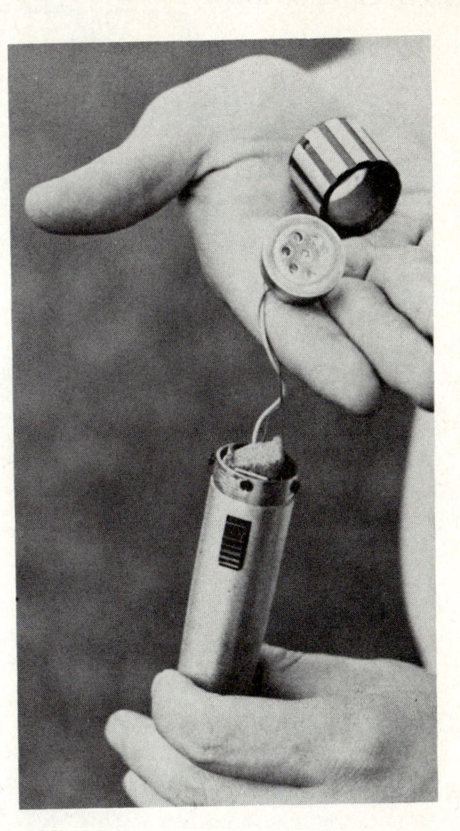

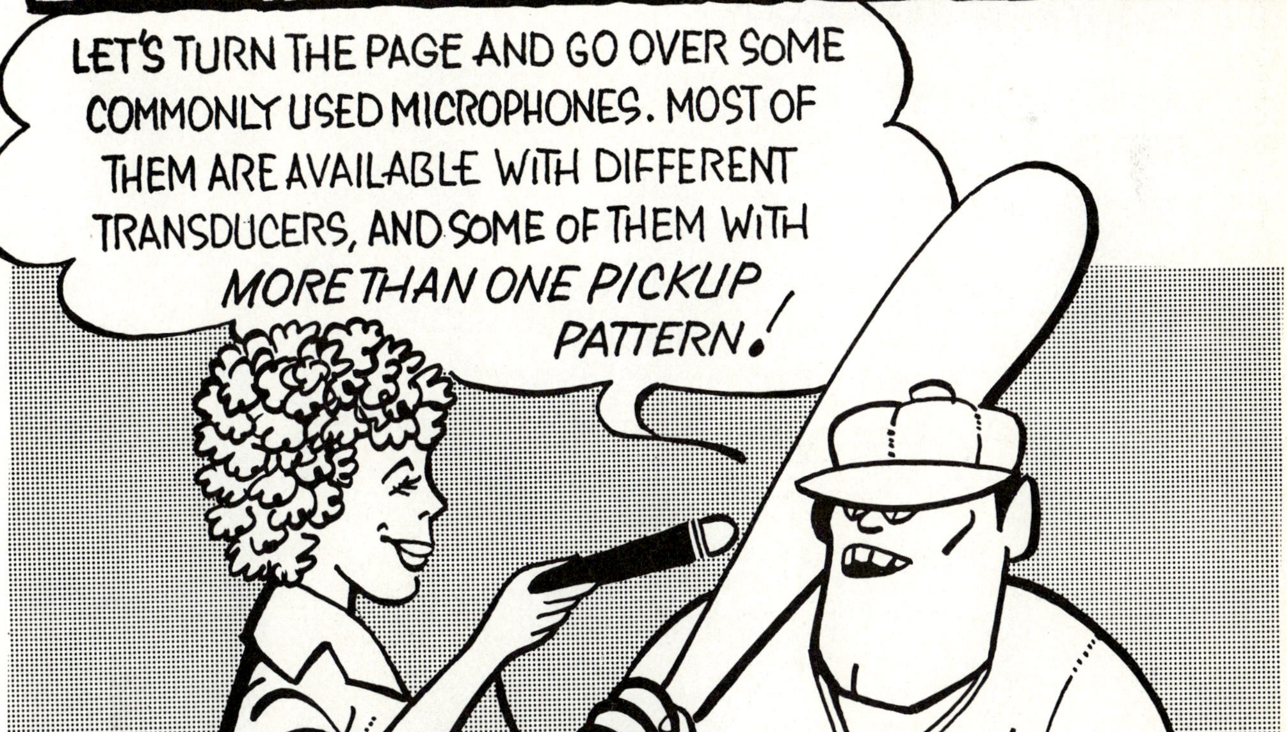

LET'S TURN THE PAGE AND GO OVER SOME COMMONLY USED MICROPHONES. MOST OF THEM ARE AVAILABLE WITH DIFFERENT TRANSDUCERS, AND SOME OF THEM WITH *MORE THAN ONE PICKUP PATTERN!*

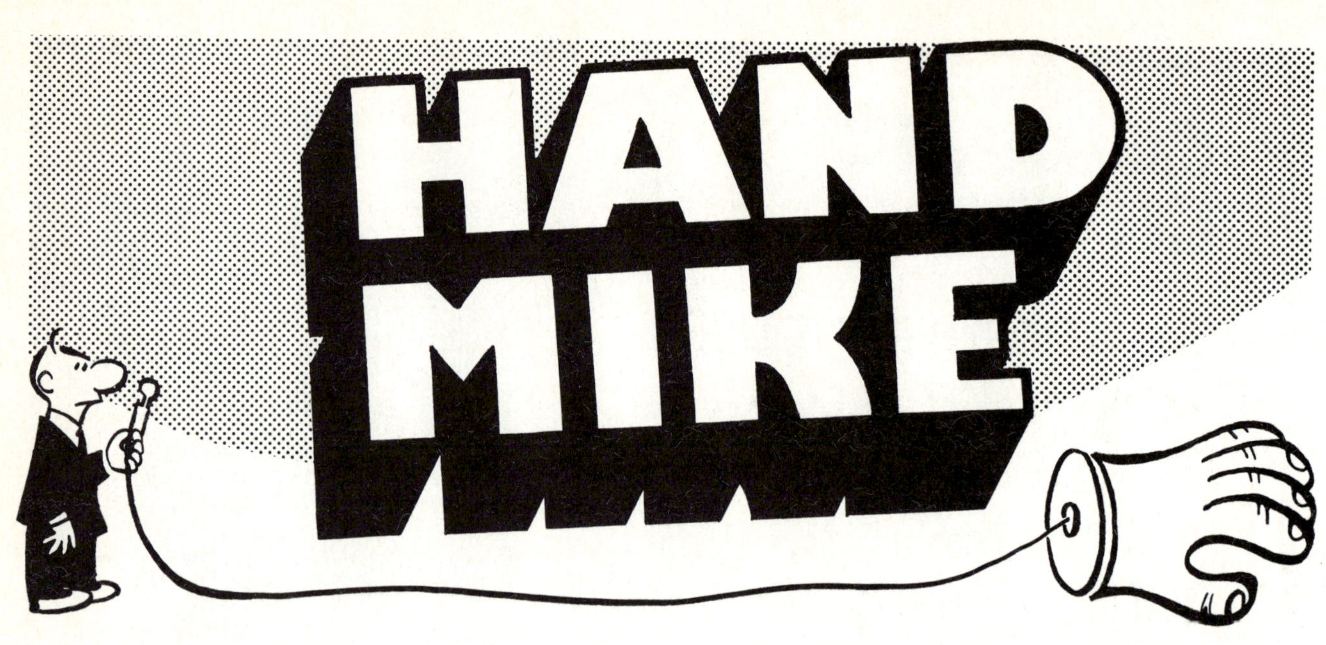

HAND MIKE

THIS IS A MICROPHONE YOU SEE USED BY SINGERS, GAME SHOW HOSTS, AND TV REPORTERS. BESIDES HAND HOLDING THE MIKE, IT CAN BE PUT INTO A DESK OR FLOOR STAND. THE PICKUP PATTERN IS USUALLY CARDIOID OR OMNIDIRECTIONAL. THIS IS USUALLY DYNAMIC, BUT ANY TRANSDUCER TYPE MAY BE USED.

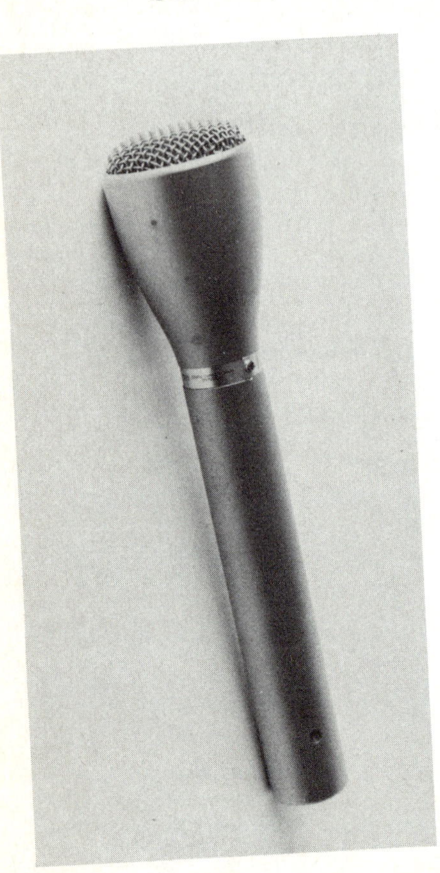

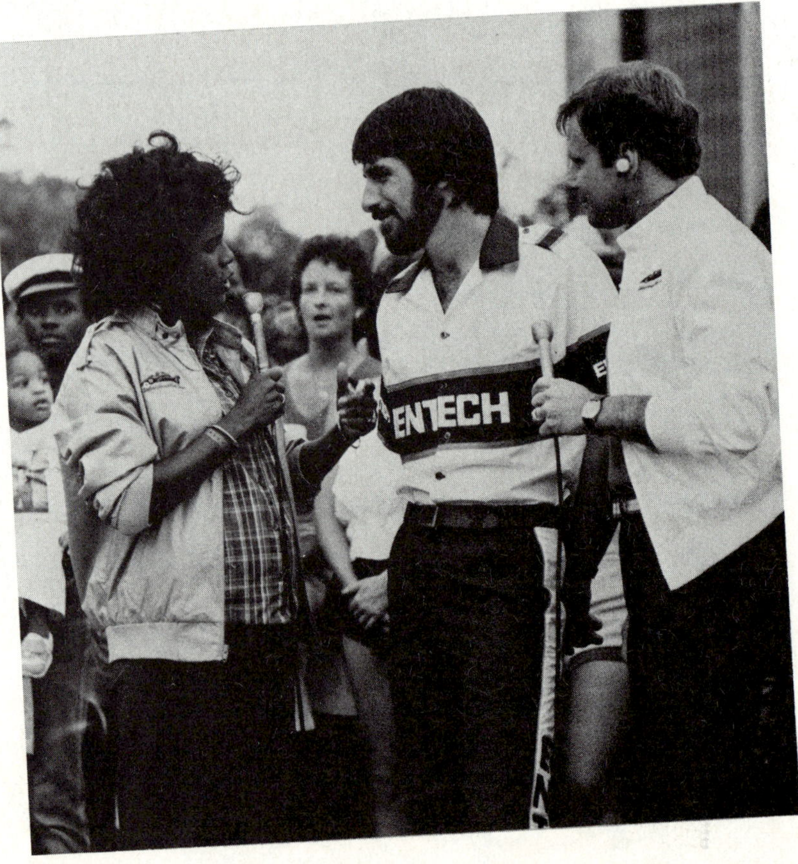

SHOTGUN MIKE

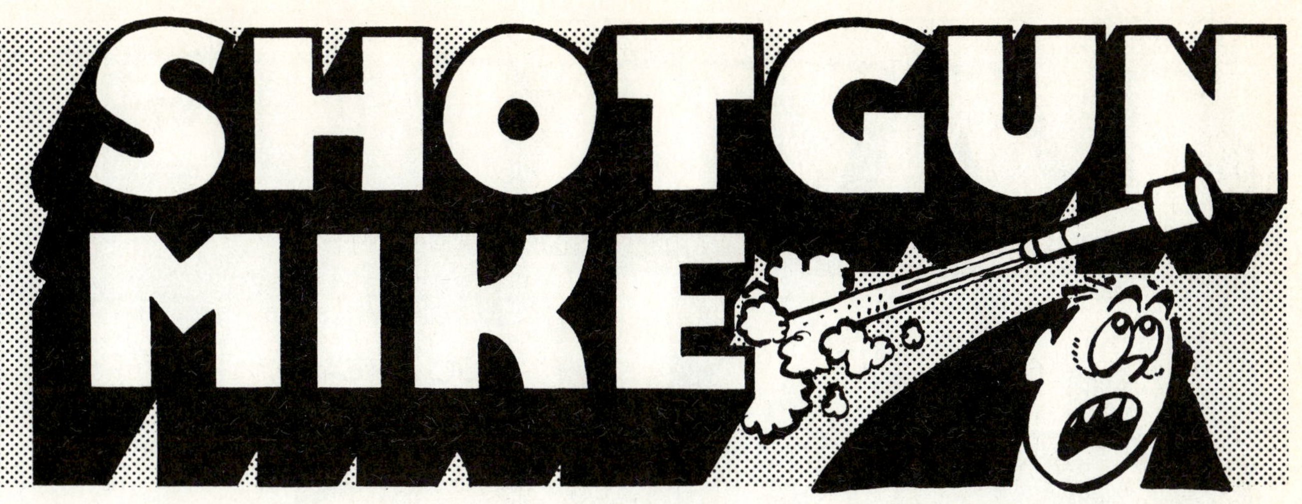

THE NAME FOR THIS MIKE COMES FROM ITS LONG **CYLINDRICAL** APPEARANCE AND **UNIDIRECTIONAL** PICKUP PATTERN, WHICH NECESSITATES AIMING IT LIKE A SHOTGUN. TO COMPLETE THE ANALOGY, A **PISTOL GRIP** IS OFTEN USED WITH IT. IT'S AN EX-CELLENT MICROPHONE FOR LONG-DISTANCE RECORDING OR PICKING UP VOICES OUT OF A CROWD. **A CONDENSER TYPE** TRANSDUCER IS USUALLY USED.

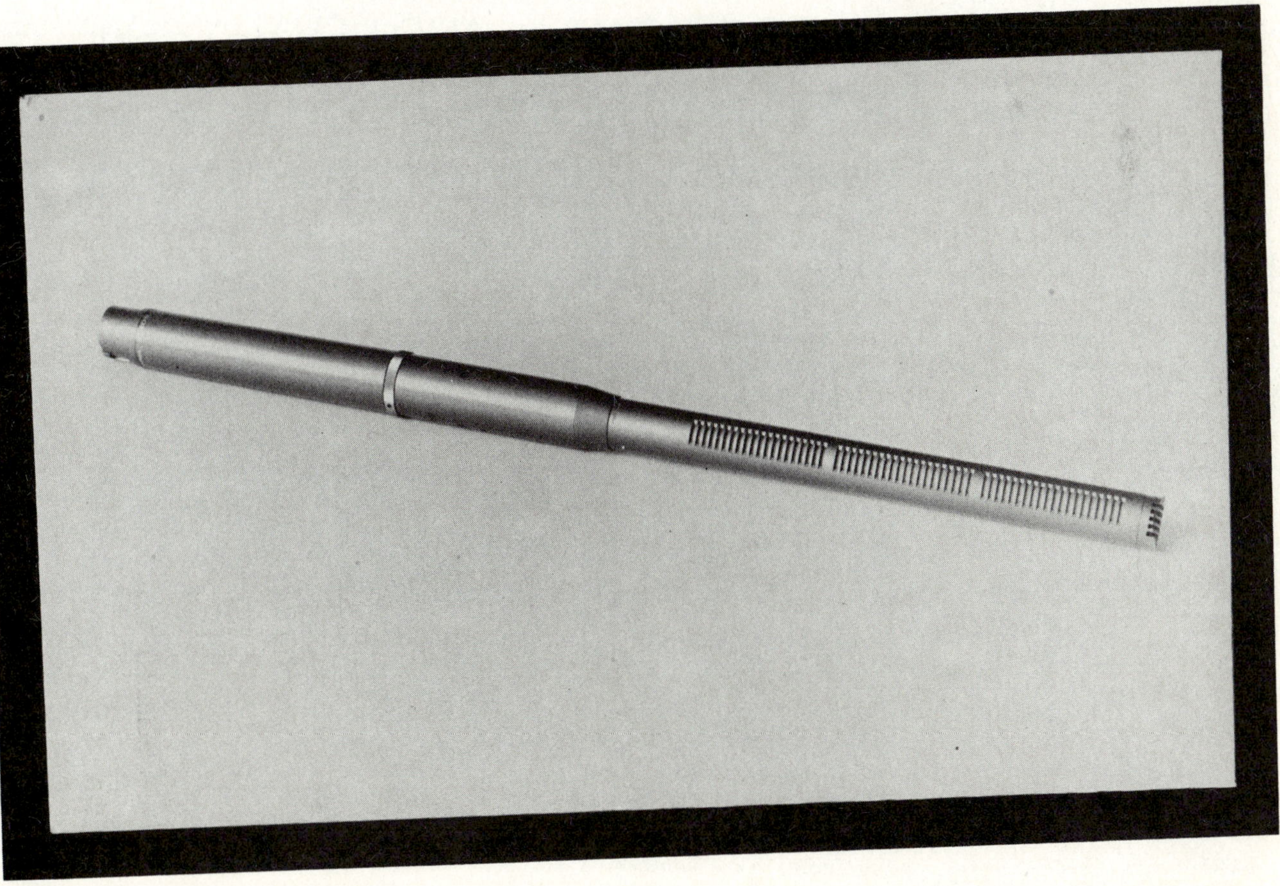

LAVALIER MIKE

THIS IS A SMALL MICRO-PHONE THAT IS DESIGNED SPECIFICALLY TO BE WORN ON THE CLOTHING OF YOUR SUBJECT. BECAUSE OF ITS SMALL SIZE, IT CAN BE EASILY HIDDEN BEHIND A TIE OR INSIDE A JACKET. THIS MIKE IS A GOOD CHOICE WHEN YOU NEED QUALITY SOUND BUT EITHER CAN'T GET YOUR MIKE CLOSE OR DON'T WANT TO SEE IT IN THE SHOT. LAVALIER TYPES ARE USUALLY **OMNIDIRECTIONAL** AND USUALLY HAVE **CONDENSER TRANSDUCERS!**

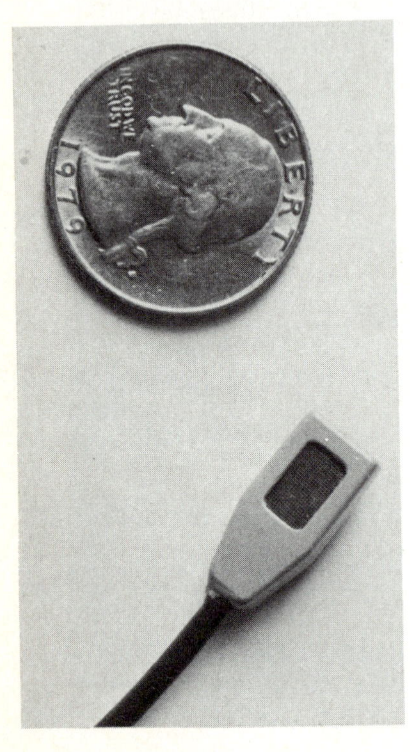

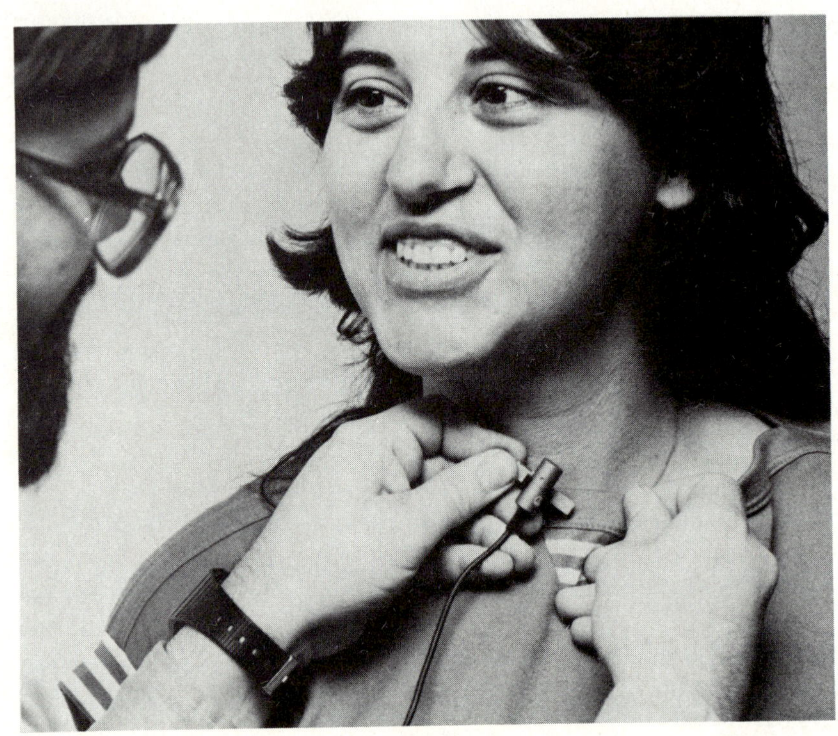

PRESSURE ZONE MIKE

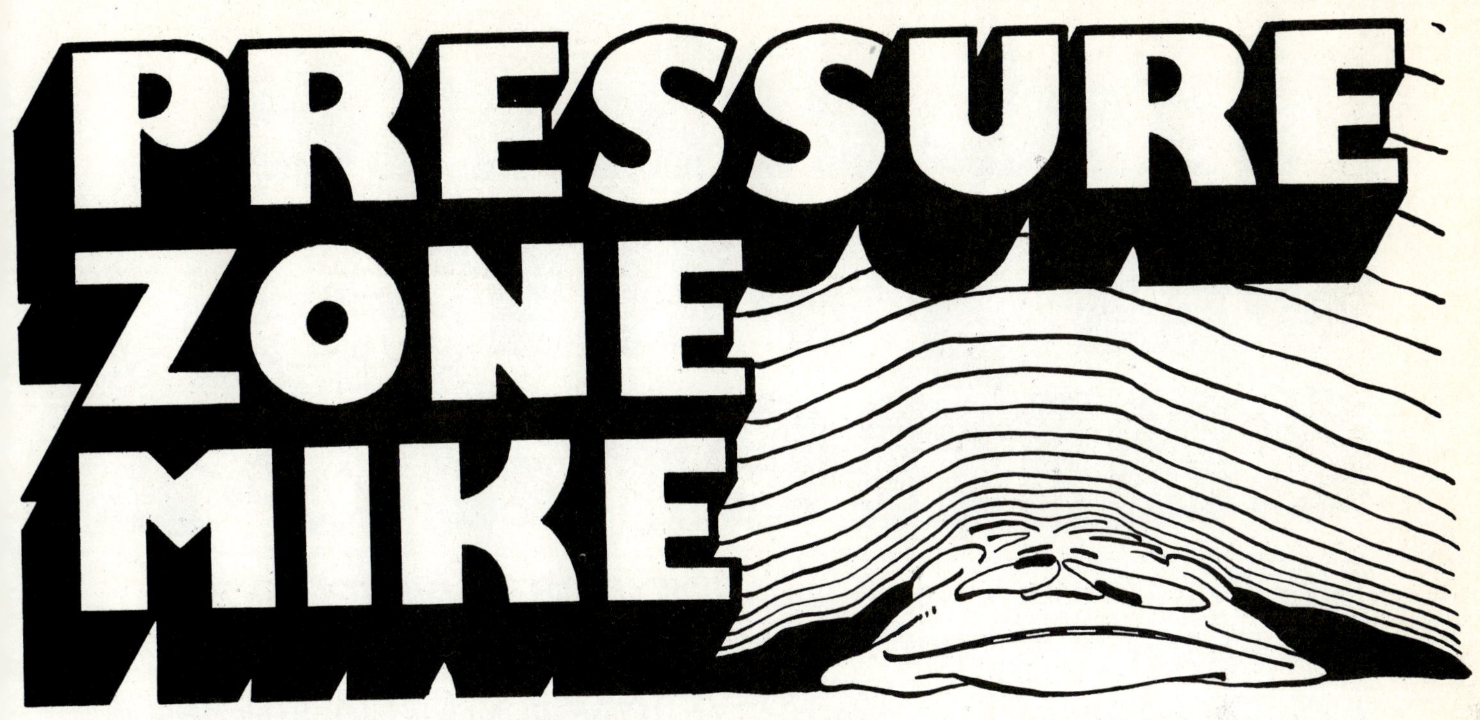

A RELATIVELY NEW MICROPHONE, THE **PZM** USES A ZONE OF CONTROLLED SOUND PRESSURE TO CREATE AN IMPROVED OMNI-DIRECTIONAL PICKUP PATTERN. THE RESULT IS A MICROPHONE THAT HAS BETTER **"REACH"** (CLARITY OF SOUND AT A DISTANCE) THAN SIMILAR MIKES. THIS IS AN EXCELLENT MIKE TO PUT ON THE PODIUM OF A SPEAKER, OR INTO THE MIDDLE OF A TABLE DISCUSSION, OR UNDERNEATH THE LID OF A PIANO. IT CAN BE MADE MORE DIRECTIONAL BY PLACING IT INTO THE CORNER OF A ROOM OR PODIUM. A FLAT SURFACE ENHANCES ITS UNIQUE QUALITIES.

PZM'S ARE TYPICALLY CONDENSER MIKES!

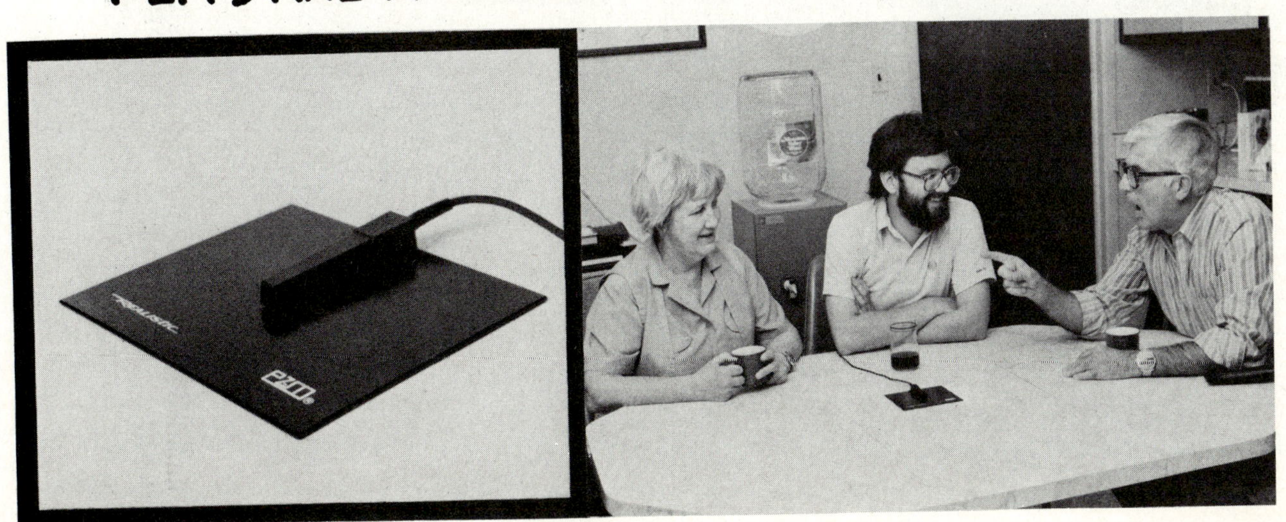

the mike on your camera

THIS IS PROBABLY EITHER A CARDIOID OR *A UNIDIRECTIONAL* CONDENSER TYPE MIKE. MANY TIMES IT IS ALSO FILTERED OR TUNED TO BE THE MOST RECEPTIVE TO VOICE FREQUENCIES! THIS LETS IT PICK UP VOICES WITH REASONABLE CLARITY— EVEN AT A DISTANCE— UNFORTUNATELY, IT IS NOT A VERY GOOD **MIKE FOR ANYTHING ELSE!**

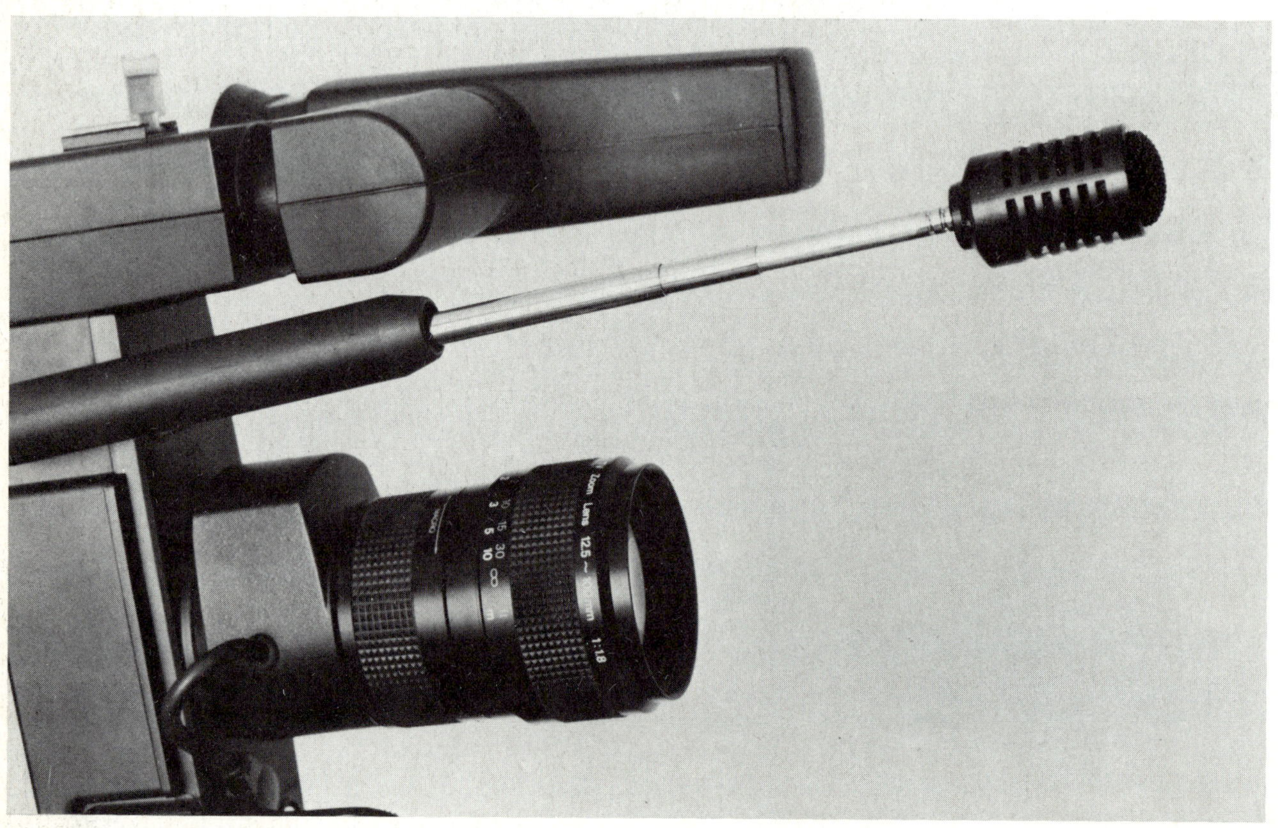

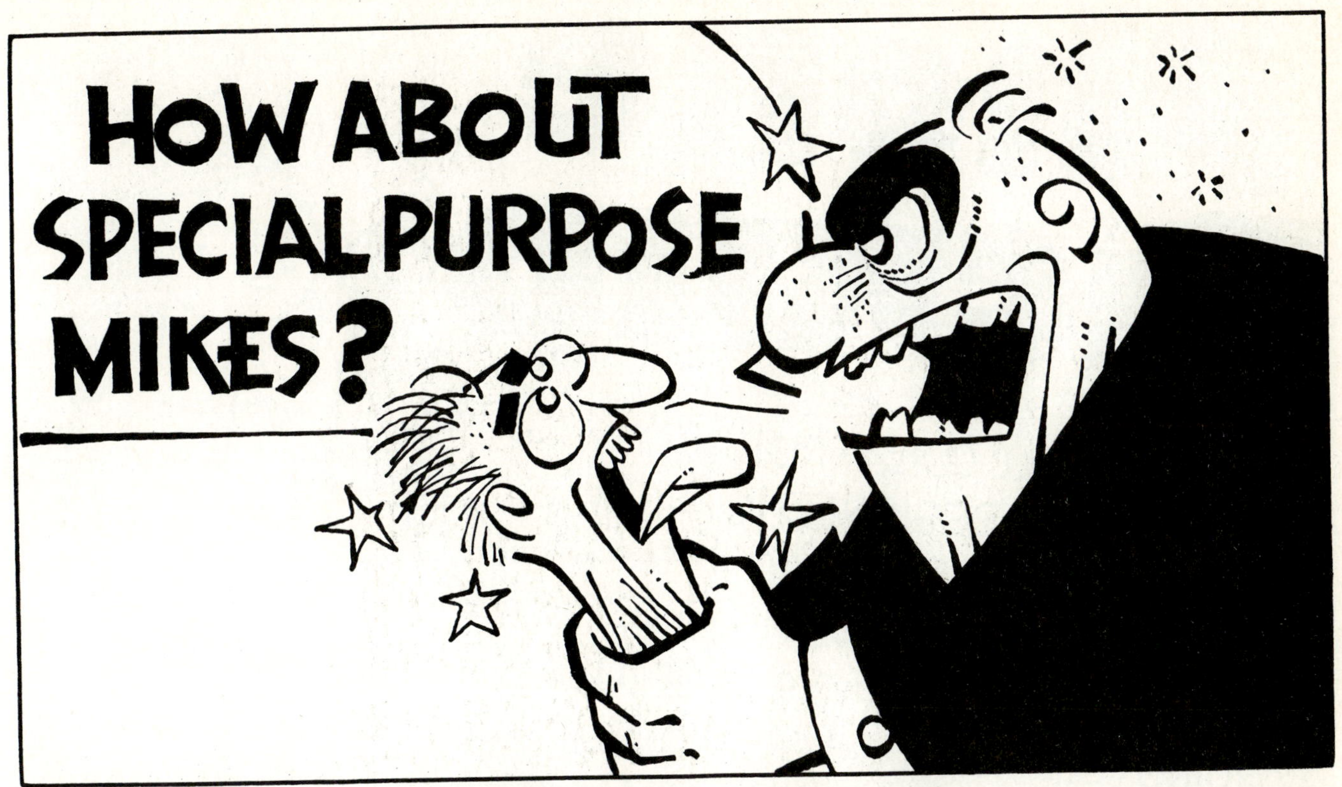

contact mike

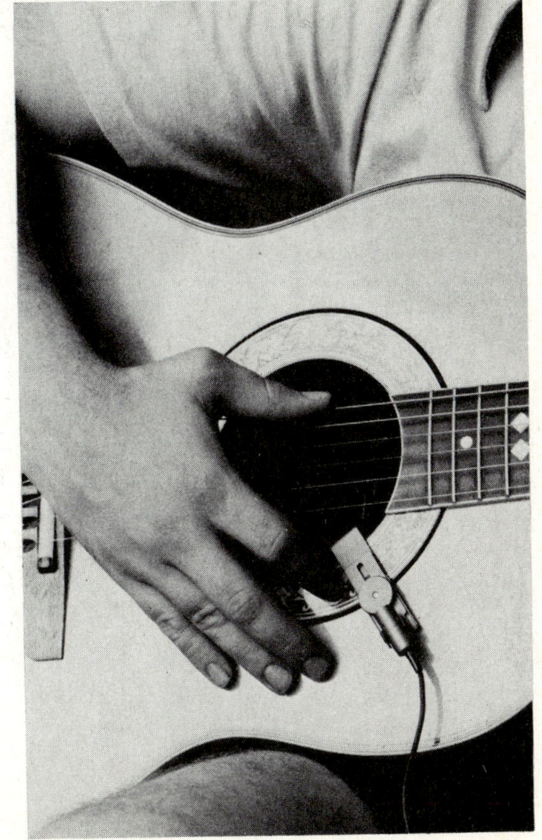

A CONTACT MIKE IS DESIGNED TO BE CLIPPED OR FASTENED DIRECTLY TO A **MUSICAL INSTRUMENT**. THE MIKE'S APPEARANCE WILL VARY DEPENDING ON THE INSTRUMENT IT'S DESIGNED FOR !

phone pickup

THIS IS A SMALL COIL, PROBABLY WITH A SUCTION CUP DESIGNED TO STICK TO A TELEPHONE RECEIVER. YOU MAY HAVE TO EXPERIMENT WITH PLACING THE PICKUP FOR THE BEST SOUND. IT IS A USEFUL ACCESSORY FOR RECORDING TELEPHONE CONVERSATIONS. ATTACH IT TO AN EXTENSION PHONE **SO IT'S NOT ON CAMERA!**

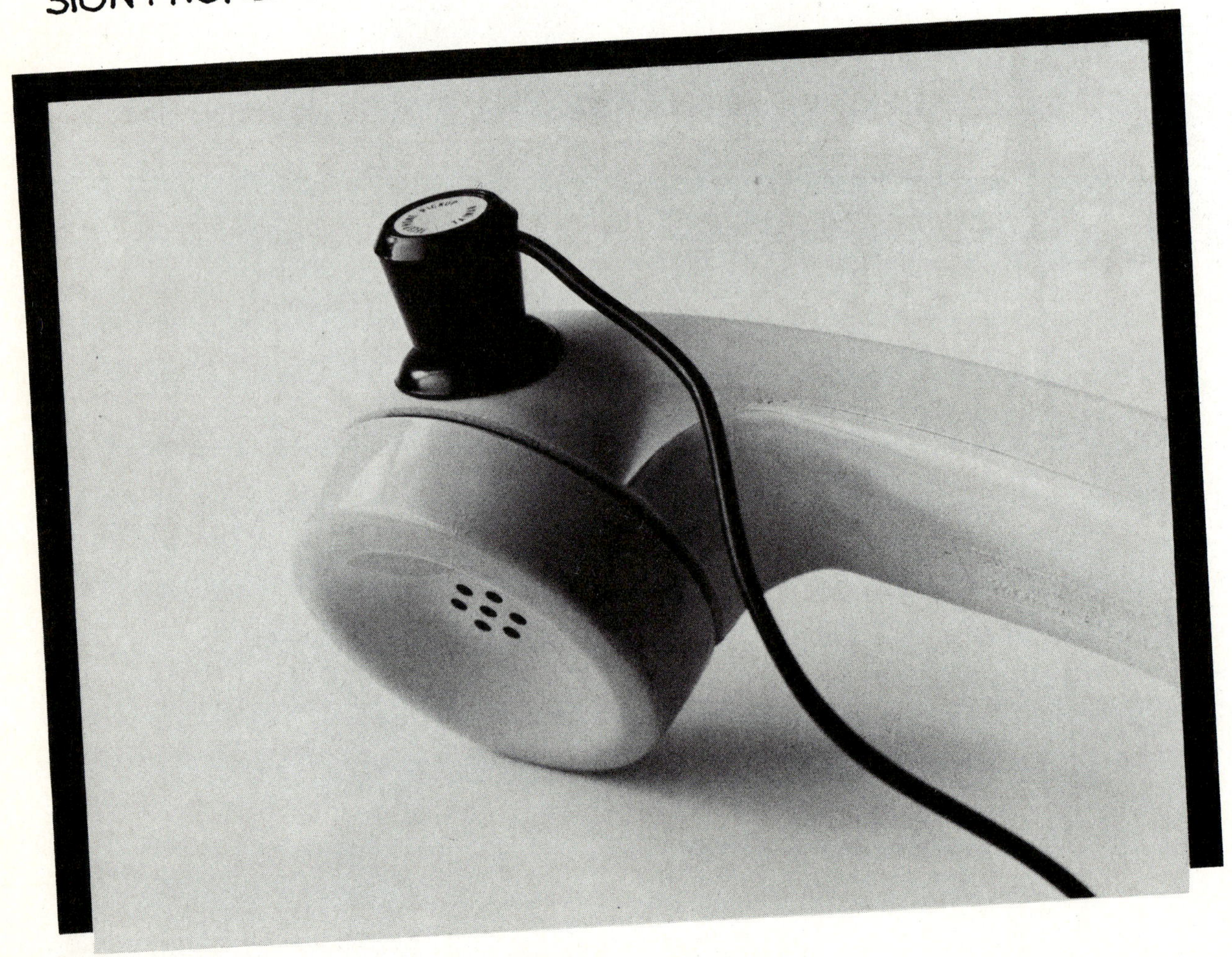

the Parabolic reflector

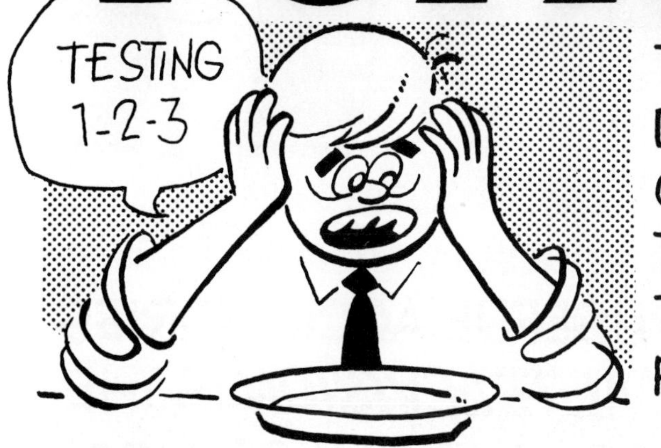

THIS IS NOTHING MORE THAN A PARA-BOLIC (CURVED) DISH WITH AN OMNIDIRECTIONAL TYPE MIKE IN THE MIDDLE. THE DISH FOCUSES THE SOUND THE SAME WAY A LENS FOCUSES LIGHT!

THE RESULT IS A VERY SENSITIVE AND DIRECTIONAL MICROPHONE. USE THE PARABOLIC MIKE TO RECORD BIRD CALLS, OR PEOPLE WHISPERING. LIKE THE SHOTGUN MIKE, THE PARABOLIC MIKE MUST BE *CAREFULLY AIMED!*

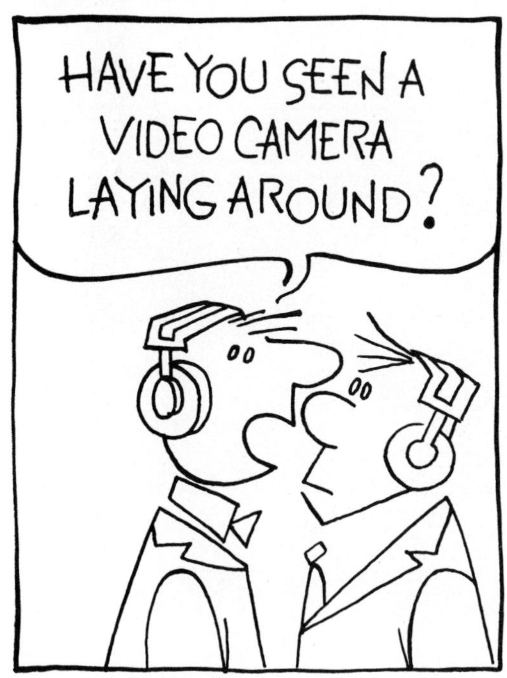

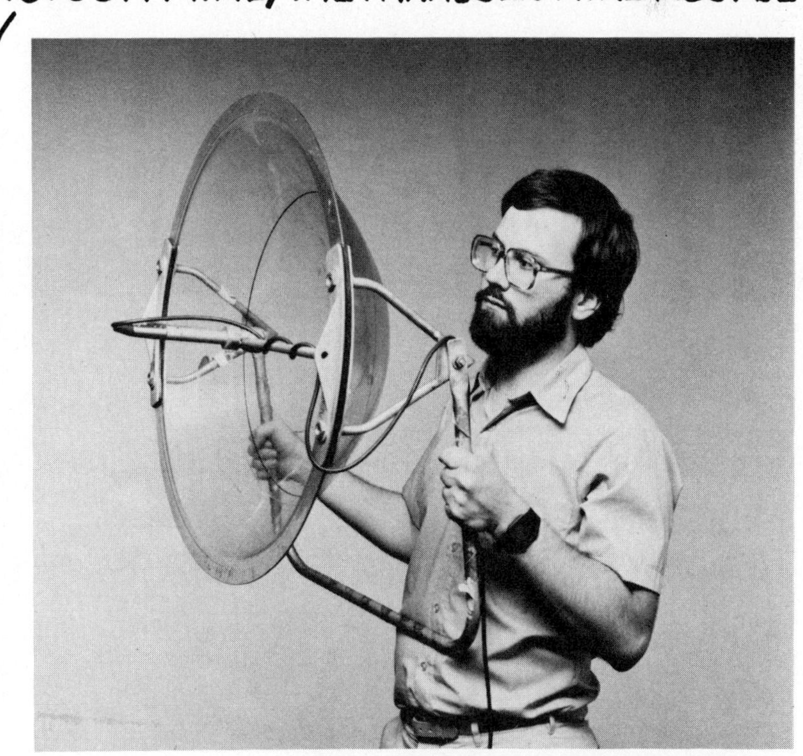
AUTHOR WITH PARABOLIC REFLECTOR MIKE

the wireless mike

ONE OF THE MOST GENUINELY USEFUL ACCESSORIES WE USE ALMOST DAILY ON *LOCAL TELEVISION* IS THE WIRELESS MIKE. THE WIRELESS MIKE CAN GO ANY-WHERE, UP TO A *HUNDRED FEET* OR SO FROM THE CAMERA, COMPLETELY UNENCUMBERED BY CABLES.

A WIRELESS MIKE SET CONSISTS OF A TRANSMITTER UNIT INTO WHICH A MICROPHONE (USUALLY A SMALL LAVALIER TYPE) CAN BE PLUGGED, AND A RECEIVER UNIT WHICH IS CONNECTED TO THE MICROPHONE JACK OF YOUR EQUIPMENT. THE TRANSMITTER/ MICROPHONE CAN THEN BE HIDDEN IN THE CLOTHING OF YOUR SUBJECTS, GIVING THEM COMPLETE FREEDOM TO MOVE ABOUT.!

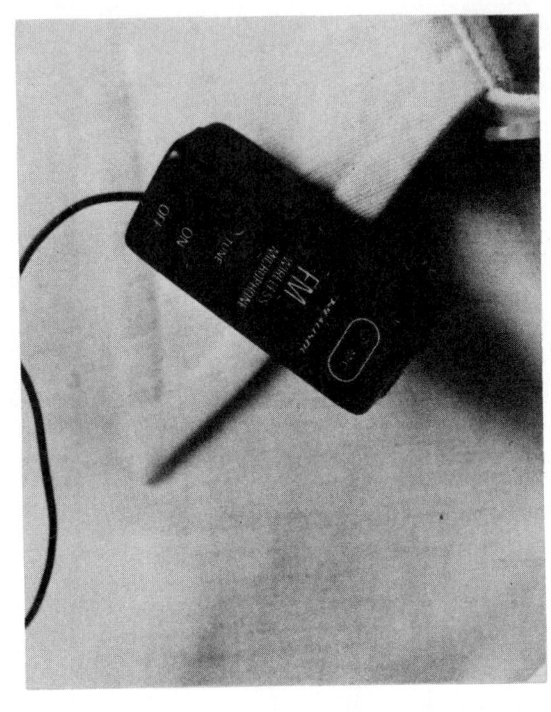

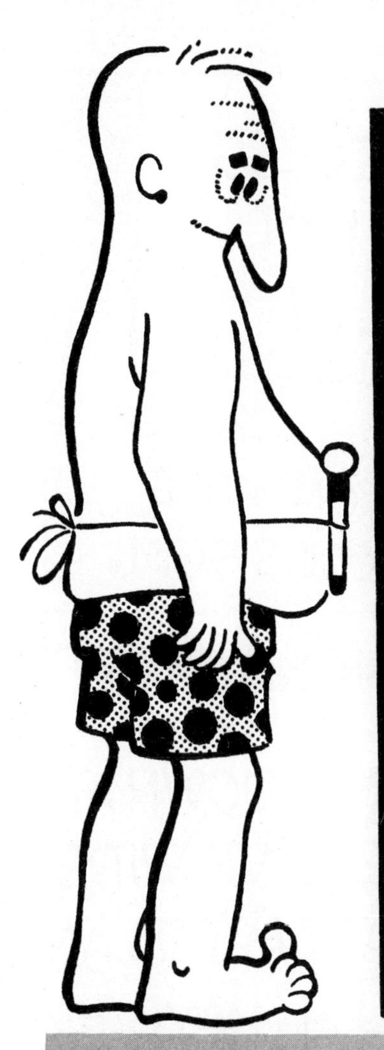

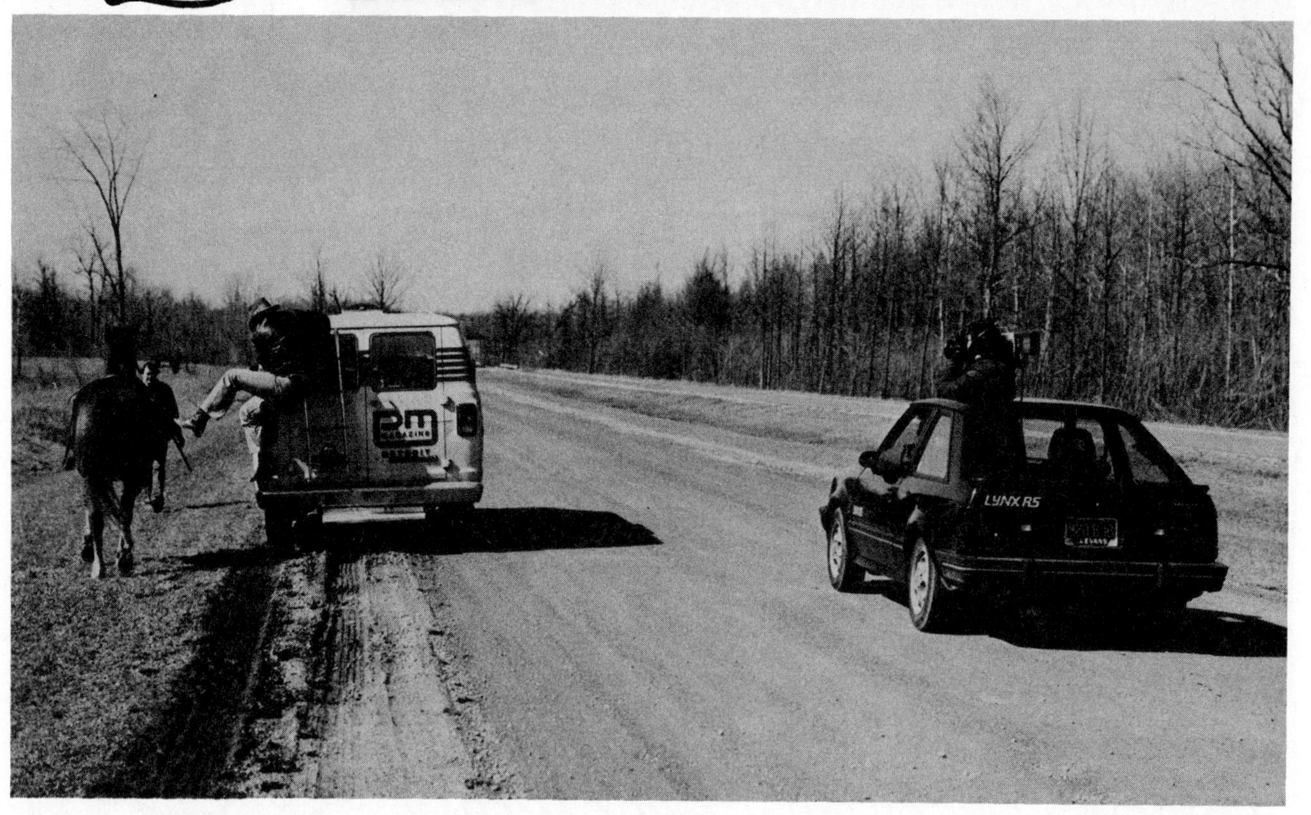
THE WIRELESS MICROPHONE CAN ALSO BE PUT PLACES YOU COULDN'T POSSIBLY REACH BY CABLE, LIKE ON A RAFT IN THE MIDDLE OF A SWIMMING POOL...

OR HIGH IN THE BRANCHES OF A TREE, TO RECORD BIRD CALLS... OR ON A HANG GLIDER PILOT AS HE JUMPS OFF A CLIFF...

OR ON A GROOM DURING A WEDDING CEREMONY. THE POSSIBILITIES ARE ENDLESS!
BUT THE WIRELESS MIKE HAS DRAWBACKS!

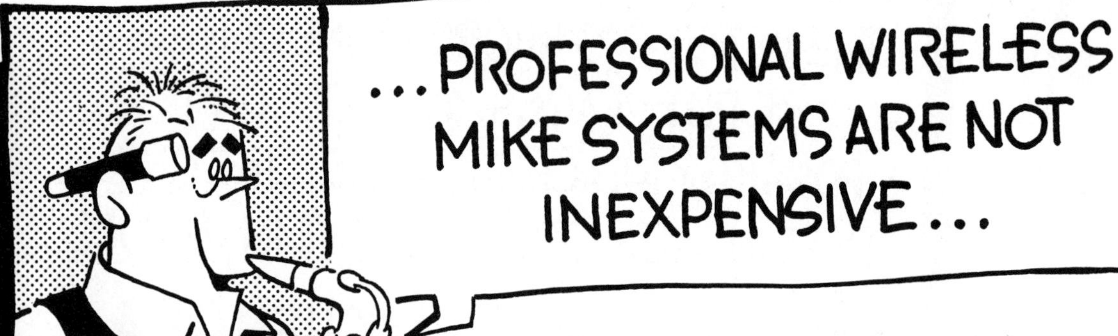

LESSER SYSTEMS CAN BE HAD, OF COURSE, DOWN AT YOUR ELECTRONICS STORE. AN INEXPENSIVE WIRELESS MIKE WILL BE DESIGNED TO BROADCAST TO AN ORDINARY FM RADIO. THIS MEANS YOU'LL HAVE TO BUY A PORTABLE FM RECEIVER TO CONNECT TO YOUR VCR *(SEE THE CHAPTER ON CONNECTING ANYTHING TO ANYTHING).*

THE RANGE IS LIMITED. YOUR WIRELESS MIKE MAY HAVE A BROADCAST RANGE OF 100 FEET OR **LESS**! GET OUT-OF RANGE, AND YOUR AUDIO WILL FADE OUT. YOU MAY LOSE THE SIGNAL TEMPORARILY FROM TIME TO TIME EVEN WHEN IN RANGE. IF TROUBLED BY FADE-OUTS, TRY A BETTER ANTENNA ON THE RECEIVER...
OR PUT THE RECEIVER & ANTENNA UP HIGH... *LIKE ON TOP OF YOUR CAMERA!*

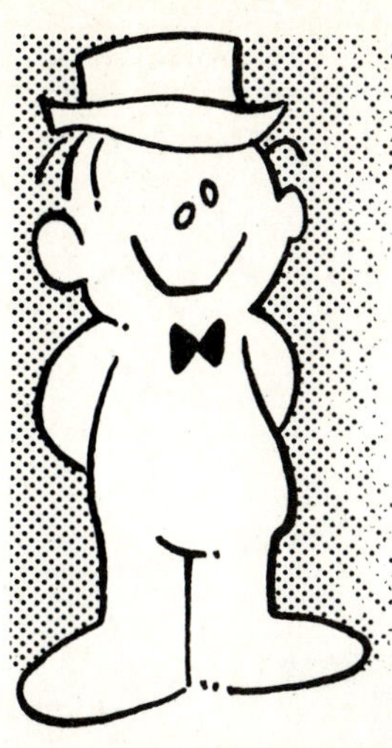

...AND REMEMBER, WIRELESS MIKES ARE HARD TO CONNECT, DIFFICULT TO ADJUST, AND YOUR BATTERIES WILL GO DEAD WHEN YOU NEED THEM MOST. IT WILL TAKE SOME PATIENCE AT FIRST TO MASTER YOUR WIRELESS.

HAVE A SPARE MIKE READY WHEN SOMETHING GOES WRONG!

WHAT DO I DO WITH ALL THESE MIKES?

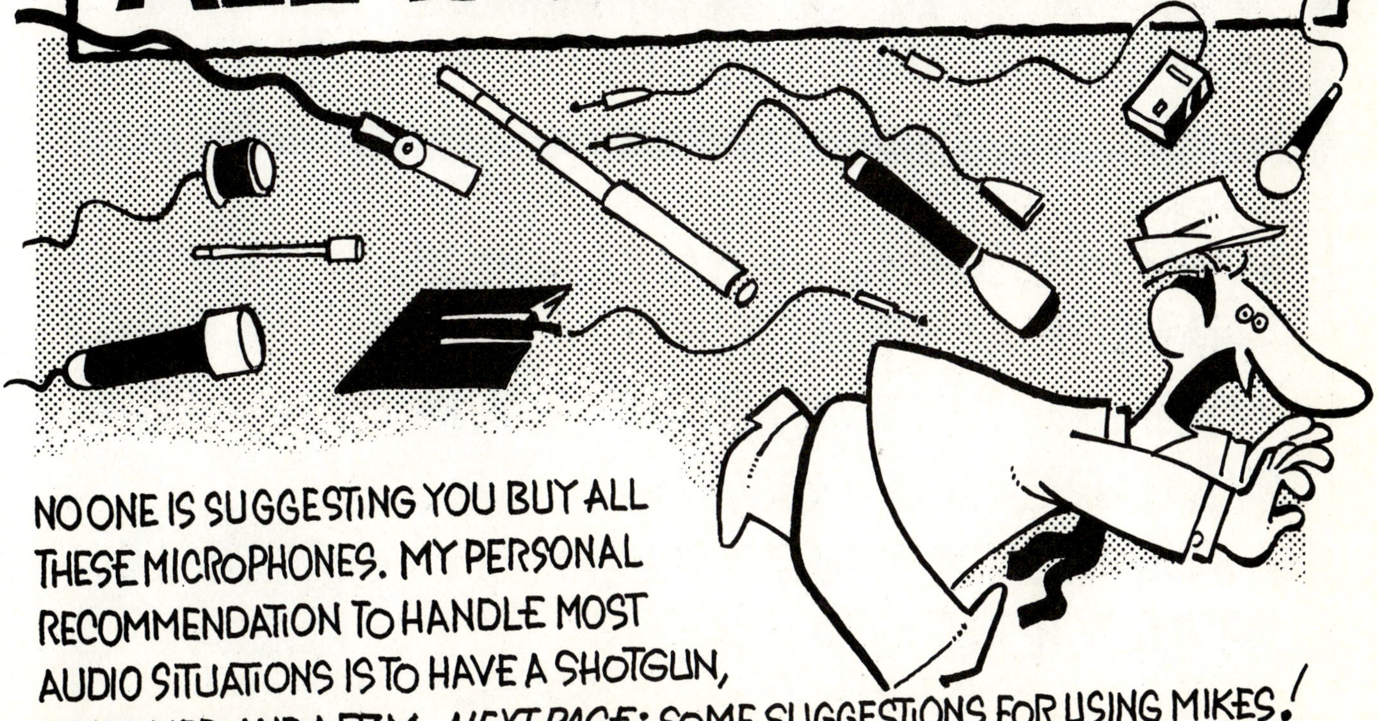

NO ONE IS SUGGESTING YOU BUY ALL THESE MICROPHONES. MY PERSONAL RECOMMENDATION TO HANDLE MOST AUDIO SITUATIONS IS TO HAVE A SHOTGUN, A LAVALIER, AND A PZM. *NEXT PAGE:* SOME SUGGESTIONS FOR USING MIKES!

SPEAKING INTO A HAND MIKE

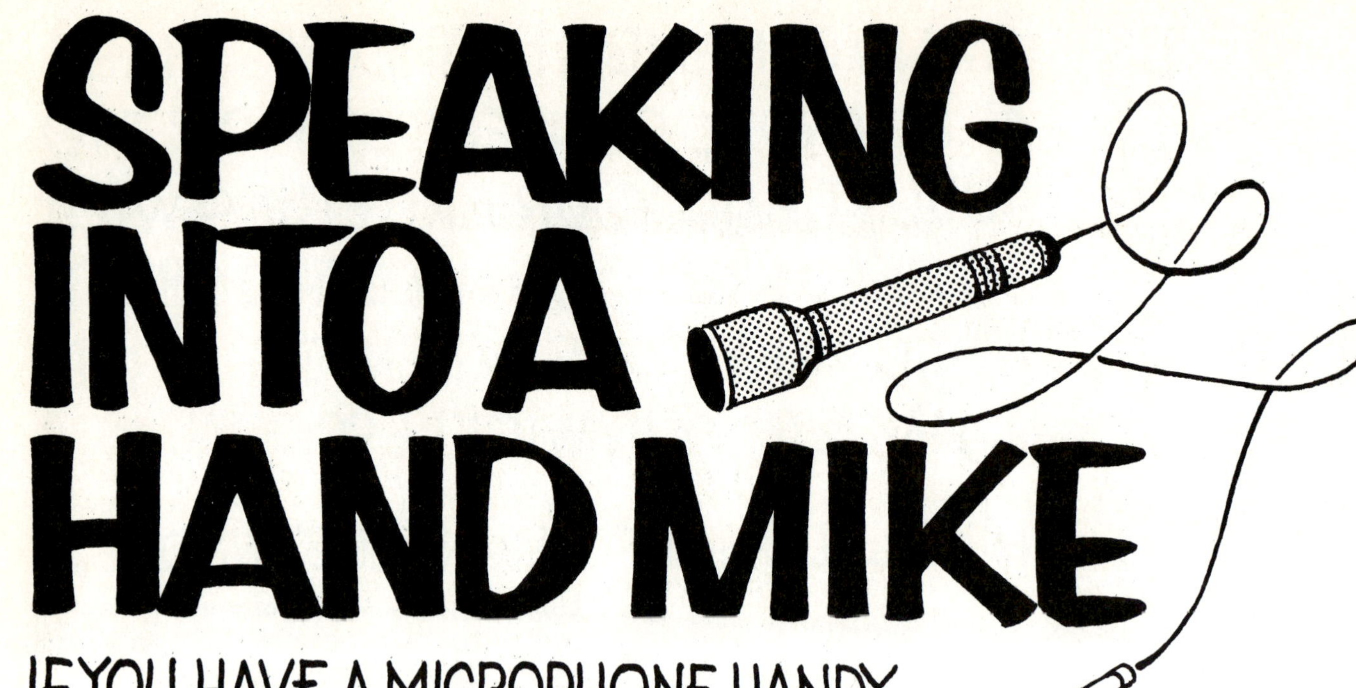

IF YOU HAVE A MICROPHONE HANDY,
TRY THIS EXPERIMENT:

HOLD THE MIKE DIRECTLY IN FRONT OF YOUR MOUTH AND SAY: "PETER PIPER PICKED A PECK OF PICKLED PEPPERS". PLAY THE TAPE BACK AND NOTICE WHAT HAPPENED TO THE P'S. WHY DO THEY SOUND SO BAD? TO ANSWER THAT QUESTION, HOLD YOUR HAND IN FRONT OF YOUR MOUTH AND SAY THE SAME THING.
FEEL ALL THAT AIR EXPLODING FROM YOUR MOUTH?

YOUR MICROPHONE CAN'T HANDLE ALL THAT AIR COMING AT IT, SO IT *DISTORTS THE SOUND!* THE SOLUTION TO THE PROBLEM IS ON THE NEXT PAGE.

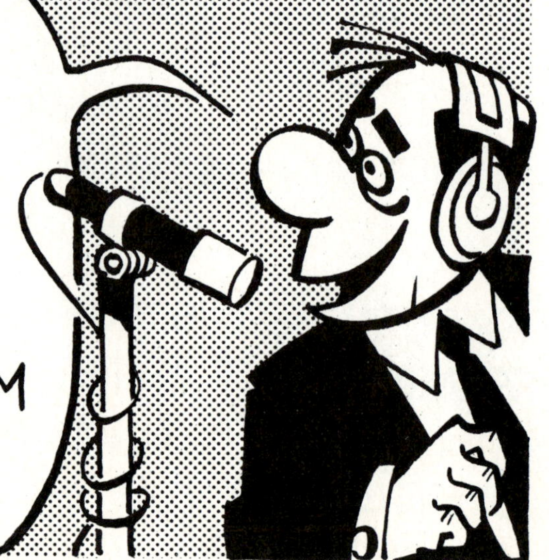

HERE IS THE CORRECT WAY TO USE A HAND MIKE:

POINT THE MIKE AT YOUR MOUTH, BUT DON'T POINT YOUR MOUTH AT THE MIKE!

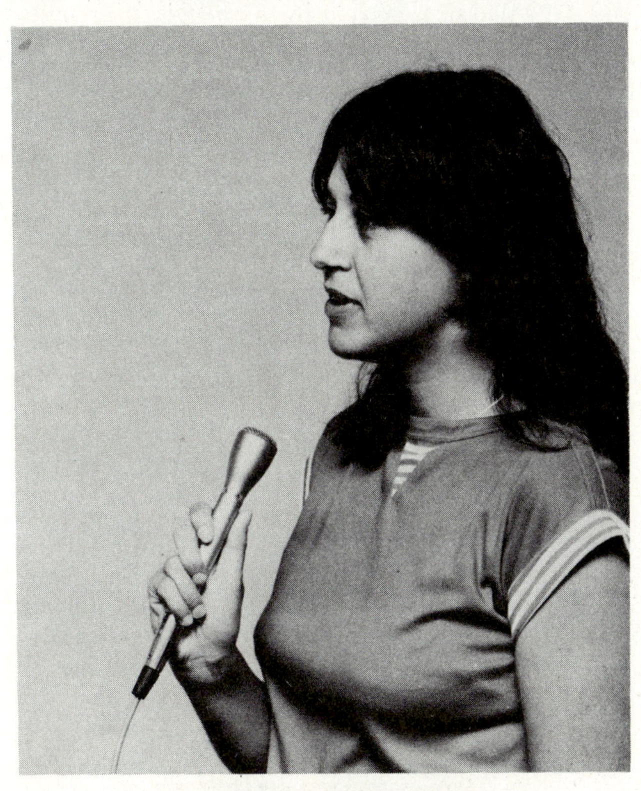

LIKE *THIS*

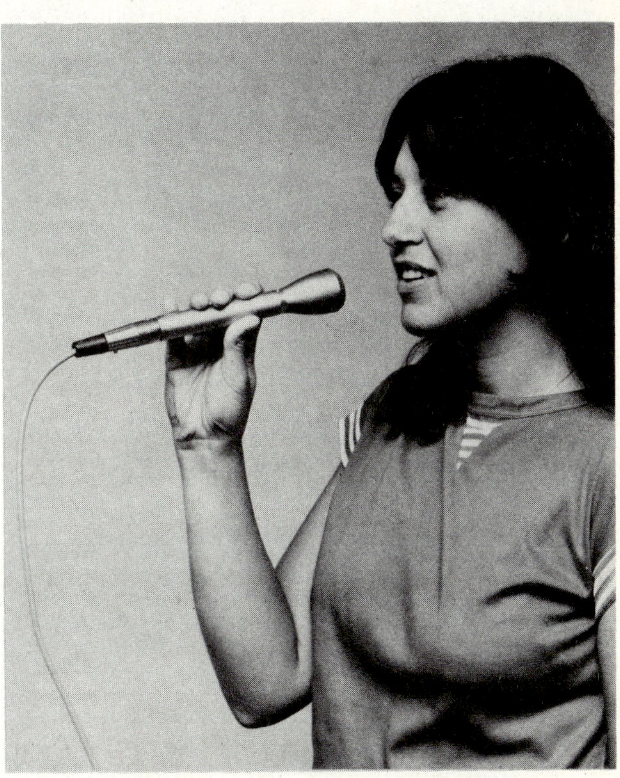

NOT LIKE THIS

HIDING MIKES

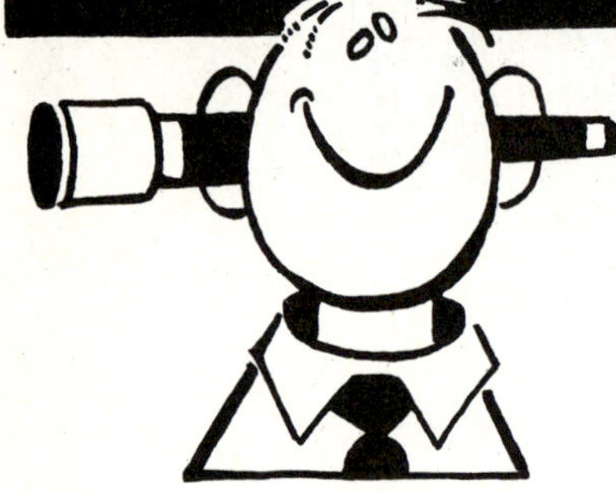

SOMETIMES, HAVING A MICROPHONE IN THE PICTURE ISN'T ACCEPTABLE. HAVING A SMALL LAVALIER MIKE ATTACHED TO YOUR SUBJECT IS ONE SOLUTION. THAT SAME MIKE, BECAUSE OF ITS SMALL SIZE, CAN ALSO BE HIDDEN IN A BOWL OF FRUIT, TAPED TO THE SIDE OF A CHAIR, OR DANGLED FROM A LIGHT FIXTURE (LARGER MIKES CAN BE HIDDEN TOO).

HERE ARE PLACES TO HIDE ALL THOSE MIKES

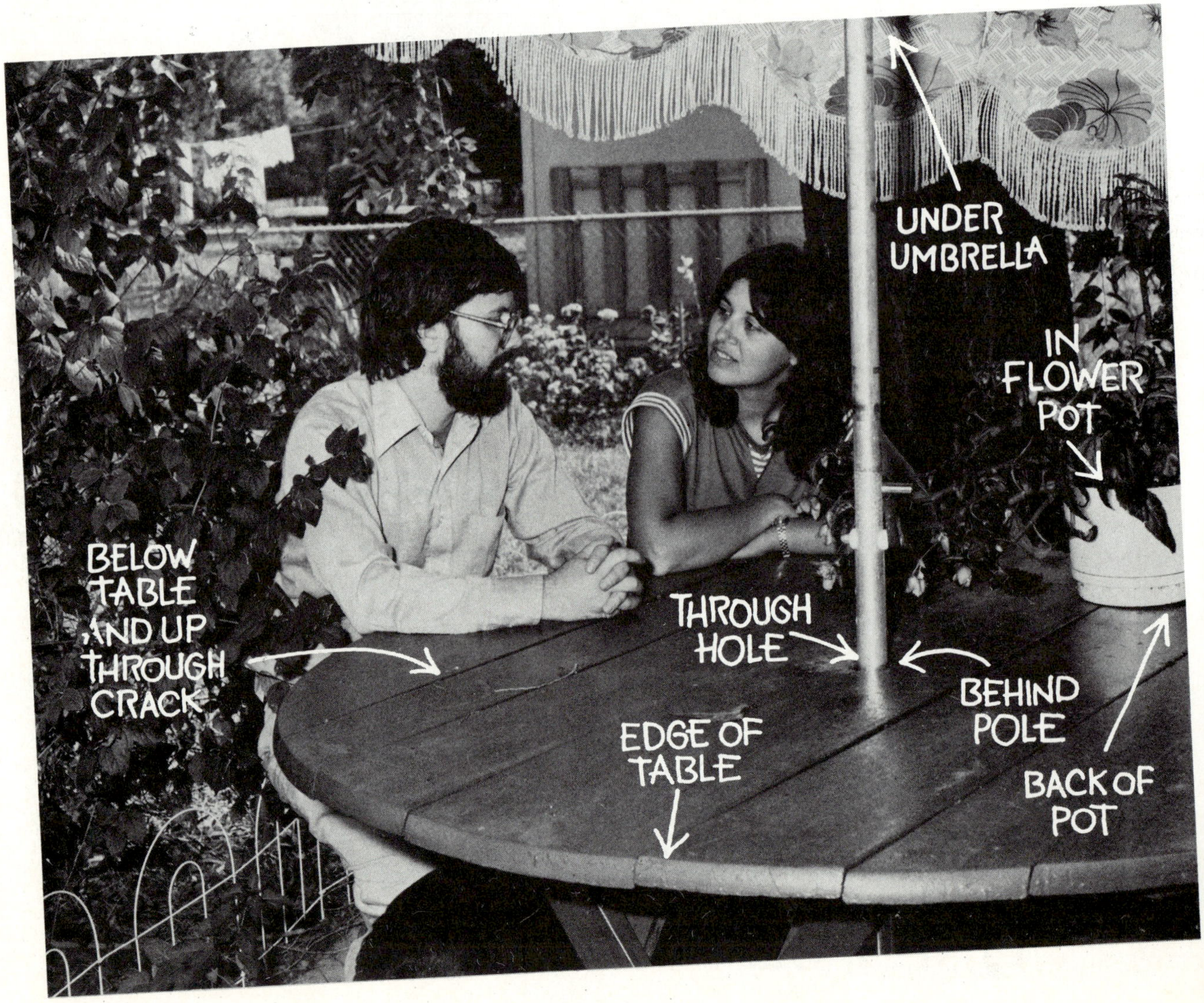

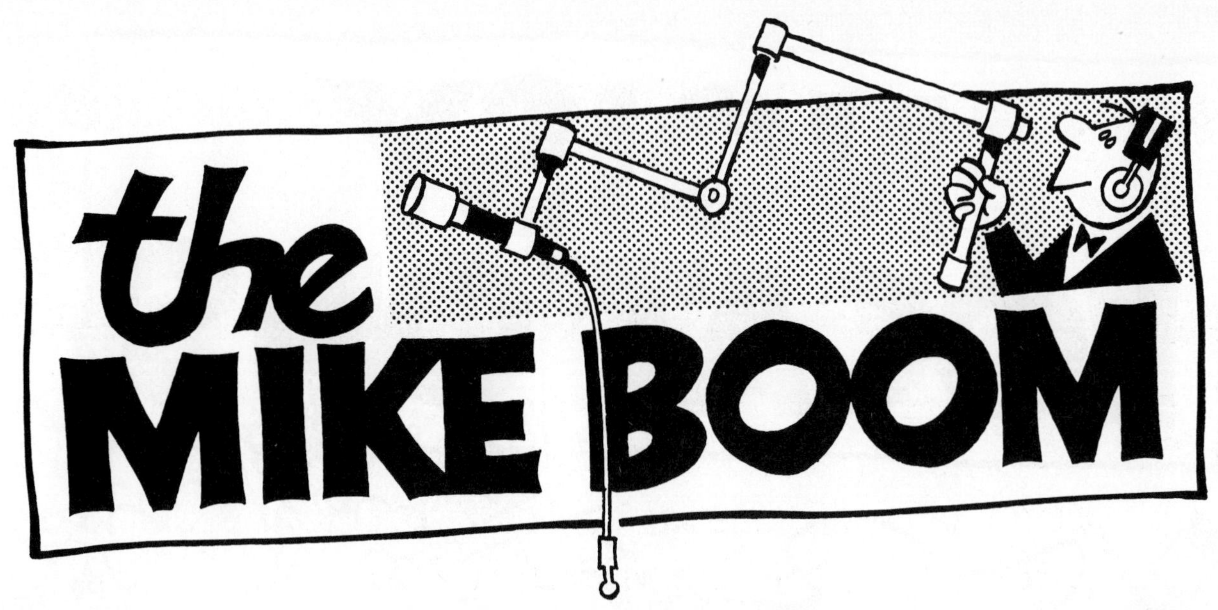

the MIKE BOOM

EVERYBODY HAS SEEN THESE IN PICTURES OF MOVIE SETS AND TV STUDIOS. A LONG EXTENDIBLE ARM HOLDS THE MIKE (USUALLY A UNIDIRECTIONAL TYPE) JUST ABOVE THE CAMERA FRAME.

A LESS EXPENSIVE AND MORE PORTABLE VERSION IS CALLED A *FISHPOLE*. THE FISHPOLE IS A LIGHT EXTENDIBLE POLE ONTO WHICH A MIKE CAN BE ATTACHED.

A SHOTGUN TYPE OF MIKE IS RECOMMENDED TO MINIMIZE BACKGROUND NOISE PICKUP (SINCE THE MIKE HAS TO BE KEPT OUT OF CAMERA FRAME, WHICH MAY BE SEVERAL FEET FROM YOUR SUBJECT).

TRY MAKING ONE OF THESE OUT OF AN OLD BROOMPOLE. YOU'LL NEED A FRIEND TO HOLD IT WHILE YOU SHOOT!

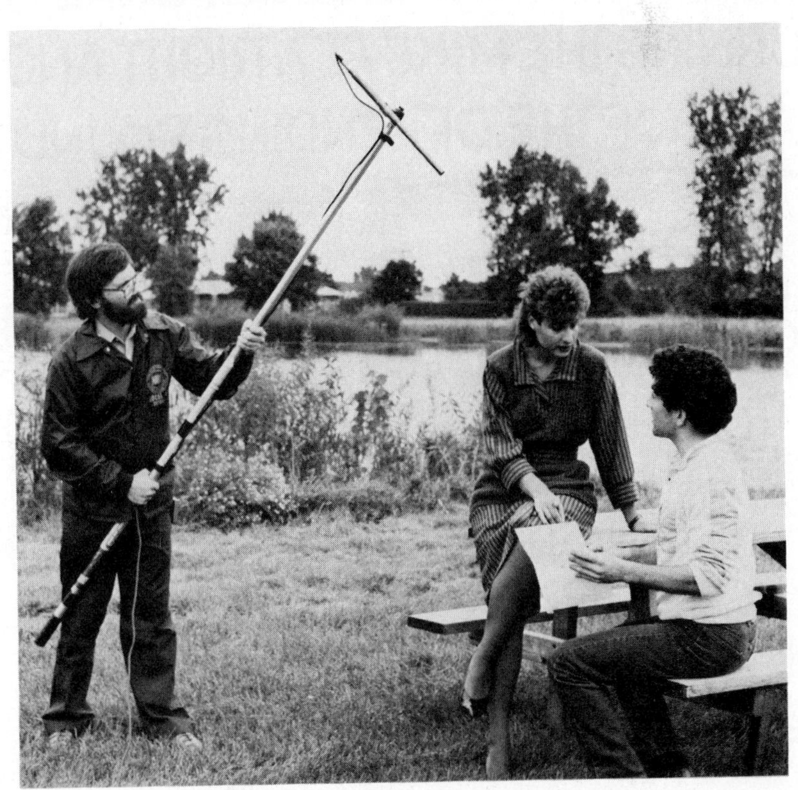

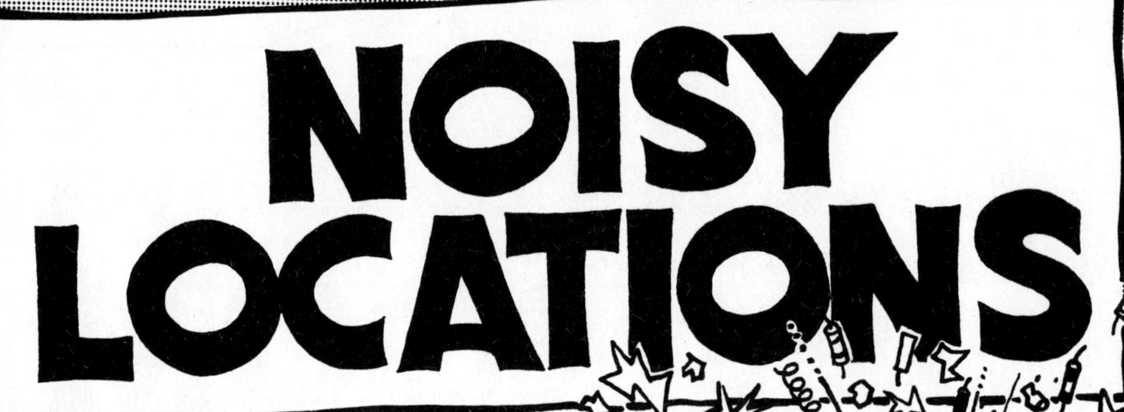

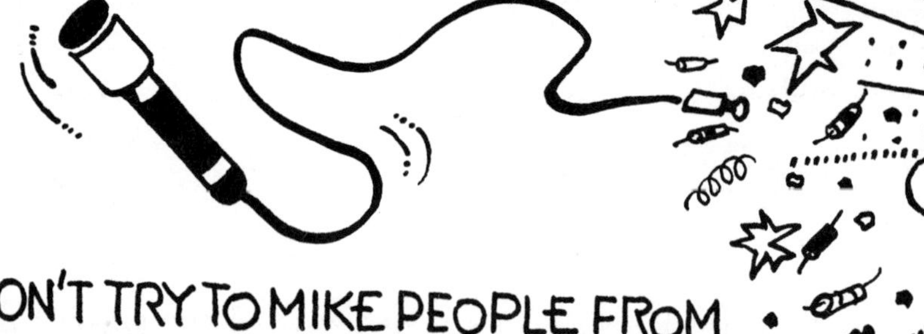

DON'T TRY TO MIKE PEOPLE FROM SEVERAL FEET AWAY UNDER NOISY CONDITIONS. IN PARTICULARY NOISY PLACES YOU WILL FIND IT NECESSARY TO GET YOUR MIKE CLOSER THAN EVER IN ORDER TO HEAR YOUR SUBJECT AT ALL.

IF THE MIKE IS UNIDIRECTIONAL OR CARDIOID, THEN TURNING THE MIKE AT A RIGHT ANGLE TO THE SOURCE OF THE OFFENDING SOUND MAY HELP!

PUTTING YOUR SUBJECT'S BACK TO THE NOISE (USING THEIR BODY TO BLOCK IT) IS ANOTHER POSSIBILITY! THE BEST THING TO DO IS MOVE TO A QUIETER PLACE.

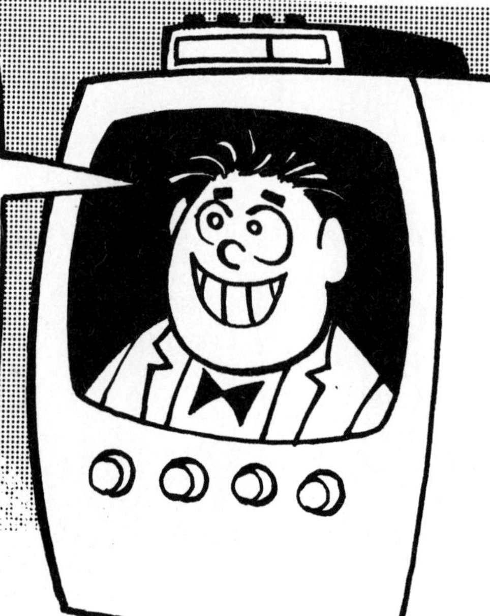

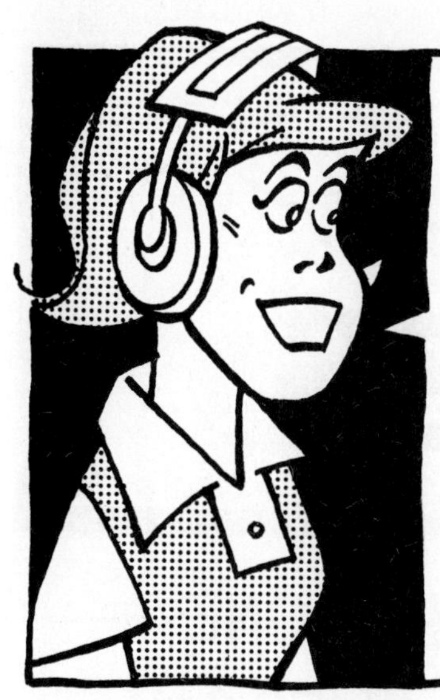

THE WIND IS ANOTHER NOISE PROBLEM TO BE DEALT WITH WHEN SHOOTING OUTDOORS. EVEN A SLIGHT BREEZE CAN SET UP AN OFFENSIVE RUMBLING SOUND IN YOUR AUDIO!

WIND SCREENS ARE AVAILABLE FOR MOST MICROPHONES!

THESE ARE OPEN-PORE FOAM COVERS WHICH FIT OVER THE MIKE AND SERVE TO BREAK THE WIND'S VELOCITY (THEY'RE ALSO GOOD FOR THE POPPING P PROBLEM DISCUSSED EARLIER). LAVALIER MIKES CAN BE PLACED INSIDE CLOTHING TO KEEP THE WIND AWAY. TAPE THE MIKE TO THE INSIDE OF A SHIRT WITH THE ELEMENT (THE HOLE WHERE THE SOUND ENTERS) FACING TOWARD THE FABRIC.

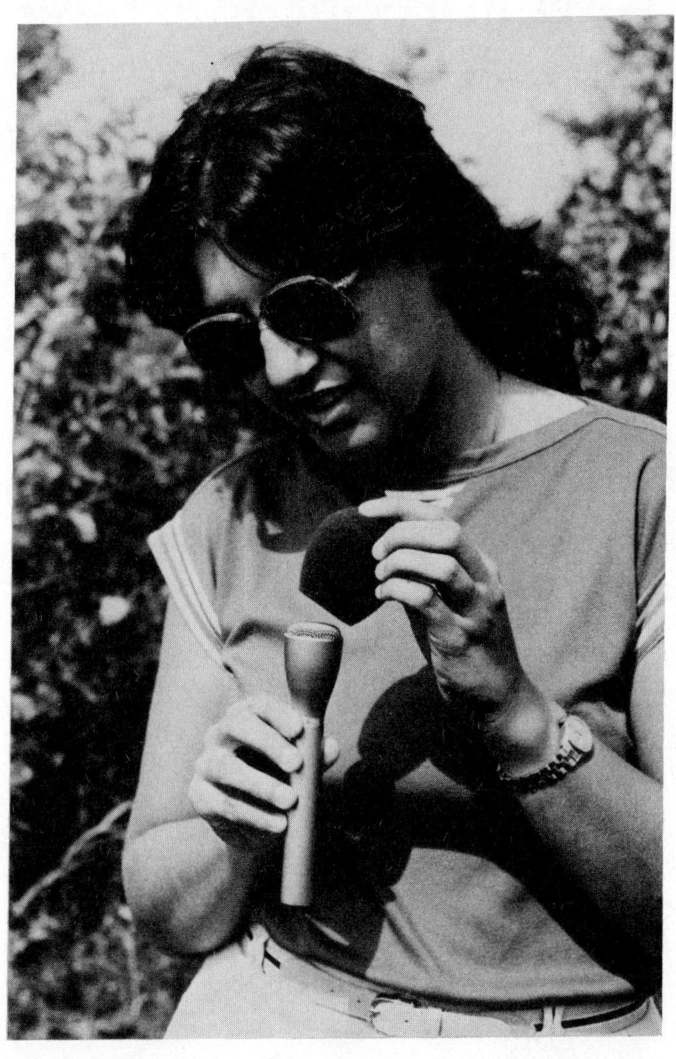

IF THE FABRIC IS TOO THICK, YOUR SOUND MAY SUFFER. AS A LAST RESORT, A *HI-PASS* FILTER CAN BE PLUGGED IN BETWEEN YOUR MIKE AND RECORDER...IT WILL REMOVE MOST OF THE SOUND RUMBLE!

MULTIPLE MICROPHONES

A FEW SITUATIONS MAY ARISE WHERE ONE MICROPHONE WON'T DO. SEVERAL MIKES CAN GIVE YOU AN EXTRA MEASURE OF CLARITY AND CONTROL OF THE SOUND, ESPECIALLY WHEN RECORDING MUSIC!

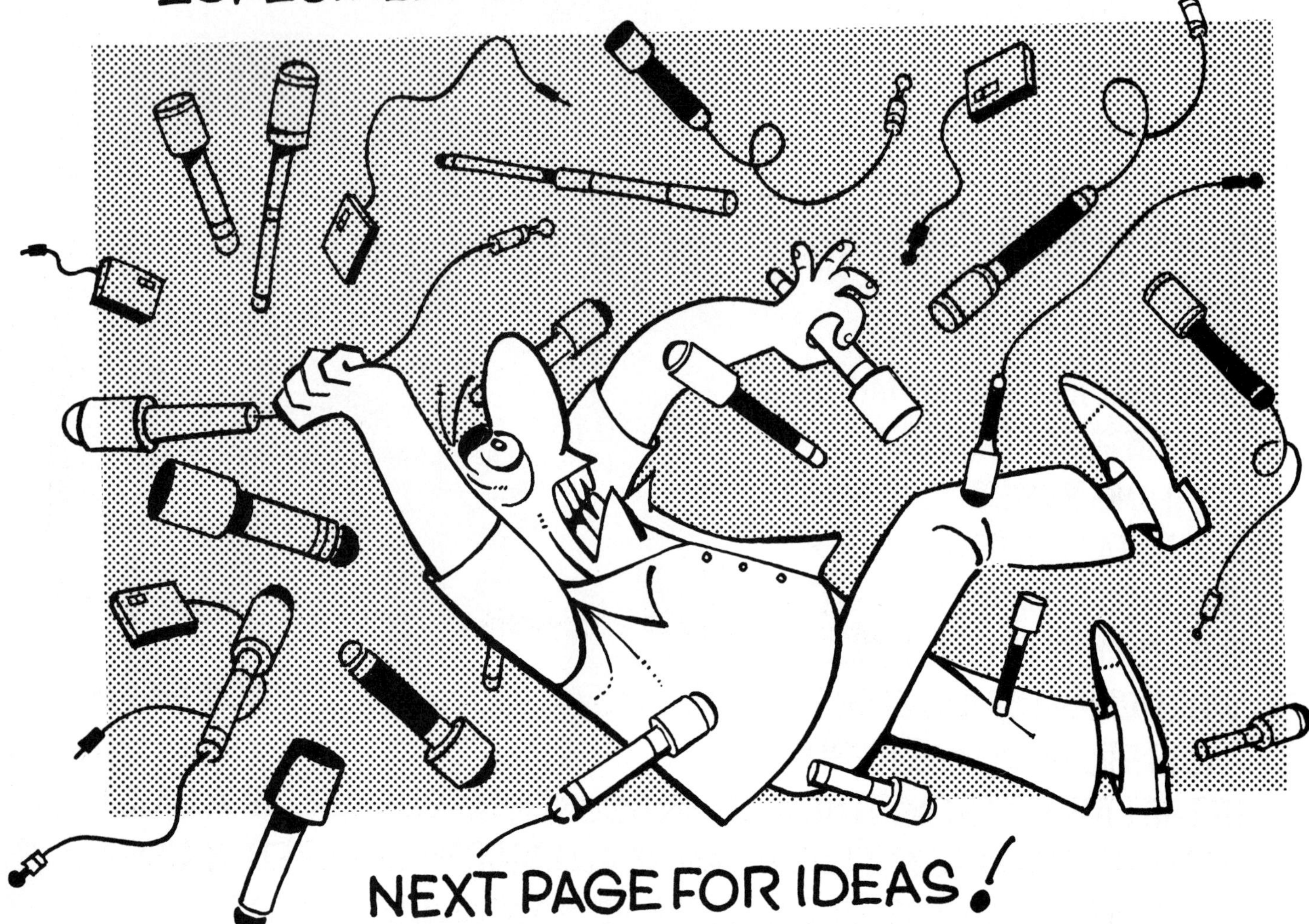

THE MIKE MIXER

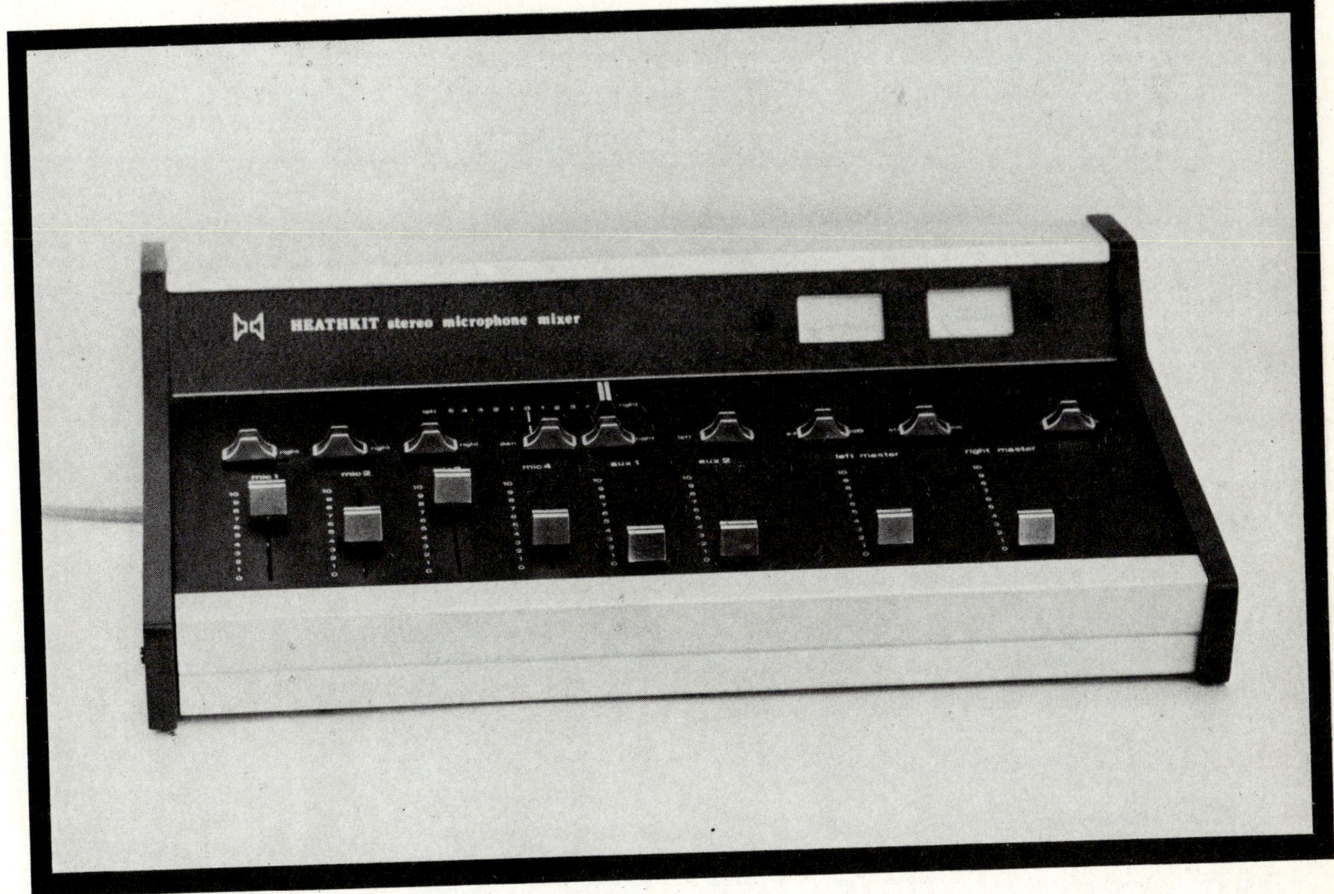

YOU WILL HAVE INDEPENDENT CONTROL OVER *ALL* THE MIKES
AS WELL AS AUXILIARY SOURCES LIKE RECORD TURNTABLES AND
AUDIO TAPE PLAYERS. YOU COULD, FOR EXAMPLE, GIVE EACH MUSI-
CIAN IN A SMALL BAND A SEPARATE MICROPHONE. USING THE MIXING
CONSOLE, YOU WOULD THEN ADJUST THE LEVEL!

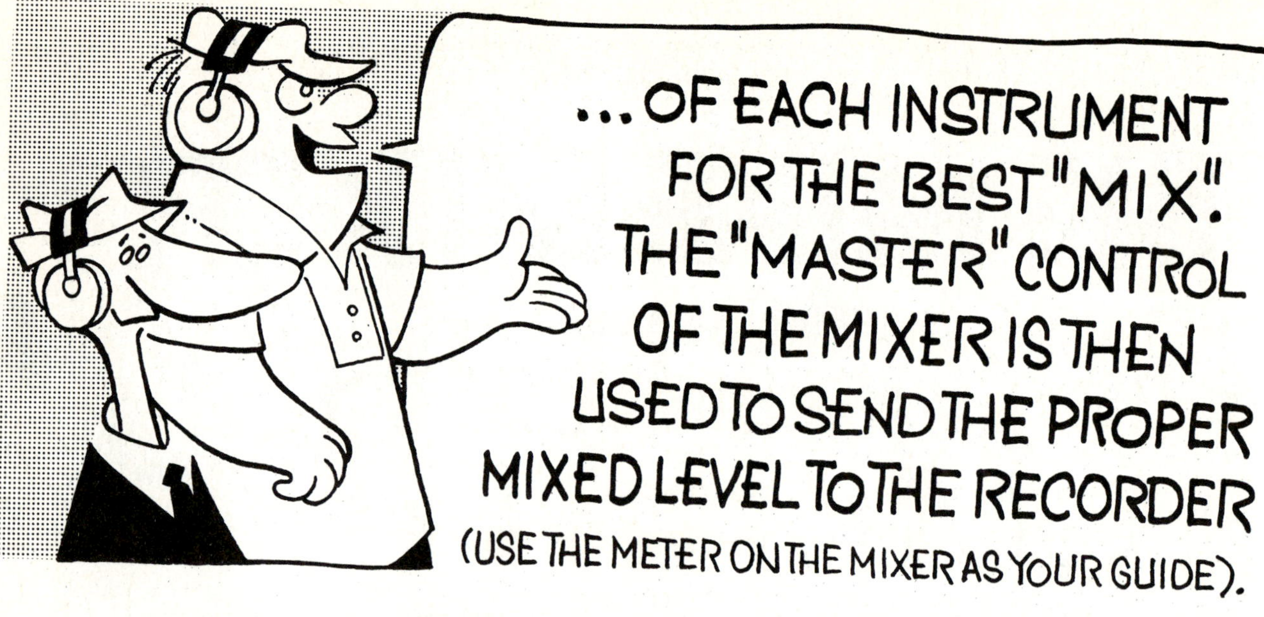

THE "Y" CONNECTOR

AN INEXPENSIVE ALTERNATIVE TO A MIXER IS A "Y" CONNECTOR. THE MICROPHONES PLUG INTO IT WHICH IN TURN PLUGS INTO YOUR MIKE JACK. INDEPENDENT LEVEL CONTROL IS IMPOSSIBLE, SO BOTH MIKES ARE *EQUALLY* SENSITIVE. FOR BEST RESULTS, BOTH MIKES SHOULD BE THE SAME, OR AT LEAST THE SAME *IMPEDANCE!*

OTHERWISE, ONE OF THEM WILL BE MUCH MORE SENSITIVE (LOUDER) THAN THE OTHER, WITH DISAPPOINTING RESULTS.

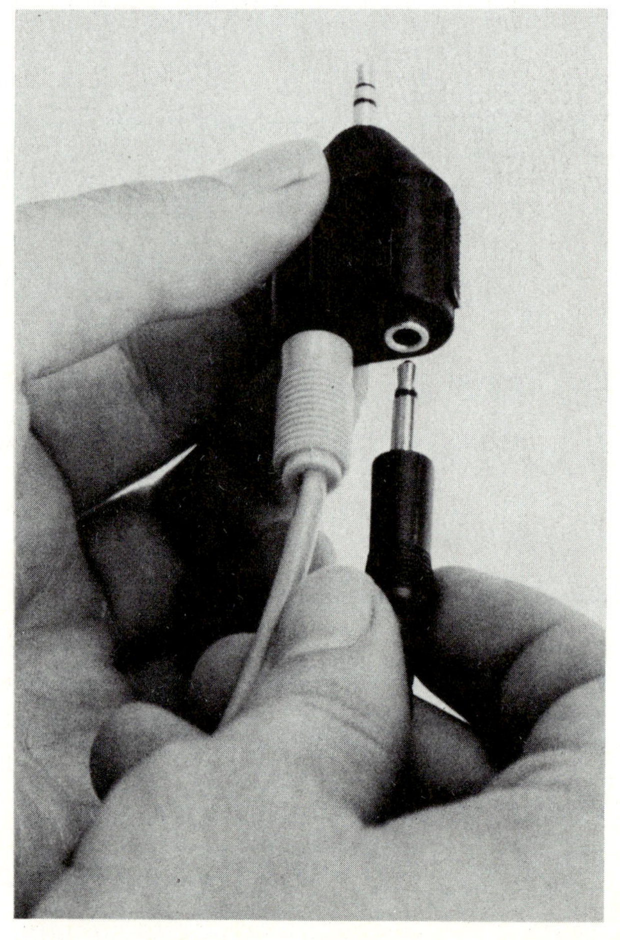

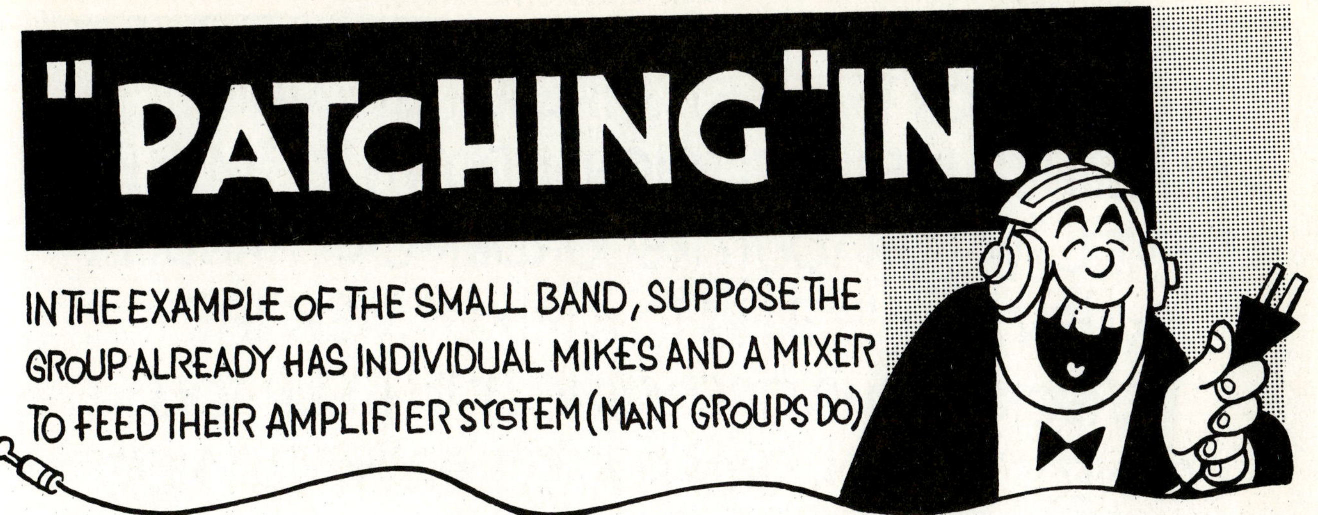

IN THAT CASE, MUCH TROUBLE CAN BE SAVED BY CONNECTING YOUR EQUIPMENT TO THEIR SYSTEM!

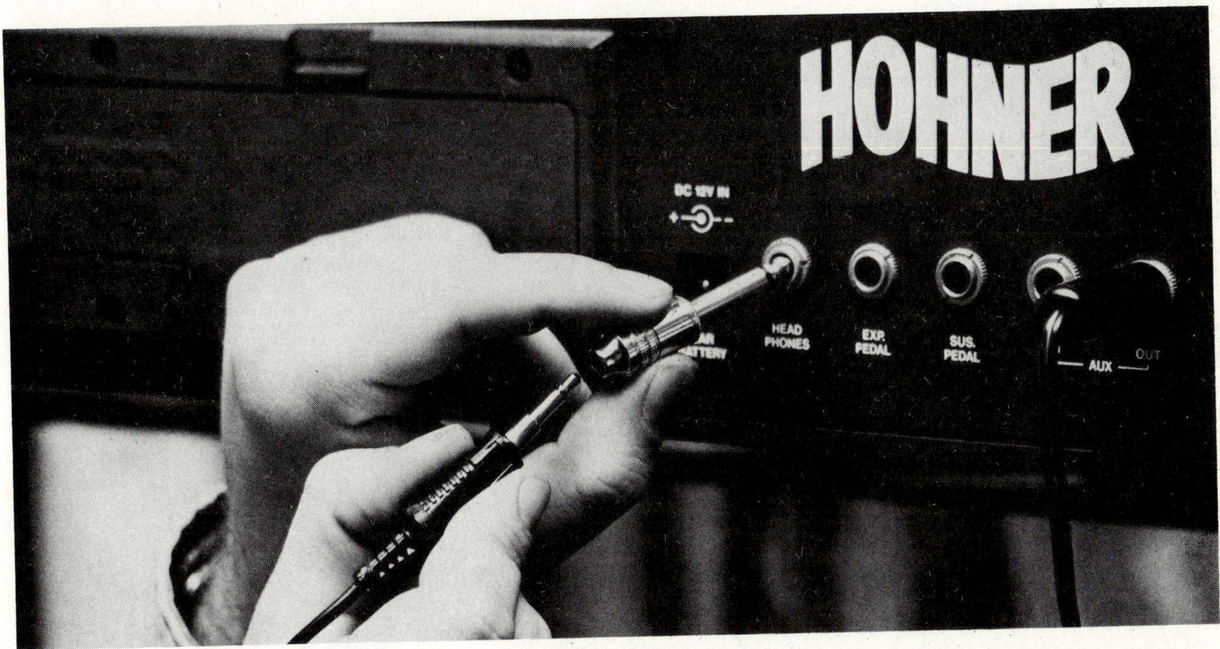

YOU WILL NEED AN ASSORTMENT OF CONNECTOR ADAPTORS IN ORDER TO BE READY TO CONNECT TO ANYBODY'S SOUND SYSTEM. *ANOTHER ITEM YOU WILL NEED IS AN ATTENUATOR*, OR LINE LEVEL ADAPTOR. IF THE MIXER YOU CONNECT TO HAS A *LINE LEVEL* OUTPUT, THE AUDIO LEVEL WILL BE TOO HIGH (TOO POWERFUL) TO CONNECT TO YOUR "MIC" INPUT. NO DAMAGE WILL LIKELY OCCUR....BUT THE SOUND WILL BE DISTORTED!

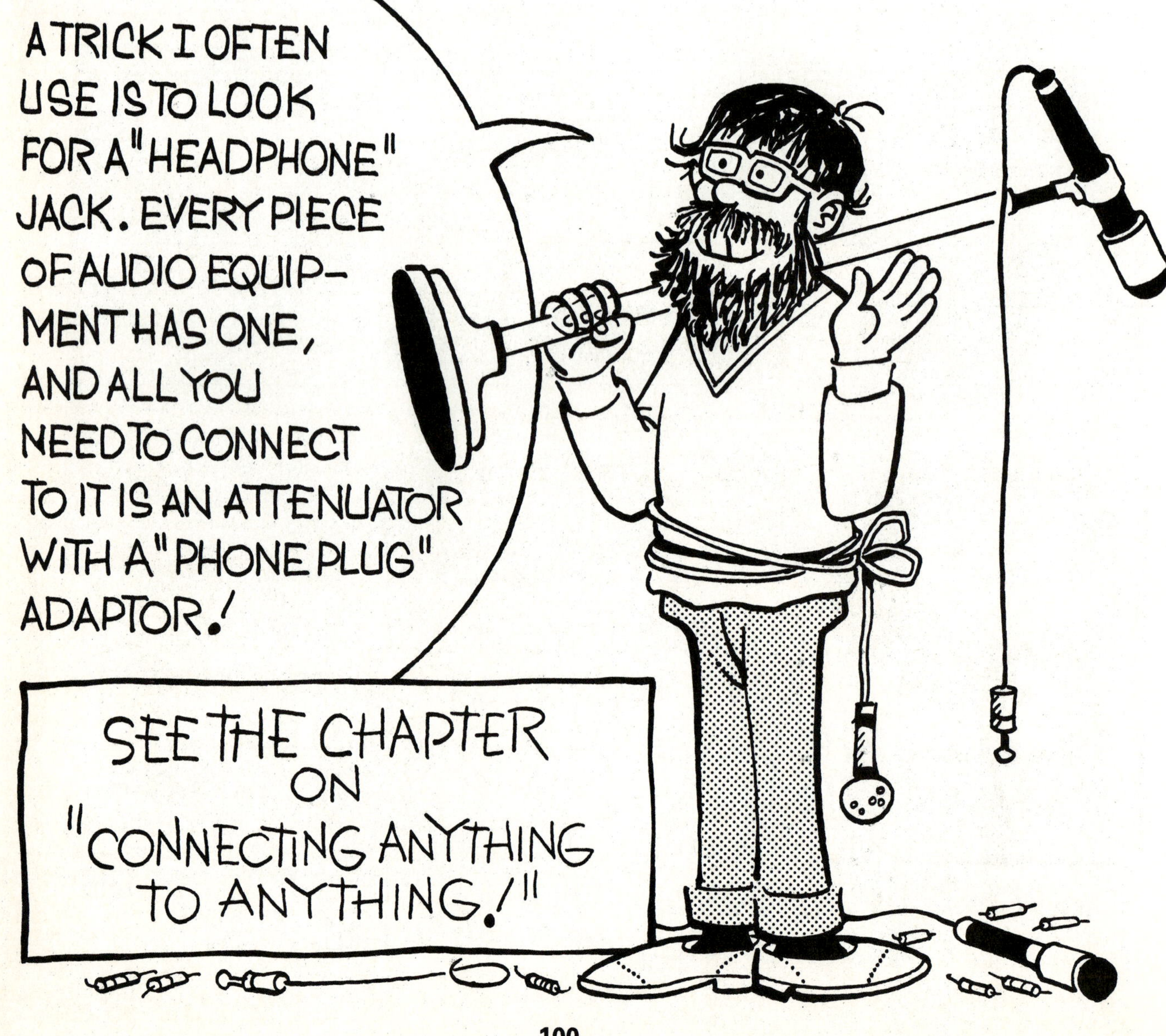
...AND DON'T FORGET... THE ATTENUATOR CUTS THE "LINE LEVEL" SIGNAL DOWN TO "MIKE LEVEL," WHICH YOUR RECORDER CAN HANDLE. WHEN CONNECTING TO A MIXER, ASK THE PERSON WHO IS OPERATING IT TO HELP YOU CONNECT TO IT. CHANCES ARE THEY WILL KNOW EXACTLY WHERE TO CONNECT YOU!
A TRICK I OFTEN USE IS TO LOOK FOR A "HEADPHONE" JACK. EVERY PIECE OF AUDIO EQUIPMENT HAS ONE, AND ALL YOU NEED TO CONNECT TO IT IS AN ATTENUATOR WITH A "PHONE PLUG" ADAPTOR!
SEE THE CHAPTER ON "CONNECTING ANYTHING TO ANYTHING!"

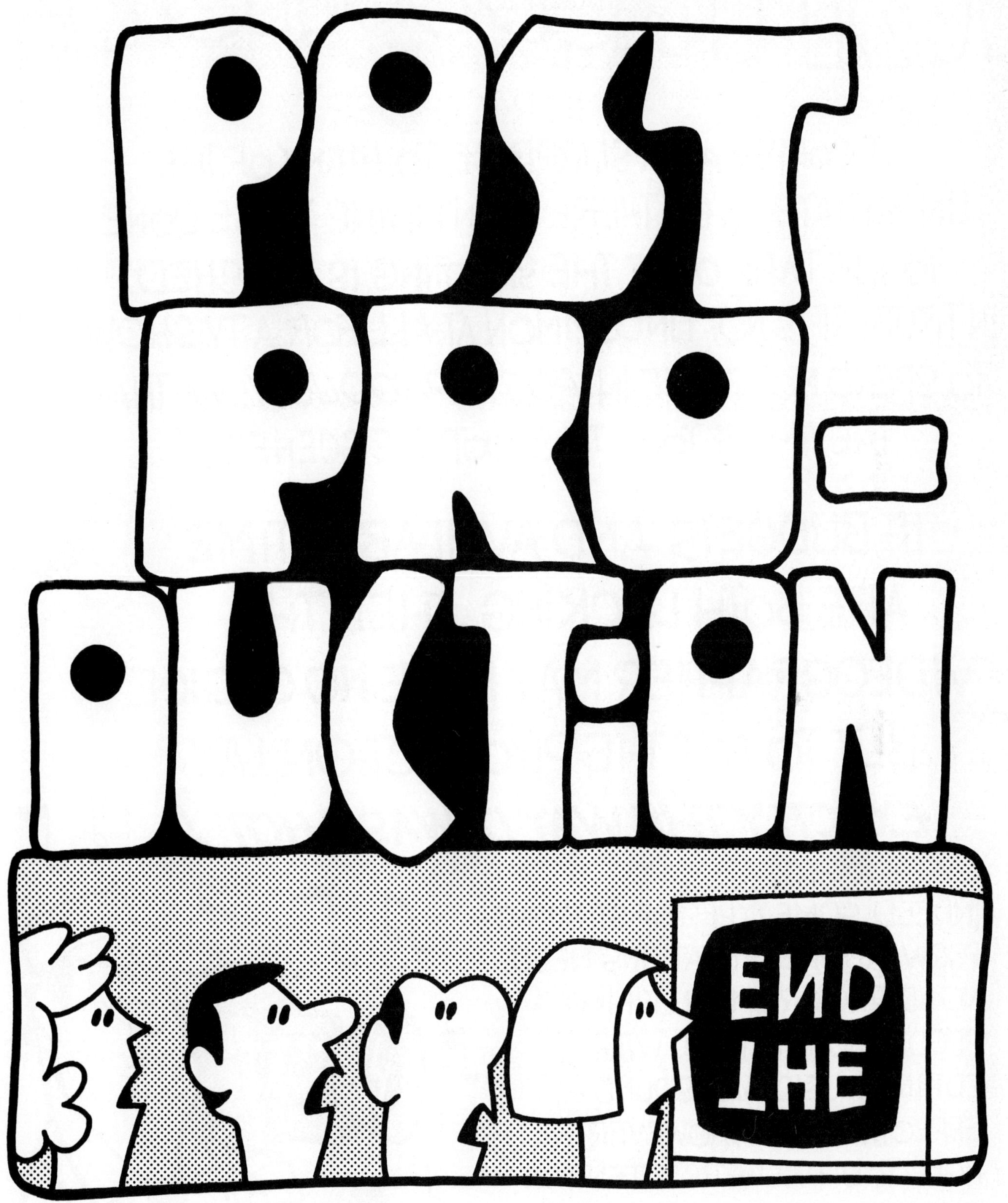

POST
PRO-
DUCTION
END
THE

POST PRODUCTION!

IT COMES AS A SURPRISE TO MANY OF THE UNINITIATED THAT THERE IS ANYTHING TO BE DONE TO THE TAPE ONCE THE SHOOTING IS FINISHED. IN TRUTH, IT IS NOT UNCOMMON AT ALL FOR A TV SHOW TO SPEND MORE TIME IN *POST PRODUCTION* THAN THE TIME IT TOOK TO SHOOT THE SCENES!

IF BUDGETS AND AVAILABLE TIME ARE BOTH LACKING, THEN THE VIDEOGRAPHER MAY HAVE NO CHOICE BUT TO LET THE PRODUCTION LAY *EXACTLY THE WAY IT WAS SHOT!*

INDEED, SOME TYPES OF STRAIGHT-FORWARD PRESENTATIONS NEED NO EDITING OR EMBELLISHING. A PRODUCTION PLANNED WITH EDITING, MUSIC, AND SOUND EFFECTS IN MIND, HOWEVER, WILL HOLD YOUR VIEWERS' ATTENTION FAR BETTER THAN SUCH A *LESSER EFFORT!*

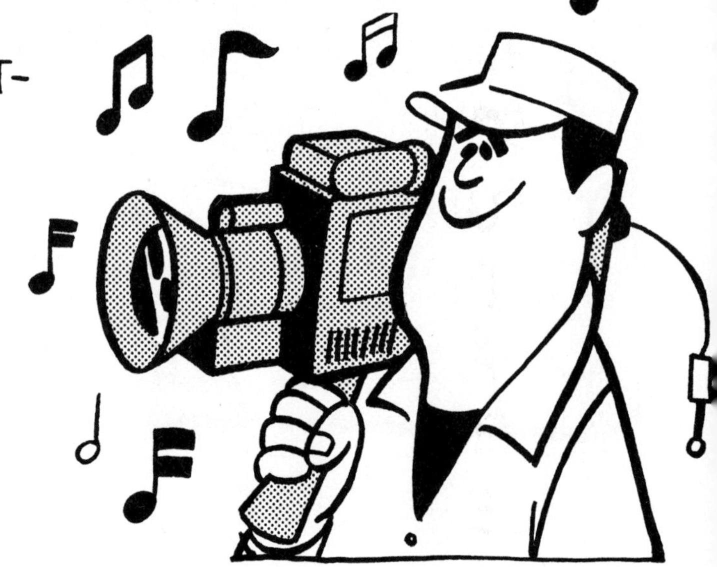

A PROFESSIONAL EDIT ROOM!

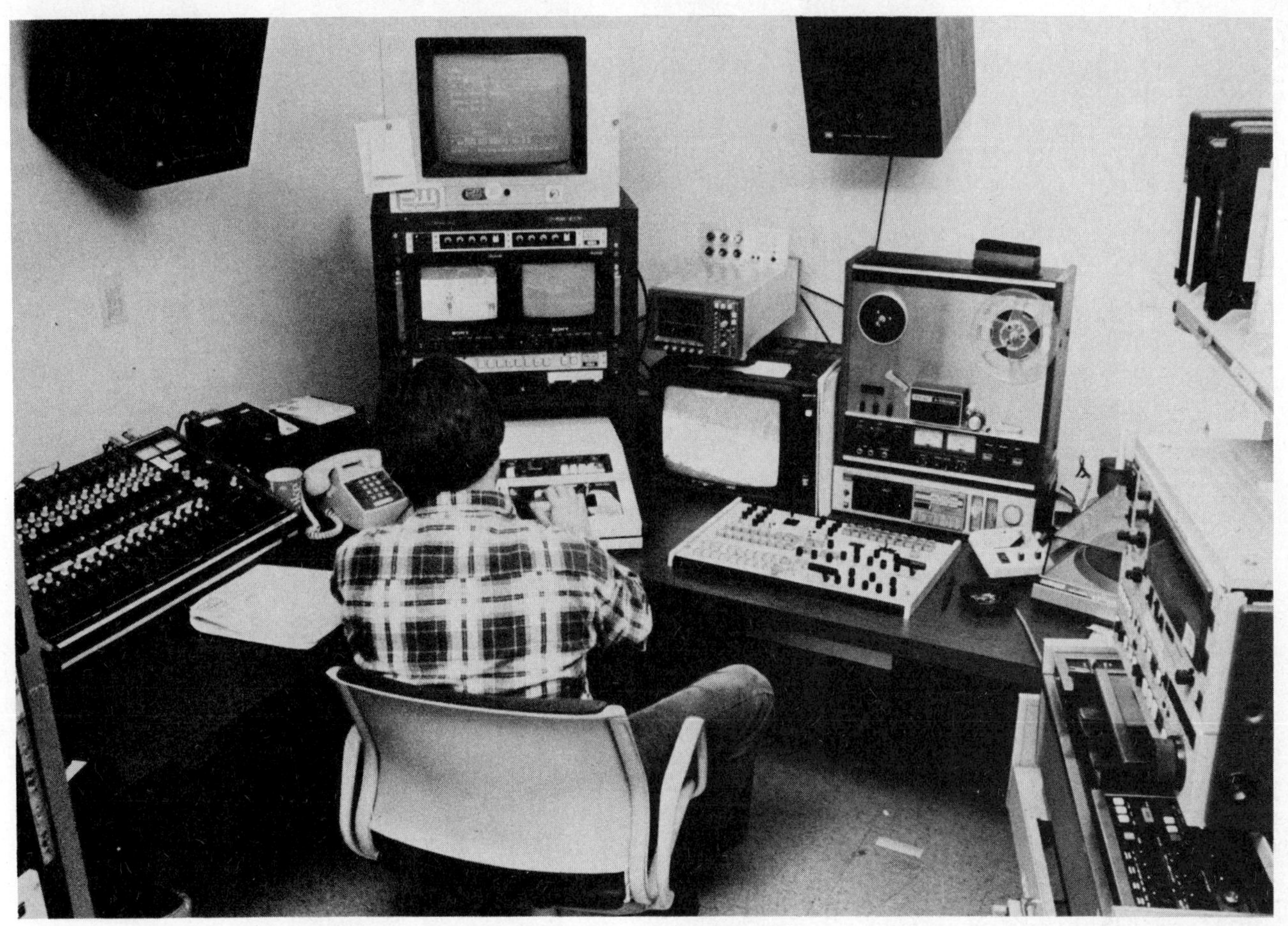

PROFESSIONAL POST-PRODUCTION FACILITIES CAN CONTAIN **HUNDREDS OF THOUSANDS** OF DOLLARS WORTH OF EDITING, AUDIO MIXING, AND **VIDEO SPECIAL-EFFECTS** EQUIPMENT. THERE IS NO WAY, ON A SHOESTRING BUDGET, TO DUPLICATE THE LEVEL OF QUALITY POSSIBLE WITH SUCH EQUIPMENT. THE **IDEAS** BEHIND POST PRODUCTION ARE FREE, THOUGH, AND SOME OF THEM, WITH A LITTLE EFFORT, CAN BE APPLIED TO YOUR OWN TV SHOWS!

WHY EDIT?
PM DETROIT

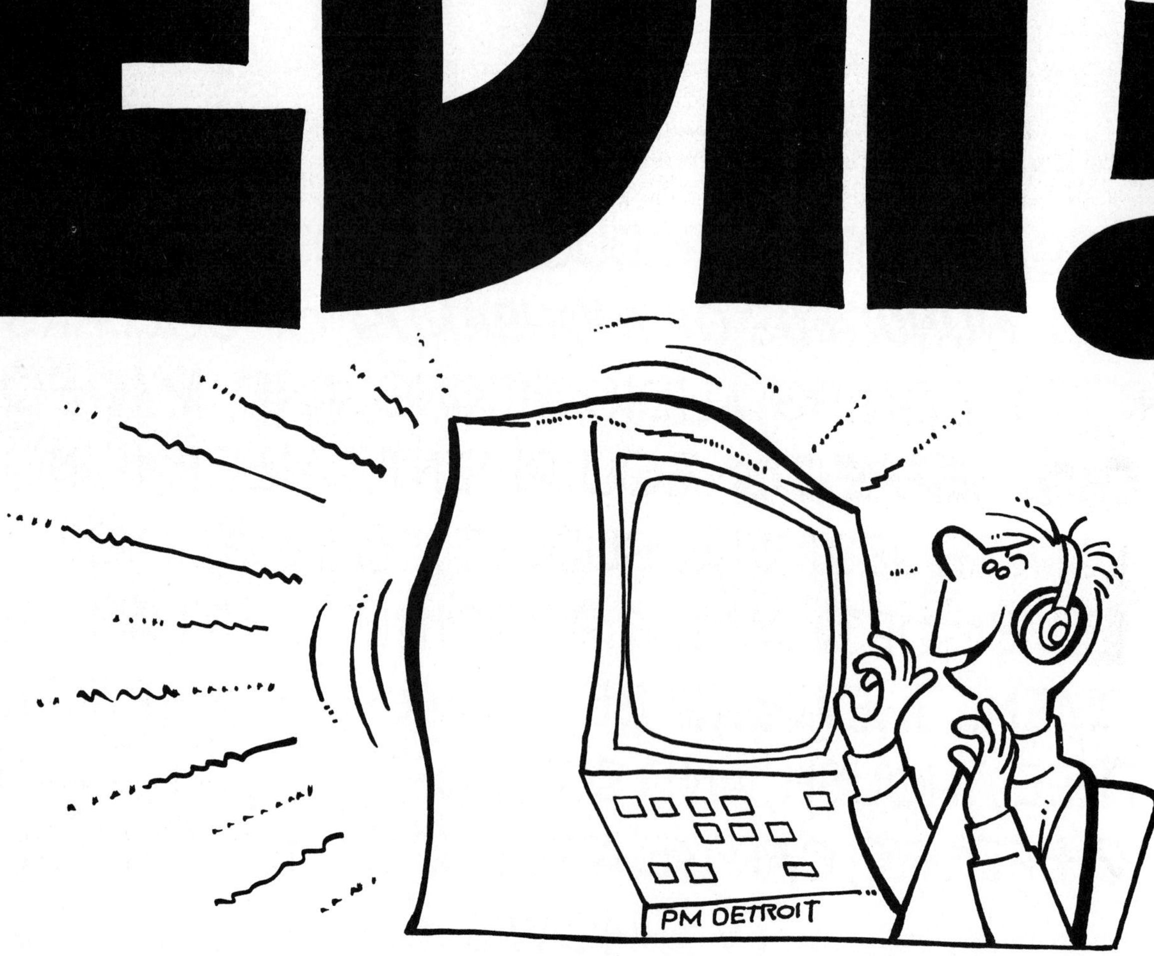

HERE ARE SOME GOOD REASONS FOR EDITING:

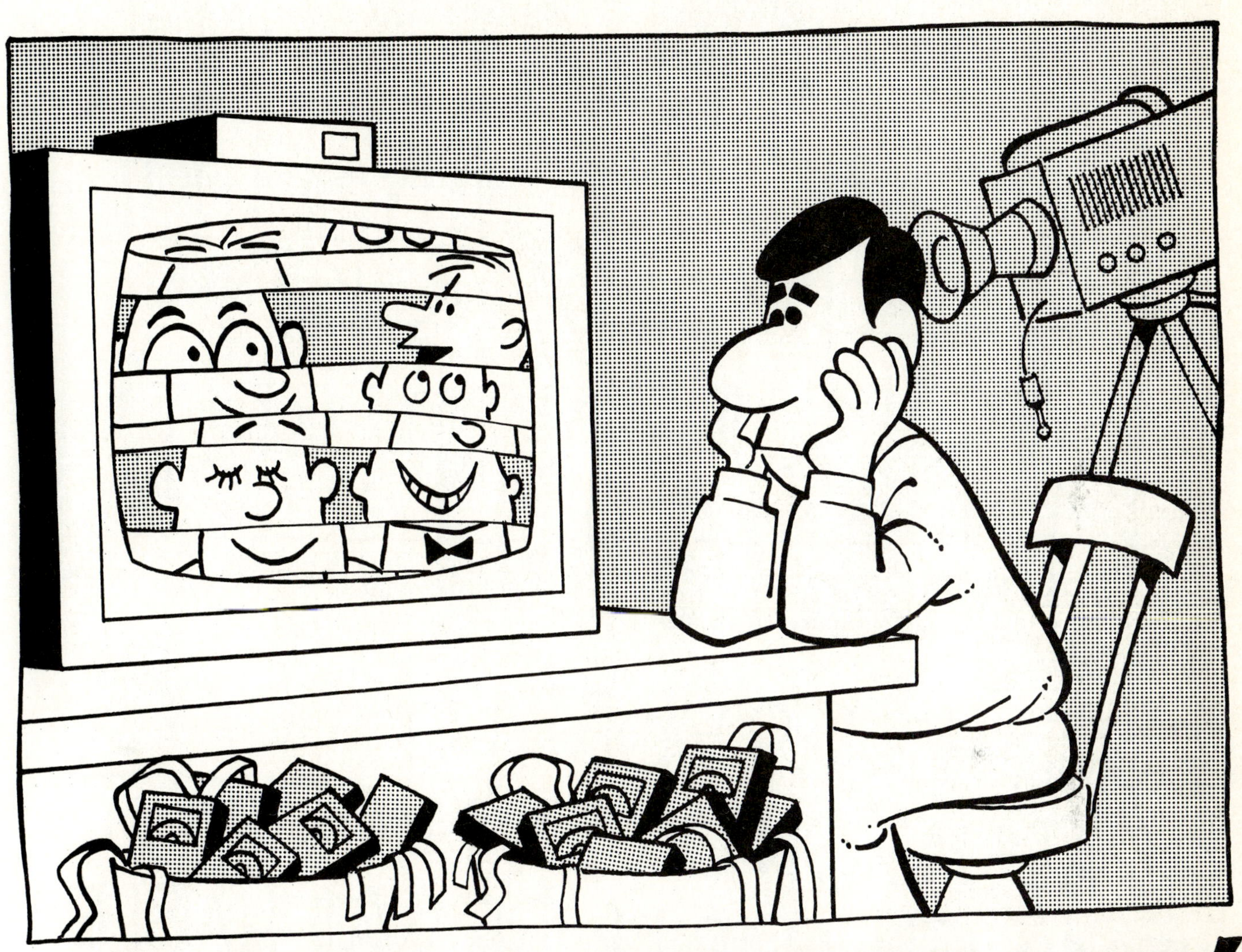

TO "NEATEN UP" YOUR TAPE!

(THAT IS, REMOVE ALL YOUR EMBARRASSING MISTAKES)

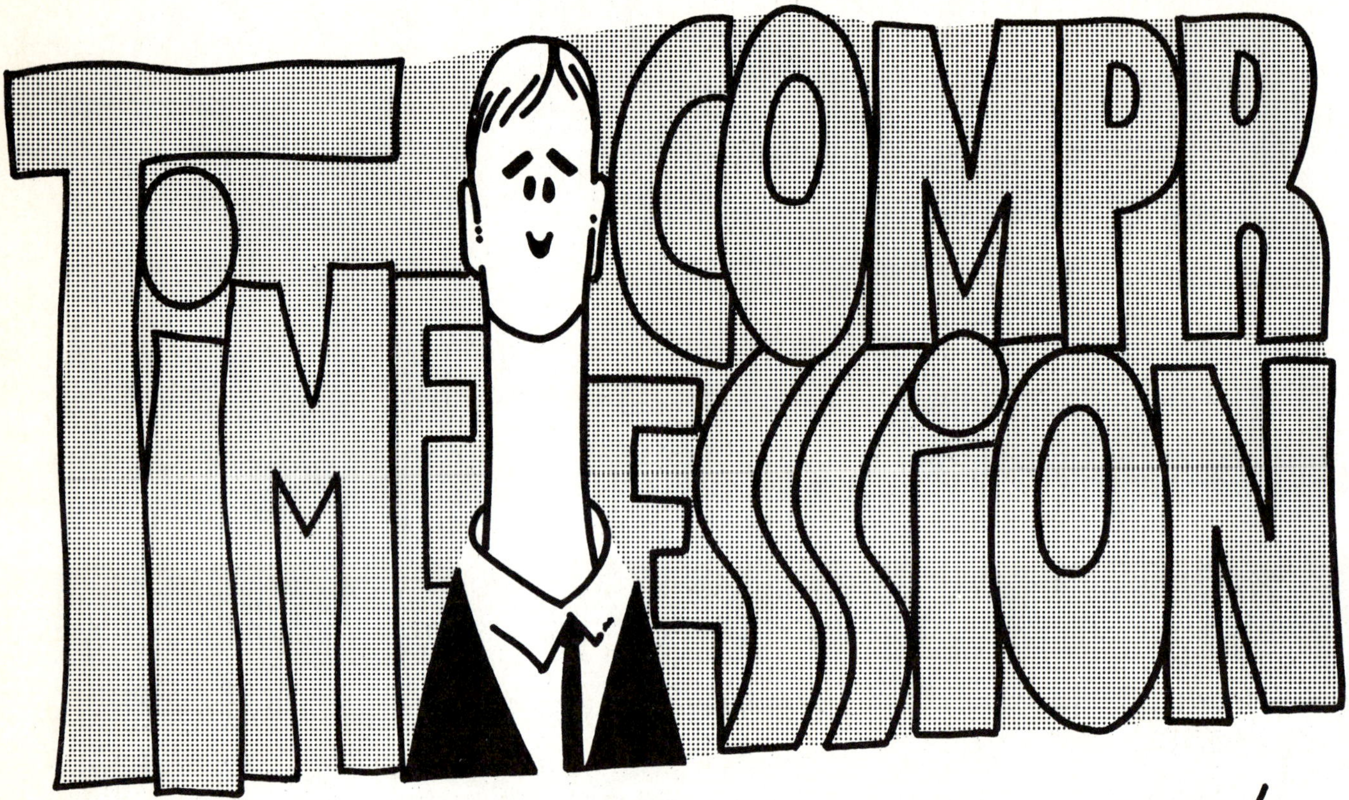

TIME COMPRESSION

(FOUR HOURS WORTH OF SUZY'S GRADUATION DAY IS NICE, BUT 15 MINUTES IS MORE WATCHABLE.)

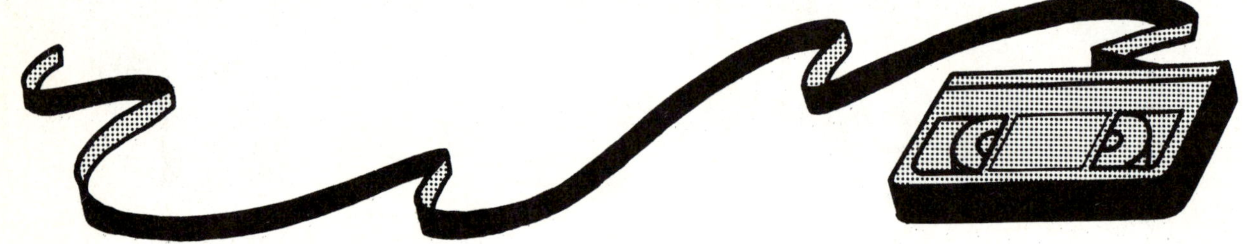

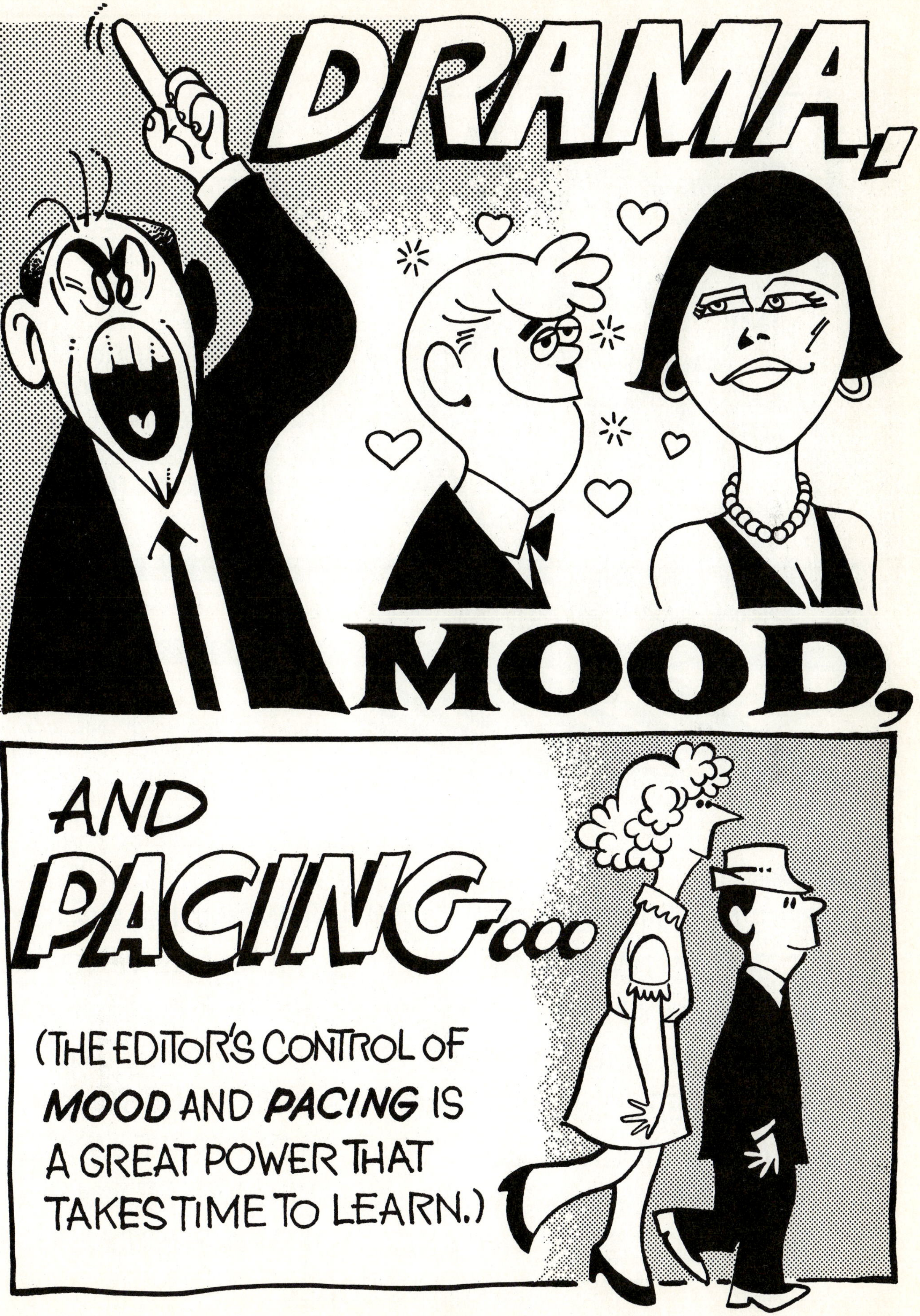

DRAMA,
MOOD,
AND
PACING...
(THE EDITOR'S CONTROL OF
MOOD AND PACING IS
A GREAT POWER THAT
TAKES TIME TO LEARN.)

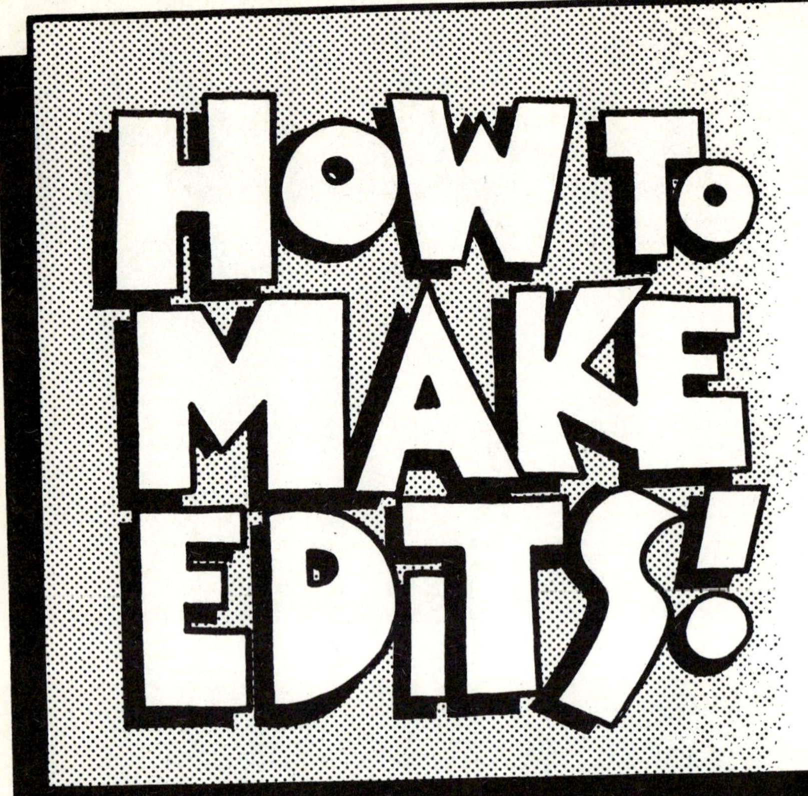

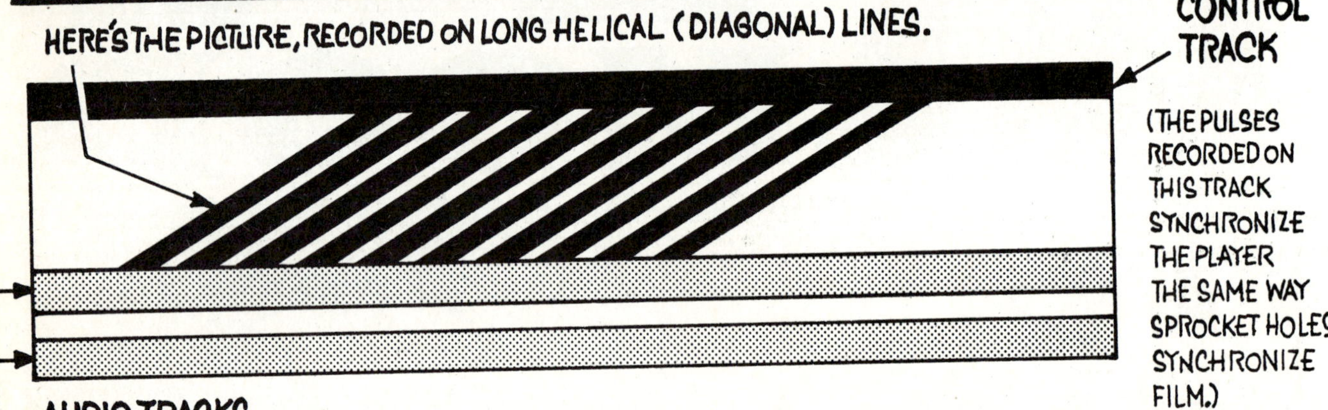

THERE IS A LOT MORE TO THIS EXPLANATION, BUT THE BOTTOM LINE IS THAT YOU CAN'T PHYSICALLY CUT AND SPLICE VIDEOTAPE THE WAY YOU WOULD AUDIO TAPE OR FILM. THE RESULT, IF YOU DID, WOULD BE VERY SLOPPY-LOOKING ROLLING AND TEARING PICTURES. IMPERFECT SPLICES OF THIS TYPE CAN ALSO RUIN THE HEADS OF YOUR VIDEO PLAYER. THE ONLY SAFE WAY TO EDIT TAPE IS TO USE TWO VCR'S— A **PLAYER**, WHERE YOU PUT THE TAPE YOU'VE SHOT— AND A **RECORDER**, WHERE YOU PUT A FRESH TAPE TO RECORD!

BASIC EDITING SYSTEM

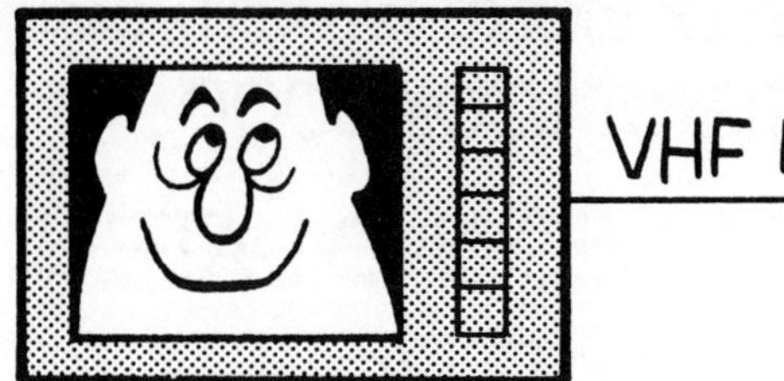

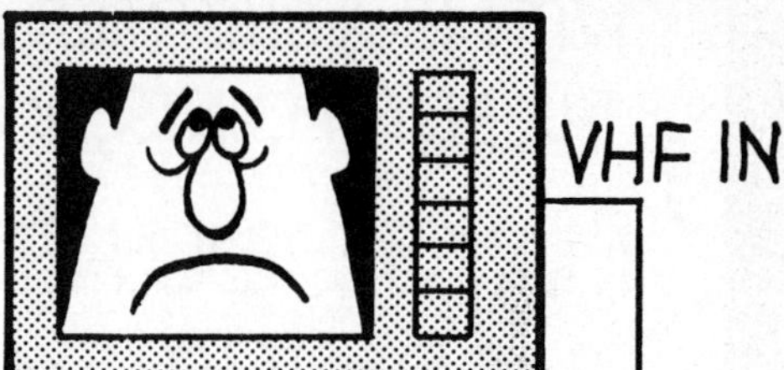

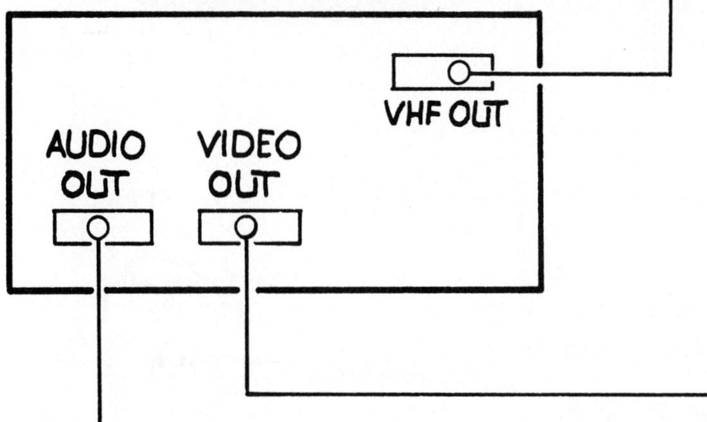

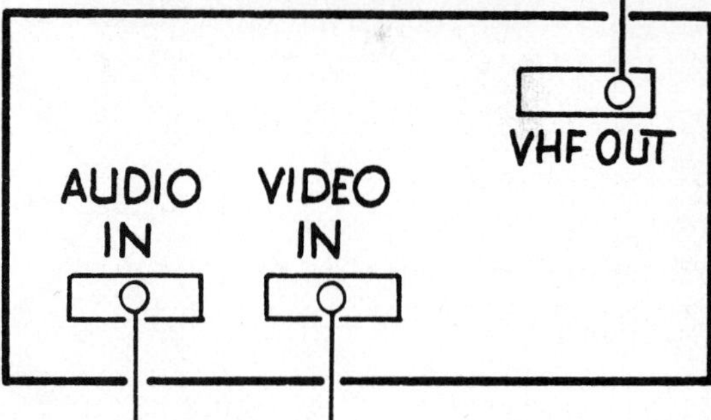

ONCE THE TWO MACHINES ARE CONNECTED TOGETHER, YOU CAN USE THE RECORDER TO SELECTIVELY RECORD THE VIDEO FROM THE PLAYER.

THIS PROCESS IS CALLED *ELECTRONIC EDITING!*

THE "PAUSE AND ROLL" METHOD

THE SIMPLEST WAY TO EDIT YOUR MATERIAL WITH A SIMPLE TWO MACHINE SETUP IS TO KEEP YOUR FINGER ON THE **PAUSE** BUTTON OF THE RECORDER. AS YOUR CAMERA TAPE PLAYS – AND YOUR RE-CORDER RECORDS IT– BE READY TO **PAUSE** THE RECORDER EVERY TIME A SHOT COMES UP THAT YOU **DON'T** WANT–AND UN-PAUSE IT WHEN THE SHOT IS OVER. WHAT YOU WILL WIND UP WITH IS A SHORTER AND PROBABLY MORE WATCHABLE TAPE. THE EDIT POINTS, HOWEVER, MAY NOT LOOK GOOD!

MAYBE YOU HIT A PAUSE A SECOND LATE...OR THE PICTURE MIGHT "FLIP" OR ROLL AT THE EDIT. EDITING LIKE THIS ISN'T TOO HARD — BUT THE RESULTS ARE A BIT ROUGH!

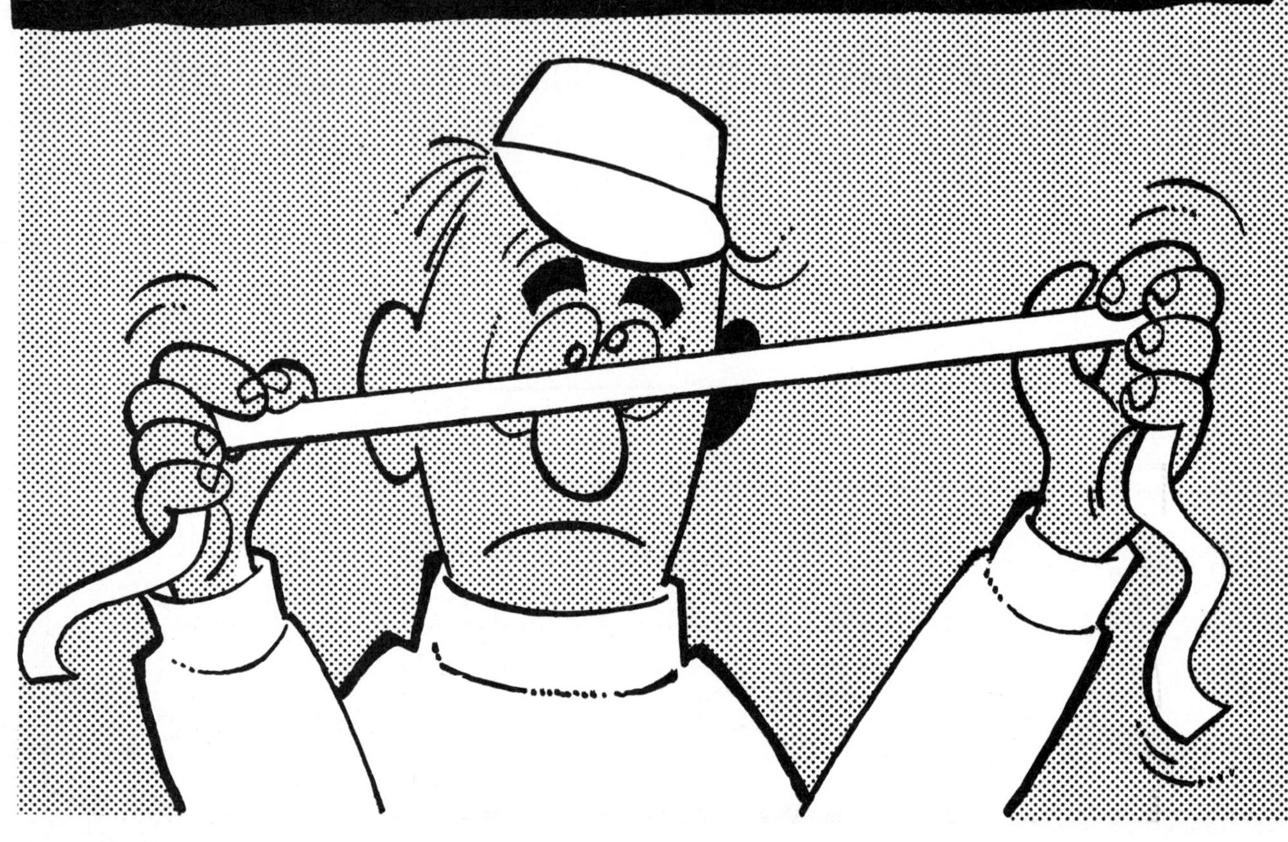

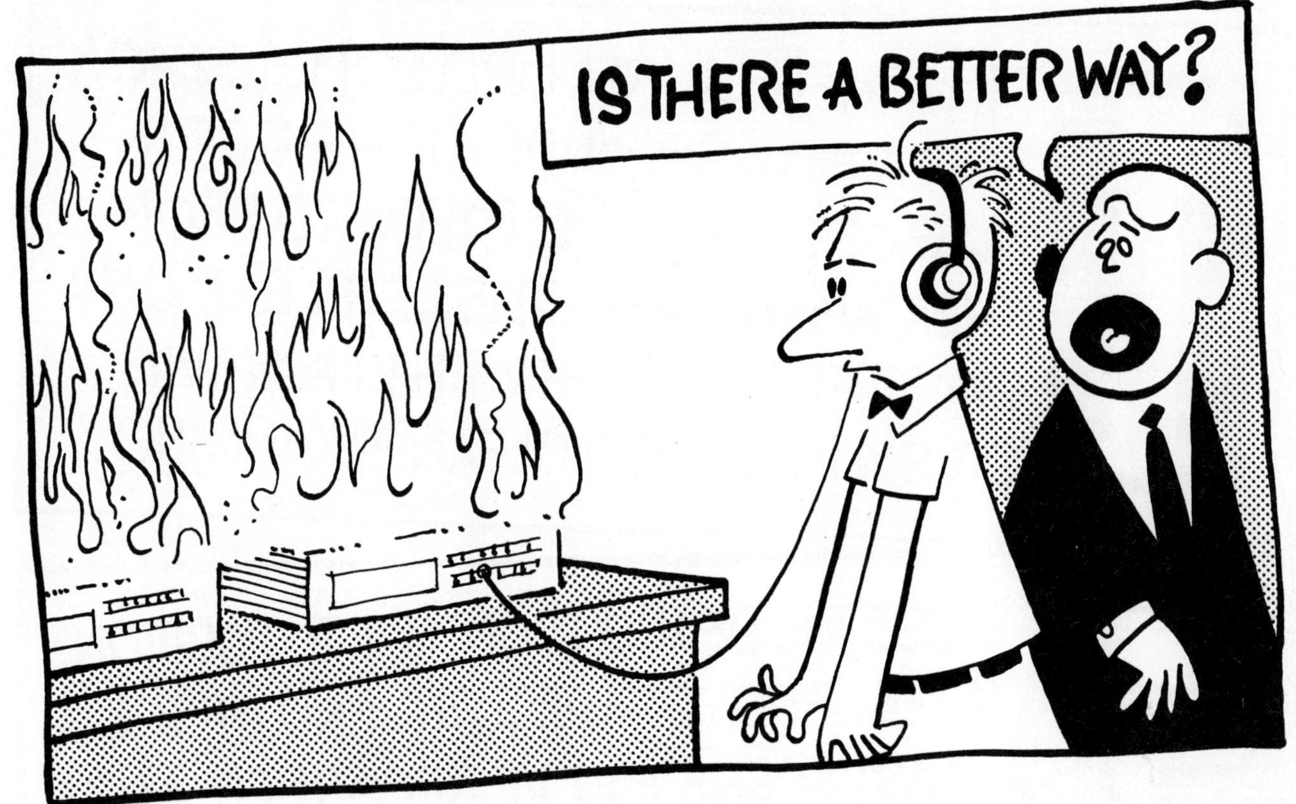

IN ORDER TO BE ABSOLUTELY ACCURATE WITH YOUR EDITS, YOU NEED TO BE ABLE TO **"CUE UP"** YOUR TAPES... THAT IS, TO SEARCH FOR THE EXACT PLACE ON BOTH MACHINES WHERE THE EDIT SHOULD HAPPEN. HERE IS THE BEST EDITING METHOD I'VE FOUND FOR AMATEUR EQUIPMENT **(YOU'LL NEED TWO MACHINES THAT HAVE "SEARCH" BUTTONS).**

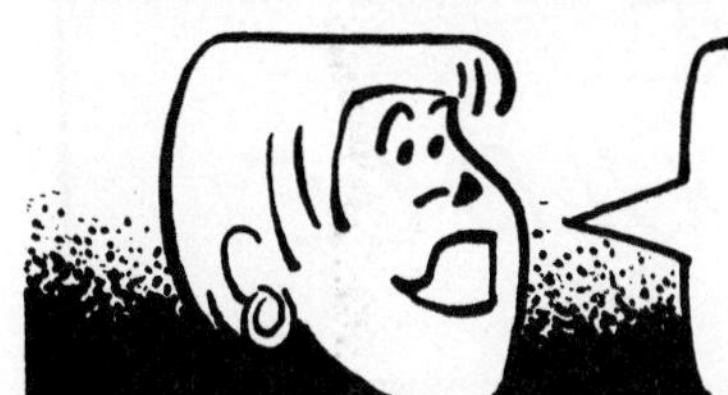

1 FIRST OF ALL, RECORD SOME **BLACK** FOR A FEW SECONDS AT THE BEGINNING OF YOUR TAPE (**RECORD FROM THE CAMERA WITH THE LENS CAP ON**). STARTING YOUR TAPE WITH BLACK WILL GIVE YOU A GOOD CLEAN BEGINNING.

2 USE THE SEARCH CONTROL TO POSITION THE *RECORD* TAPE TO THE END OF THE LAST SCENE YOU'VE RECORDED, AND *PAUSE* THERE. FOR THE FIRST EDIT, THIS WOULD BE AT THE END OF THE BLACK YOU'VE JUST RECORDED.

3 USE THE SEARCH ON THE **PLAYBACK** MACHINE TO POSITION THE TAPE TO THE BEGINNING OF THE SCENE YOU WANT TO ADD NEXT. IF THIS IS THE FIRST EDIT, SEARCH FOR THE START OF YOUR FIRST SCENE AND **PAUSE** THE TAPE THERE. *BOTH MACHINES SHOULD BE IN PAUSE NOW!*

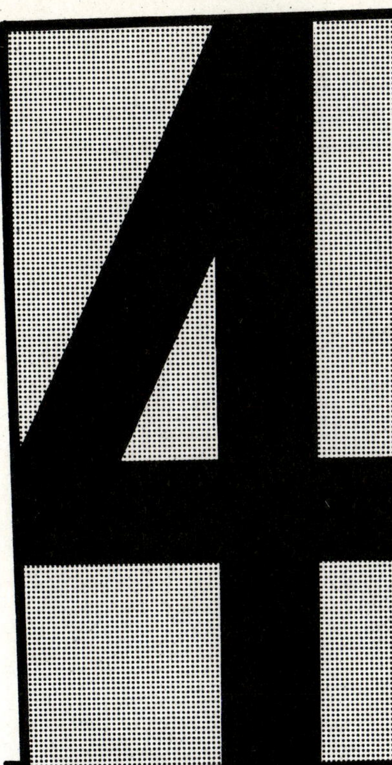

4 AT THE EXACT SAME TIME, PUSH THE *REVERSE* SEARCH ON BOTH MACHINES. LET THE TAPES BACK UP FOR A COUNT OF THREE, THEN RELEASE. THEY SHOULD *PAUSE* **AGAIN** (IF THEY DON'T, YOU'LL HAVE TO HIT PAUSE IMMEDIATELY AFTER THE REVERSE SEARCH). **BOTH TAPES ARE NOW PAUSED SEVERAL SECONDS BEFORE YOUR EDIT POINTS!**

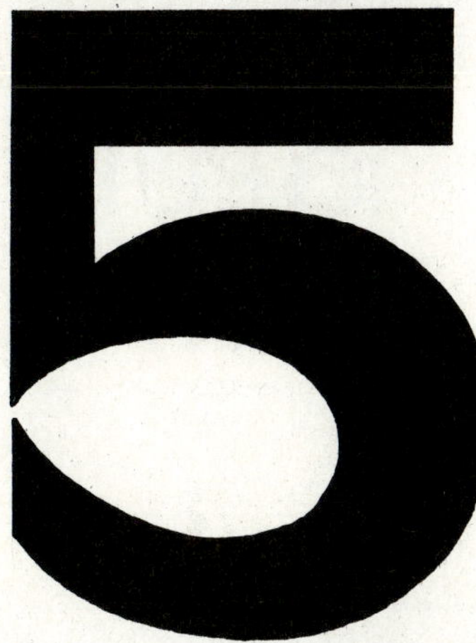

5 SIMULTANEOUSLY PUSH THE PAUSE BUTTONS OF BOTH MACHINES (**UNPAUSING THEM**). AS BOTH MACHINES ROLL TOWARD THE EDIT POINT, KEEP YOUR FINGERS ON THE *PLAY* AND *RECORD* BUTTONS OF THE RECORDER. WATCH THE SCREEN, AND WAIT. WHEN IT'S TIME FOR THE EDIT TO HAPPEN, PUSH *RECORD* AND *PLAY!*

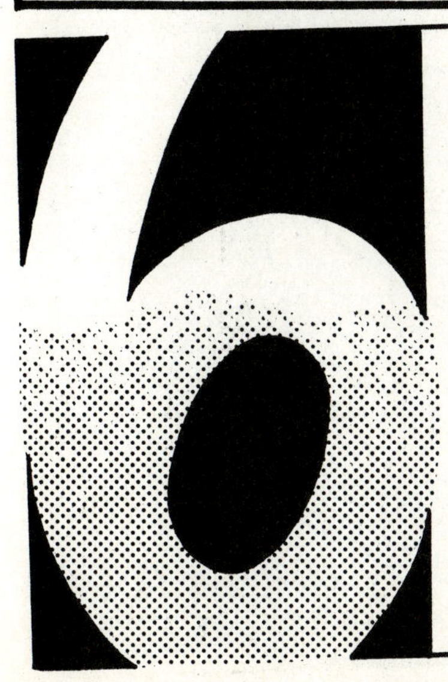

6 LET THE MACHINES CONTINUE UNTIL YOU'VE RECORDED ALL OF THE SCENE THAT YOU WANT. IT'S OK TO LET IT RECORD A LITTLE LONGER THAN YOU NEED, BECAUSE YOU CAN EDIT YOUR NEXT SHOT AT ANY POINT ON THE END OF WHAT YOU'VE RECORDED. PUSH *STOP* OR *PLAY* TO END YOUR EDIT. REPEAT STEPS 2 THROUGH 6 FOR EACH ADDITIONAL EDIT!

THE "PRE-ROLL" THAT THE PREVIOUS METHOD INCORPORATES MAKES FOR A SMOOTHER LOOKING EDIT BECAUSE THE MOTORS IN THE MACHINES HAVE HAD A FEW SECONDS TO STABILIZE BEFORE RECORDING STARTS. ANOTHER THING THIS METHOD GIVES YOU IS THE FREEDOM TO PUT TOGETHER YOUR SCENES IN ANY ORDER YOU WANT—

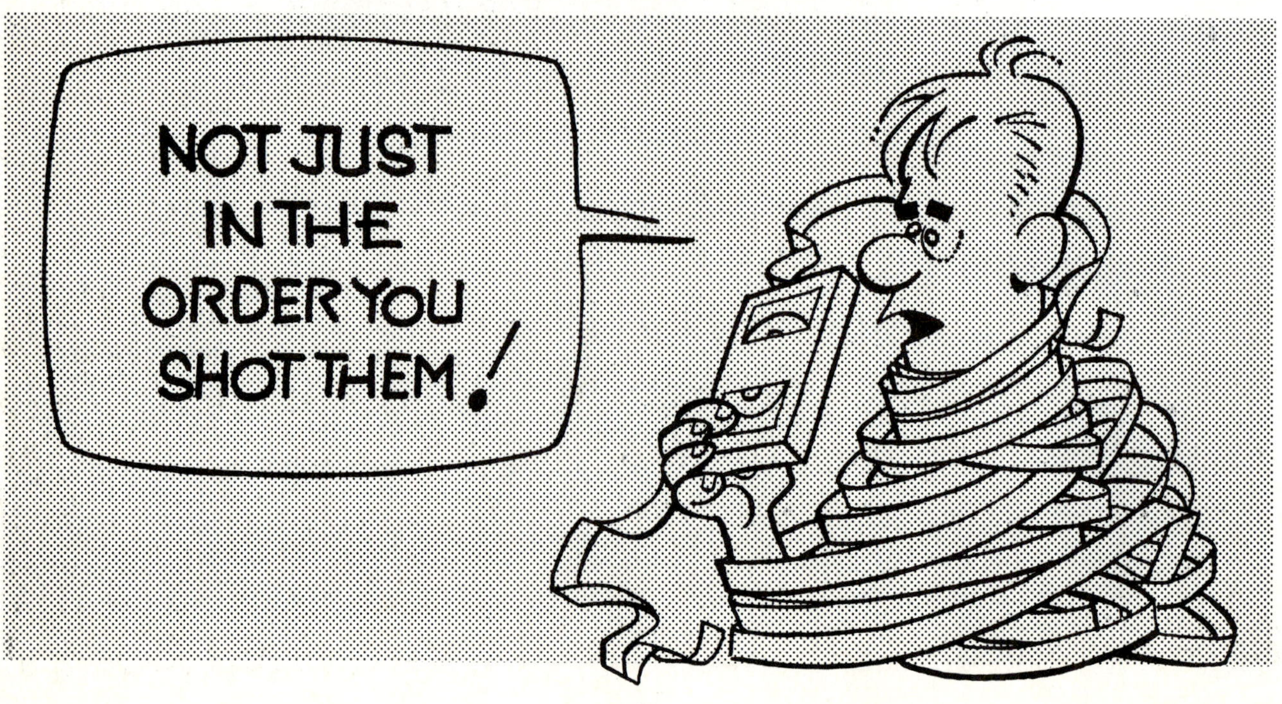

PROFESSIONAL EDITING

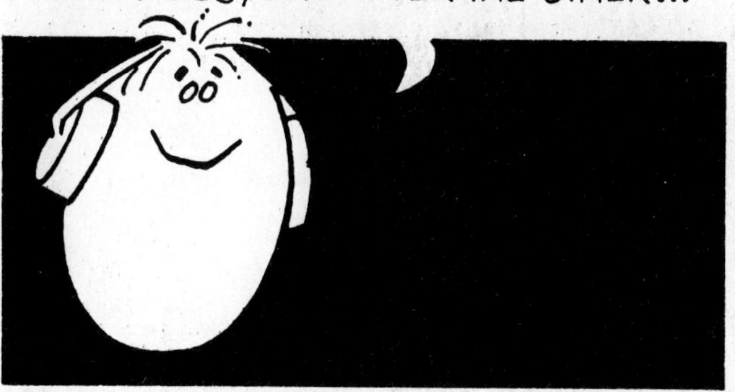

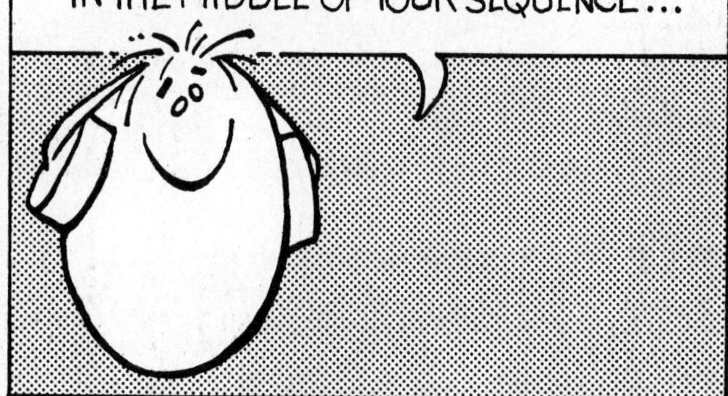

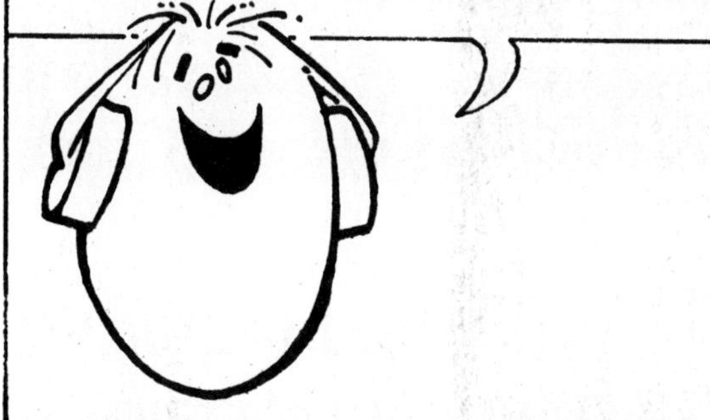

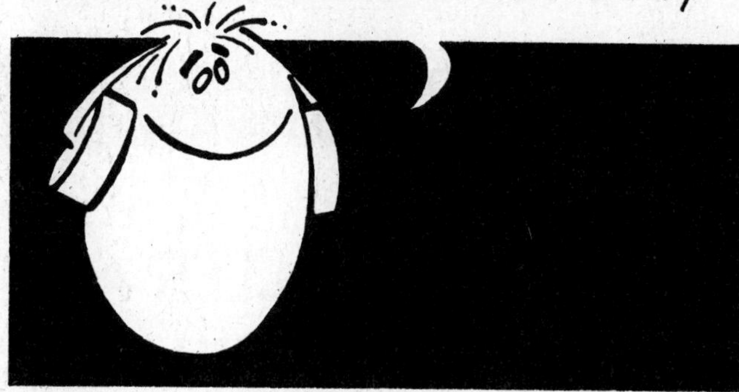

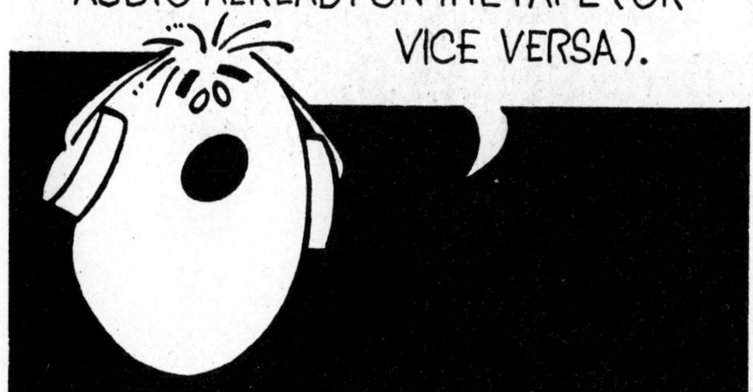

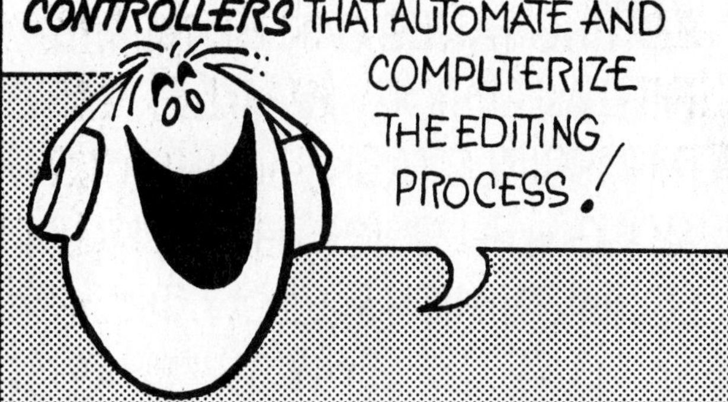

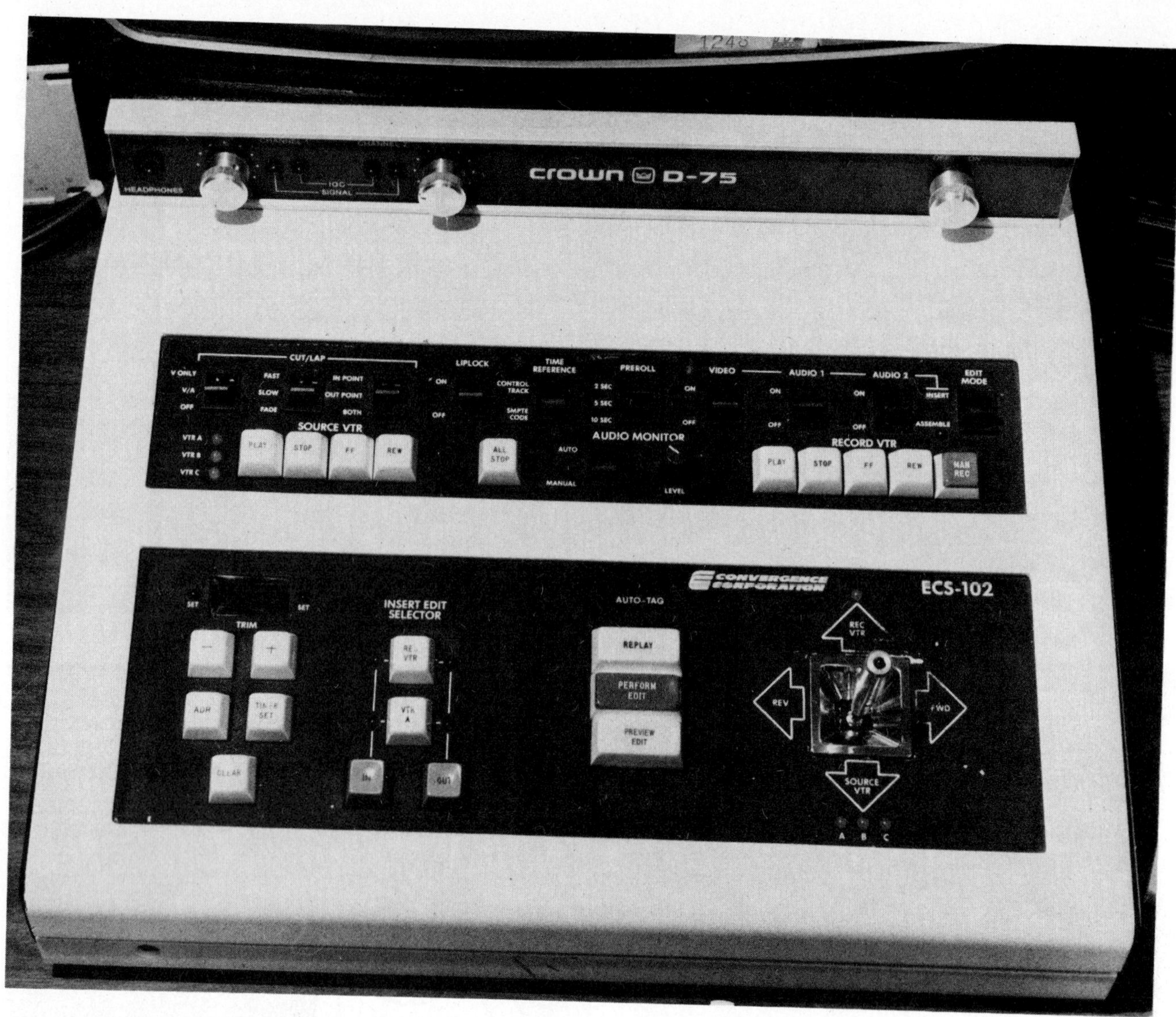

AN EDIT CONTROLLER AND INSERT EDITING MACHINES ARE MUSTS FOR THE VIDEOGRAPHER WHO IS SERIOUS ABOUT DOING INTRICATE EDITING !

EDITING WITHOUT EDITING – THE EXTRA TIME AND EXPENSE THAT EDITING TAKES CAN BE MINIMIZED IF THE VIDEOGRAPHER THINKS LIKE AN EDITOR **WHILE SHOOTING SCENES.** IT'S NOT AN IMPOSSIBLE TASK, BUT IT DOES TAKE SOME ADVANCE PLANNING ALONG WITH QUICK THINKING ON LOCATION. READ THE RULES FOR EDITING WHICH FOLLOW. THEY CAN BE APPLIED **DURING** SHOOTING AS WELL AS AFTERWARDS !

RULES FOR EDITING

RULES, AS THEY SAY,
ARE MEANT
TO BE BROKEN.

SINCE VIDEO CAN BE
CONSIDERED AN ART FORM,
"RULES" CAN BE SUSPENDED
IF THEY INTERFERE
WITH THE ARTIST'S EXPRESSION.

THE ARTIST, HOWEVER, MUST
HAVE AN UNDERSTANDING OF
THE RULES TO KNOW
HOW TO TRANSCEND THEM.

NOT UNDERSTANDING THE RULES
ISN'T GROUNDS FOR DISREGARDING THEM!

PACING

THE PACING OF YOUR PRODUCTION HAS LOTS TO DO WITH ITS MOOD. QUICK CUTTING CONVEYS A SENSE OF EXCITEMENT (WATCH A FIGHT SCENE IN AN ACTION MOVIE, FOR EXAMPLE). FAST CUTTING (NO SHOT LASTS LONGER THAN A FEW SECONDS) CAN ALSO BE USED TO HOLD THE INTEREST OF YOUR AUDIENCE WHEN THE SUBJECT OF THE PRODUCTION IS LESS THAN COMPELLING (TV COMMERCIALS ARE A GOOD EXAMPLE). SLOW CUTTING WOULD BE USED TO PORTRAY QUIETER EMOTIONS (PEACE, RELAXATION, SADNESS, ETC.). NATURE PHOTOGRAPHY SET TO CLASSICAL MUSIC, FOR EXAMPLE, CALLS FOR SLOWER PACED EDITING!

IN ANY PRODUCTION, WATCH OUT FOR LONG, BORING SHOTS WITH LITTLE OR NO ACTION. BREAK YOUR SCENE UP INTO SEVERAL SHOTS, VARYING THE CAMERA ANGLES AND COMPOSITION WITH EACH ONE!

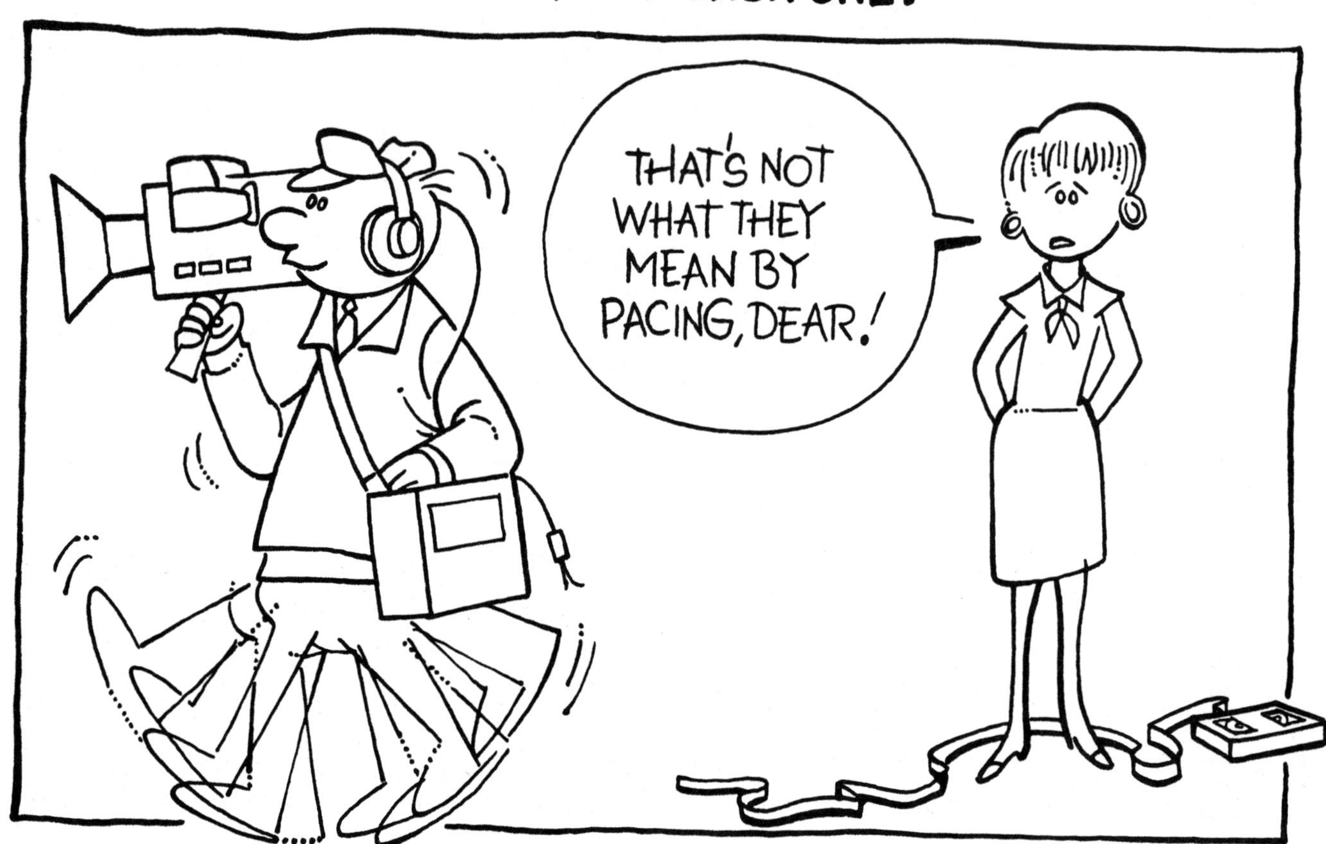

PUTTING SHOTS TOGETHER

SAY, FOR EXAMPLE, YOUR *FRIEND* MAKES A GREAT BOLOGNA SANDWICH. YOU HAVE DECIDED TO VIDEOTAPE THE CREATION OF ONE OF HIS CULINARY DELIGHTS. THE CAMERA COULD SIMPLY BE SET UP AND ALLOWED TO RUN WHILE HE DOES HIS THING, OF COURSE. IF HE HAS THE PATIENCE TO WAIT WHILE YOU MOVE THE CAMERA AROUND, HOWEVER, YOU CAN PLAN A SEQUENCE OF CAMERA SHOTS TO BE EDITED TOGETHER!

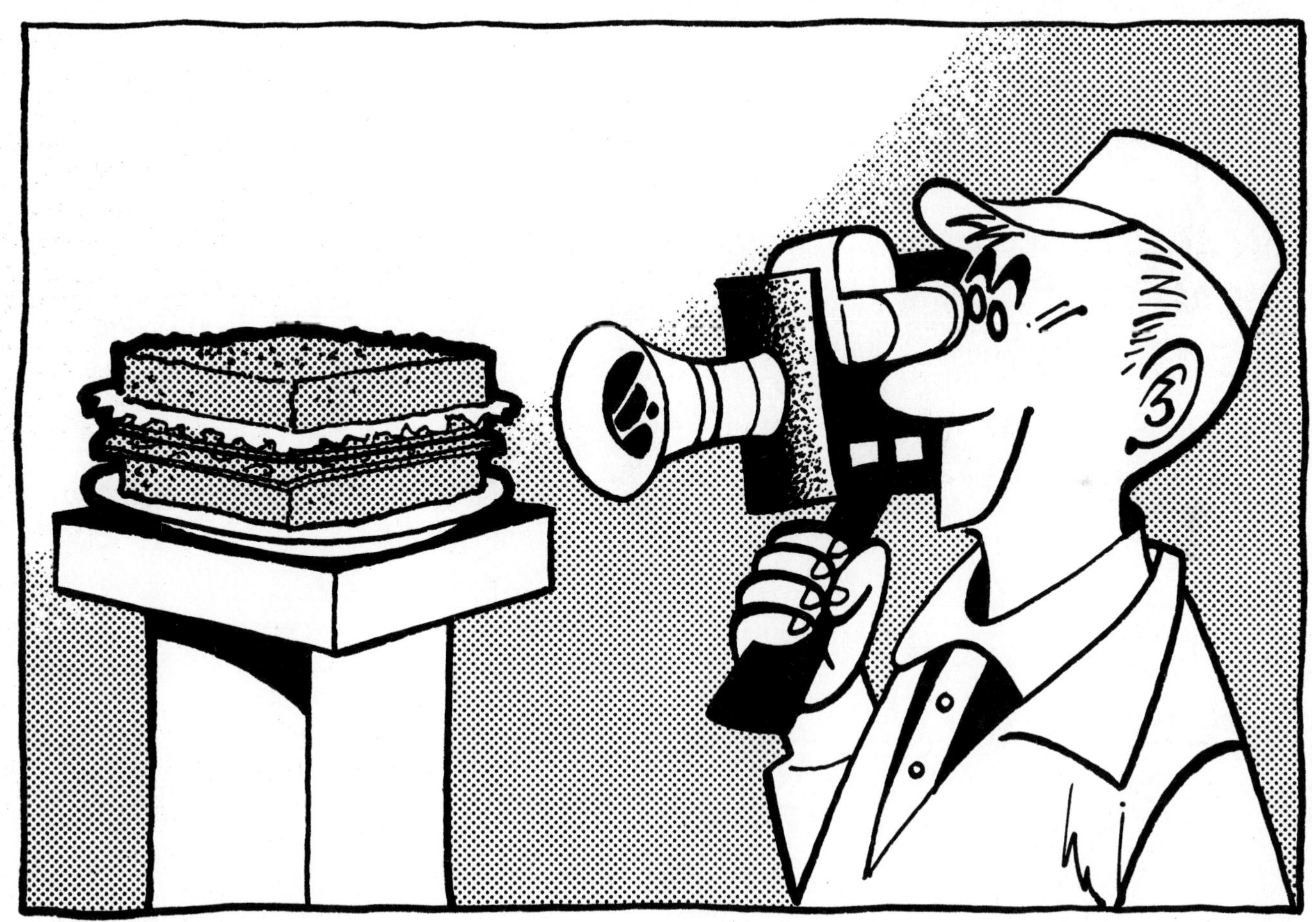

TURN THE PAGE AND LET'S SEE HOW THE STORYBOARD IS USED TO PLAN THE SEQUENCE OF CAMERA SHOTS!

STORYBOARD – THE BOLOGNA SANDWICH!

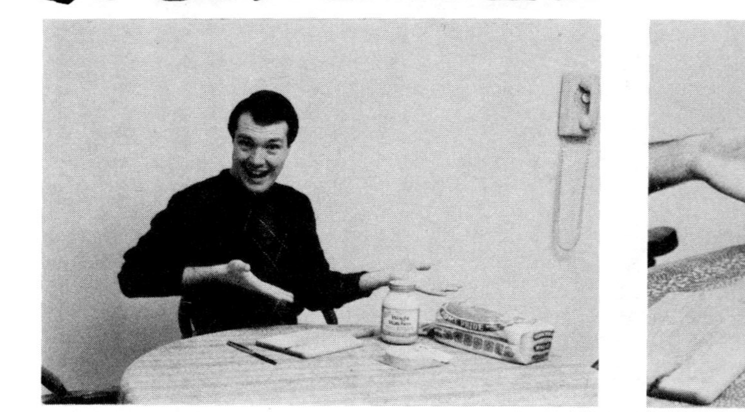
"I'M GOING TO SHOW YOU HOW TO MAKE A BOLOGNA SANDWICH"

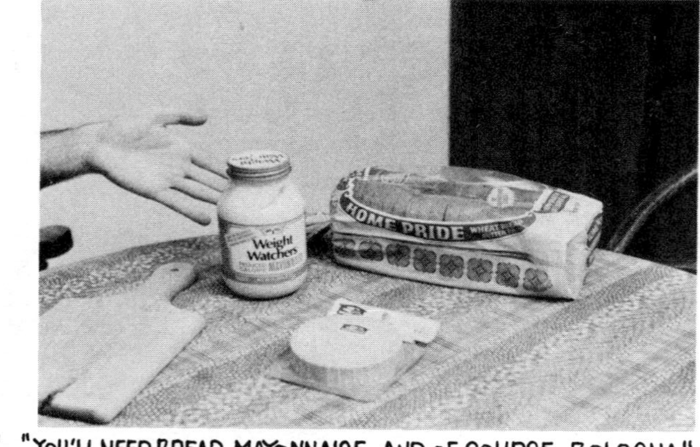
"YOU'LL NEED BREAD, MAYONNAISE, AND OF COURSE, BOLOGNA"

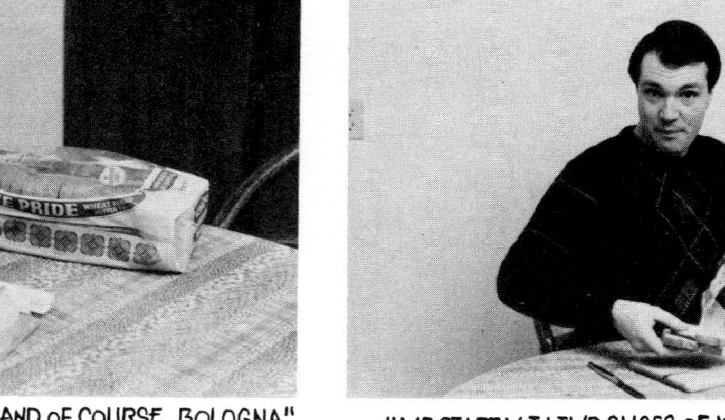
"WE START WITH TWO SLICES OF WHEAT BREAD"

"NEXT COMES THE MAYONNAISE"

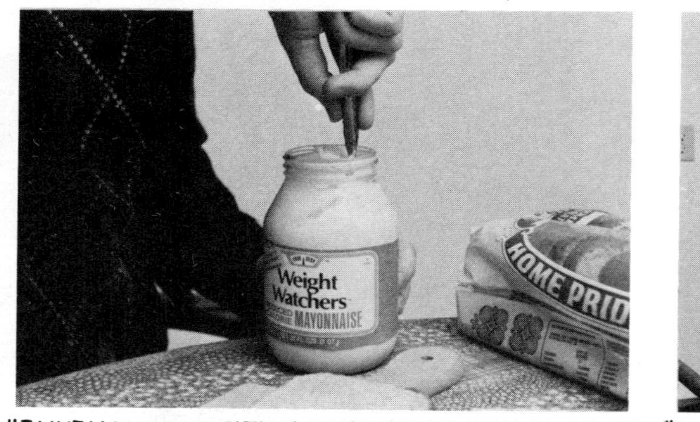
"I LIKE MAYONNAISE, BUT YOU CAN SUBSTITUTE SALAD DRESSING"

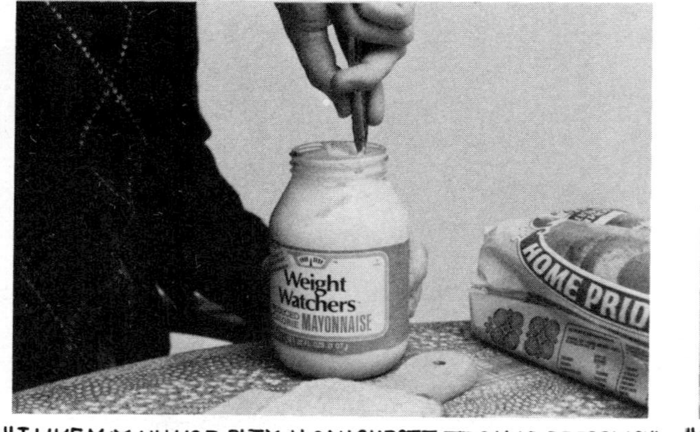
"SOME PEOPLE LIKE MUSTARD ON THEIR SANDWICH, BUT NOT ME"

"AND FINALLY, THE BOLOGNA GOES IN THE MIDDLE"

"NOW FOR THE TEST OF A BOLOGNA SANDWICH...THE TASTE"

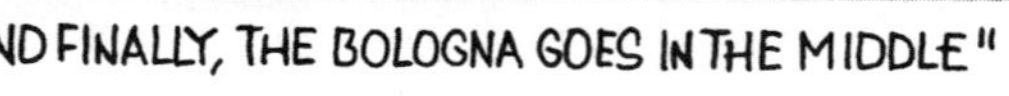
"MMMM...DELICIOUS"

THE STORYBOARD
DRAWINGS OR PHOTOS WITH CAPTIONS

A WIDE SHOT, MAN AT TABLE WITH LOAF OF BREAD, JAR OF MAYONNAISE, AND A PACKAGE OF BOLOGNA

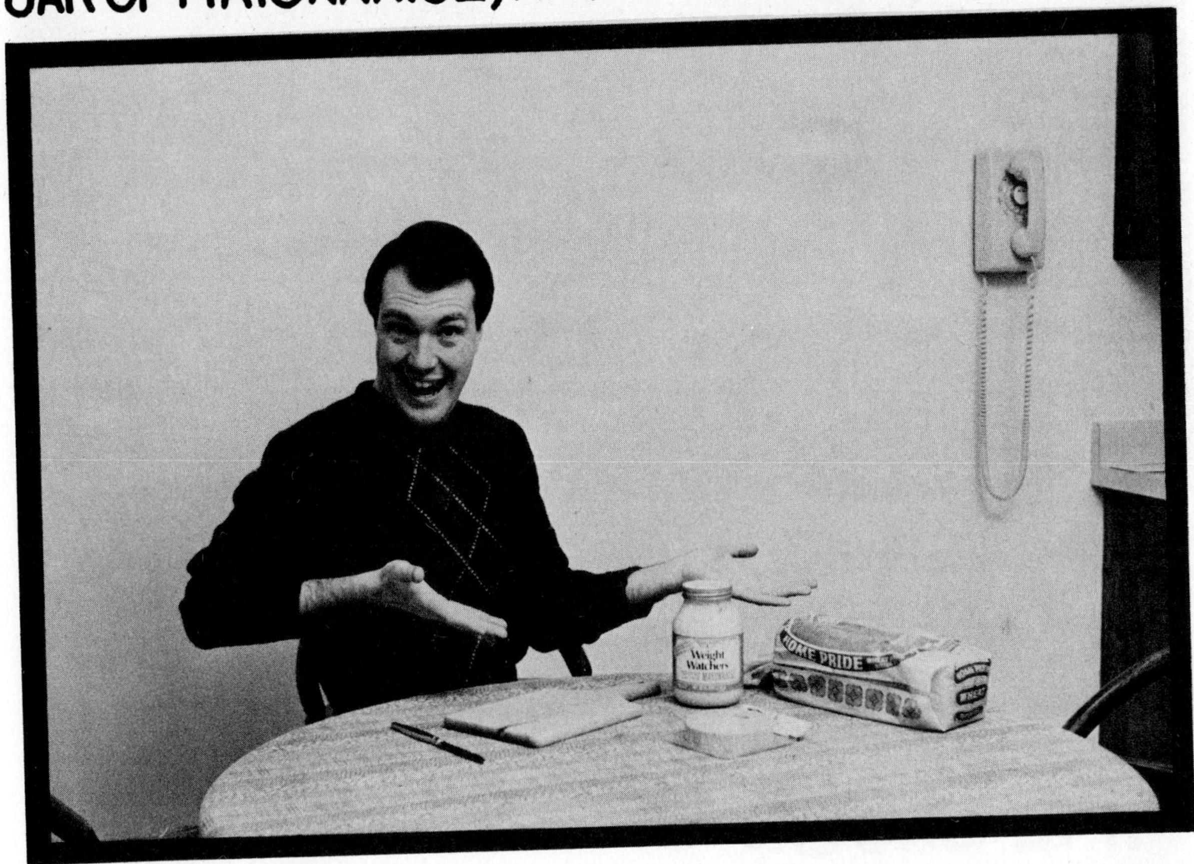

"TODAY I'M GOING TO SHOW YOU HOW TO MAKE ONE OF THE BEST BOLOGNA SANDWICHES AROUND."

MAKING YOUR FIRST SHOT A **WIDE SHOT** (ALSO KNOWN AS AN **ESTABLISHING** SHOT) HELPS ESTABLISH YOUR LOCATION FOR YOUR AUDIENCE AND ORIENT THEM FOR THE SHOTS THAT FOLLOW!

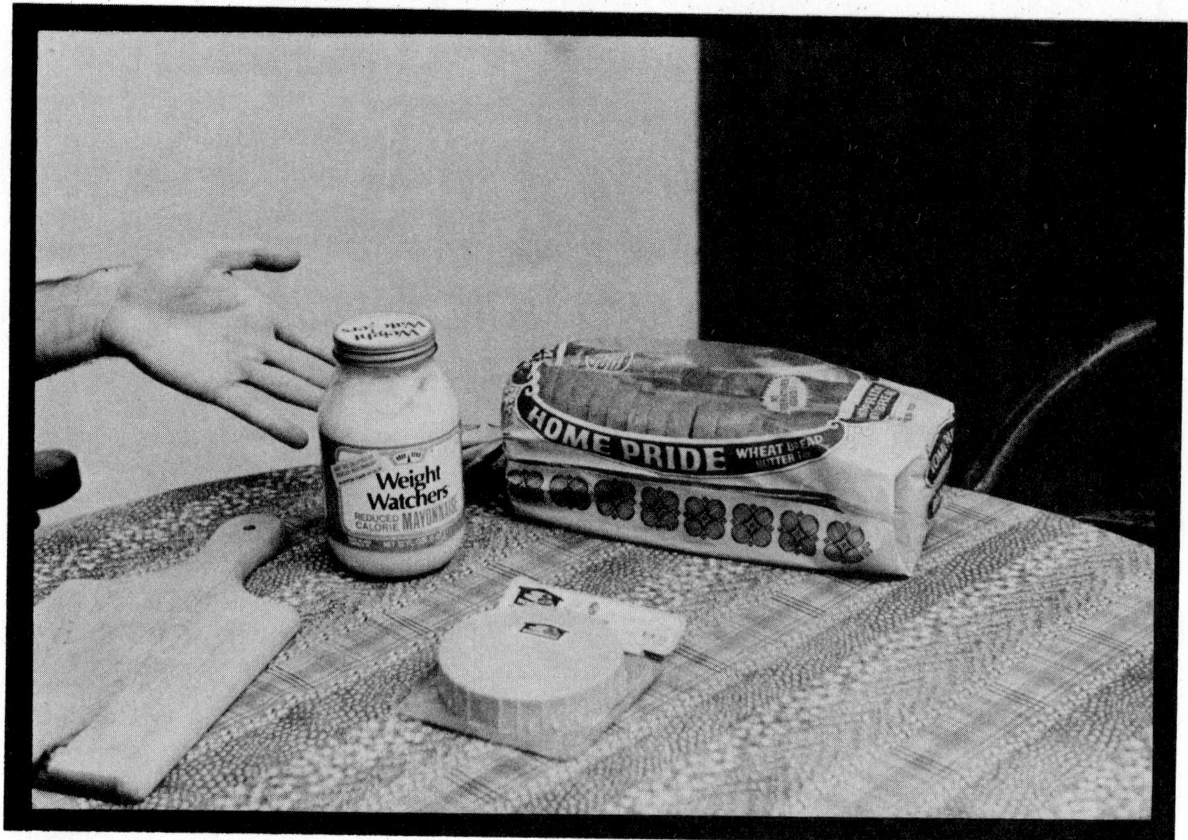

"YOU'LL NEED QUALITY INGREDIENTS, LIKE BREAD, MAYONNAISE, AND OF COURSE, BOLOGNA."

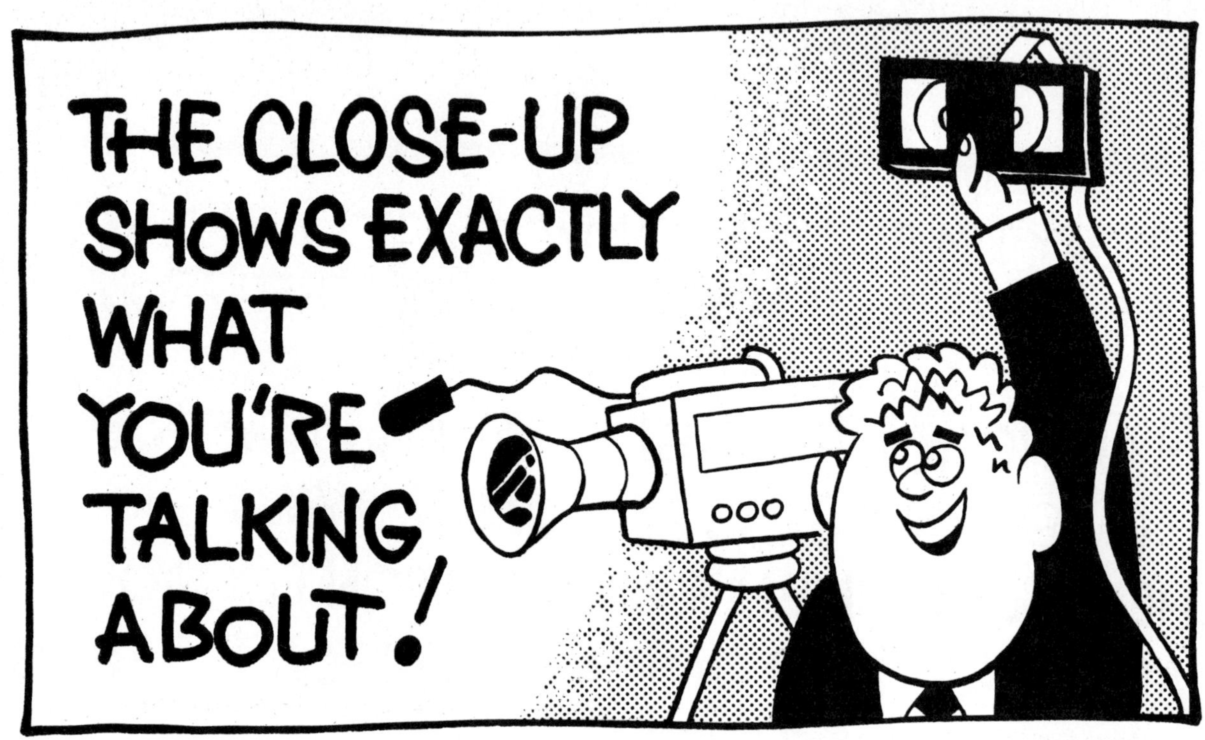

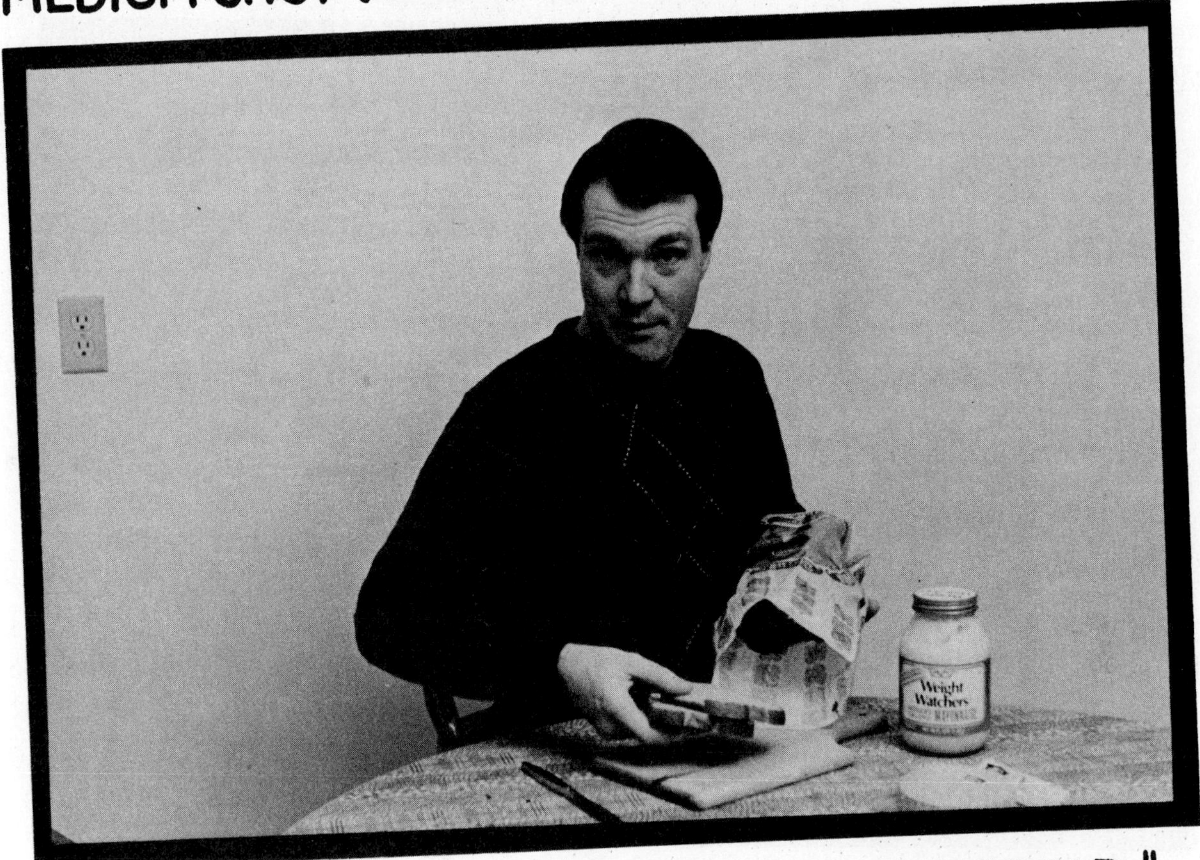

"WE START WITH TWO SLICES OF WHEAT BREAD."

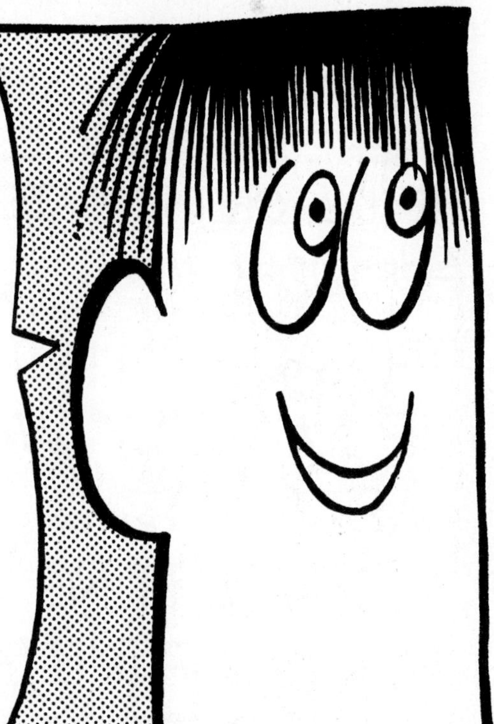

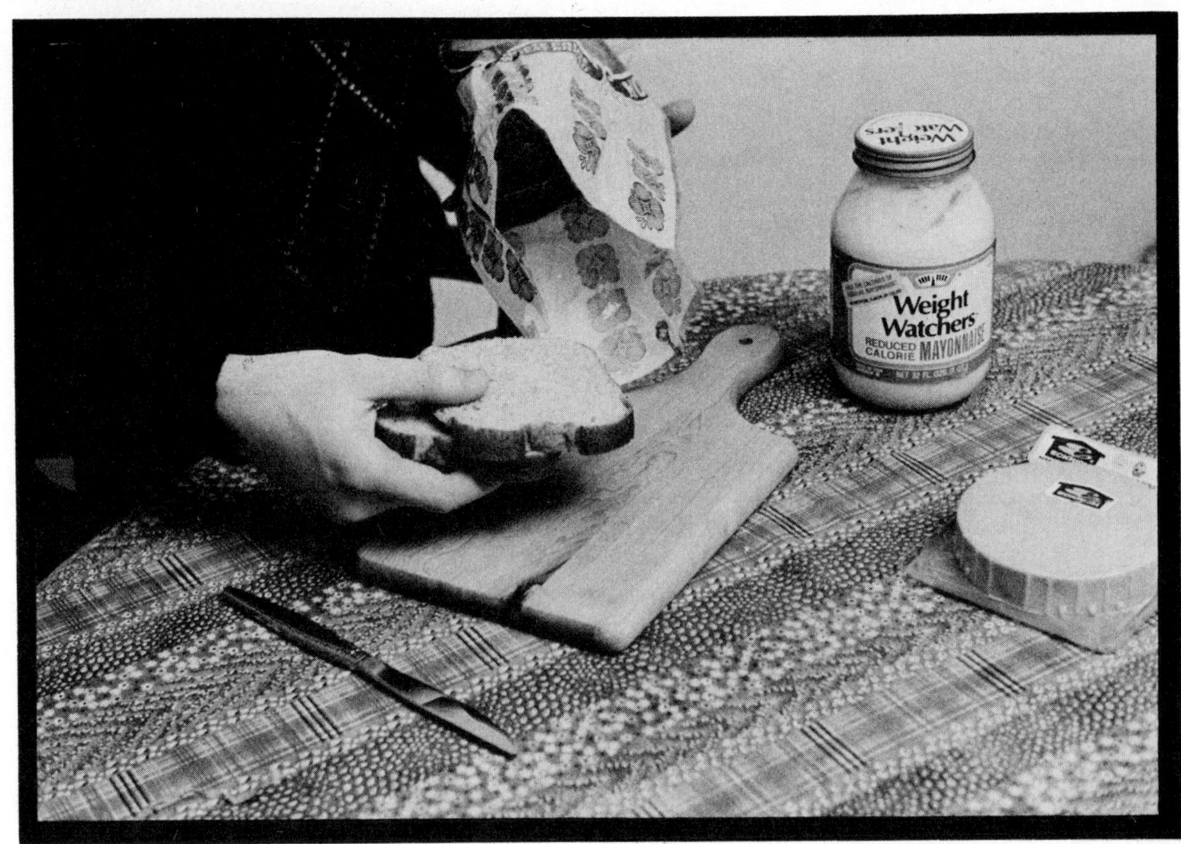

"NEXT COMES THE MAYONNAISE."

HERE WE TRY TO MAKE OUR EDIT RIGHT AT THE POINT WHERE THE BREAD COMES OUT OF THE WRAPPER AND HEADS FOR THE PLATE. THE TRICK IS TO MAKE THE NEXT SHOT *MATCH!*

THE ACTION IN THIS SHOT SHOULD PICK UP *EXACTLY* WHERE IT LEFT OFF IN THE LAST SHOT.

ALSO, CUTTING *ON* OR *BEFORE* THE ACTION OF THE BREAD HITTING THE PLATE LOOKS BETTER THAN CUTTING *AFTERWARD!*

TIGHT SHOT OF KNIFE IN JAR OF MAYONNAISE

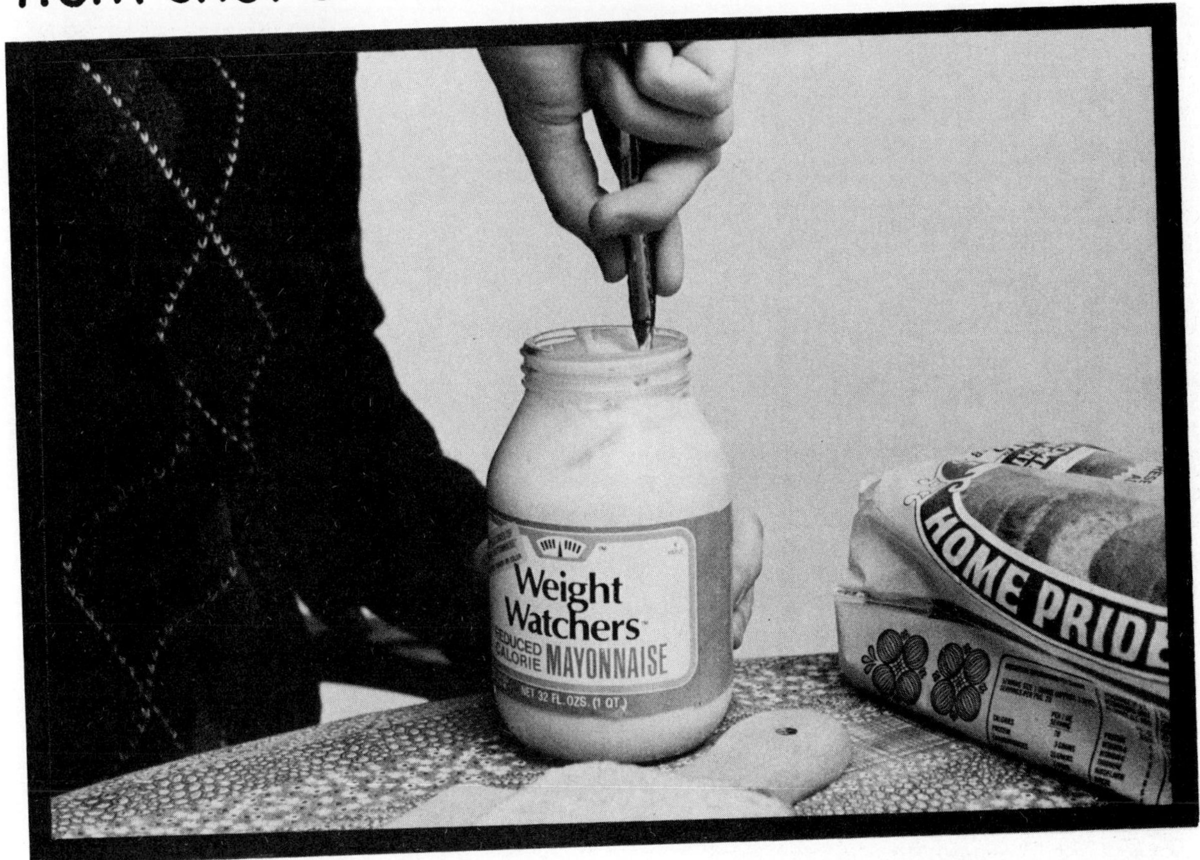

"I LIKE MAYONNAISE, BUT YOU CAN SUBSTITUTE SALAD DRESSING IF YOU LIKE."

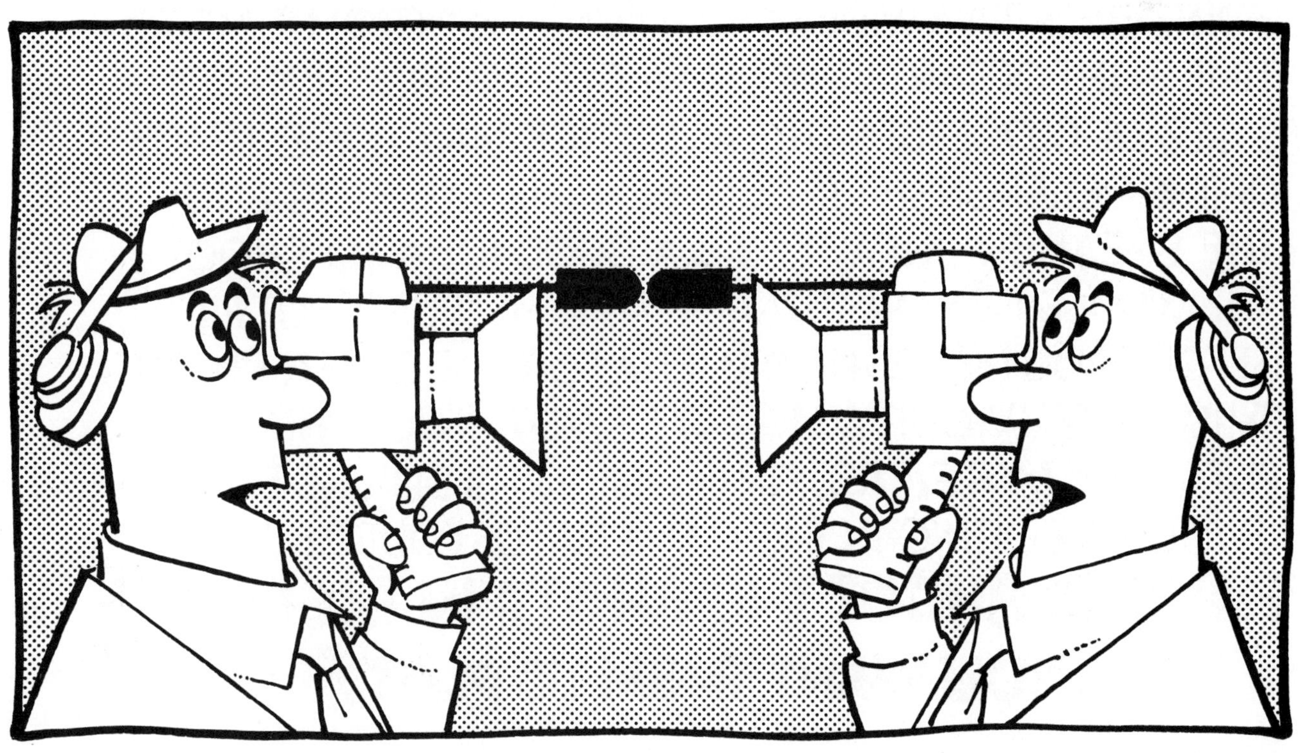

WIDE SHOT SPREADING MAYONNAISE

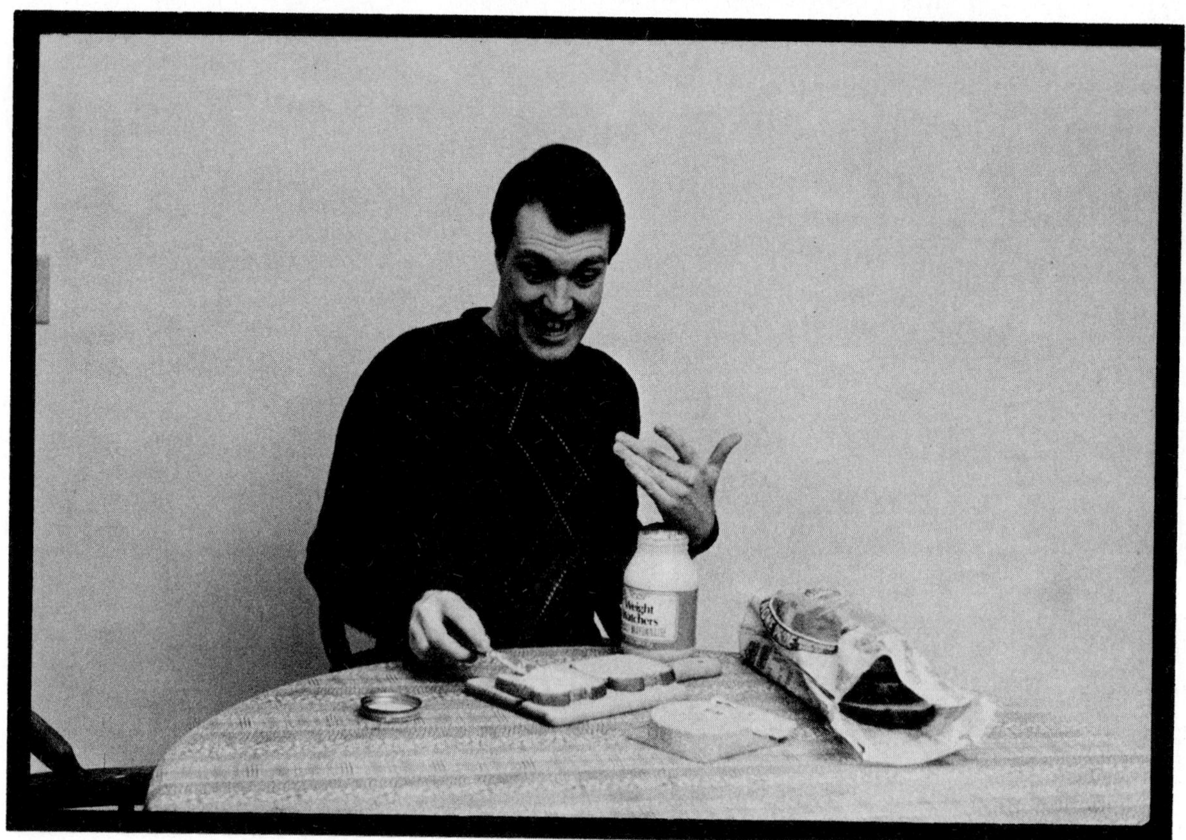

"SOME PEOPLE LIKE MUSTARD ON THEIR SANDWICHES, BUT NOT ME!"

GOING BACK TO A WIDE OR MEDIUM SHOT FROM TIME TO TIME IS IMPORTANT. IF YOUR WHOLE PRODUCTION CONSISTS OF CLOSE-UPS, THE AUDIENCE MAY *LOSE* TRACK OF THE RELATIONSHIPS BETWEEN THE OBJECTS AND THE SPEAKER. INFACT, IT'S A GOOD IDEA TO SHOOT THE WHOLE DEMONSTRATION AS A MEDIUM SHOT FIRST, BEFORE YOU MOVE THE CAMERA FOR THE OTHER SHOTS. THIS SHOT IS YOUR **MASTER SHOT,** INTO WHICH YOU PUT YOUR **INSERTS,** OR CLOSE-UPS DURING EDITING. IF YOU'RE EDITING IN THE CAMERA, OF COURSE, YOU'LL **HAVE TO SHOOT THE SHOTS IN THE ORDER YOU WANT THEM TO PLAY!**

CLOSE-UP OF BOLOGNA GOING INTO SANDWICH

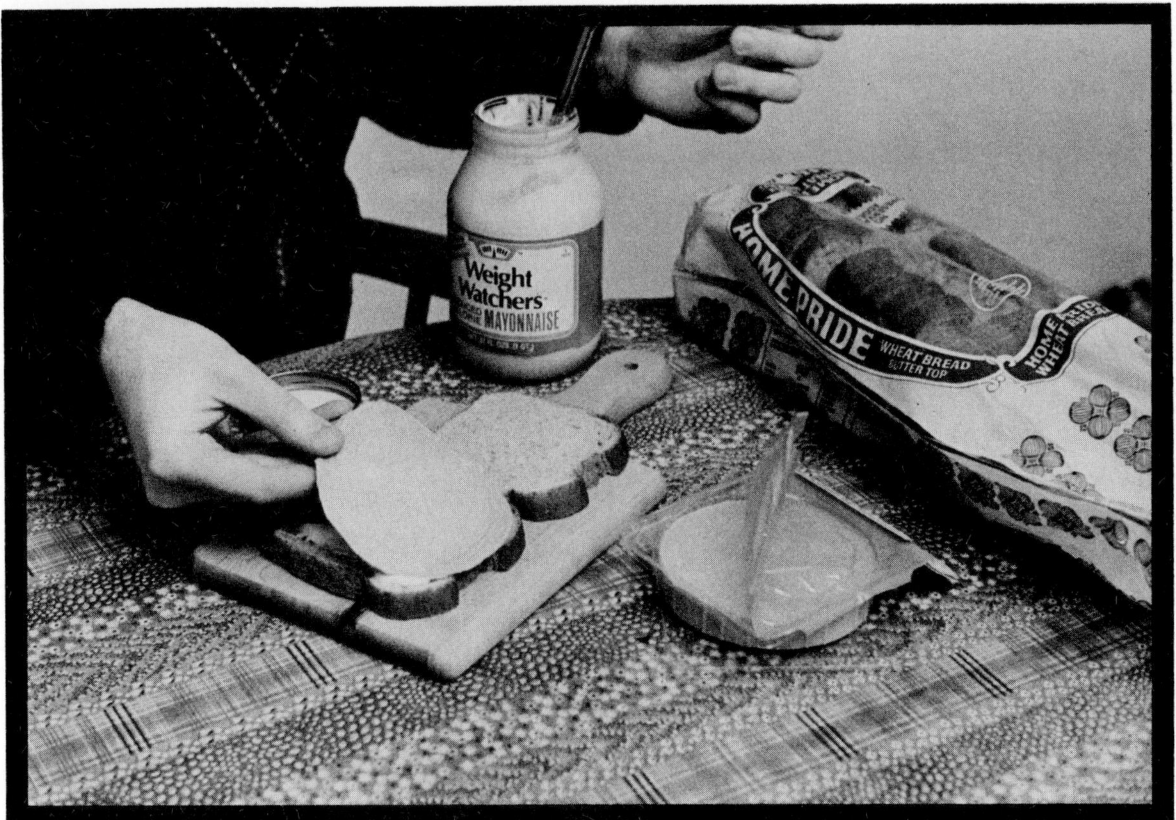

"AND FINALLY, THE BOLOGNA GOES IN THE MIDDLE."

WIDE SHOT PICKING UP BOLOGNA

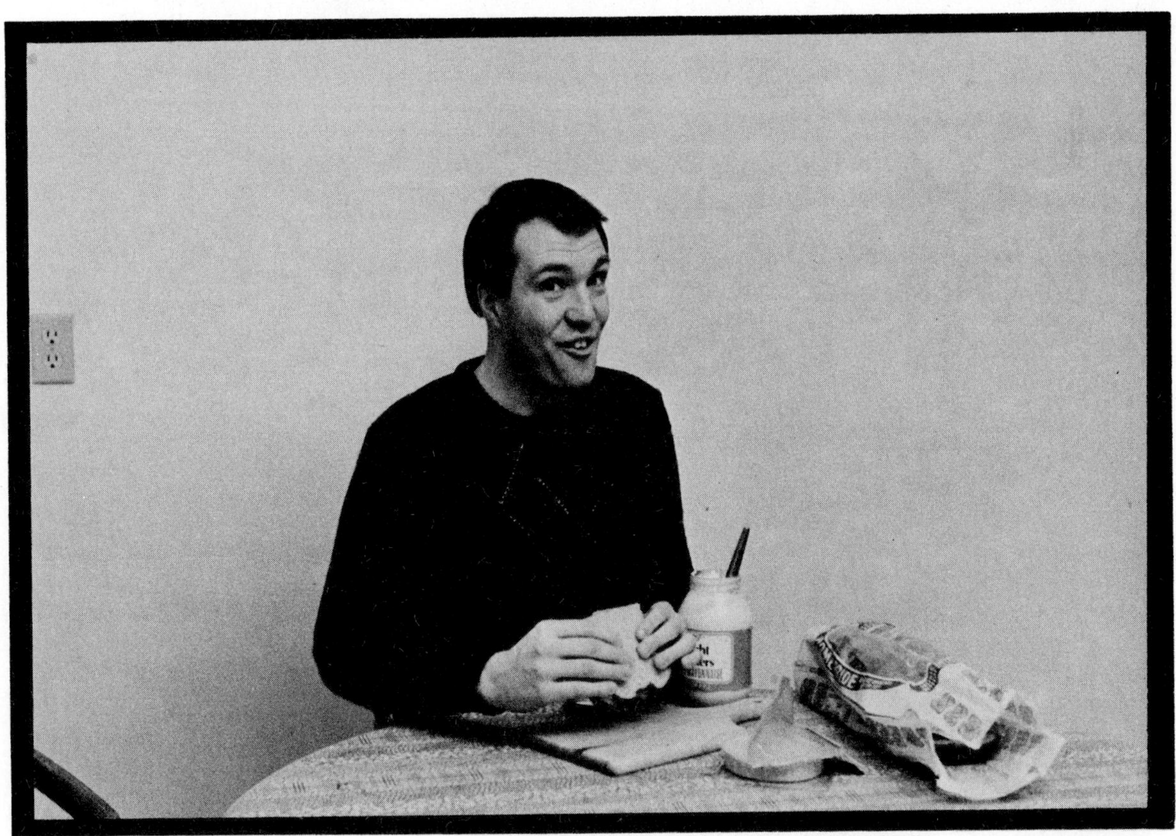

"NOW FOR THE TEST OF A REALLY FINE BOLOGNA SANDWICH ... THE TASTE."

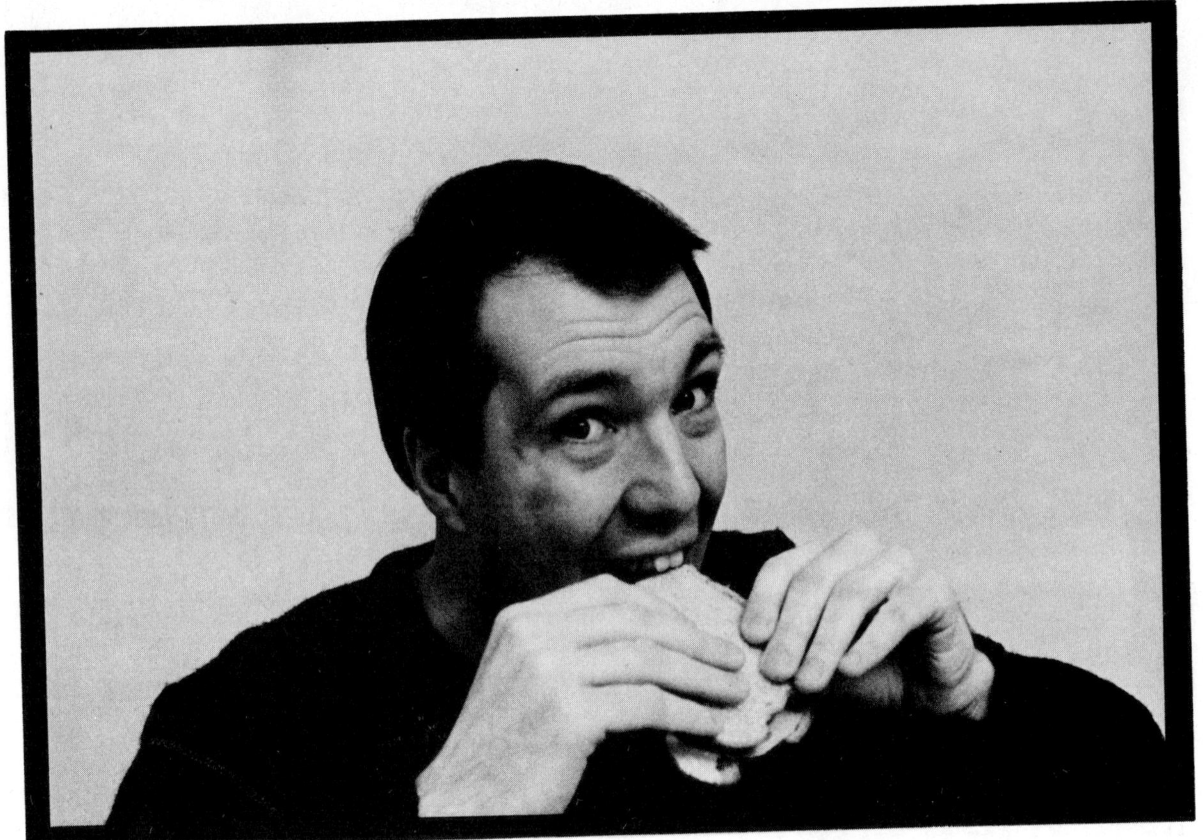

"MMMM . . . . DELICIOUS!"

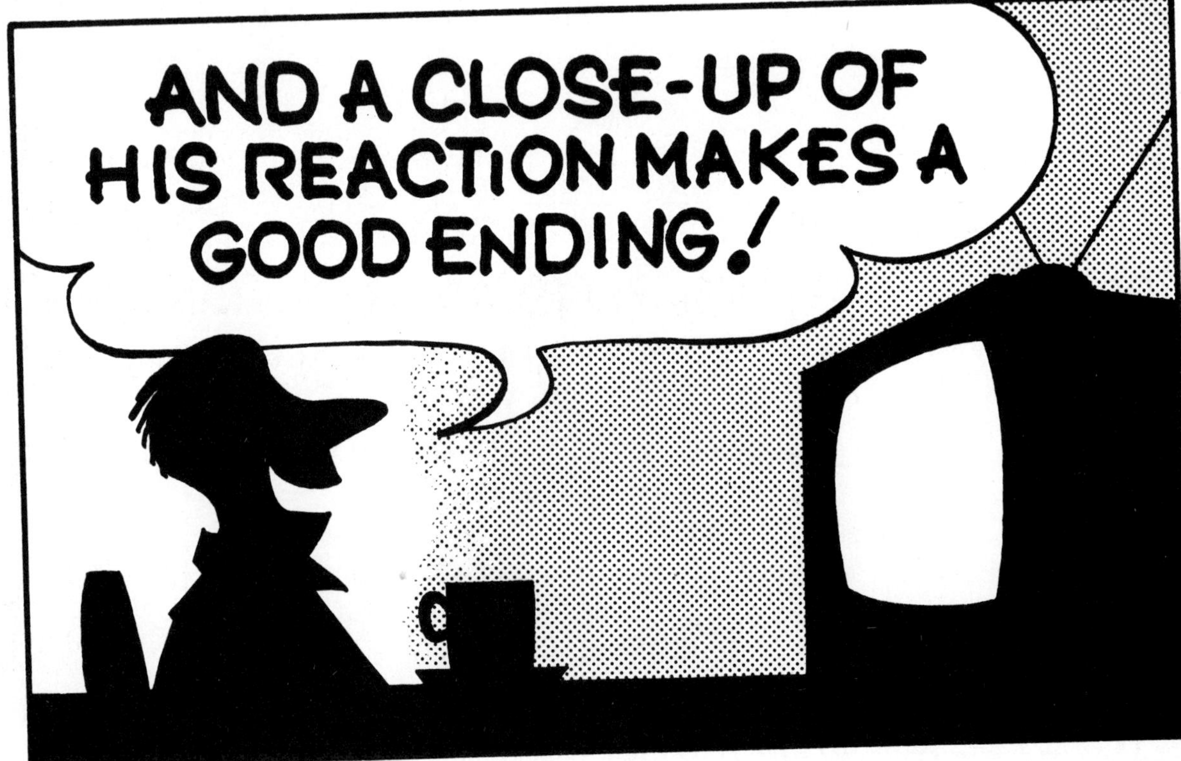

CONTINUITY!

THE *STORYBOARD* WE HAVE JUST LOOKED AT ILLUS-TRATES AN IMPORTANT CONCEPT IN EDITING . . . . THAT OF *CONTINUITY.* WE ARE MAKING THE DEMON-STRATION APPEAR *CONTINUOUS* EVEN THOUGH THE SEPARATE PARTS MAY HAVE BEEN SHOT *OUT OF ORDER!* WHEN EDITED TOGETHER PROPERLY, THE ACTION SHOULD SEEM TO *FLOW* NATURALLY FROM SHOT TO SHOT. SPECIAL ATTENTION NEEDS TO BE PAID TO THE ACTION OF YOUR FRIEND AND THE EXACT POSITION OF ALL THE OBJECTS HE'S HANDLING SO THAT EVERYTHING *MATCHES* WHEN CUTTING FROM ONE SHOT TO ANOTHER.

SOMETIMES A *STORYBOARD* CAN BE MADE, USING DRAWINGS OR PHOTOGRAPHS OF EACH SHOT YOU NEED TO GET. THE STORYBOARD IS YOUR OUTLINE, AND IT WILL GUIDE YOU DURING YOUR PRODUCTION, RE-MINDING YOU EXACTLY WHAT YOUR SHOTS ARE!

MANY TV COMMERCIALS, HOLLYWOOD MOTION PIC-TURES AND OTHER PRECISELY SCRIPTED PRODUC-TIONS USE STORYBOARDS!

TiME ComPRESSioN!

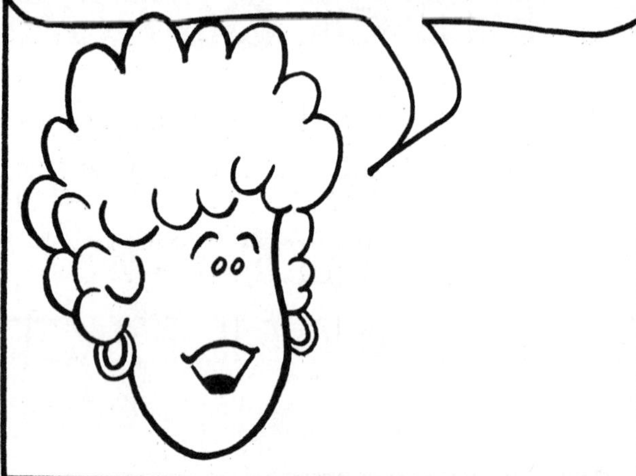

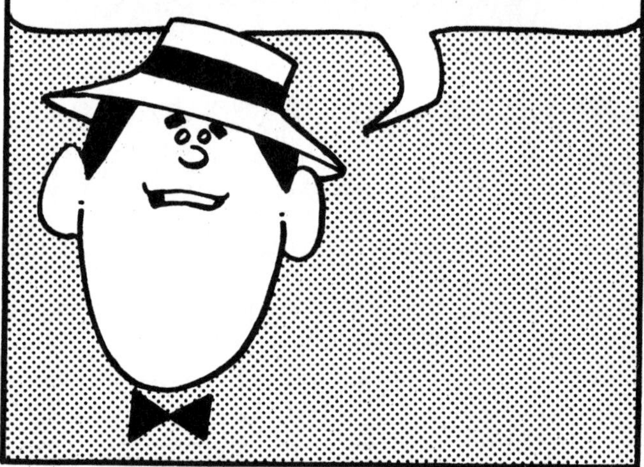

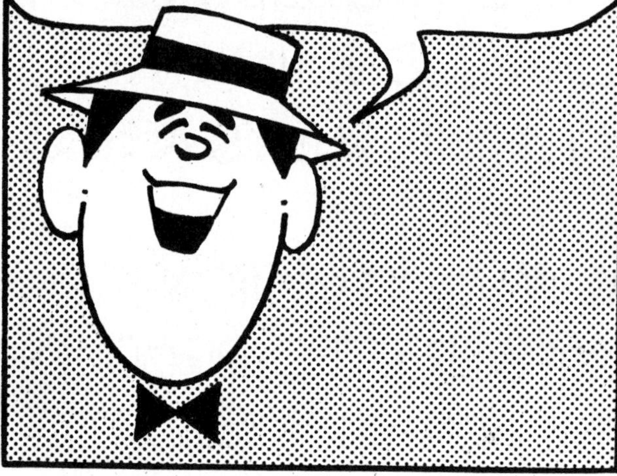

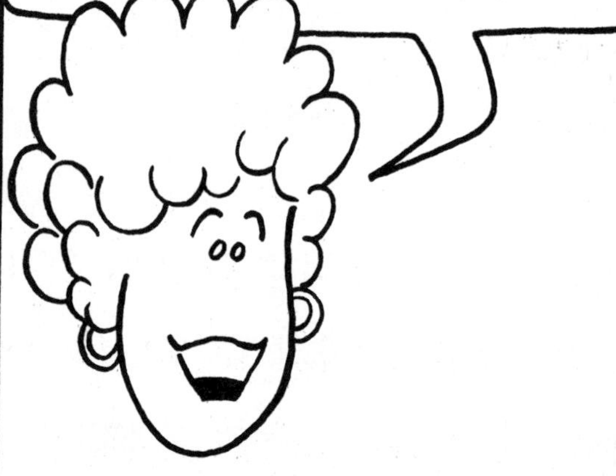

ALAS, MOST OF OUR PRODUCTIONS AREN'T SO NEATLY STRUCTURED. GIVEN THE CHANCE, MIKE WOULD PROBABLY RAMBLE ON, SAYING MUCH THAT YOU DON'T NEED, OR IN THE WRONG ORDER. IF THIS HAPPENS, DON'T DESPAIR. CARRY ON, AND SHOOT THE CLOSE-UPS AFTERWARD ANYWAY. WHEN YOU EDIT, USE NOTHING ***BUT*** CLOSE-UPS FOR THE DEMONSTRATION (*USE YOUR WIDE SHOT AT THE BEGINNING AND END, BUT NOWHERE ELSE.*)

NOW, GO BACK TO THE BEGINNING OF YOUR TAPE AND EDIT *JUST THE SOUND* TO GO WITH THE PICTURES YOU'VE EDITED. USE THE ***AUDIO DUB*** FEATURE OF YOUR RECORDER (*INSTEAD OF THE RECORD BUTTON*) TO MAKE AUDIO ONLY EDITS.

OTHER THAN THIS DIFFERENCE, THE EDITS ARE MADE EXACTLY THE SAME WAY. YOU CAN CHOOSE EXACTLY WHAT YOU WANT HIM TO SAY FROM EVERYTHING HE TALKED ABOUT AND EDIT IT TOGETHER.

AS LONG AS WE DON'T SEE HIS FACE AT THE TIME, NO ONE WILL KNOW THE DIFFERENCE!

CUT-AWAYS

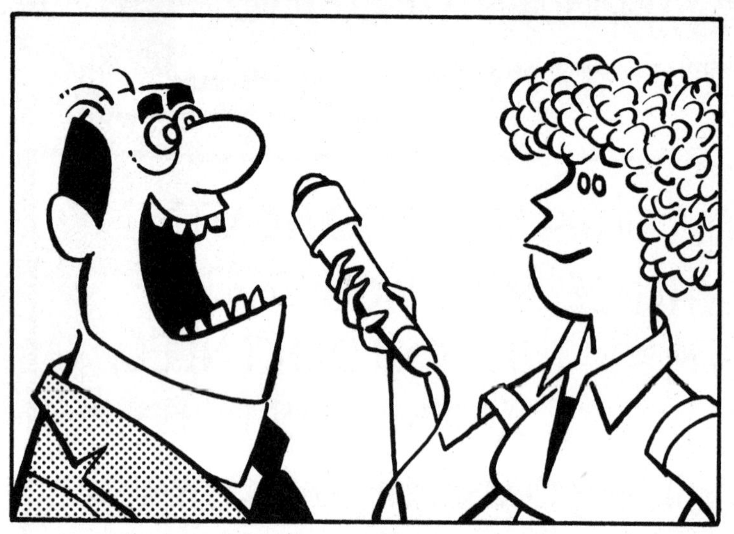

HERE'S A TRICK YOU'VE PROBABLY SEEN ON THE EVENING NEWS: THE MAYOR IS SPEAKING TO A LOCAL TV REPORTER.
AFTER HE HAS SPOKEN FOR A FEW SECONDS,

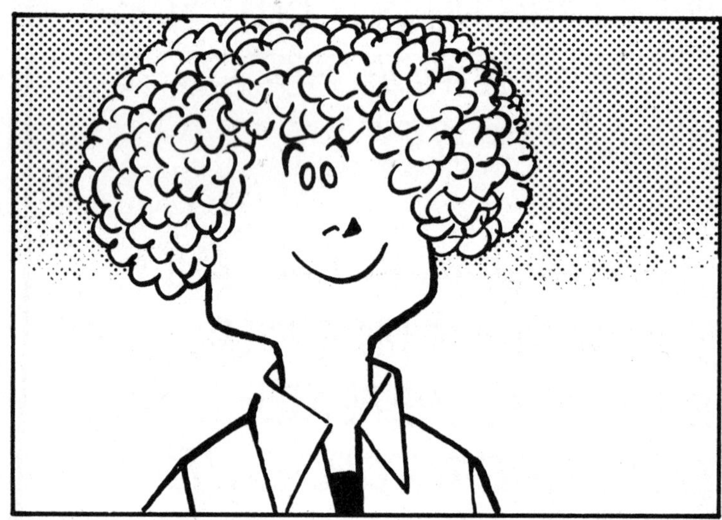

WE CUT TO A SHOT OF THE REPORTER LISTENING,

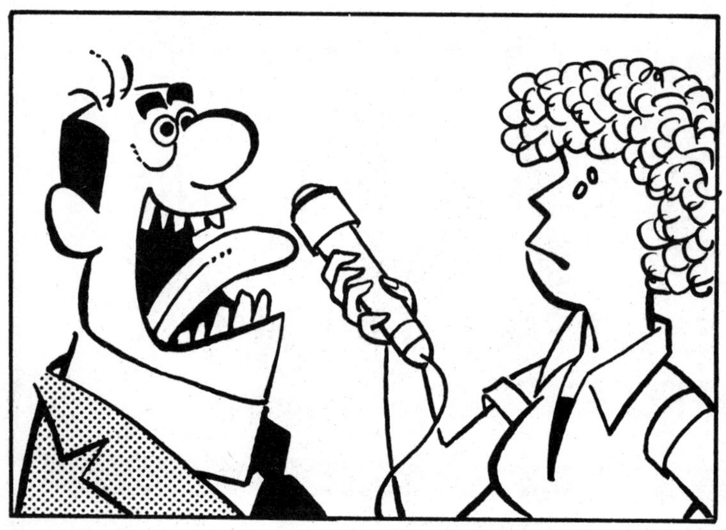

THEN BACK TO THE MAYOR SPEAKING!

DURING THE TIME WE SAW THE REPORTER, AN EDIT WAS MADE IN THE MAYOR'S COMMENT! THE **CUT-AWAY** OF THE REPORTER WAS USED TO SHORTEN THE LENGTH OF THE STORY WITHOUT LETTING THE AUDIENCE SEE THE EDIT!

HOW CAN YOU USE THIS TRICK?

IF LITTLE GILLIAN IS TAKING TEN MINUTES TO OPEN HER BIRTHDAY PRESENT, YOU COULD SHOW THE FIRST FEW SECONDS OF IT, CUT-AWAY TO MOM'S REACTION, THEN CUT BACK TO THE LAST FEW MOMENTS OF THE WRAPPER COMING OFF!

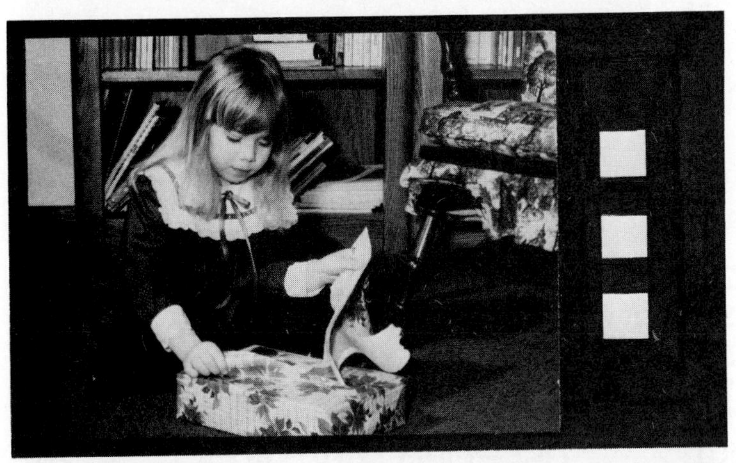

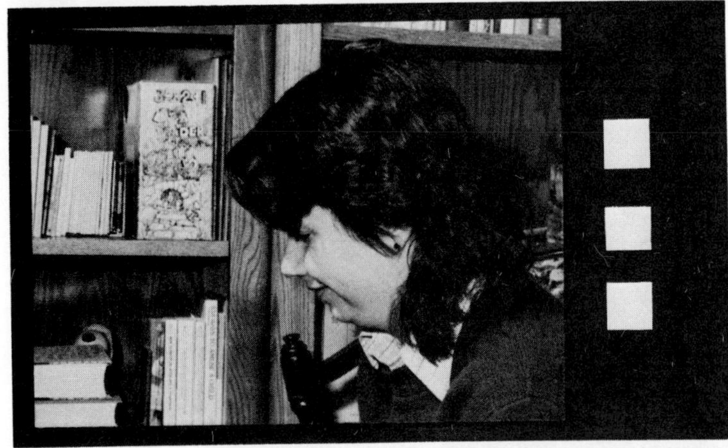

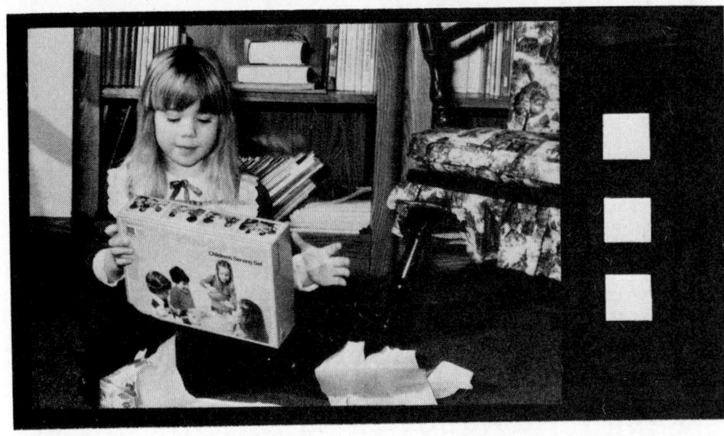

WE'VE JUST MADE TEN MINUTES INTO TEN SECONDS, AND THE VIEWER WON'T EVEN KNOW IT! IN BOTH THESE EXAMPLES, NOTE THAT THE CUT-AWAY SHOT IS *RELATED* TO THE ACTION. AN *UNRELATED* CUT-AWAY WILL HAMPER THE CONTINUITY OF YOUR SCENE.

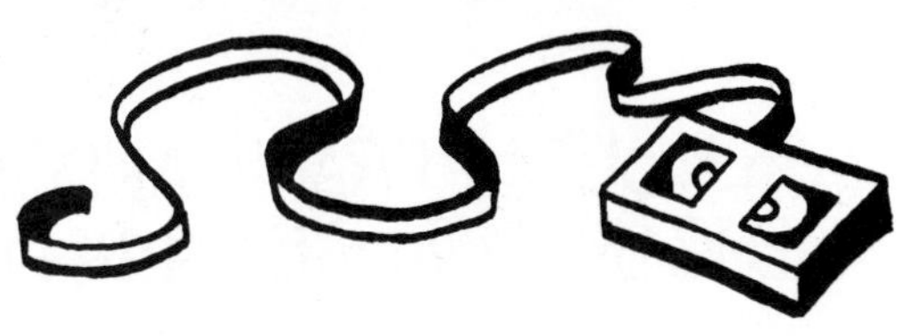

A TRANSITION IS A LESS SUBTLE DEVICE FOR ILLUSTRATING THE PASSAGE OF TIME OR A CHANGE OF LOCATION!

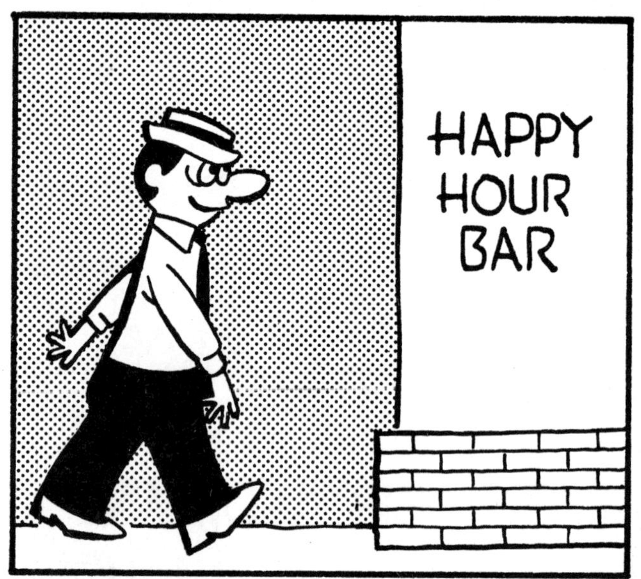

IF YOUR BROTHER IMBIBES TOO MUCH, YOU COULD DEMONSTRATE THIS WITH A SHOT OF HIM ENTERING A BAR, FOLLOWED BY A *FADE-OUT*

(THE PICTURE GOES TO BLACK)

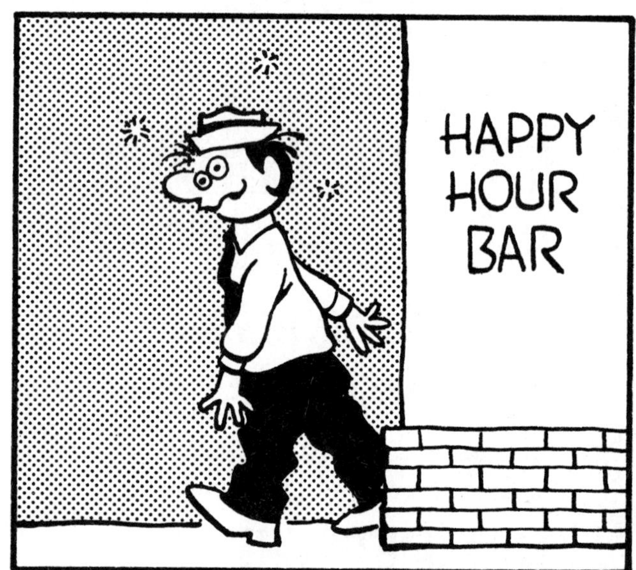

IMMEDIATELY AFTER THE FADE-OUT, *FADE-IN* ON HIM EXITING THE BAR, OBVIOUSLY INTOXICATED!

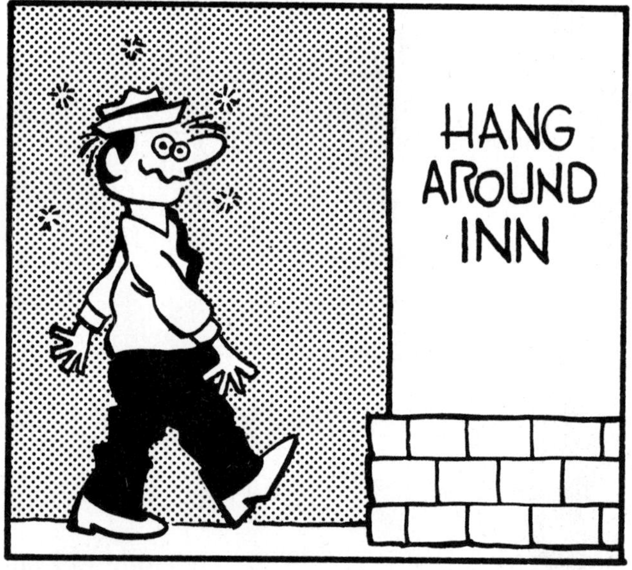

THE *FADE-OUT / FADE-IN* COMBINATION IS A *TRANSITION* THAT SUGGESTS THE PASSAGE OF TIME. NOW HE WALKS OUT OF THE FRAME AND WE CUT TO A SHOT OF ANOTHER BAR, AND OUR MAN WALKS INTO THE FRAME!

THE WALK OUT OF FRAME AND THEN INTO IT AGAIN IS ALSO A TRANSITION, AND IS USED TO GET HIM FROM ONE PLACE TO ANOTHER!

MONTAGE

A MONTAGE IS A SERIES OF VERY QUICKLY PACED SHOTS THAT CONVEY AN IDEA OR SET A MOOD. FOR EXAMPLE, IMAGINE THIS SEQUENCE AT THE BEGINNING OF A TAPE ABOUT YOUR VACATION TO HAWAII (EACH SHOT IS ABOUT 2 TO 5 SECONDS LONG).

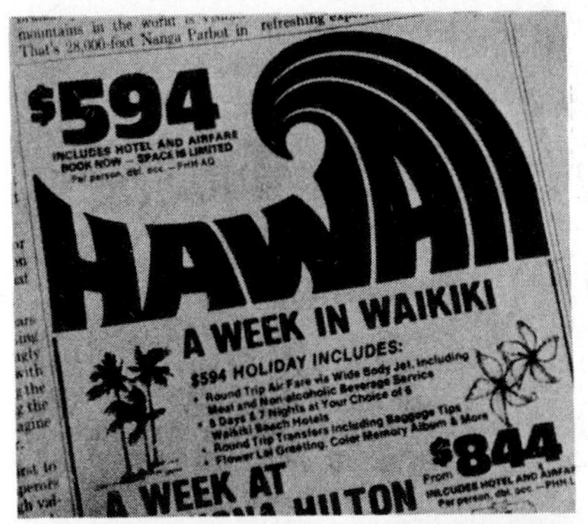

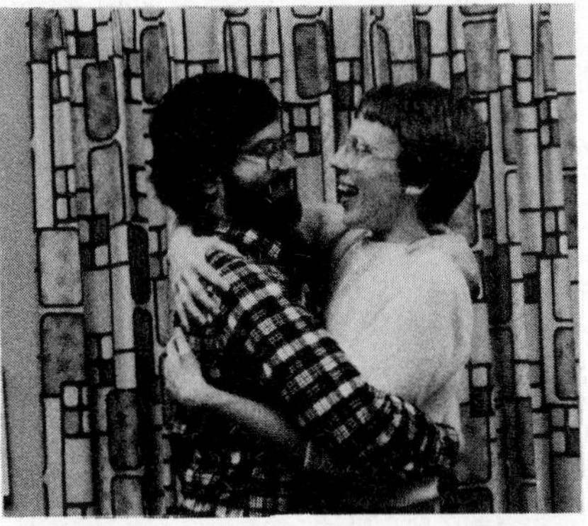

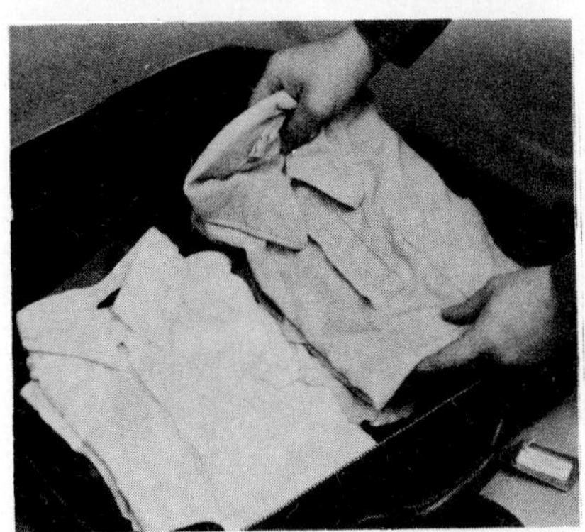

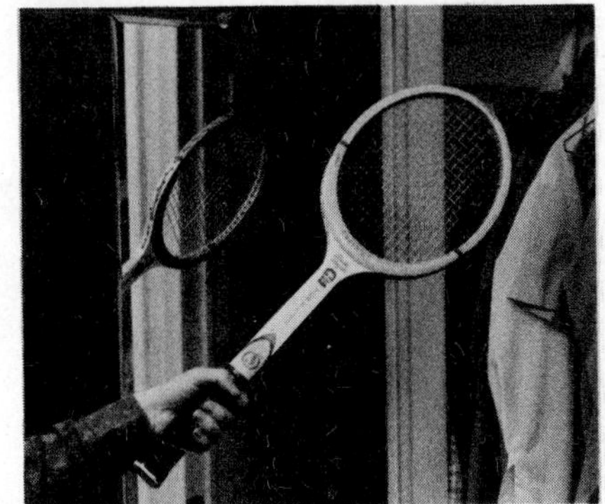

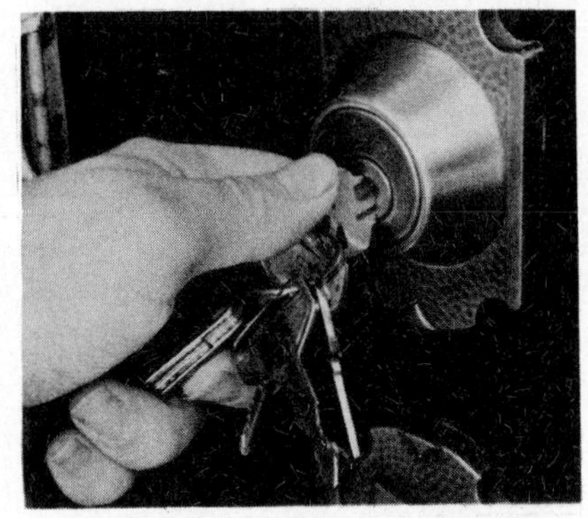

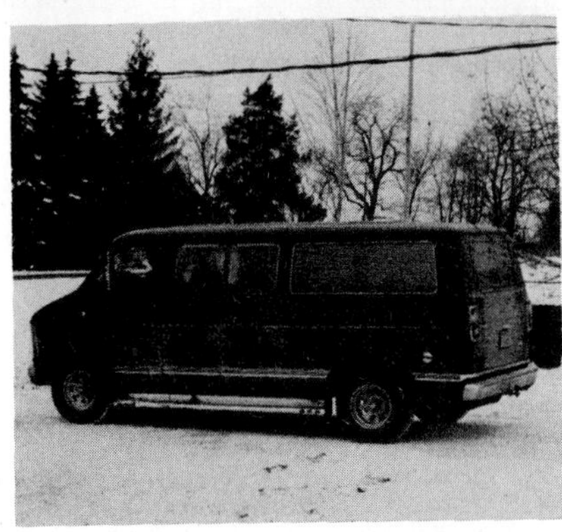

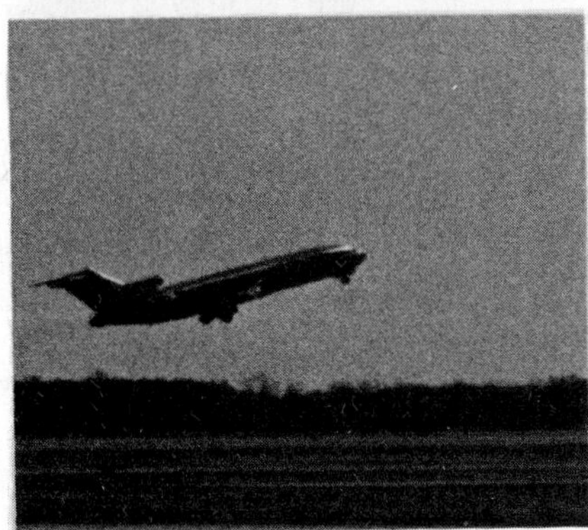

IN ONLY A FEW SECONDS OF TAPE, WE HAVE CONVEYED THE SENSE OF EXCITEMENT FELT BY THE TRAVELERS AND SHOWED THEM PREPARING FOR THEIR VACATION!

WITH AN APPROPRIATE PIECE OF MUSIC ON THE AUDIO TRACK, THIS COULD BE A VERY POWERFUL SEQUENCE.

EDITS THAT DON'T LOOK GOOD

A GOOD EDITOR STRIVES TO MAKE HIS WORK INVISIBLE!
AN EDIT THAT CALLS ATTENTION TO ITSELF IS PROBABLY A POOR ONE,
SINCE IT TAKES AWAY FROM THE SMOOTHNESS OF THE PRESENTATION.

JUMP CUTS

A JUMP CUT IS AN EDIT BETWEEN TWO
SHOTS OF NEARLY IDENTICAL COMPOSITION.

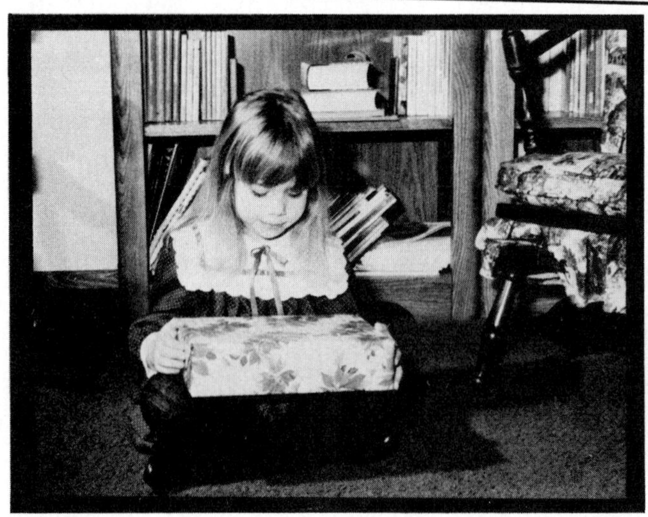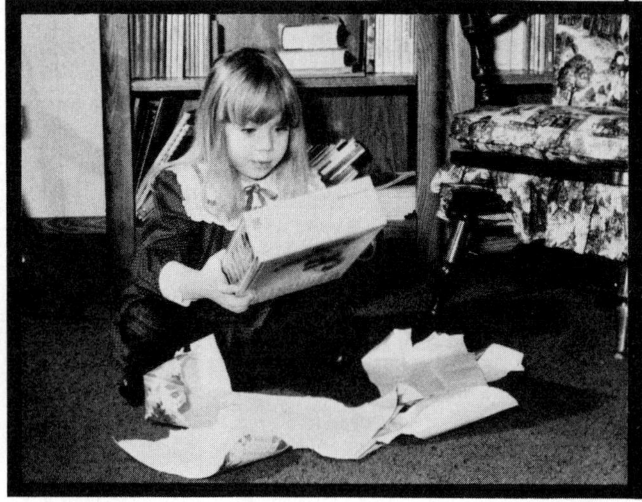

IF YOU MAKE AN EDIT FROM THE SHOT OF GILLIAN
STARTING TO OPEN HER PRESENT DIRECTLY TO THE
SHOT OF THE OPEN PACKAGE, THE RESULT LOOKS
STRANGELY DISCONTINUOUS. THE WRAPPER SEEMS TO
JUMP RIGHT OFF THE BOX! USE A CUTAWAY OR A
TRANSITION IN THIS SITUATION UNLESS A HUMOR-
OUS EFFECT IS WHAT YOU WANT!

CHANGE OF SCREEN DIRECTION.!!

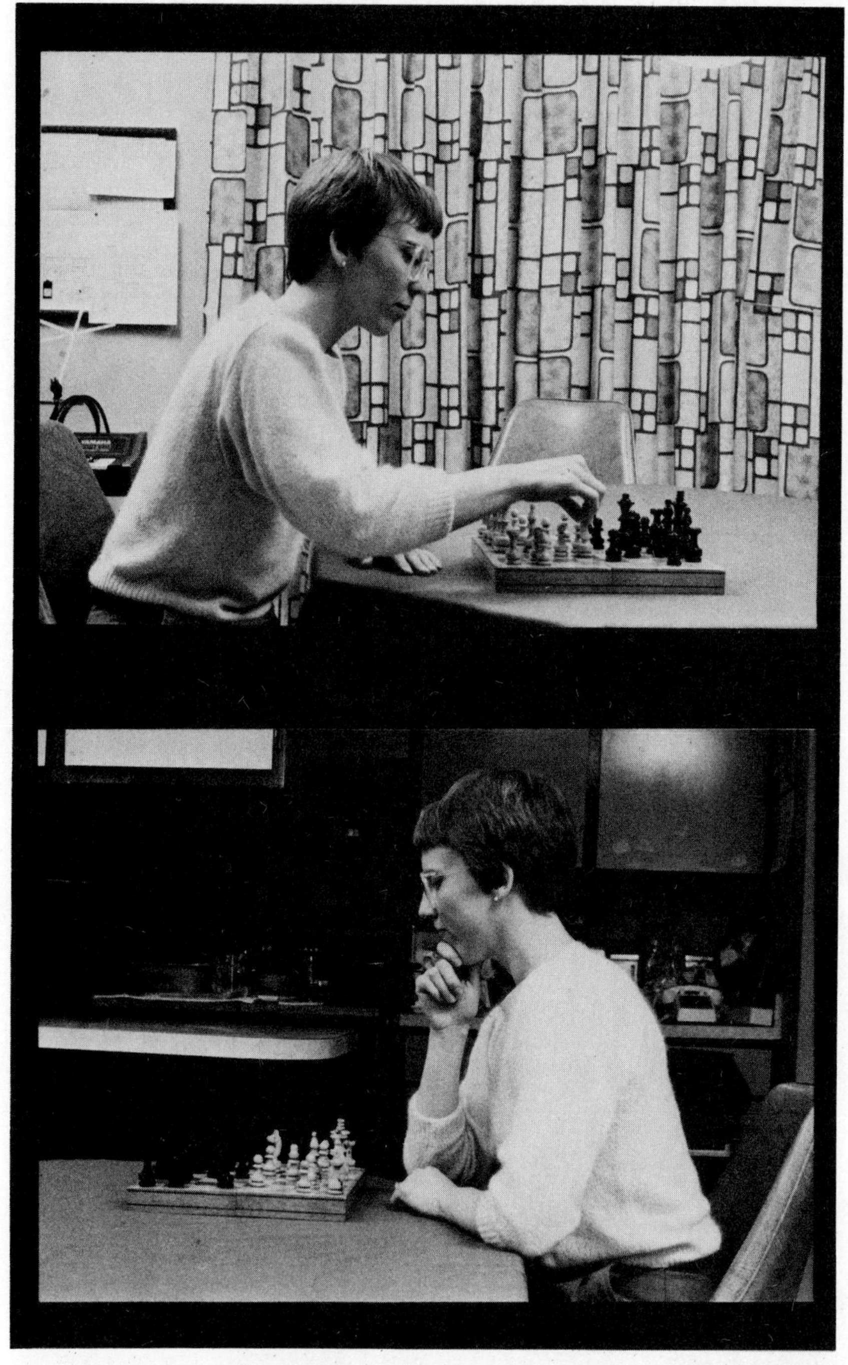

MEDIUM
PROFILE SHOT
OF **KAREN**
PLAYING CHESS

MEDIUM
PROFILE SHOT
OF KAREN
FROM EXACT
OPPOSITE
SIDE

TO THE VIEWER, IT LOOKS AS THOUGH KAREN IS PLAYING
CHESS WITH HERSELF. ACTUALLY, THE CAMERA WAS
MOVED TO THE OTHER SIDE OF THE CHESS BOARD FOR
THE SECOND SHOT. A CHANGE OF *SCREEN DIRECTION*
LIKE THIS IS CONFUSING TO THE VIEWER.!

A CHANGE OF ANGLE FROM SHOT TO SHOT
USUALLY LOOKS GOOD, BUT PEOPLE SHOULD
STILL BE FACING THE SAME *GENERAL* DIREC-
TION AS THEY WERE IN THE LAST SHOT!

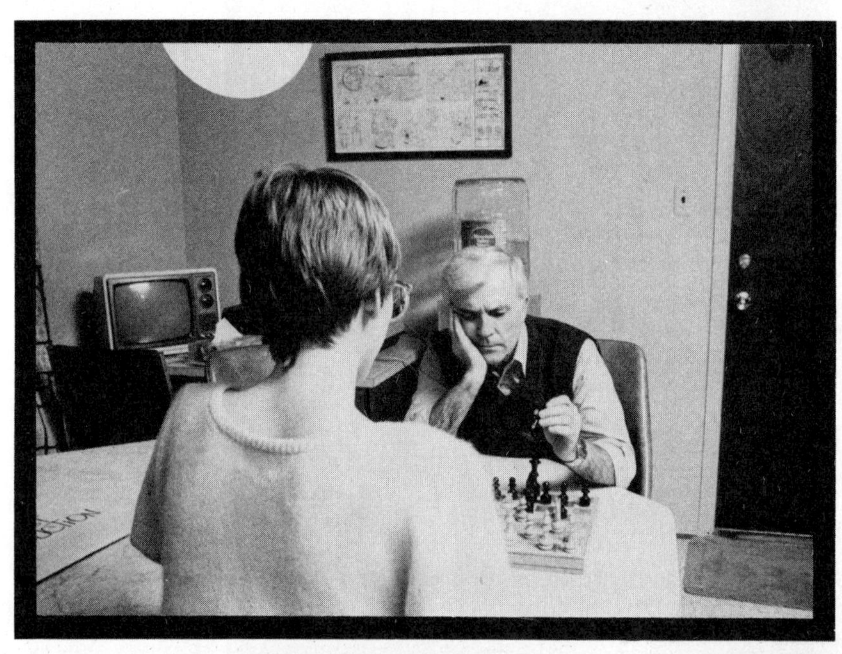

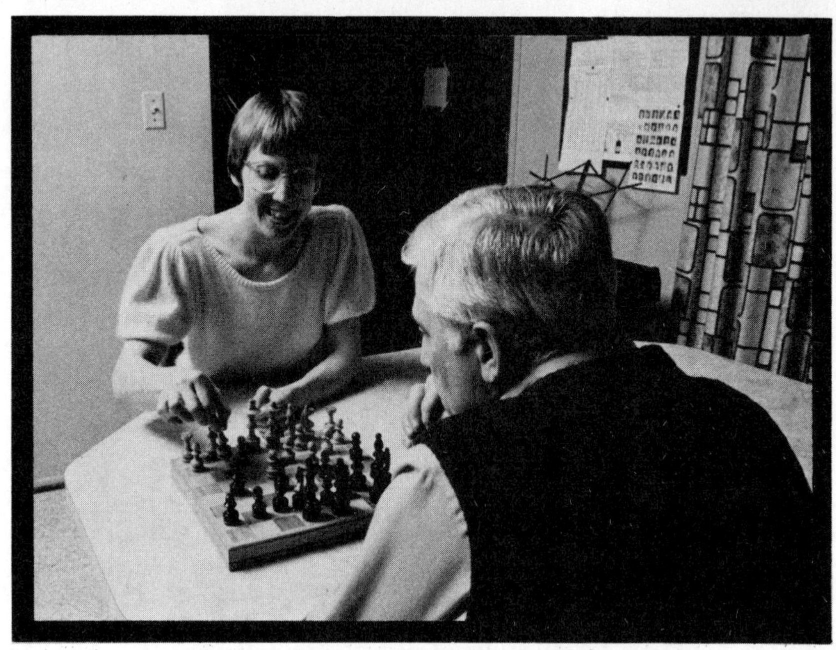

THESE TWO SHOTS
PRESERVE SCREEN DIRECTION

NON-MATCHED ACTION

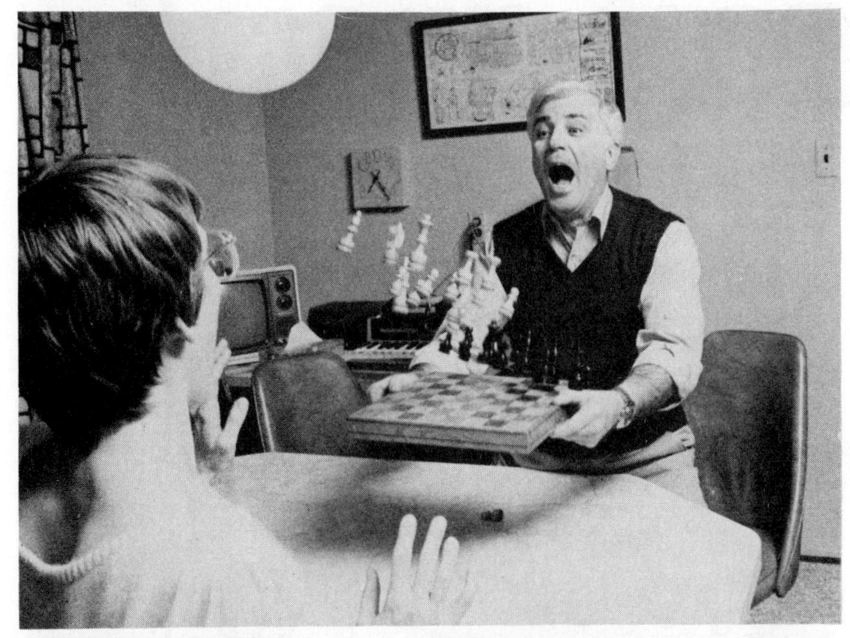

OVER SHOULDER SHOT
SORE LOSER
UPSETTING
CHESSBOARD.

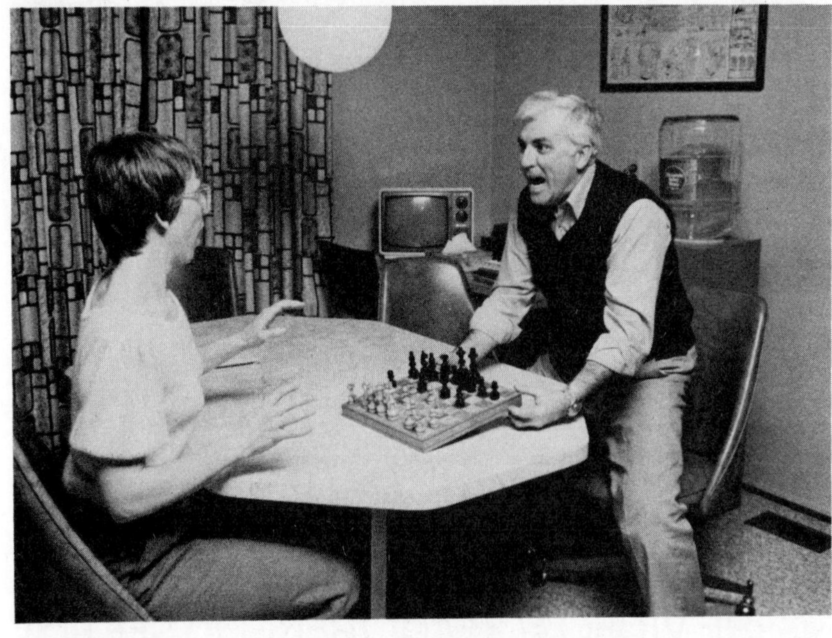

UNMATCHED
ACTION
WIDE SHOT
OF SAME.

IF THE EDIT BETWEEN THESE TWO SHOTS ISN'T MADE IN EXACTLY THE RIGHT PLACE, THE ACTION WILL APPEAR DISCONTINUOUS. UNLESS YOU HAVE ACCURATE EDITING EQUIPMENT, IT'S SAFER TO MAKE THE CUT *BEFORE* THE SORE LOSER UPSETS THE CHESSBOARD. IF IT'S IMPOSSIBLE TO ALWAYS MAKE ACTION MATCH, SOMETIMES A DRAMATIC CHANGE IN COMPOSITION (EDITING FROM A CLOSE-UP TO A WIDE SHOT, FOR INSTANCE) WILL HELP HIDE THE MISMATCH!

AUDIO POST PRODUCTION!

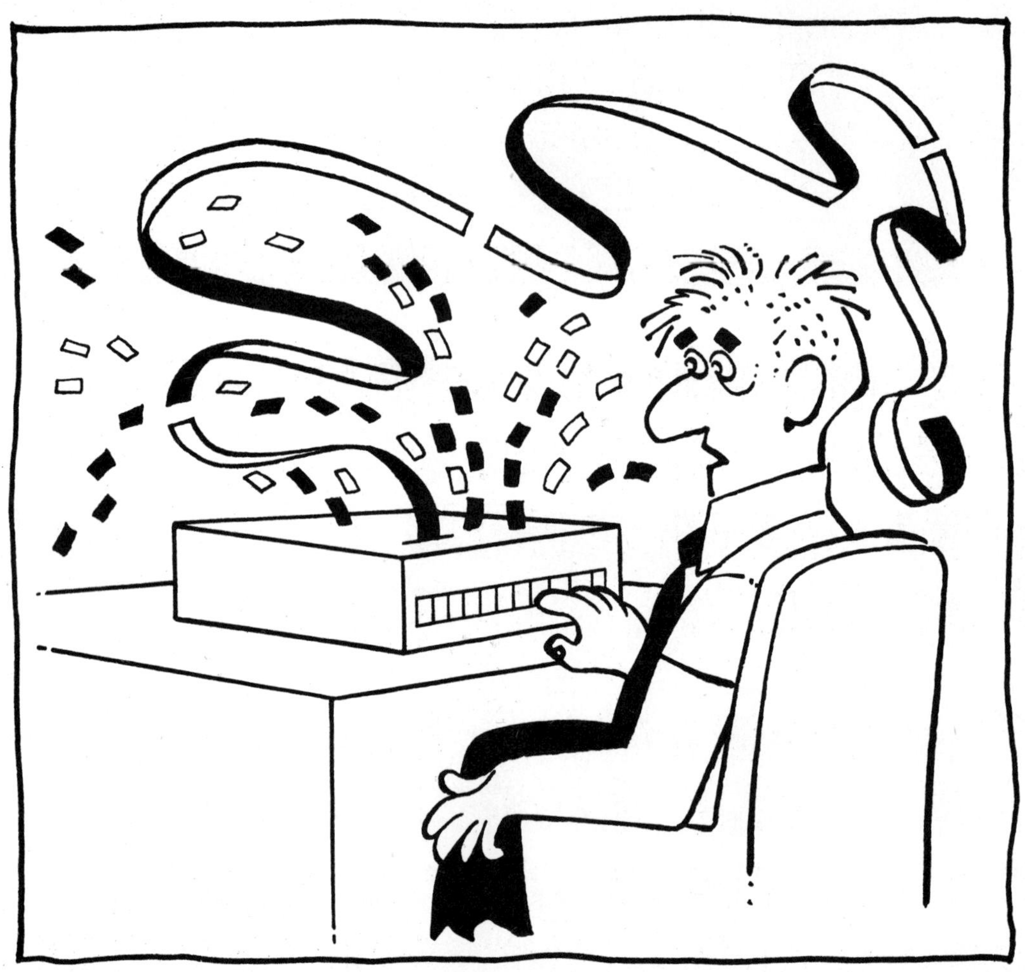

THE AUDIO DUB BUTTON - THE AUDIO DUB FEATURE FOUND ON MOST VCRs MAKES IT POSSIBLE TO RECORD NEW SOUND ONTO A TAPE WITHOUT DESTROYING THE VIDEO ALREADY THERE. TO SEE HOW THIS WORKS, PLUG A MICROPHONE INTO YOUR RECORDER AND TRY RECORDING SOME NARRATION TO GO WITH THAT VACATION TAPE YOU SHOT. IF YOU MAKE A MISTAKE, JUST BACK UP THE TAPE AND RECORD THAT PART AGAIN. YOU CAN EVEN **"POST-DUB"** YOUR OWN DRAMATIC PRODUCTIONS: HAVE YOUR ACTORS GATHER AROUND THE MICROPHONE AND TRY TO **"LIP-SYNC"** THEMSELVES ON THE SCREEN (THIS USUALLY LOOKS HILARIOUS AND SHOULD BE RESERVED FOR COMEDY PRODUCTIONS).

MUSIC AND SOUND EFFECTS

AUDIO DUB CAN ALSO BE USED TO ADD MUSIC OR APPRO-PRIATE SOUND EFFECTS TO YOUR TAPE. A LIVELY PIECE OF MUSIC OR A HUMOROUS SOUND EFFECT CAN DO WONDERS TO AN OTHERWISE DULL PRODUCTION. HERE IS A WAY TO **CUE** YOUR RECORD TURNTABLE SO THAT THE MUSIC OR SOUND EFFECT STARTS EXACTLY WHEN YOU NEED IT (THE TECHNIQUE IS CALLED **SLIPCUEING**):

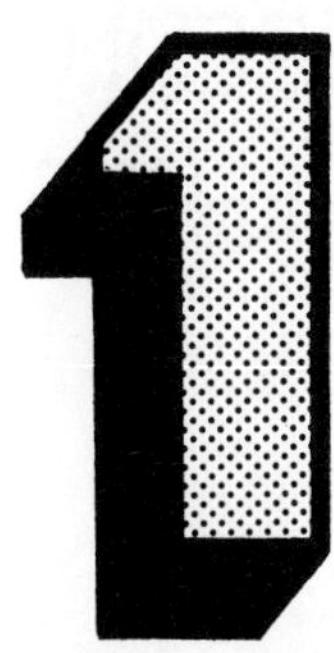

1 PLACE A PIECE OF FELT ON THE TURNTABLE AND PUT THE RECORD ON TOP OF THE FELT. THE FELT WILL LET THE RECORD **SLIP** AGAINST THE TURNTABLE!

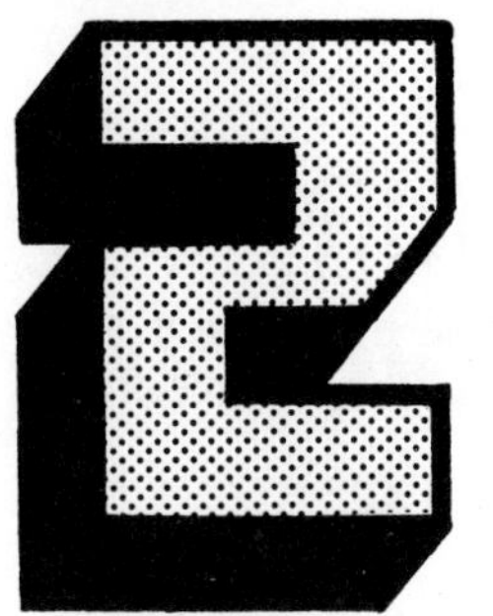

2 PUT THE NEEDLE ON THE RECORD AND SPIN THE RECORD BY HAND TO FIND THE START OF YOUR MUSIC OR **SFX** (THE RECORD SHOULD SPIN EASILY AGAINST THE FELT). WHEN YOU FIND THE SPOT, CAREFULLY BACK UP THE RECORD UNTIL YOU'RE A COUPLE OF INCHES IN FRONT OF WHERE THE SOUND STARTS!

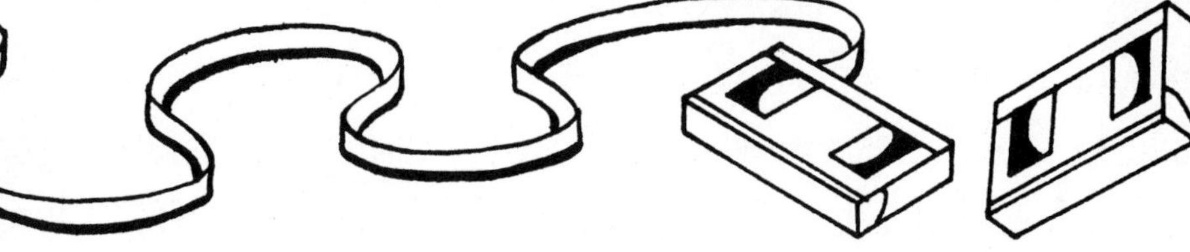

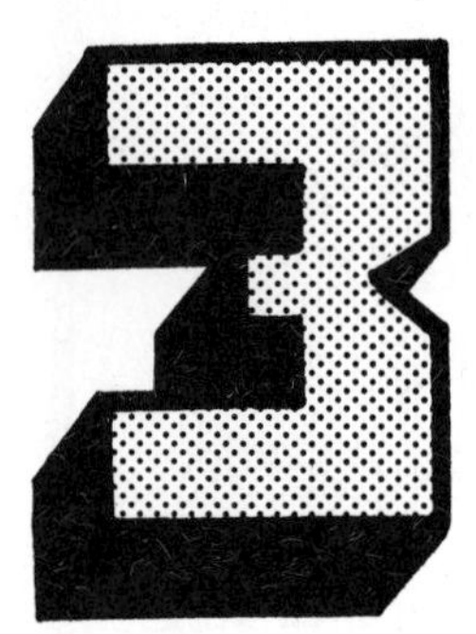

3 BACK UP YOUR VIDEOTAPE (USING THE RE-VERSE SEARCH CONTROL) UNTIL YOU'RE A FEW SECONDS BEFORE THE PLACE WHERE YOU WANT THE SOUND TO START, AND PAUSE IT THERE.

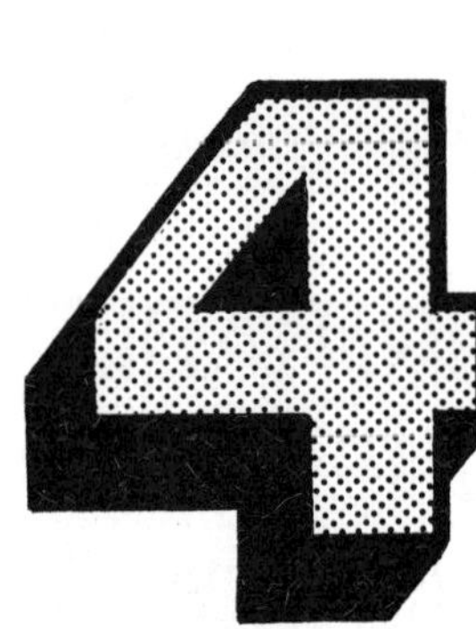

4 HERE'S THE TRICKY PART. PUT YOUR FINGER ON THE RECORD SO THAT IT WON'T MOVE. START THE TURNTABLE. IT SHOULD SPIN UNDERNEATH THE RECORD (IF THE NEEDLE JUMPS AROUND A LOT, SET IT FOR A HIGHER TRACKING FORCE).
DON'T LET GO OF THE RECORD YET!

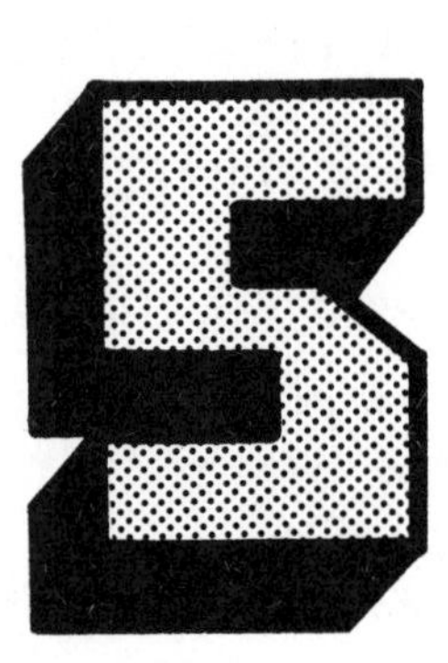

5 UNPAUSE THE RECORDER. WATCH THE SCREEN. WHEN IT'S TIME FOR YOUR SOUND, HIT THE **PLAY** AND **AUDIO DUB** BUTTONS, AND THEN RELEASE THE RECORD. IF YOU PRACTICE THIS A FEW TIMES, YOU'LL BE ABLE TO RECORD YOUR SOUNDS RIGHT ON CUE!

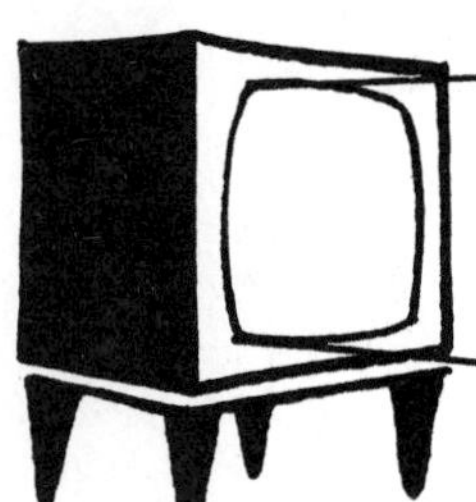

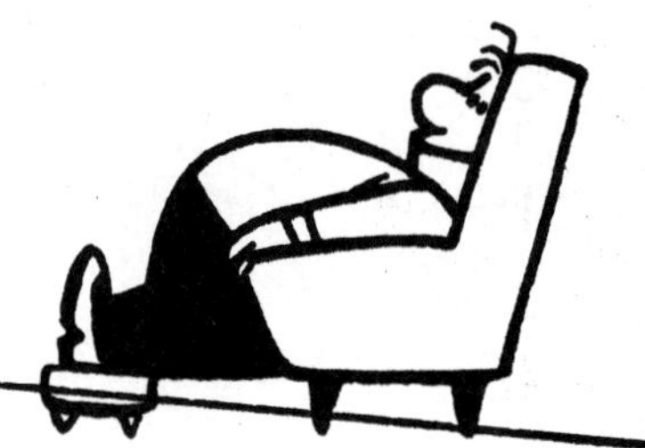

MULTIPLE TRACKS

HOW ABOUT MUSIC AND NARRATION AT THE SAME TIME? WELL, IF YOU HAVE A STEREO VCR, YOU COULD CONNECT THE MIKE TO THE LEFT CHANNEL AND YOUR TURNTABLE TO THE RIGHT. IF YOU'VE ONLY GOT ONE AUDIO CHANNEL, IT'S A BIT HARDER.

THE EASIEST WAY IS TO PUT THE SPEAKER FROM YOUR STEREO NEAR YOUR MIKE. AS YOU NARRATE, YOU WOULD OPERATE THE VOLUME CONTROL ON THE STEREO TO TURN THE MUSIC UP OR DOWN. THE QUALITY OF THE MUSIC WILL BE BETTER, HOWEVER, IF YOU CAN CONNECT IT DIRECTLY TO YOUR MACHINE. A MIXER COULD PERFORM THIS FUNCTION.

AN UNFORTUNATE DRAWBACK TO AUDIO DUB IS THAT ANYTHING ALREADY ON THE AUDIO TRACK WILL BE ERASED AND REPLACED WITH YOUR NEW AUDIO. WHAT IF YOU WANT TO MIX MUSIC WITH THE SOUND ALREADY ON THE TAPE? THE ONLY WAY TO DO THIS IS WITH A **SOUND-ON-SOUND** MIX, FOR WHICH YOU'LL NEED TWO VCRs AND A MIXER. AS YOU MAKE A COPY OF YOUR TAPE FROM ONE MACHINE TO THE OTHER, THE NEW MUSIC IS MIXED IN WITH THE ORIGINAL SOUND USING THE MIXER!

THE NEW TAPE (THE COPY) HAS THE MIXED AUDIO!

SEE THE CHAPTER ON "CONNECTING ANYTHING TO ANYTHING" FOR MIXER CONNECTIONS.

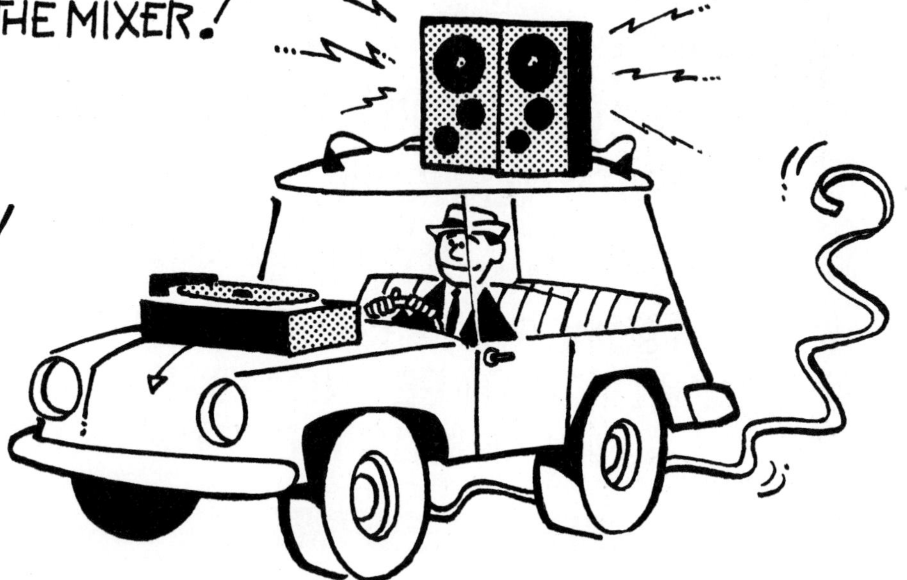

FUN WITH POST PRODUCTION

POST DUB YOUR OWN MOVIE

HAVE YOU EVER WATCHED A FOREIGN MOVIE THAT'S BEEN DUBBED REALLY BADLY? THE SIGHT OF ACTORS WHO DON'T MATCH THE VOICES COMING OUT OF THEIR MOUTHS CAN BE HILARIOUS.

WITH AN ACTIVE SENSE OF HUMOR, YOU CAN EXPLOIT THIS CONCEPT (AS WOODY ALLEN ONCE DID IN THE FILM "WHAT'S UP TIGER LILY"). RECORD AN OLD MOVIE (THE MORE ACTION, THE BETTER. WESTERNS OR SCIENCE-FICTION SERIALS ARE GOOD.) NOW, WITH A MIKE PLUGGED INTO YOUR VCR, **ERASE** THE ORIGINAL SOUND TRACK (WITH THE **AUDIO DUB** CONTROL) AND CREATE YOUR OWN! GET A COUPLE OF FRIENDS IN FRONT OF THE SET AND DECIDE WHO WILL PLAY EACH CHARACTER.

WHENEVER YOUR CHARACTER SPEAKS ON SCREEN, BE READY TO DO HIS VOICE. MAKE UP YOUR OWN DIALOGUE...THE MORE RIDICULOUS THE BETTER!

WITH SOME REHEARSAL (REMEMBER, YOU CAN ALWAYS BACK UP THE TAPE AND DO IT AGAIN) YOU'LL HAVE A HILARIOUS PIECE OF ENTERTAINMENT!

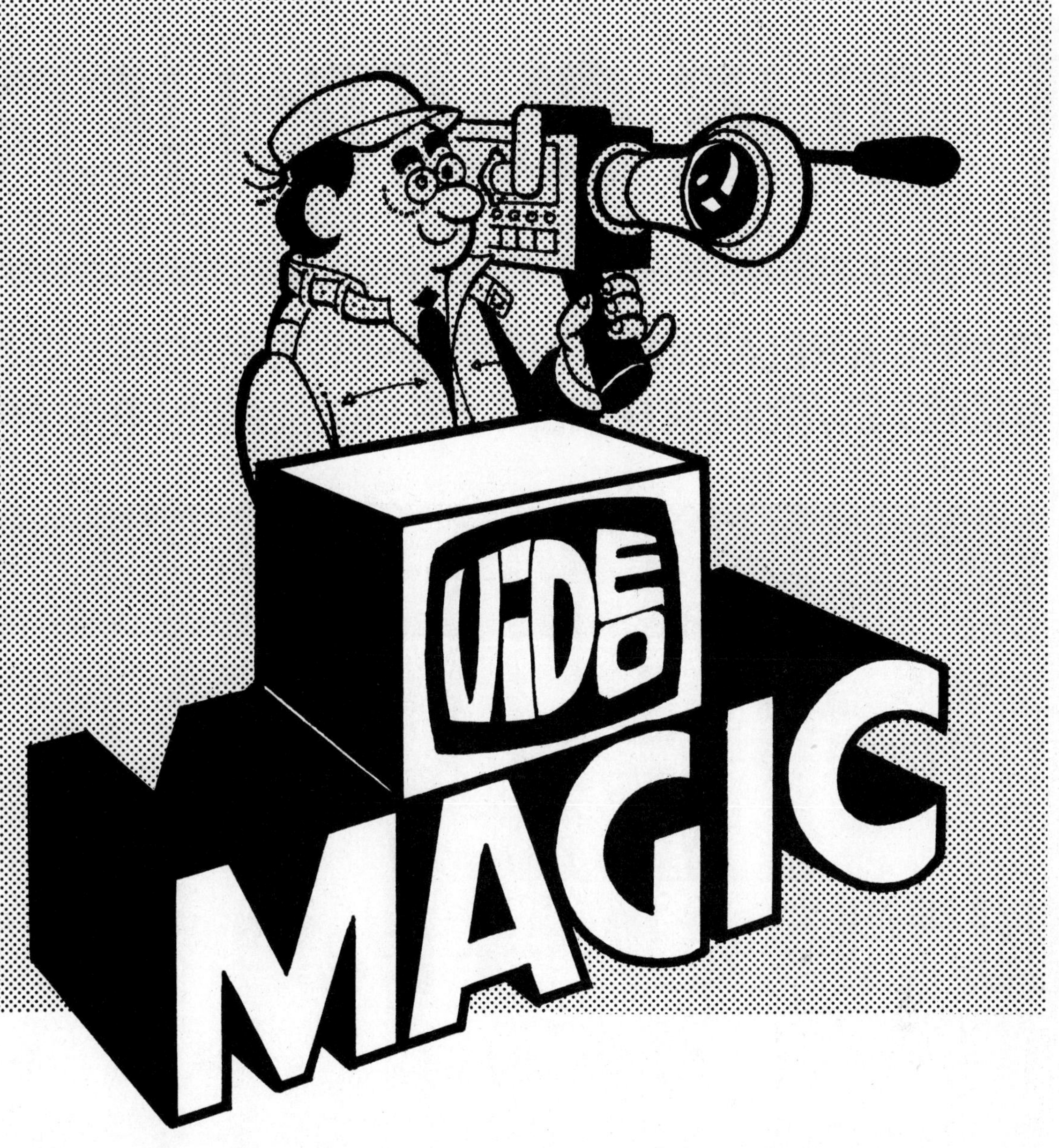

A SPECIAL EFFECT IS A PROFESSIONAL TOUCH THAT WILL MAKE A GENUINE IMPRESSION ON THE VIEWERS OF YOUR PRODUCTION. WHILE IT IS QUITE IMPOSSIBLE TO COMPETE WITH MULTIMILLION DOLLAR HOLLYWOOD OPTICS, THERE ARE NONETHELESS DOZENS OF FEATS OF VIDEO MAGIC AWAITING THOSE BOLD ENOUGH TO *EXPERIMENT!*

THE SWITCHER

THIS IS A RELATIVELY INEXPENSIVE PROFESSIONAL VIDEO SWITCHER (ONLY FIVE FIGURES IN THE PRICE).

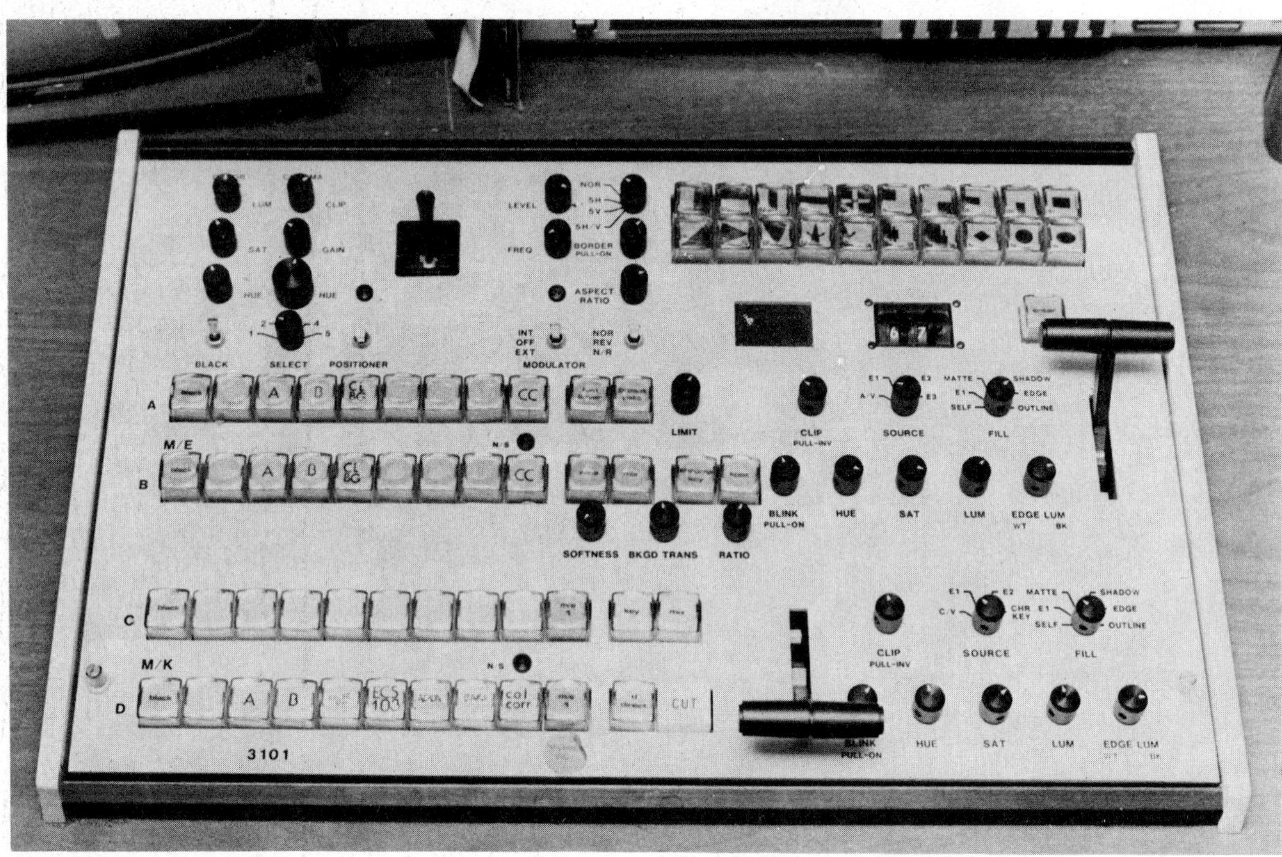

DISSOLVES, SPLIT SCREENS, KEYS (WHERE LETTERING APPEARS OVER THE PICTURE), AND OTHER SPECIAL EFFECTS COMMONLY SEEN IN TV PRODUCTIONS ARE CREATED IN ONE OF THESE! THERE ARE INEXPENSIVE HOME VIDEO SWITCHERS ON THE MARKET THAT CAN DO SOME OF THE THINGS A PROFESSIONAL SWITCHER CAN DO....AND THERE ARE SOME SPECIAL EFFECTS THAT REQUIRE *NO* SWITCHER TO DO. *HERE ARE SOME IDEAS:*

MORE ABOUT TRANSITIONS

A TRANSITION (SEE THE LAST CHAPTER) IS A WAY TO ILLUSTRATE A CHANGE OF TIME OR PLACE TO YOUR AUDIENCE. THERE ARE QUITE A FEW DIFFERENT TRANSITIONS TO CHOOSE FROM... IN FACT, YOU CAN PROBABLY INVENT SOME OF YOUR OWN! *HERE ARE SOME IDEAS:*

A SWISH PAN GIVES THE ILLUSION OF RAPIDLY PANNING THE CAMERA FROM ONE SCENE TO THE NEXT ONE!

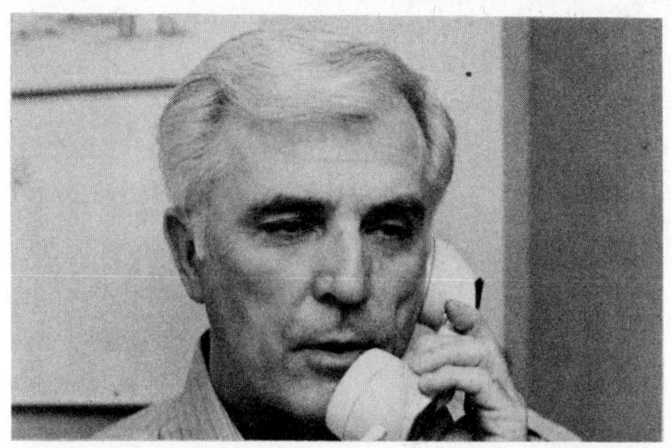

AT THE END OF YOUR FIRST SCENE, QUICKLY PAN THE CAMERA TO THE RIGHT OR LEFT, THEN STOP THE RECORDER WHILE THE CAMERA IS STILL MOVING!

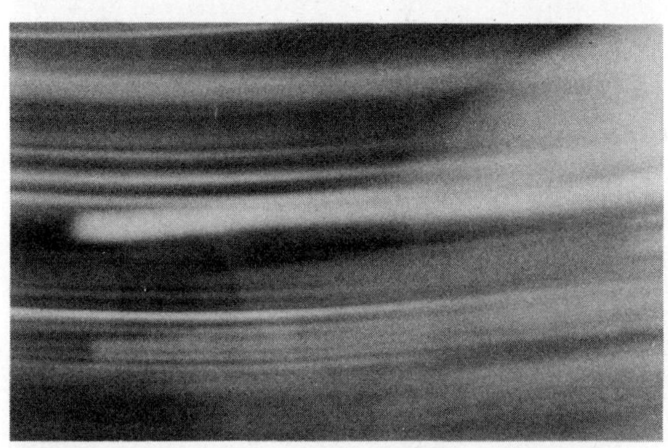

WHEN YOU START YOUR NEXT SCENE, PAN THE CAMERA WHEN YOU START THE RECORDER-AND STOP THE PAN ON YOUR SECOND SCENE.

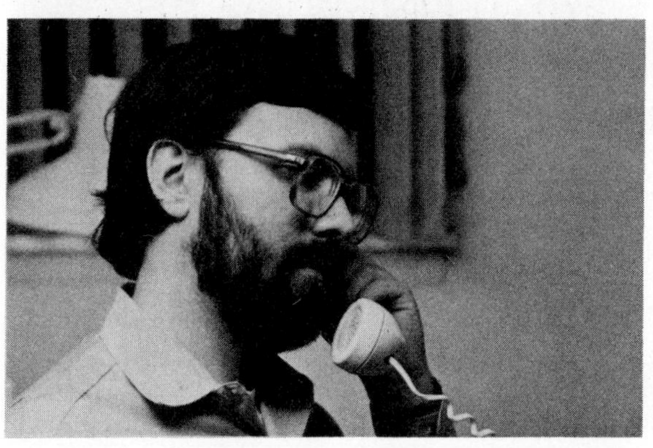

THE TWO PANS WILL LOOK LIKE ONE CONTINUOUS PAN FROM ONE PLACE TO ANOTHER! USE A LONG (TELEPHOTO) SETTING ON YOUR ZOOM LENS!

FADE TO/FROM BLACK

IF YOUR CAMERA HAS A "FADE" BUTTON, YOU CAN DO A "BLACK OUT" TO END YOUR FIRST SCENE AND START THE NEXT.!

YOU CAN ALSO DO A **WHITE OUT** BY FINDING A WHITE WALL AND ZOOMING INTO IT AT THE END OF SCENE 1...THEN ZOOMING OUT OF A SIMILAR WHITE WALL AT YOUR NEXT LOCATION. HOW ABOUT A **RED OUT?** HAVE YOUR SUBJECT WEAR A RED SHIRT... AND WALK INTO THE CAMERA AT THE END OF SCENE 1 (SO THAT NOTHING BUT RED FILLS THE SCREEN). YOUR SUBJECT STARTS IN THE SAME POSITION TO BEGIN SCENE 2, AND WALKS AWAY FROM THE LENS.

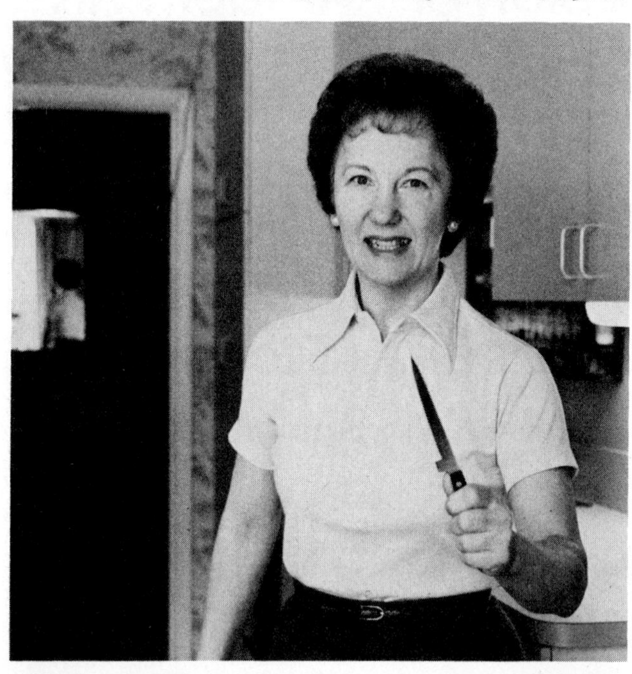

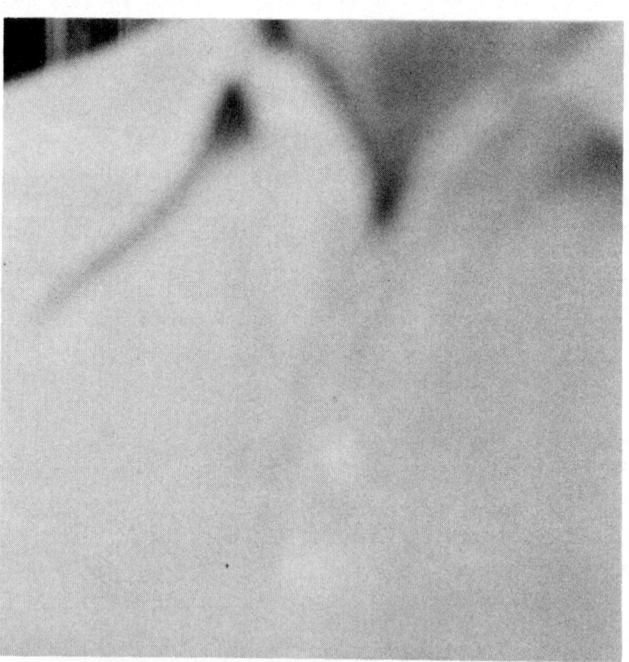

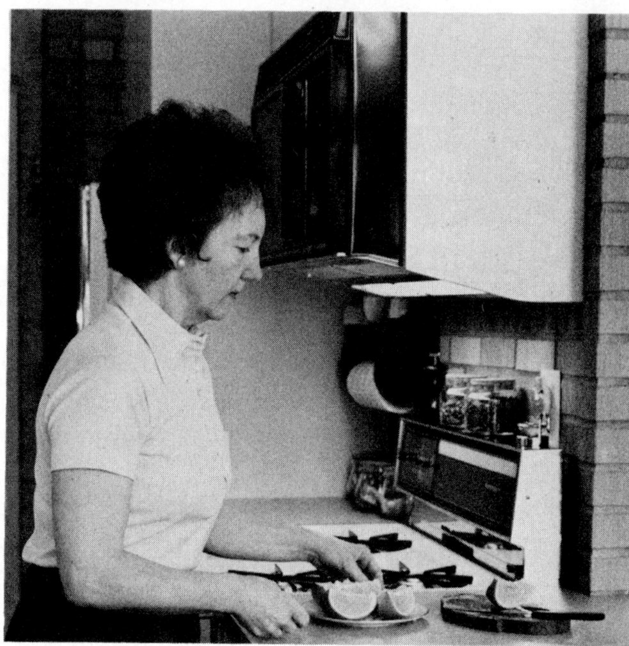

WIPES

A *SWITCHER* IS USUALLY USED TO PERFORM A *WIPE*, WHERE BLACK (OR ANOTHER SCENE) IS 'PUSHED ON TOP' OF YOUR VIDEO. IF YOU DON'T HAVE A *SWITCHER*, TRY PUSHING A BLACK CARD IN FRONT OF YOUR LENS. HAVE IT ABOUT A FOOT AWAY FROM THE LENS, & EXPERIMENT WITH DIFFERENT ZOOM LENS SETTINGS *FOR THE BEST RESULTS!*

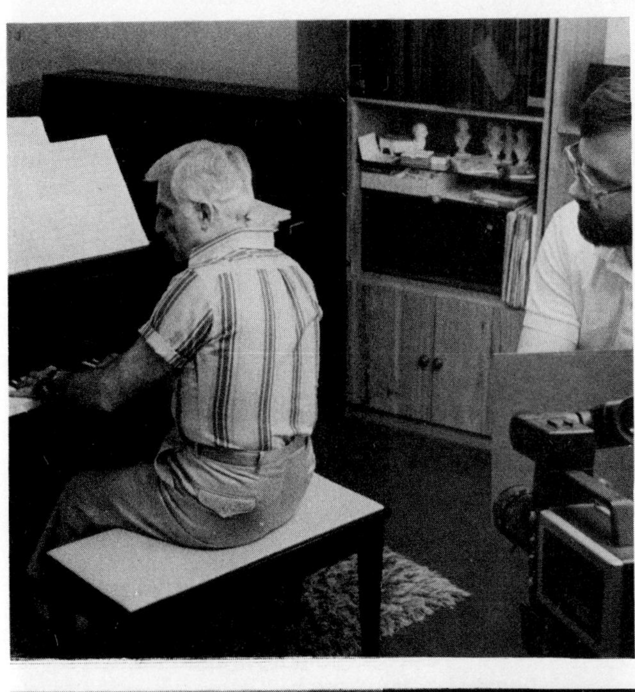
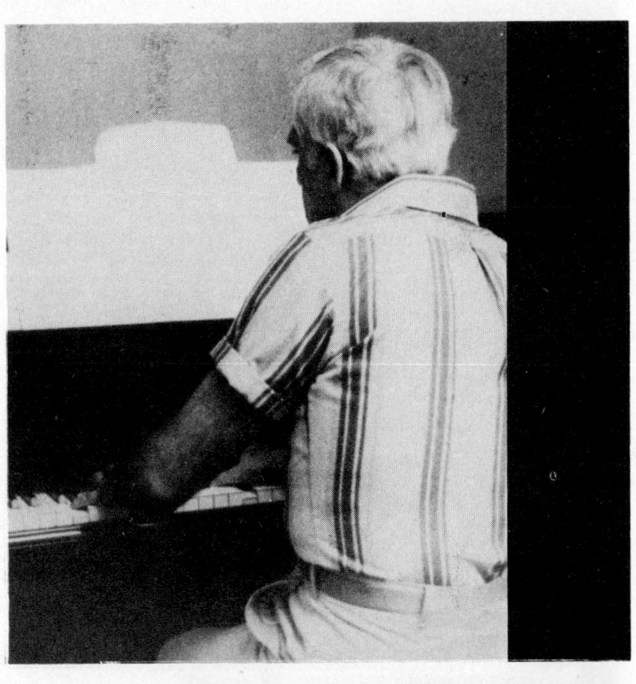
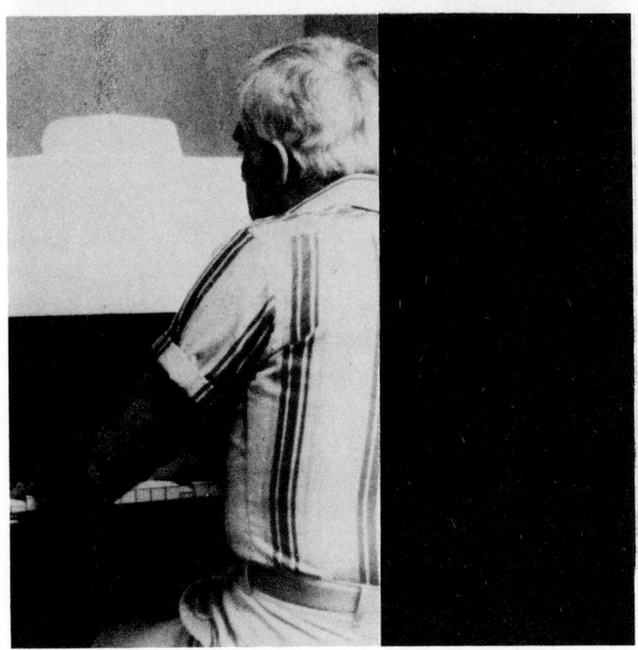

FOCUS OUT

AT THE END OF SCENE 1, TURN THE **FOCUS** RING SO THAT THE PICTURE GOES OUT OF FOCUS. START SCENE 2 WITH THE CAMERA OUT OF FOCUS, AND TURN THE FOCUS RING TO BRING YOUR SUBJECT INTO FOCUS. YOU WILL PROBABLY NOT BE ABLE TO DE-FOCUS ENOUGH UNLESS YOUR ZOOM LENS IS SET TO **TELEPHOTO**!

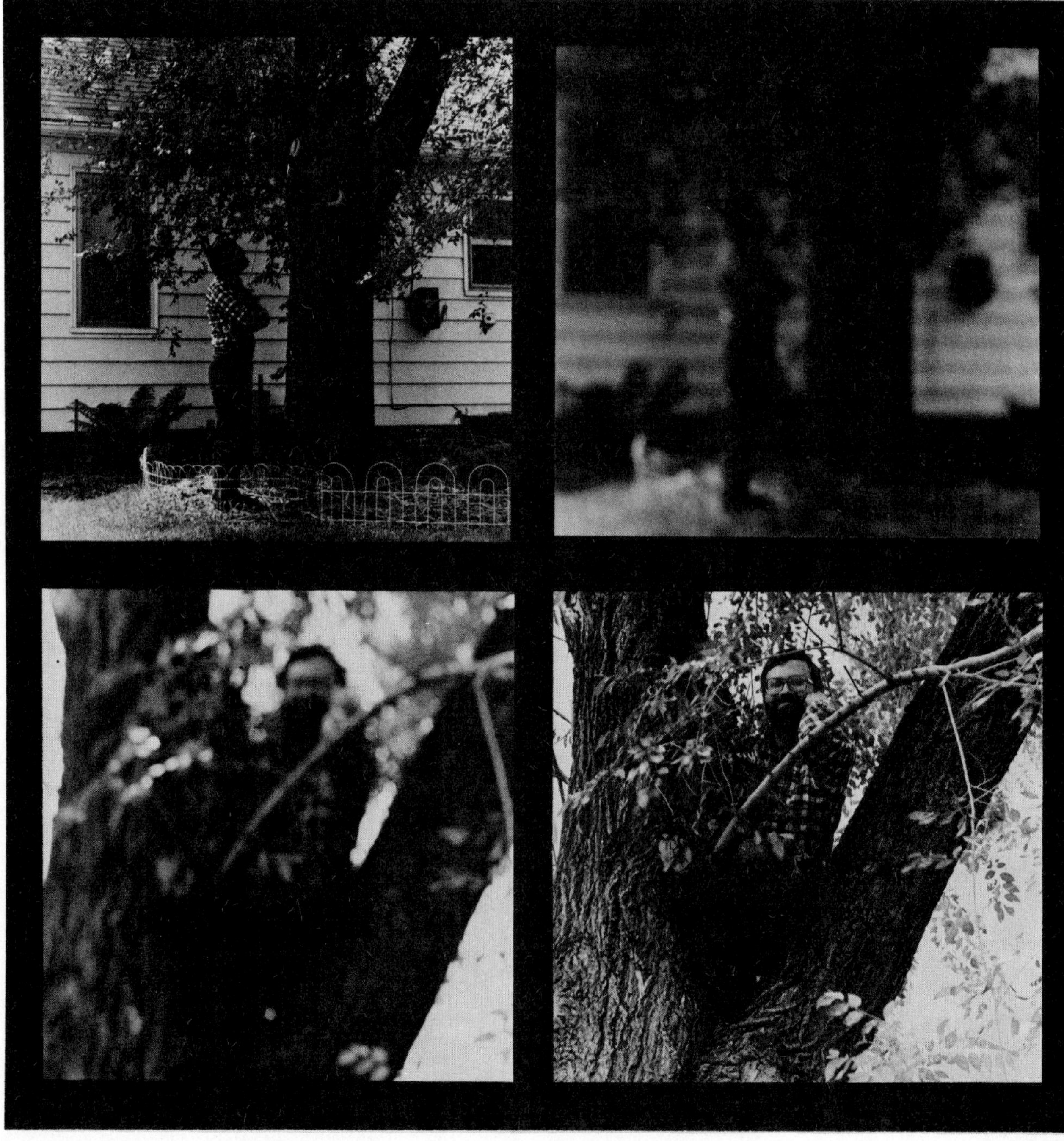

DISAPPEARANCES....

VIDEOTAPE YOUR NEIGHBOR IN HIS FAVORITE CHAIR. THEN WITHOUT MOVING THE CAMERA (VERY IMPORTANT), *STOP* RECORDING, HAVE THE NEIGHBOR LEAVE THE CHAIR, THEN *START* RECORDING AGAIN!

WHEN THE TAPE IS PLAYED, YOU WILL SEE YOUR SUBJECT *DISAPPEAR* FROM THE CHAIR! USE A GOOD STEADY TRIPOD FOR THIS KIND OF SHOT!

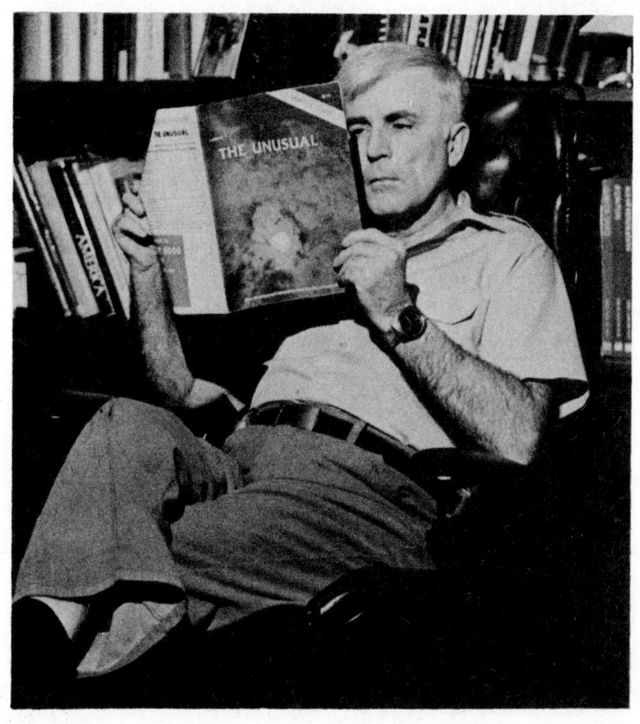

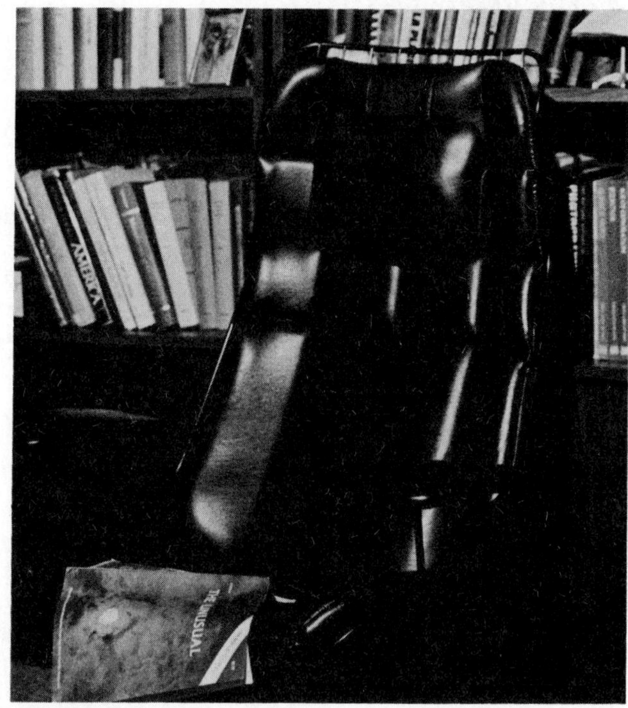

ANIMATION

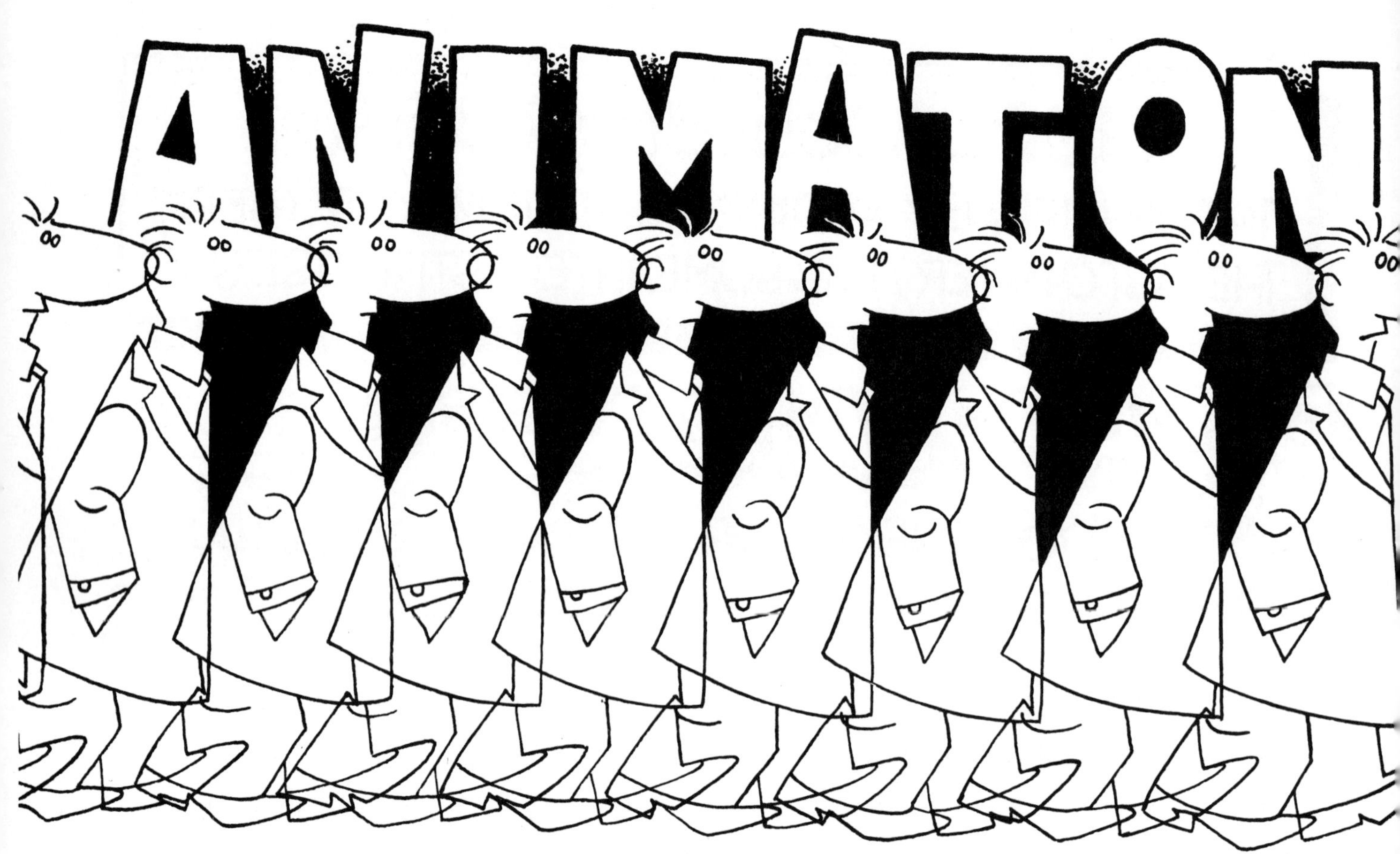

To understand **ANIMATION,** it's important to realize that the video camera actually creates **STILL** pictures...but it makes **THOUSANDS** of them (60 every second), and your recorder plays them back so fast that the **ILLUSION** of motion is created. If you can present your camera with a series of still pictures and record them one at a time, it's possible to create an illusion of motion with objects that can't move!

In reality, this is a very difficult thing to do. You cannot tell your recorder to record only one frame at a time, as you could with a motion picture camera. It might be possible to **EDIT** individual frames together, if you have an accurate edit controller. With only a basic camera and recorder, however, you can still get **ROUGH** looking animation.

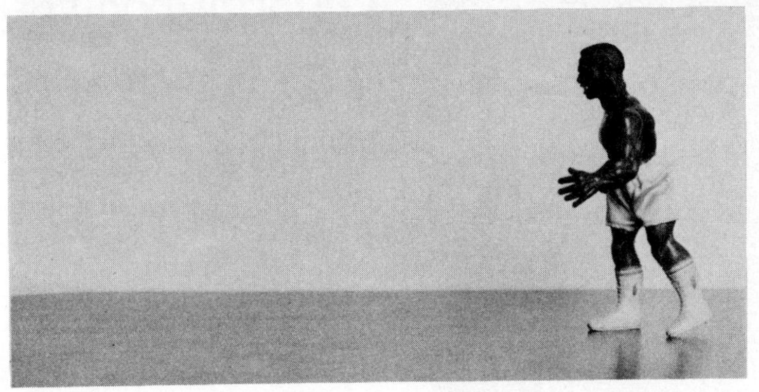

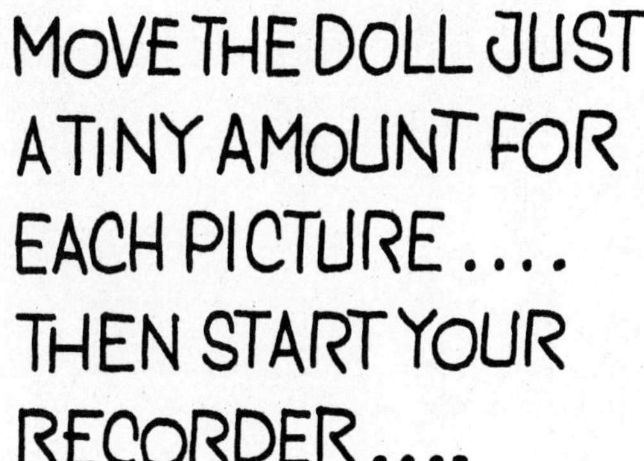

MOVE THE DOLL JUST A TINY AMOUNT FOR EACH PICTURE.... THEN START YOUR RECORDER....

AND ALMOST IMME- DIATELY STOP IT. (YOU'LL WANT TO RECORD JUST A VERY TINY BIT OF EACH PICTURE).

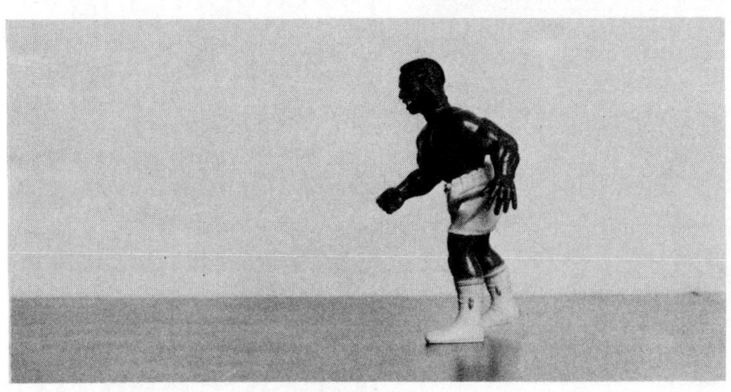

KEEP DOING THIS UNTIL THE DOLL HAS COVERED THE DISTANCE YOU WANT IT TO MOVE!

MAKE SURE THE CAMERA IS ON A GOOD STEADY TRIPOD!

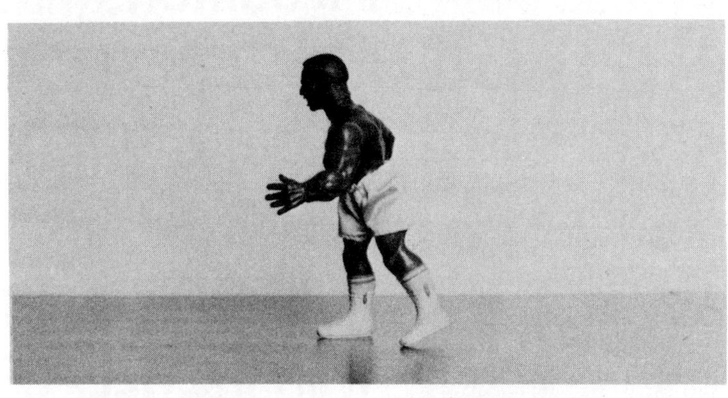

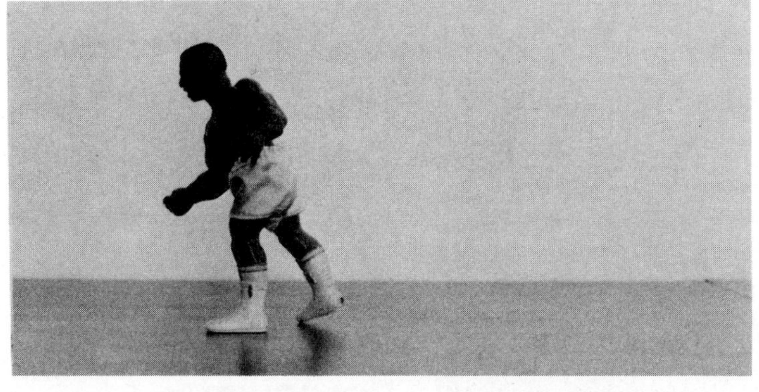

SUPERIMPOSITIONS

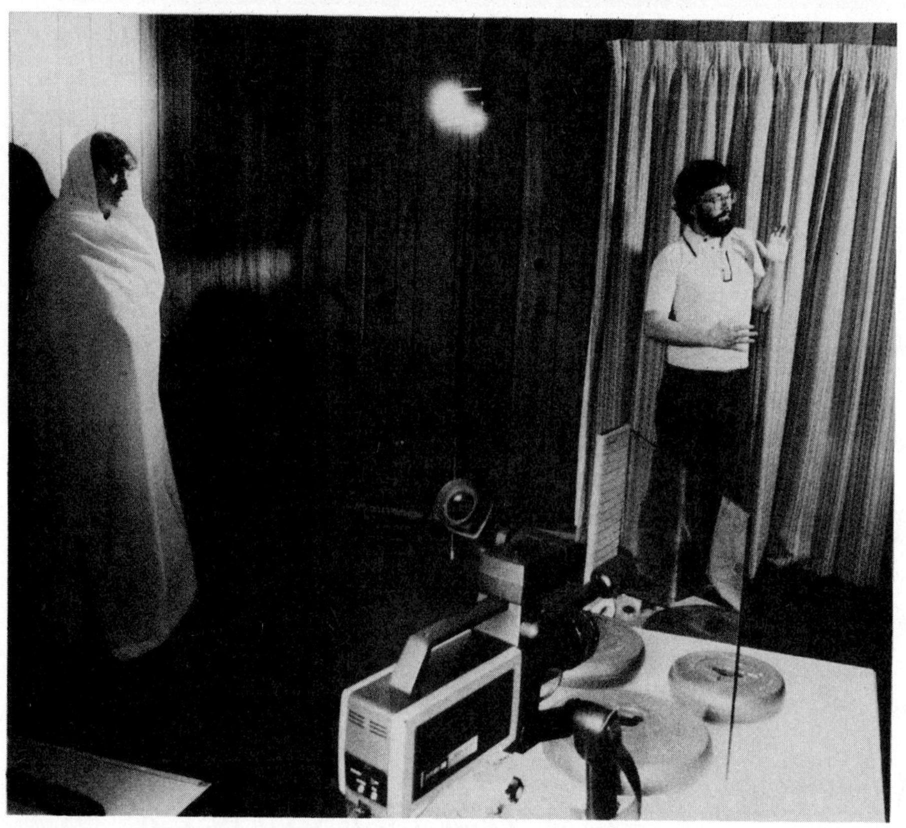

A SUPERIMPOSITION (THE EQUIVALENT OF A DOUBLE EXPOSURE ON FILM) IS WHERE ONE IMAGE IS SUPERIMPOSED ON, OR MIXED WITH ANOTHER!

SINCE VIDEOTAPE CAN'T BE "DOUBLE EXPOSED", SUPERIMPOSITIONS (AND RELATED EFFECTS, LIKE DISSOLVES AND KEYS) ARE TYPICALLY CREATED WITH THE HELP OF A SWITCHER!

HERE'S AN EASY (IF SOMEWHAT LIMITED) WAY TO PERFORM A SUPERIMPOSITION WITHOUT ANY SPECIAL EQUIPMENT!

A PIECE OF GLASS AT A 45 DEGREE ANGLE TO THE LENS WILL COMBINE THE IMAGE IN FRONT OF THE CAMERA WITH THE IMAGE REFLECTED FROM THE GLASS!

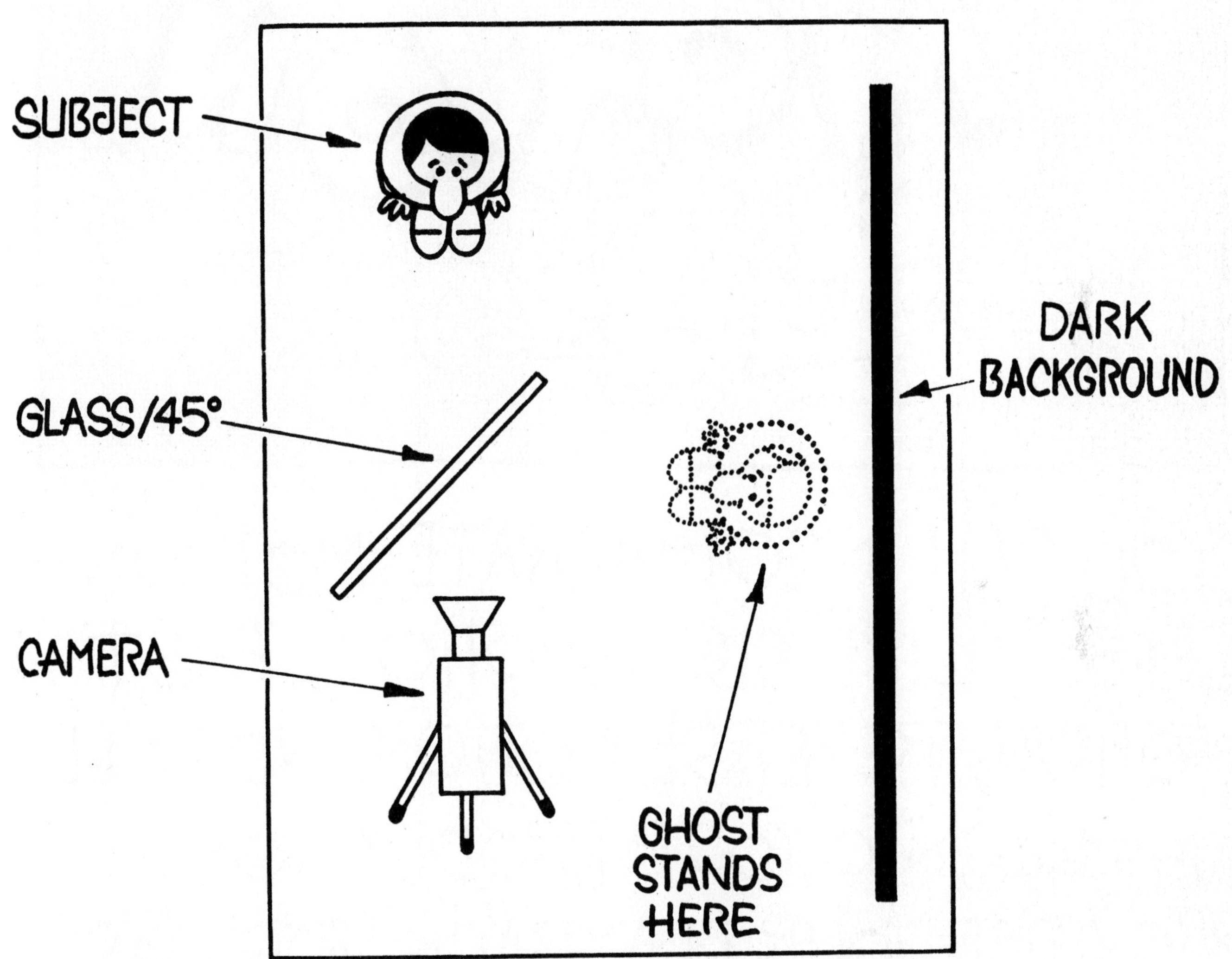

THE IMAGE TO BE REFLECTED SHOULD BE BRIGHTLY LIT, AND PLACED AGAINST A DARK BACKGROUND. IF YOU MAKE SOME TITLES (BRIGHT LETTERS ON A PIECE OF BLACK CARDBOARD) YOU CAN SUPERIMPOSE THEM ONTO WHATEVER THE CAMERA IS POINTED AT. BY TURNING THE LIGHT ON AND OFF, THE TITLE CAN "FADE IN" OR "FADE OUT." SINCE THE REFLECTION IS A MIRROR IMAGE, HOWEVER, MAKE SURE YOU PRINT *BACKWARDS!*

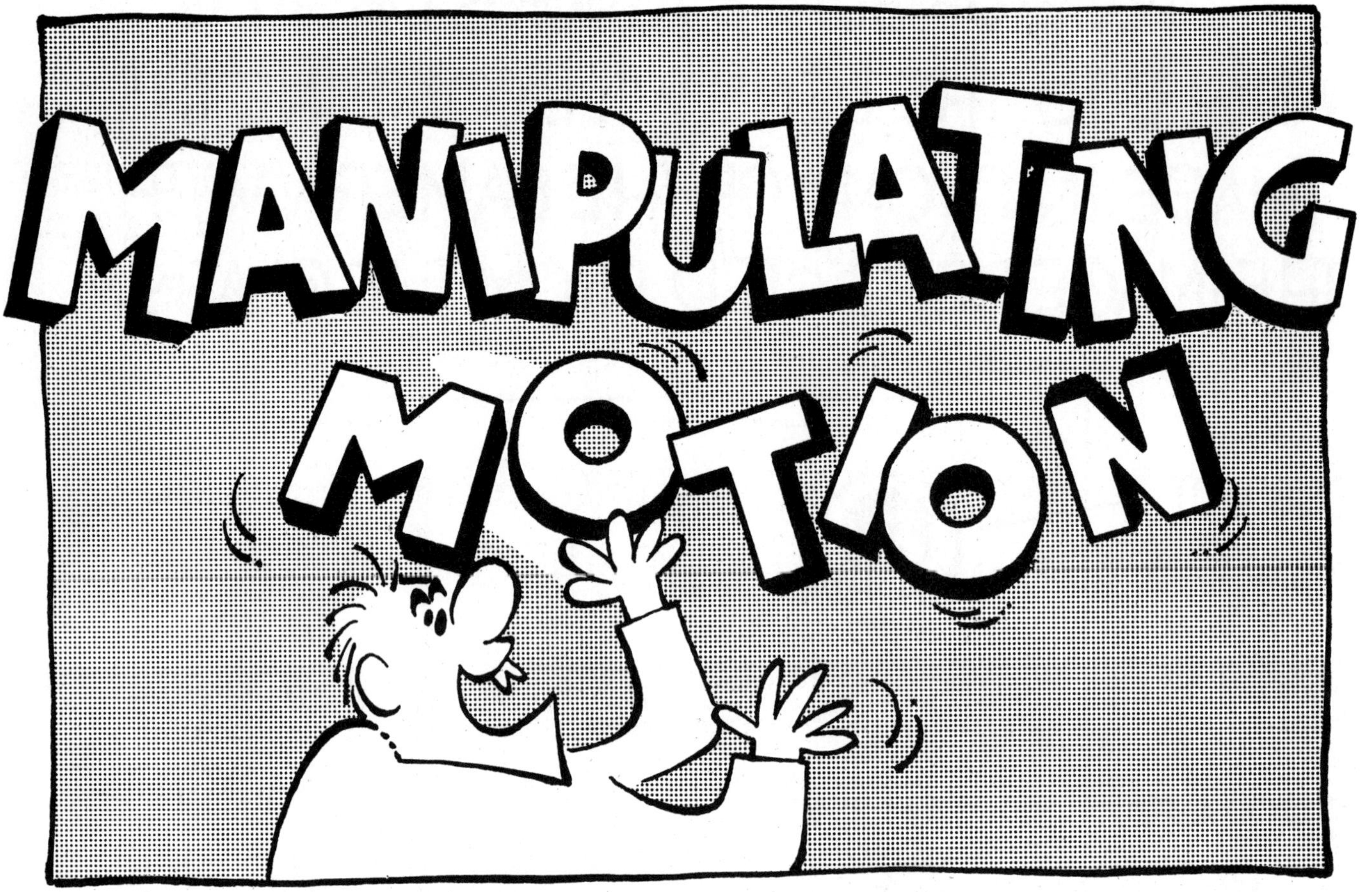

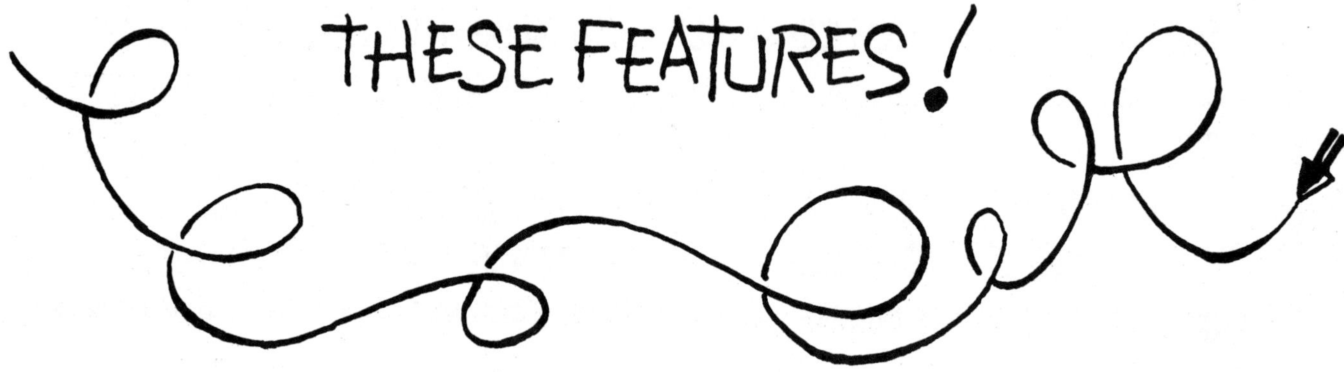

YOU CAN INCORPORATE MOTION EFFECTS LIKE SLOW MOTION, FAST MOTION, REVERSE MOTION AND STILL FRAMES INTO YOUR PRODUCTION, PROVIDED YOUR PLAYBACK VCR HAS THESE FEATURES!

WHEN YOU EDIT, PUT YOUR PLAYER INTO THE MODE (FAST, SLOW, REVERSE, OR STILL) THAT YOU WANT, AND RECORD THE RESULT ONTO YOUR RECORD TAPE. AS AN EXAMPLE, YOU COULD INSERT A SLOW MOTION REPLAY AT APPROPRIATE PLACES WHILE EDITING A TAPE OF A SOFTBALL GAME. EVERYTIME YOU PLAY THE FINISHED TAPE (AT NORMAL SPEED), YOU WILL SEE THE REPLAYS IN SLO-MO!

THE RESULTS OF RE-RECORDING FROM A "SPECIAL EFFECTS" MODE WILL LARGELY DEPEND ON THE PARTICULAR VCR YOU USE. THE SPECIAL EFFECTS MAY PERFORM BETTER AT SOME RECORDING SPEEDS THAN OTHERS (TRY THE SLOWER SPEEDS WHEN RECORDING). YOU MAY HAVE TO PUT UP WITH LINES OR BANDS OF "SNOW" IN THE PICTURE. IT MAY EVEN BE IMPOSSIBLE TO GET USABLE RESULTS, DUE TO THE DISTORTION OF THE SYNCHRONIZING SIGNALS WHICH ARE IMPORTANT TO THE VCR.

ONE WAY TO DEFEAT PROBLEMS WHEN RE-RECORDING IS TO PLAY YOUR MOTION EFFECT ON THE TV SET AND RE-RECORD IT BY POINTING YOUR CAMERA AT THE SCREEN (THE QUALITY OF YOUR RESULTS WILL BE SOMEWHAT INFERIOR, SO MAKE THIS A LAST RESORT).

EXPERIMENT!

A WORD ABOUT FILM

I KNOW *FILM* IS A DIRTY WORD IN A VIDEO BOOK, BUT HEAR ME OUT. A SMALL 8mm MOVIE CAMERA CAN DO A FEW (NOT MANY, BUT A FEW) THINGS BETTER THAN VIDEO CAN. ITS SMALLER, SIMPLER MECHANISM CAN TAKE MORE ROUGH HANDLING, AND WOULD BE A BETTER CHOICE FOR SKY DIVING OR WHITE WATER RAFTING. THE ABILITY TO EXPOSE THE FILM AT DIFFERENT FRAME RATES WILL MAKE MORE REALISTIC-LOOKING SLOW MOTION, AND YOU CAN EVEN SINGLE-FRAME FOR SMOOTH ANIMATION!

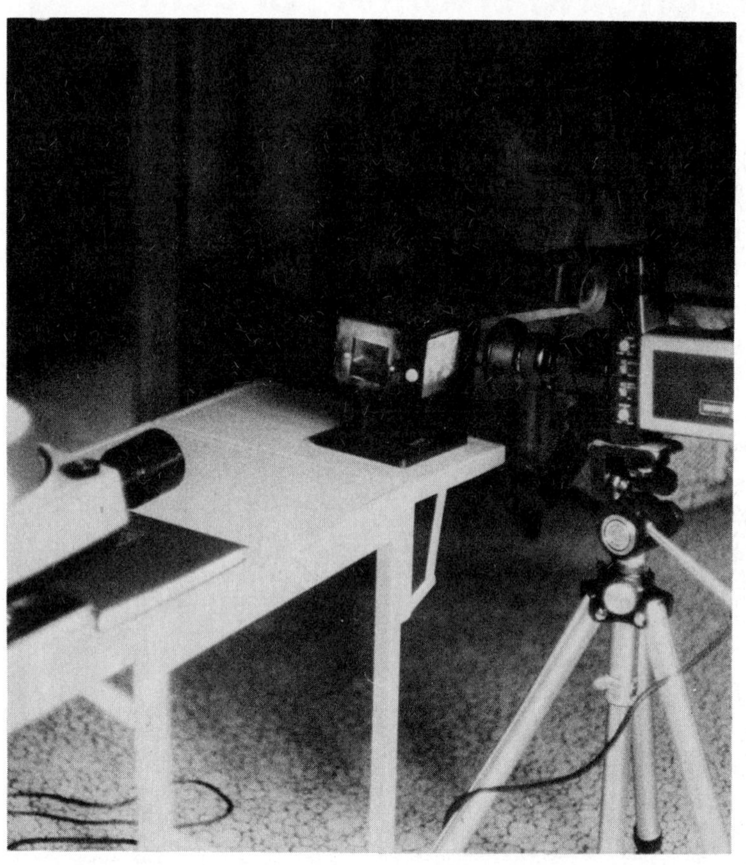

TO TRANSFER YOUR FILM ONTO TAPE, PROJECT IT ONTO A SMOOTH WHITE SURFACE AND LINE UP THE IMAGE IN YOUR VIEWFINDER SO IT JUST BARELY MEETS ALL FOUR CORNERS OF YOUR FRAME. MAKE THE PICTURE AS BRIGHT AS YOU CAN, BY MOVING THE PROJECTOR CLOSE TO THE SCREEN. YOU MIGHT WANT TO PURCHASE A SMALL REAR-SCREEN PROJECTION SYSTEM, WHICH WILL PROVIDE *MAXIMUM BRIGHTNESS!*

YOU'LL WANT TO SHOOT THE PROJECTED IMAGE STRAIGHT ON, NOT AT AN ANGLE. IF YOUR PROJECTOR HAS A VARIABLE SPEED CONTROL, YOU CAN MINIMIZE *FLICKER* IN YOUR VIDEO BY ADJUSTING IT *SLIGHTLY.* DON'T FORGET TO WHITE BALANCE WITH THE LIGHT FROM THE PROJECTOR!

CAMERA FILTERS

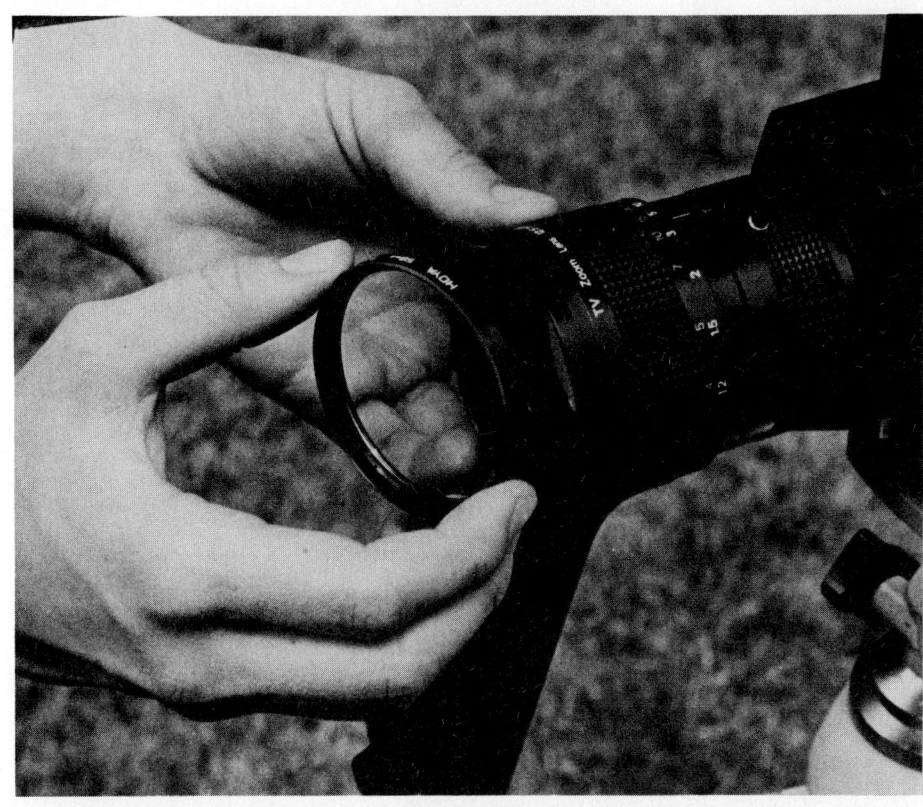

SCREW-ON CAMERA FILTERS CAN BE USED TO CREATE INTERESTING EFFECTS. HERE ARE SOME EXAMPLES:

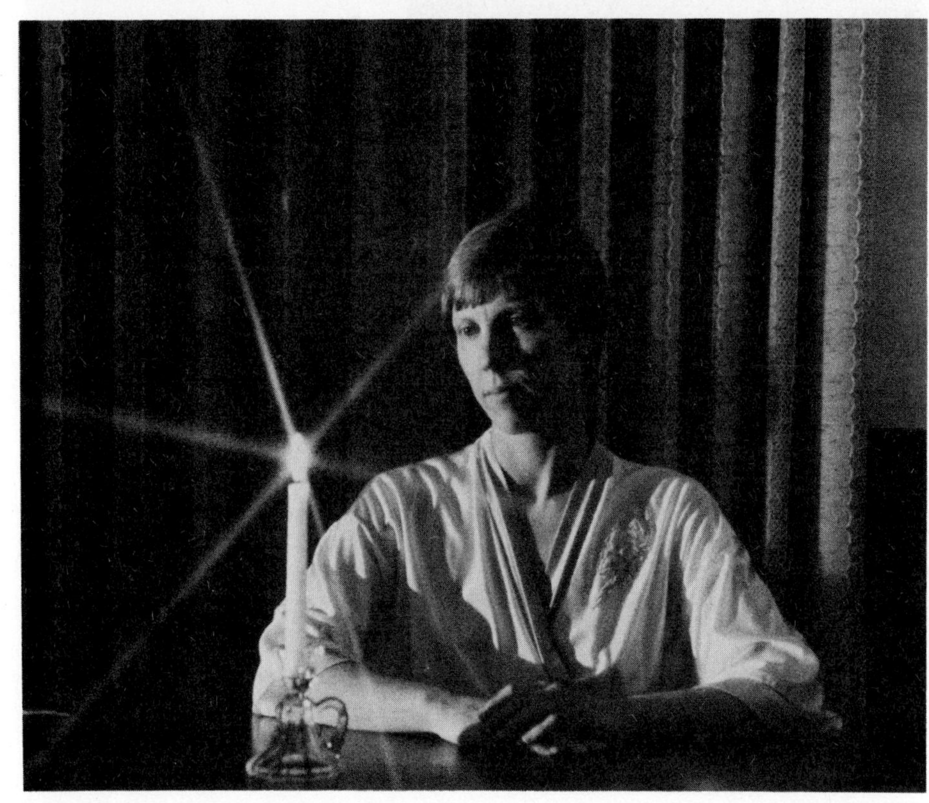

THE **STAR** FILTER ADDS A "STAR" PATTERN OF STREAKS TO THE "SPECULAR HIGHLIGHTS" BRIGHT SPOTS IN THE SCENE.

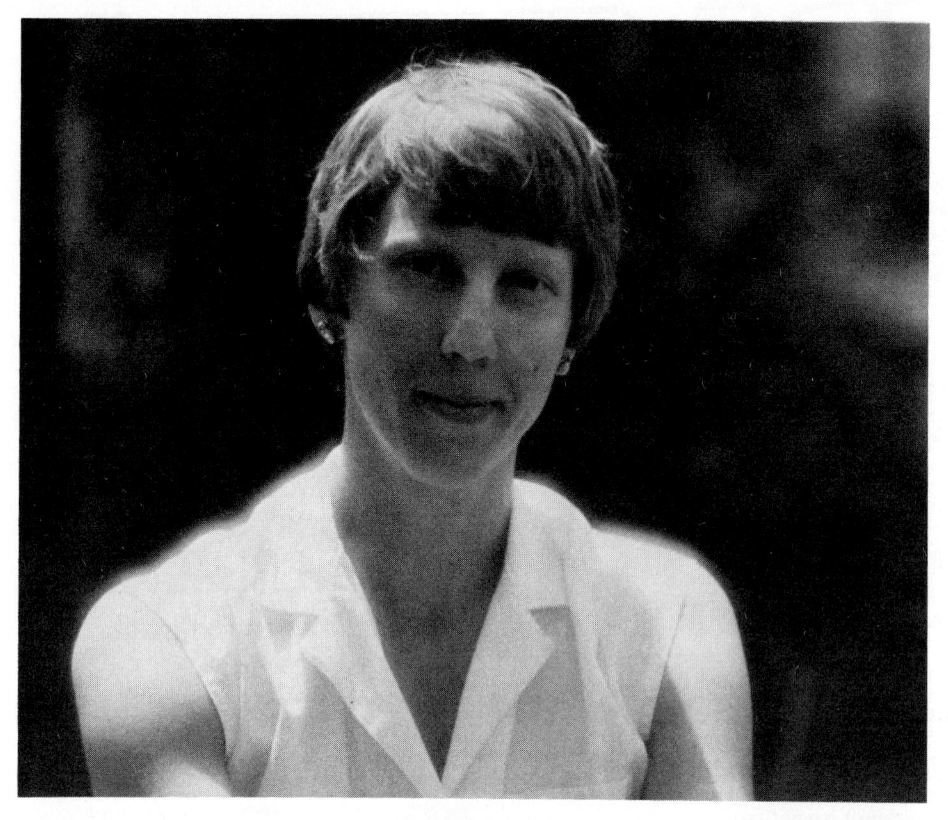

THE *DIFFUSION* FILTER SUBTLY SOFTENS THE IMAGE AND IMPARTS A SLIGHT HAZE.

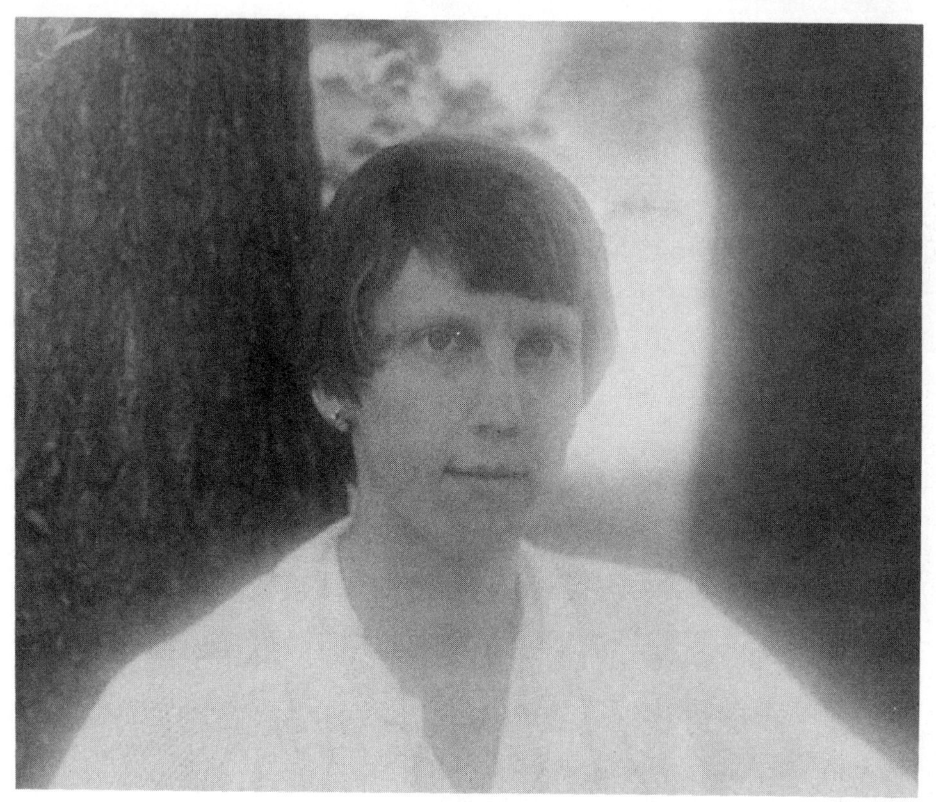

THE *FOG* FILTER ADDS A DEFINITE HAZE AND REDUCES CONTRAST.

CENTERSPOT FILTER

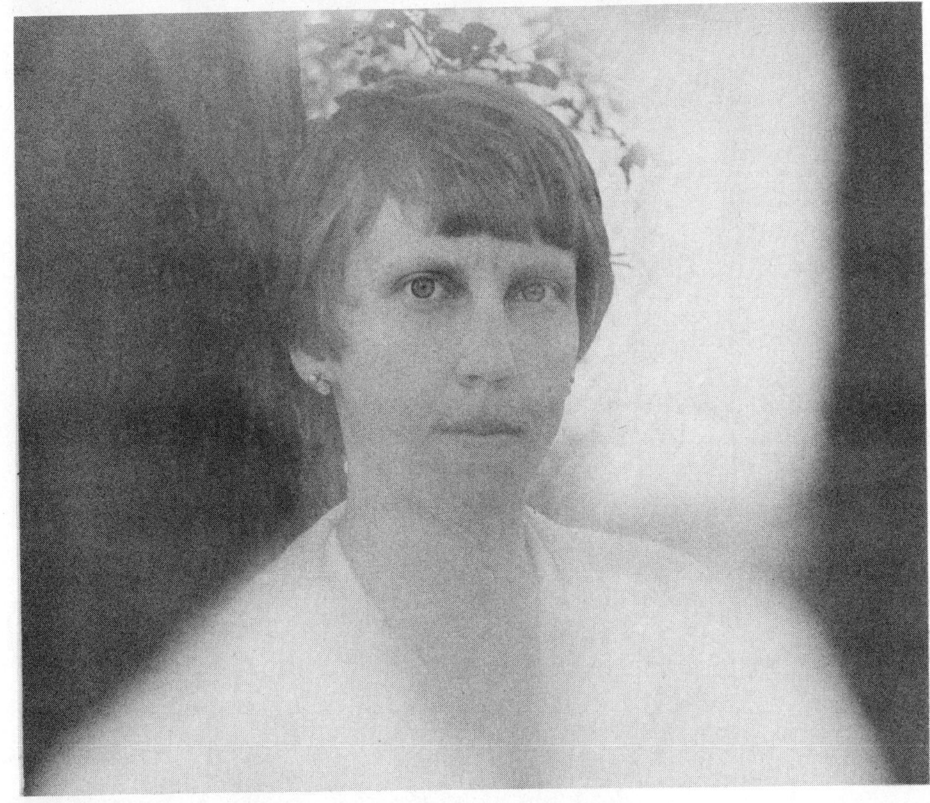

THE "CENTERSPOT" FILTER SOFTENS THE FOCUS AROUND THE EDGES OF THE PICTURE.

POLARIZING FILTER

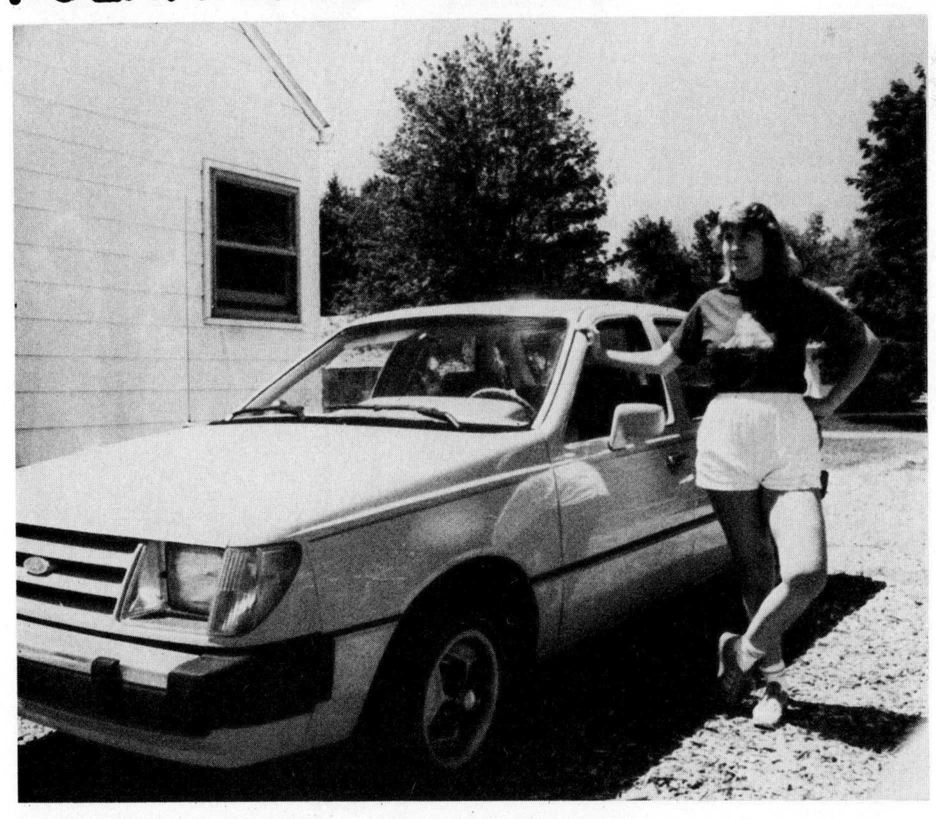

THE POLARIZING FILTER DARKENS THE SKY AND REDUCES GLARE.

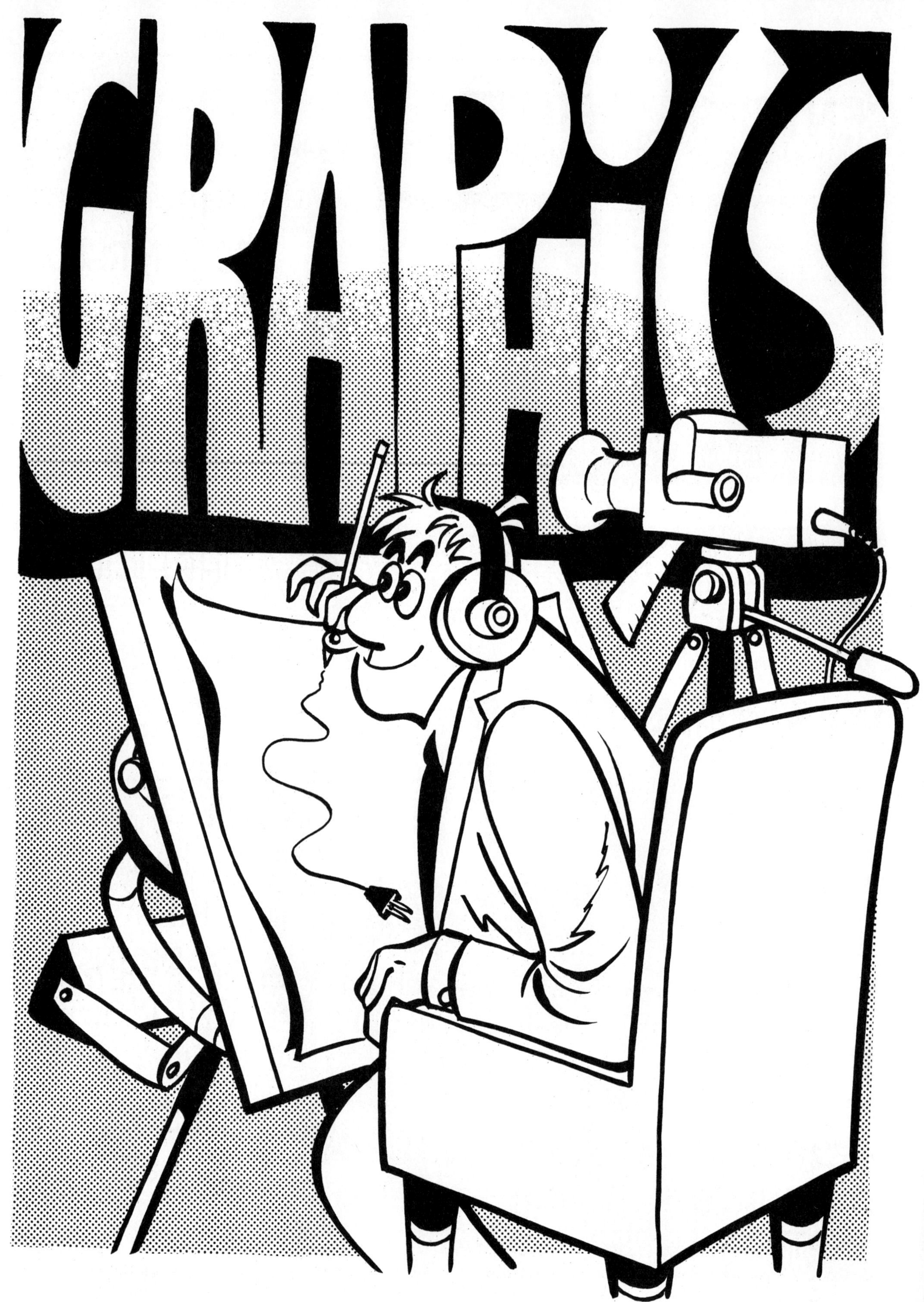
GRAPHICS

YOU CAN MAKE YOUR OWN TITLES OR OTHER ARTWORK TO USE IN YOUR PRODUCTIONS IF YOU FOLLOW A FEW SIMPLE RULES:

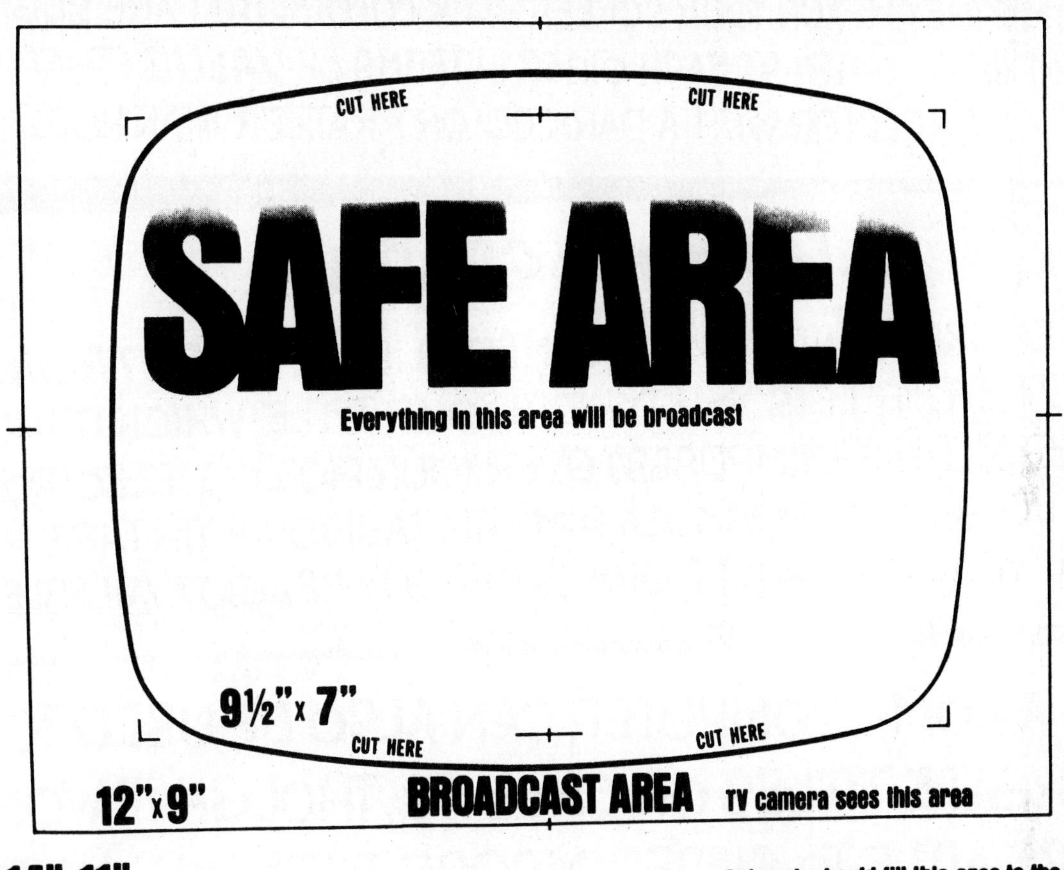

1. CORRECT ASPECT RATIO. IF YOU LOOK AT YOUR TV SCREEN YOU'LL NOTICE IT'S SHAPED LIKE THIS.

THIS SHAPE HAS AN *ASPECT RATIO* of 1.4/1, WHICH IS THE RATIO OF ITS WIDTH TO ITS HEIGHT. IT MAKES SENSE TO CREATE YOUR ARTWORK IN THIS SHAPE, BECAUSE ANY OTHER SHAPE WON'T PRECISELY FIT ONTO THE TV SCREEN.

2. SAFE AREA. MOST TV SETS "CHOP" A LITTLE BIT OFF THE EDGES OF YOUR PICTURE BEFORE IT REACHES THE SCREEN. TO BE SAFE, KEEP THE TITLES NEAR THE CENTER OF YOUR CARDBOARD (IN THE SAFE AREA), LEAVING A BLANK AREA ALL THE WAY AROUND IT.

3. CHOICE OF COLORS

AS A GENERAL RULE, AVOID THE REALLY BRIGHT, VIBRANT COLORS. THEY WILL ONLY LOOK FUZZY, GRAINY, AND OFF-COLOR BY THE TIME THEY REACH YOUR SCREEN. PICK COLORS THAT ARE SUBTLE AND THAT CONTRAST EACH OTHER IN TERMS OF *VALUE* (THAT IS, A LIGHT COLOR WITH A DARK COLOR) RATHER THAN HUE.

ELECTRONIC GRAPHICS

A FEATURE FOUND IN SOME CAMERAS IS THE *ELECTRONIC TITLER.* IT LETS YOU TYPE IN YOUR TITLE WHICH IT THEN *KEYS* (SUPERIMPOSES) OVER YOUR PICTURE. ELECTRONIC TITLERS WHICH WORK IN A SIMILAR FASHION WITH TAPE YOU'VE ALREADY SHOT (DURING EDITING) ARE ALSO AVAILABLE.

A HOME COMPUTER CAN ALSO BE USED TO CREATE TITLES OR CREDITS, THOUGH IT WON'T BE ABLE TO SUPERIMPOSE THEM ON YOUR VIDEO. SOFTWARE IS AVAILABLE TO LET YOU CREATE TITLES, CARTOONS, 3D PERSPECTIVE DRAWINGS, AND EVEN ANIMATE ALL OF THE AFOREMENTIONED.

CONNECT THE COMPUTER'S VIDEO OUTPUT DIRECTLY TO YOUR VCR'S VIDEO IN!

HERE'S A SIMPLE COMPUTER PROGRAM (IT WILL RUN ON ANY COMPUTER THAT UNDERSTANDS *BASIC*) THAT WILL "ROLL" CREDITS UP YOUR SCREEN. PUT YOUR OWN CREDITS IN PLACE OF THE SAMPLES. EXCEPT FOR THIS TYPE IT EXACTLY AS YOU SEE IT!

```
100    GOSUB 1000
110    PRINT "PRODUCED BY JOHN SOPKO"
120    GOSUB 1200
130    PRINT "DIRECTED BY JOHN SOPKO"
140    GOSUB 1200
150    PRINT "PHOTOGRAPHED BY JOHN SOPKO"
160    GOSUB 1200
170    PRINT "EDITED BY JOHN SOPKO"
180    GOSUB 1200
190    PRINT "JOHN SOPKO PRODUCED BY MR. AND MRS. SOPKO"
200    GOSUB 1000
210    END
990    REM THIS SUBROUTINE CLEARS THE SCREEN
1000   FOR Z=1 TO 6
1010   GOSUB 1200
1020   NEXT Z
1030   RETURN
1190   REM THIS SUBROUTINE PUTS BLANK LINES BETWEEN THE CREDITS
1200   FOR X=1 TO 5
1210   PRINT
1220   FOR Y=1 TO 1000
1230   NEXT Y
1240   NEXT X
1250   RETURN
```

YOU CAN MAKE THE CREDITS ROLL SLOWER BY MAKING THE NUMBER IN LINE 1220 LARGER.

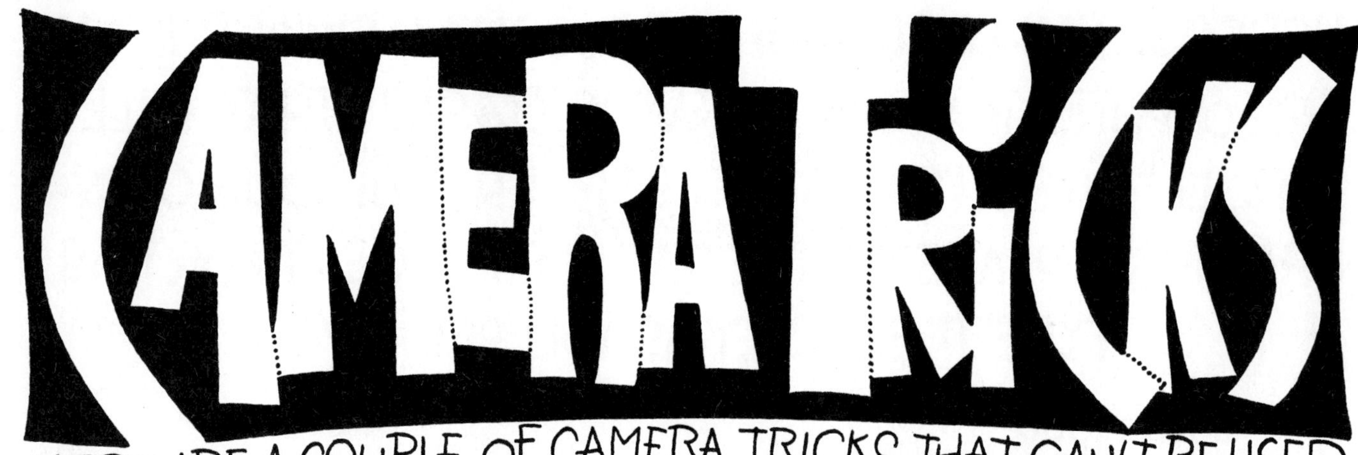

HERE ARE A COUPLE OF CAMERA TRICKS THAT CAN'T BE USED VERY OFTEN, BUT ARE LOADS OF FUN TO PLAY WITH!

VIDEO FEEDBACK

THIS IS AN ABSOLUTELY FASCINATING VISUAL EFFECT THAT'S EASY TO DO:

WITH YOUR CAMERA CONNECTED TO YOUR VCR AND TV (SO THAT THE CAMERA'S PICTURE IS ON THE SCREEN), POINT IT AT THE TV SCREEN. THE "HALL OF MIRRORS" EFFECT THAT RESULTS IS CAUSED BY THE CAMERA LOOKING AT ITS OWN PICTURE.

NOW, EXPERIMENT WITH YOUR CAMERA'S CONTROLS. ZOOM IN AND OUT. TURN THE COLOR BALANCE KNOB. TURN THE CAMERA SIDEWAYS. MOVE THE CAMERA CLOSER OR FURTHER FROM THE SET. TURN THE TINT CONTROL ON YOUR SET. PUT YOUR HAND BE-TWEEN THE CAMERA AND THE SCREEN. *EXPERIMENT!*

FOR AN EASY MUSIC VIDEO, PUT ON A PIECE OF MUSIC AND CHOREO-GRAPH YOUR SPECIAL EFFECTS TO THE BEAT.

YOUR FRIENDS WILL GASP IN AMAZEMENT! (WELL, MAYBE.)

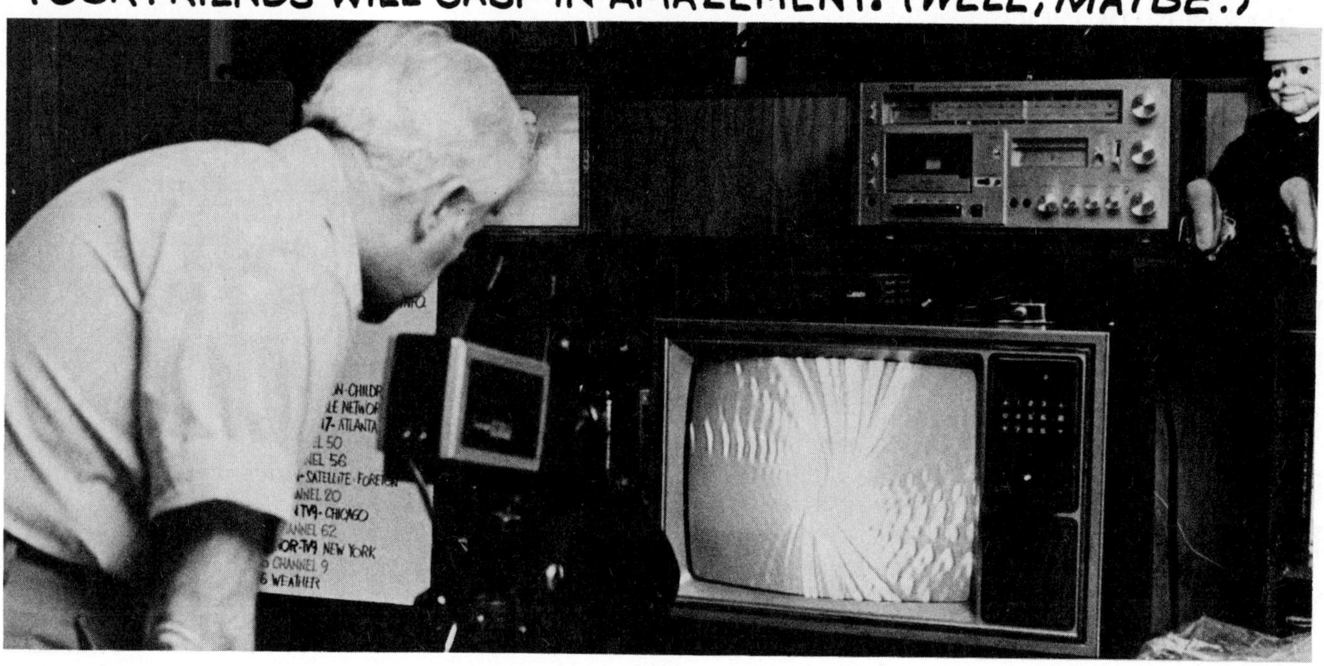

THE ZOOM/DOLLY!

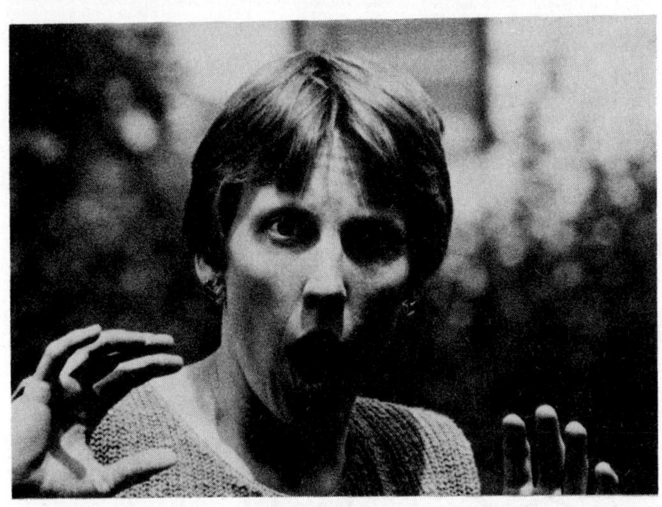

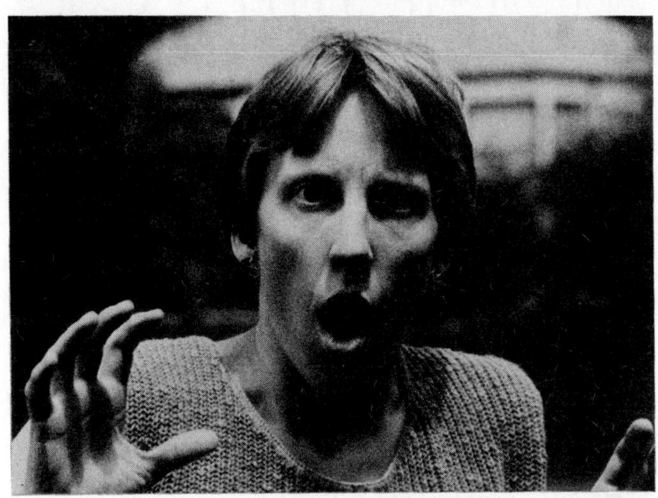

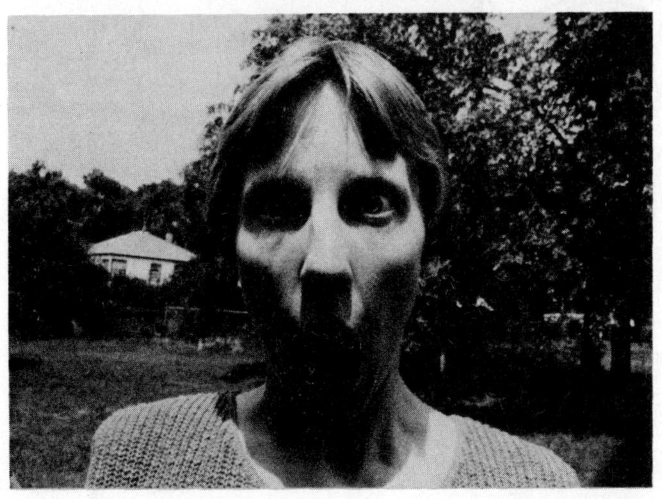

THIS TRICK EXPLOITS THE SHIFT IN PERSPECTIVE THAT OCCURS WHEN DIFFERENT FOCAL LENGTH SETTINGS ARE USED ON YOUR ZOOM LENS. *TRY THIS:* SIT IN A WHEELED CHAIR ABOUT 20 FEET FROM YOUR SUBJECT, WHO SHOULD BE POSED AGAINST A BUSY, DEEP BACKGROUND. ZOOM IN ON YOUR FRIEND'S FACE, SO THAT YOU HAVE A CLOSE-UP. *NOW* – START YOUR RECORDER AND HAVE AN ACCOMPLICE PUSH THE CHAIR TOWARD YOUR SUBJECT.

AS YOU GET CLOSER, *SIMULTANEOUSLY* ZOOM THE LENS TOWARD *WIDE* (YOU ARE ZOOMING OUT). WHAT YOU ARE TRYING TO DO IS TO KEEP THE SUBJECT'S FACE THE SAME SIZE IN YOUR VIEW-FINDER, EVEN THOUGH THE CAMERA IS GETTING CLOSER.

OBSERVE WHAT IS HAPPENING TO THE BACKGROUND! THIS IS A TRULY BIZARRE SHOT, WHICH WORKS WELL IN HORROR PRODUCTIONS.
(WATCH THE FILMS *"VERTIGO"* AND *"JAWS"* TO SEE IT IN ACTION)

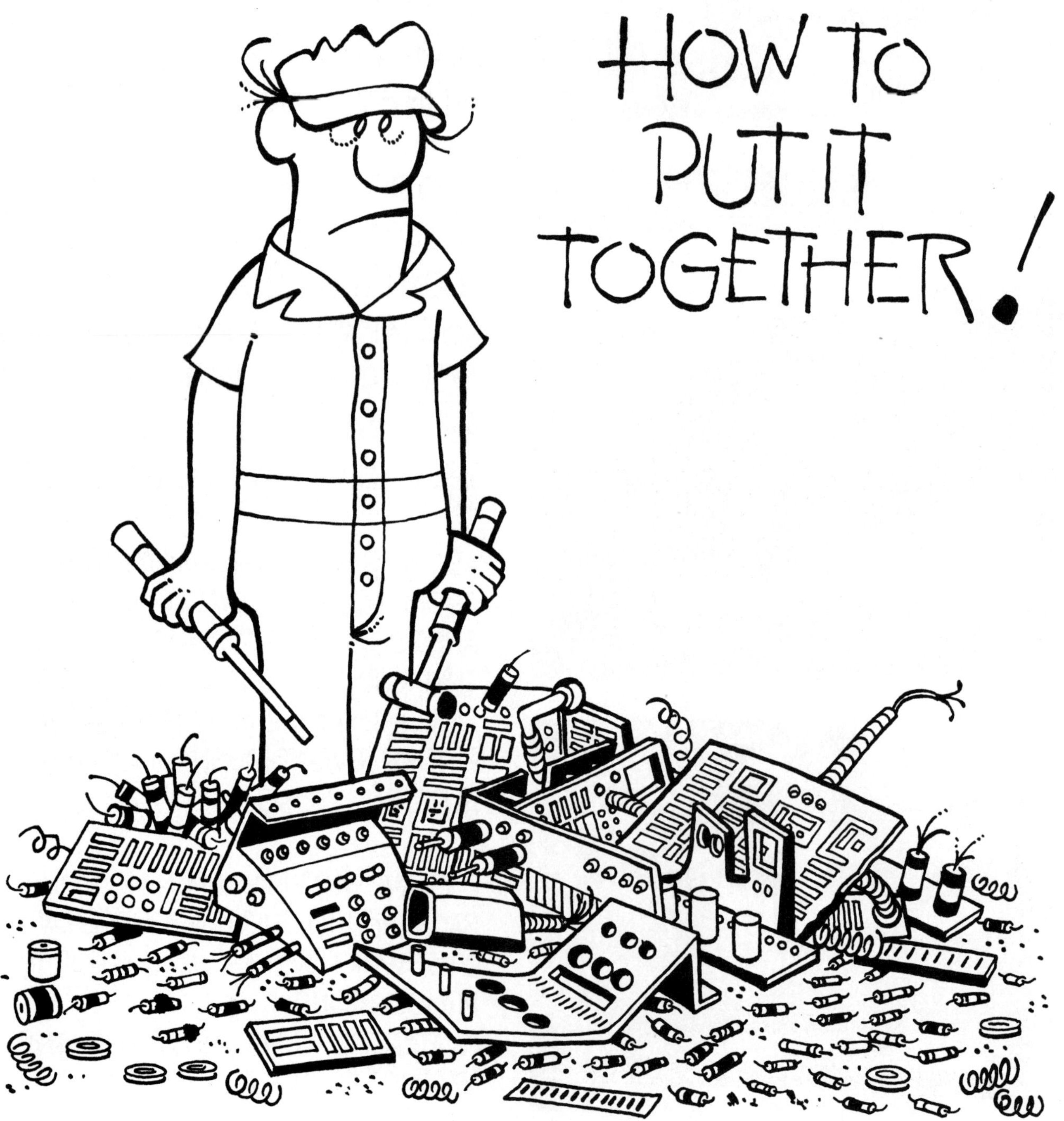
HOW TO PUT IT TOGETHER!

YOUR WORK OF VIDEO ART WILL NOT CREATE ITSELF! BEFORE YOU CAN MAKE REALLY GOOD TV, YOU'LL HAVE TO NOT ONLY MASTER YOUR EQUIPMENT, BUT MASTER YOUR *IDEAS* AS WELL.

THINK ABOUT THE TAPE YOU'RE ABOUT TO MAKE. WHAT SHOULD IT LOOK LIKE WHEN IT'S DONE? IF YOU'RE NOT SURE, THEN THE RESULT MAY REFLECT SOME DISORGANIZATION.

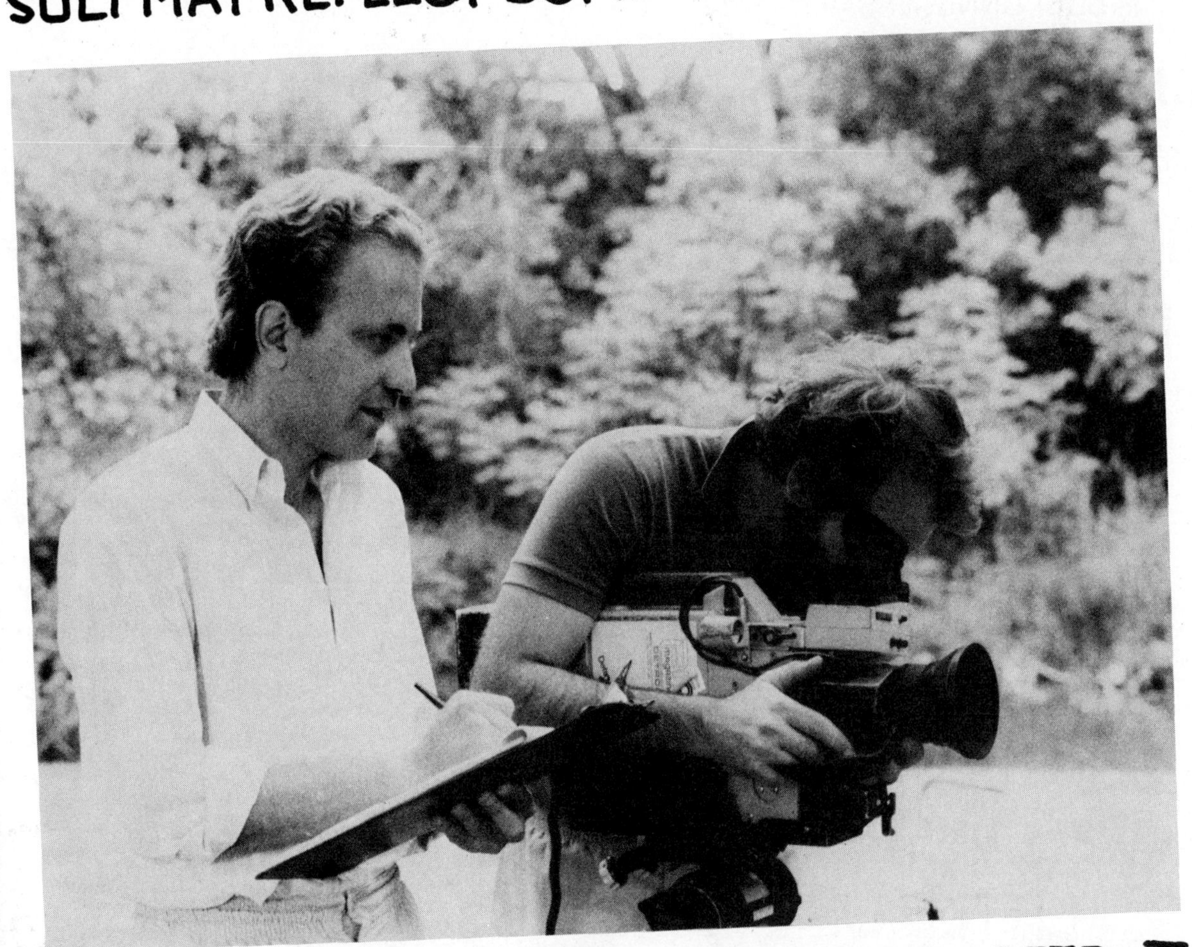

A TV PRODUCER AT WORK AT WJBK-TV, DETROIT

HOW THE BEGINNER WORKS

FEW VIDEOGRAPHERS, SETTING OUT FOR THE FIRST TIME TO VIDEOTAPE AN EVENT, HAVE A CLEAR IDEA OF WHAT THEY ARE TRYING TO CREATE. THOUGH IT MAY SEEM TO BE LESS WORK TO **"MAKE IT AS YOU GO"**, THERE ARE SOME GOOD REASONS TO THINK OTHERWISE. TAKING THE TIME TO ORGANIZE YOUR PRODUCTION MEANS THAT IT WILL TAKE LESS TIME TO SHOOT IT. WITHOUT A PLAN TO WORK FROM, YOU WILL BE TEMPTED TO TAPE *EVERYTHING* YOU CAN POINT YOUR CAMERA AT.

ANY PRE-PLANNING THAT YOU DO WILL HELP YOU TO KNOW WHAT YOU NEED VIDEO OF AND WHAT IS JUST UNNECESSARY.

TAKING THE TROUBLE TO ORGANIZE WILL ALSO SAVE YOU EDITING TIME. WITHOUT AN OUTLINE TO SHOOT FROM, YOU WILL ALMOST CERTAINLY *HAVE* TO EDIT YOUR TAPE IF IT NEEDS TO BE MORE COHERENT OR LESS BORING!

ON THE OTHER HAND, AN ORGANIZED PRODUCTION, SHOT FROM AN OUTLINE OR A SCRIPT, COULD VERY WELL WORK WITH LITTLE OR NO EDITING!

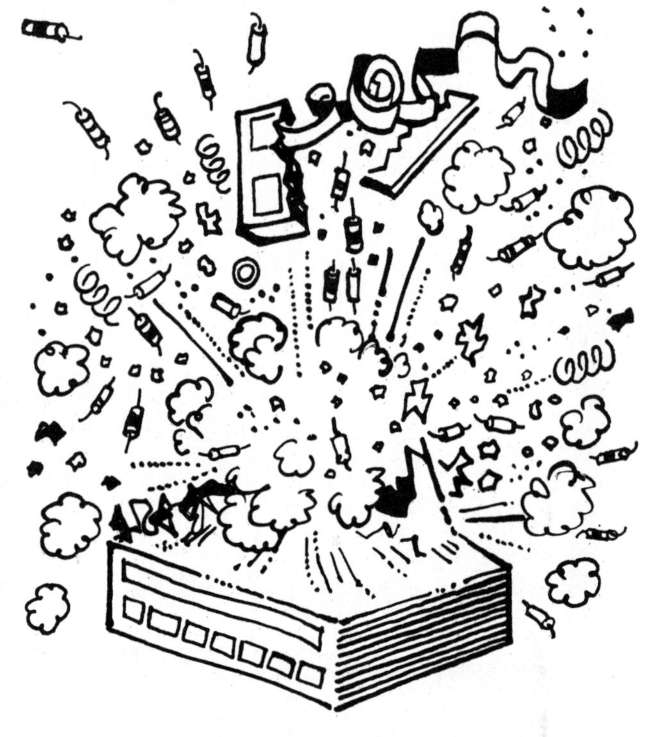

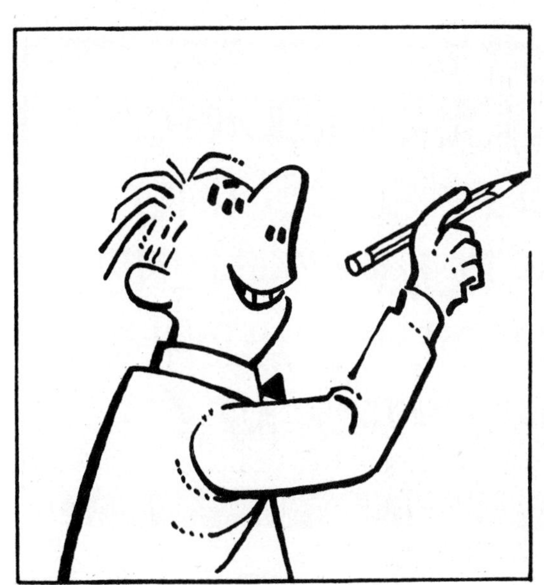

BEFORE YOU COMMIT YOUR CREATION TO PAPER OR TAPE, YOU WILL HAVE TO KNOW *FIRST* EXACTLY WHAT YOU ARE GOING TO ENCOUNTER WHEN YOU ARRIVE TO BEGIN TAPING. IF AUNT MARTHA IS ORGANIZING THE FAMILY REUNION, CALL HER AND GET A RUNDOWN OF ALL THE EVENTS SHE'S PLANNED. IF YOU'RE ABOUT TO TAPE YOUR VACATION TO AUSTRALIA, BUY A BOOK ABOUT THE COUNTRY, OR TALK TO SOMEONE WHO CAN TELL YOU WHAT'S WORTH SHOOTING!

THE *SECOND* THING YOU'LL HAVE TO KNOW IS EXACTLY HOW YOU EXPECT THE FINISHED TAPE TO LOOK!

WANT SOME IDEAS? TURN ON YOUR TV SET. RECORD SOME PROGRAMS OR MOVIES OR MUSIC VIDEOS THAT *YOU* THINK ARE GOOD EXAMPLES OF WHAT YOU'D LIKE TO DO. STUDY YOUR RECORDINGS. HOW DID THE WRITER DO HIS JOB SO WELL? HOW DO YOU SUPPOSE THE DIRECTOR GOT THE RESULTS HE WANTED? WHILE YOU'RE AT IT, WATCH THE EDITS, THE CAMERA ANGLES AND THE LIGHTING!

LISTEN TO THE SOUND, MUSIC AND SOUND EFFECTS. PAY ATTENTION TO THE PACING, AND HOW *EVERYTHING* SERVES THE STORYLINE!

WHY TELL STORIES?

VIDEO, ALONG WITH MOTION PICTURES, IS UNIQUELY SUITED TO STORYTELLING. IF YOU'VE NEVER TRIED SHOOTING TAPE WITH A STORY IN MIND, YOU MIGHT BE SURPRISED TO FIND THAT YOUR TAPES TELL STORIES ANYWAY.

PLAY THE TAPE YOU SHOT OF YOUR SON'S LAST BIRTHDAY PARTY AND NOTICE HOW THE ACTION, FOR THE MOST PART, FOLLOWS A LOGICAL PROGRESSION: FIRST THE GUESTS ARRIVE, THEN THE KIDS OPEN PRESENTS, THEY PLAY WITH THEIR GIFTS, AND EVERYONE GOES HOME!

SUPPOSE SOMEONE WERE TO TAKE YOUR TAPE AND EDIT ALL THE SHOTS TOGETHER IN THE WRONG ORDER? THE TAPE, SINCE IT NO LONGER TOLD A LOGICAL STORY, WOULDN'T BE AS MUCH FUN TO WATCH. IT FOLLOWS, THEN, THAT THE MORE ORGANIZED YOUR APPROACH TO THE STORY, THE BETTER THE FINISHED TAPE WILL BE!

HOW TO PLAN

THE AMOUNT OF ORGANIZING YOU WILL NEED TO DO DEPENDS ON THE KIND OF EVENT BEING TAPED. NOT EVERY SITUATION CALLS FOR EXTENSIVE PLANNING. A LECTURE, FOR EXAMPLE, IS PRETTY STRAIGHTFORWARD TAPING. AFTER SHOOTING THE SPEAKER AND MAYBE THE AUDIENCE, THERE'S NOTHING LEFT TO PHOTOGRAPH. THE SAME IS USUALLY TRUE FOR SPORTS EVENTS. YOU ALREADY KNOW ROUGHLY WHAT'S GOING TO HAPPEN, SO AN OUTLINE ISN'T NECESSARY!

IS AN OUTLINE NEEDED?

IN BOTH OF THE PREVIOUS EXAMPLES, THE ENTERTAINMENT VALUE OF YOUR FINISHED PRODUCTION WILL DEPEND ON THE SUBJECT FAR MORE THAN IT DEPENDS ON YOU. A DULL SPEAKER ... OR A BORING GAME CAN ONLY LEAD TO A DULL, BORING TAPE. FOR THE MOST PART, THE PRODUCTIONS THAT NEED THOUGHT AND PLANNING ARE THOSE WHERE THE ENTERTAINMENT VALUE WILL DEPEND MORE ON *YOUR* APTITUDE FOR WRITING AND DIRECTING.

THE OUTLINE ITSELF CAN TAKE MANY FORMS, FROM A SIMPLE LIST OF SHOTS OR EVENTS THAT NEED TO BE TAPED TO A VERY SPECIFIC RUNDOWN OF YOUR PRODUCTION!

HERE'S A SIMPLE OUTLINE THAT SIMPLY SERVES TO REMIND THE VIDEO GRAPHER WHAT TO SHOOT:

BILL MEADOR DEMONSTRATES HOW TO DRAW

WIDE /MEDIUM SHOT OF HIS DEMONSTRATION

CLOSE-UPS OF BILL DRAWING

CLOSE-UPS OF MATERIALS THAT HE DESCRIBES:

- PENCIL
- PEN POINTS
- BRUSHES
- INK
- ERASERS

SHOOT SOME OF BILL'S FINISHED WORK!

HERE'S A MORE ELABORATE OUTLINE, WHICH WAS WRITTEN TO SHOOT A STORY ABOUT A REAL HAUNTED HOUSE FOR WJBK-TV IN DETROIT. MOST OF THE DETAILS OF THE STORY WERE DETERMINED FROM PHONE CALLS TO FORMER RESIDENTS OF THE HOUSE, AND THE OUTLINE WAS BASED ON THAT INFORMATION. THIS OUTLINE LOOKS A LOT LIKE A SCRIPT, BUT IT IS LESS SPECIFIC THAN A SCRIPT WOULD BE. REMEMBER, THE DIRECTOR STILL HASN'T ACTUALLY *VISITED* THE HOUSE, OR INTERVIEWED THE OCCUPANTS ON CAMERA. ONCE HE DOES, HE CAN MODIFY THE OUTLINE BASED ON WHAT HE CAPTURES ON FILM.

THE "VIDEO" AND "AUDIO" COLUMNS ARE PRETTY STANDARD FEATURES OF TV SCRIPTS. "VO" IN THE AUDIO COLUMN STANDS FOR "VOICE OVER". THE VOICE OF THE INDICATED PERSON IS HEARD WHILE THE SHOT IN THE "VIDEO" COLUMN IS BEING SEEN. "SOT" (SOUND ON TAPE) MEANS THAT THE SOUND COMES FROM THE SAME SHOT AS THE VIDEO!

NORMAN'S HOUSE OUTLINE

VIDEO	:	AUDIO

-Shots of house/different angles. : (VO announcer) Welcome to
: Norman's house. It's been
: Norman's house for quite some
: time now. In fact, Norman has
-Kid is riding bike or walking by. : been living here for over 50
-Door swings open. : years. No, that's not exactly
: right. He hasn't been "living."

-Apparition appears in door :
as kid looks on - reaction- kid :
runs. :

: (VO anncr.) This historic old
: home, located in Fenton,Michigan,
: was once the home of the Reverend
-Reverend's hand on Bible in bed. : Norman Hough. He lived peacefully
-Hand goes limp. : here until his death one night in
-Hand disappears. : 1926. His body was removed and
-More house angles, : buried, but Norman remains here
or bring announcer on camera. : somehow to look after his century
: old home.

-Marilyn and husband pull up and :
unload some boxes from car. : (VO anncr.) Introducing Mr. and
: Mrs. Brumback. Marilyn fell in
: love with the house on first
: sight.Of course, nobody mentioned
: Norman. And nobody told her what
: happened to Norman's last
-She comes in front door. Dog runs : tenants.
upstairs. She follows. Dog barks :
at wall. She stares at wall. : (Sound of footsteps begins-- gets
-Eventually she becomes frightened : louder.)
and runs. : (VO Marilyn) She talks about how
: she didn't know about ghost.
-Both of them in bed... various : Talks about becoming frightened
noises to match VO. : at noises. Talks about other
-Door opens by itself. : phenomena:Door that opens itself.
-Painting falls off wall. : The wall nothing stays on.
-Sequence of shots about bowl : The flying bowl incident.
that flew across room. : The strange chamber music.
-Marilyn in bathroom hearing music : Unrolling toilet paper.
and seeing tp unroll. :

: (VO Marilyn or announcer) Talks
: about how she became aware that
: ghost is harmless... or is he?
-Setup Jan coming in, the two of : Asks Jan, her neighbor, about
them talking. : other tenants of the house.
-DISSOLVE to Betty's re-creations. :

: (VO Jan) Talks about other
: owners. Asks if Betty, the last
: owner, was nearly murdered.
:
: (VO Betty) Talks about her
: experiences. Talks about rocking
-Chair rocks. : chair that rocked itself. Then
: talks about the time Norman went
-Some kind of stylized falling : "too far" and pushed her down
down staircase. : the staircase.

-DISSOLVE to Marilyn in bed. It   : (SOT Marilyn) "Goodnight honey."
creaks as someone seems to get in. :
                                   : (VO Marilyn) Talks about whether
                                   : Norman might go too far with her
                                   : and how the house has been bad
                                   : luck.
-Bed creaks again as someone   :
seems to get in.   : (SOT Marilyn) "How many times are
-Shot of husband's incredulous   : you going to get into bed?"
look.   : (SOT husband) "This is the first
-Marilyn's incredulous reaction-PAN: time!"
to empty pillow with depression   :
in it. DISSOLVE to "moving out"   : (VO Marilyn) Talks about moving
shots.   : out.
                                   : (VO announcer)But the story isn't
-Jody moving in.   : over yet. Enter Jody Brehmer and
                                   : her daughter, -------, the newest
                                   : residents of "Norman's house."
                                   : Jody's been living here just a
                                   : few weeks, and says she's
                                   : skeptical.
                                   :
                                   : (VO Jody) Gives explanations for
-Wind blowing open door.   : door, footsteps.
-Walnut tree dropping nuts on roof.:
                                   : (VO Jody) Talks about one time
-Sequence about walking into dining: when... MAYBE she saw Norman.
room and seeing face in wall.   :
                                   : (VO announcer) Does Norman live
-Shots of house.   : here? You'll have to decide
                                   : for yourself. Will Jody ever meet
                                   : him? Well, maybe Norman is just
-Face in wall smiles.   : waiting for the... right moment.
                                   :

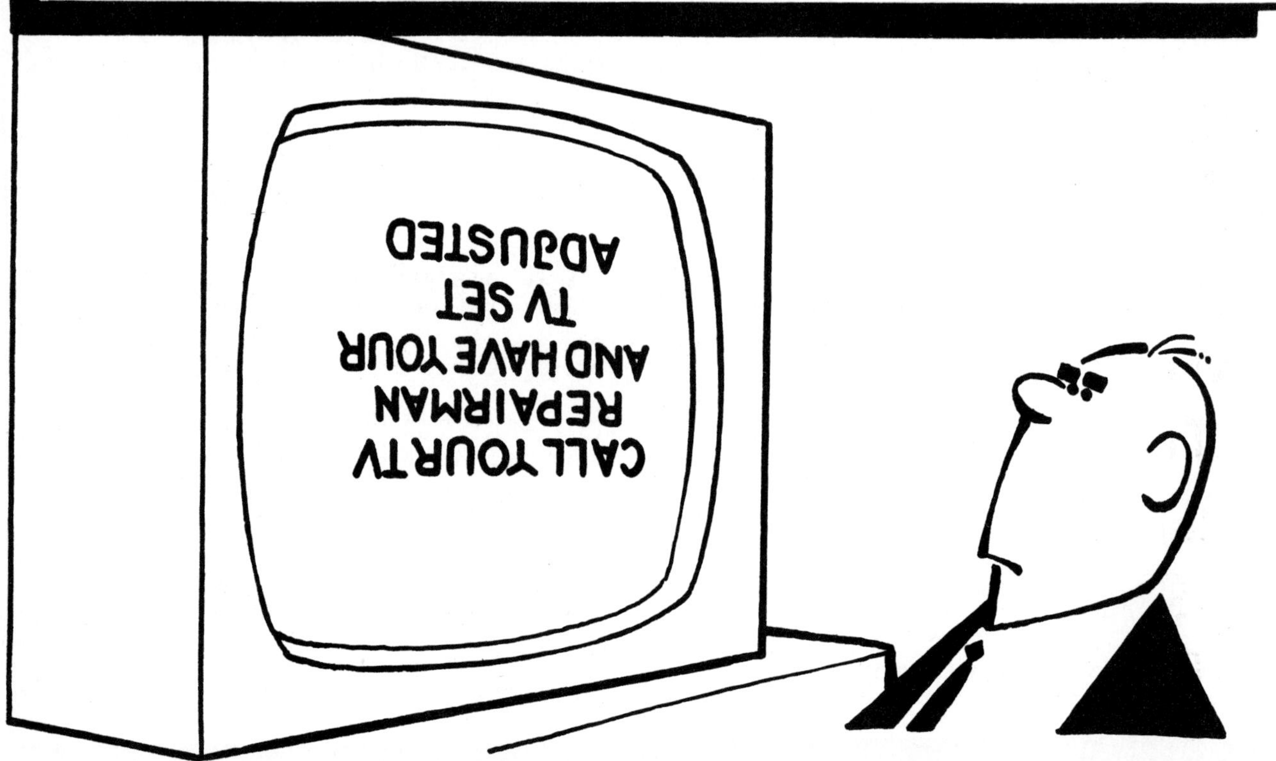

WHEN TO SCRIPT!

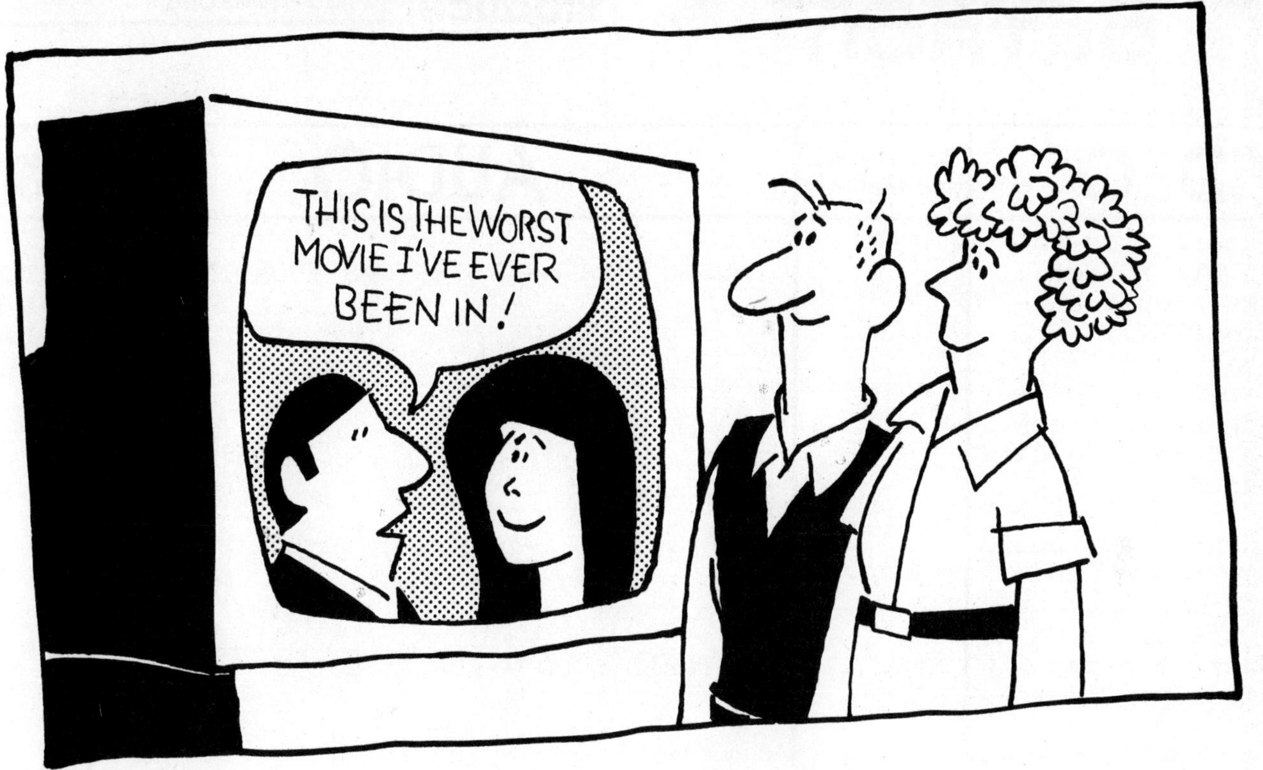

WHEN THERE ARE SPONTANEOUS ELEMENTS TO YOUR STORY, IT'S NOT REALLY POSSIBLE TO PLAN YOUR SHOOT DOWN TO THE LAST DETAIL. ON THOSE OCCASIONS WHEN THE PRODUCTION IS ENTIRELY UNDER YOUR CONTROL, HOWEVER, YOU MAY WANT TO WRITE A SCRIPT OR STORYBOARD PRIOR TO SHOOTING.

A SCRIPT IS TYPICALLY A PRECISE SHOT-BY-SHOT BREAK-DOWN OF YOUR SHOW. ON THE FOLLOWING PAGE IS PART OF A SCRIPT FOR A COMEDY PRESENTATION PRO-DUCED AT WJBK-TV, DETROIT. SINCE ALL THE ACTION WAS STAGED, THE SCRIPT COULD BE WRITTEN BE-FOREHAND AND FOLLOWED RIGOROUSLY!

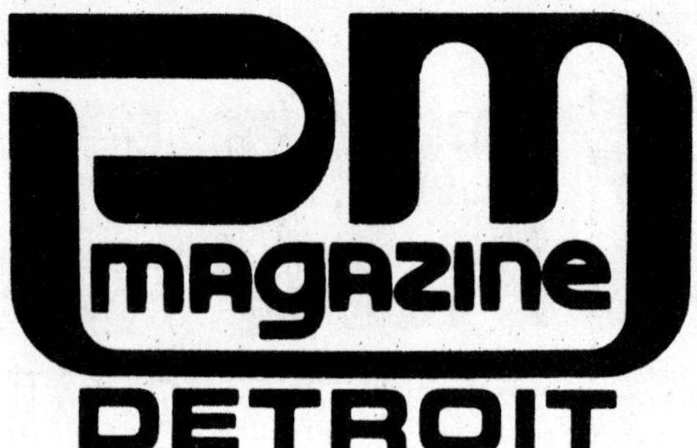

Page No. THREE

Story "Todd Hissong & the Temple
of Donuts"

Producer Todd Hissong

VIDEO	Cassette No. and Memory	AUDIO	Cassette No. and Memory
WS door. Todd enters his office... looks around suspiciously... leaves frame.		MUSIC UNDER--MYSTERIOUS SOUNDING	"Temple of Doom" album.
WS desk. Todd enters frame and sits at desk.			
MS desk. Todd pulls a bag of potato chips out from under his coat. He attacks the bag viciously, and raises a handful of chips to his mouth.		NATURAL SOUND--RUSTLING BAG	
CU phone.		SOUND EFFECT--PHONE RINGS	Sound Effects album.
CU Todd. He looks at phone.		TODD: "Nah... it couldn't be..."	
MS Todd. He answers phone.		TODD: "Hello?"	
MS Anonymous caller in silhouette.		ANONYMOUS CALLER: "Hello again..."	
MS Todd. He reacts.			
MS caller.		CALLER: "It's me... remember? So you lost nine pounds... (laughs) big deal! I challenge you to lose another ten!"	
CU Todd. (CUTAWAY)			
MS Todd.		TODD: "Mattie, we did this last year. I'm not amused. It's ridiculous. I told you that...	
WS Mattie, looking at Todd. PAN as she walks over, stands behind him. Todd looks at Mattie, then at phone.		MATTIE: "Hi, Todd."	
MS caller.		CALLER: "I'll donate a dollar to your favorite charity for every pound you lose."	

PM 021

PAT AND JANET'S WEDDING

MY FRIEND PAT CALLED ME THE OTHER DAY TO ANNOUNCE HIS IMPENDING MARRIAGE AND ASKED ME TO VIDEOTAPE IT FOR HIM. "OF COURSE," I SAID, AND I SET OUT TO ORGANIZE MY PRODUCTION.

SINCE PAT IS A GOOD FRIEND, I DECIDED TO GO *ALL OUT* AND DO THE BEST JOB I COULD. FIRST, I TALKED TO PAT AT LENGTH TO FIND OUT AS MUCH AS I COULD ABOUT HIS WEDDING DAY. SINCE PAT AND JANET HAD BEEN CHILDHOOD FRIENDS, THEY HAD A SCRAPBOOK OF PHOTOS OF THE TWO OF THEM GROWING UP TOGETHER.

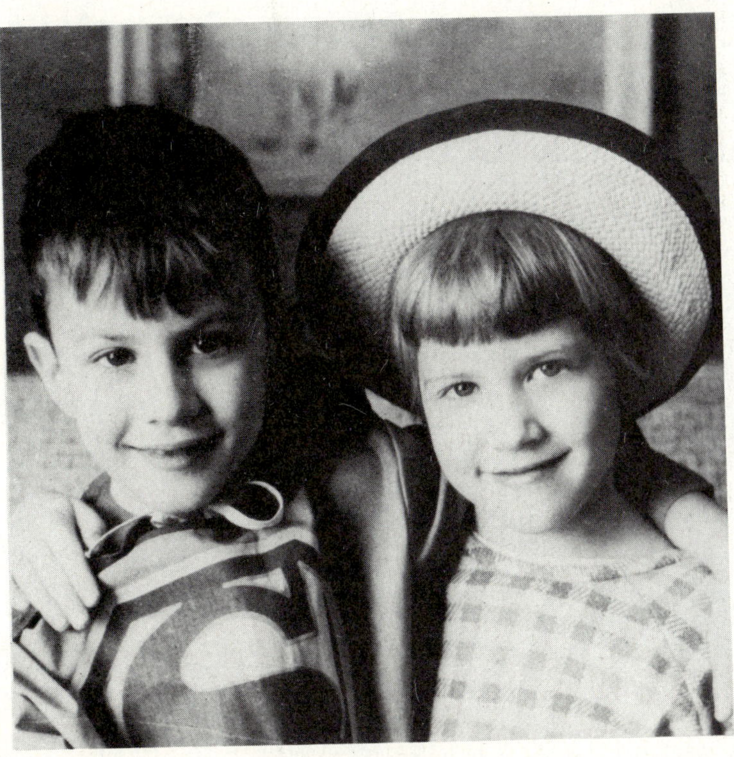

I DECIDED TO INCORPORATE THESE, SET TO MUSIC, AT THE BEGINNING OF MY TAPE. STILL PHOTOS TAKEN BY A PHOTOGRAPHER AT THE WEDDING WOULD BE USED AT THE END.

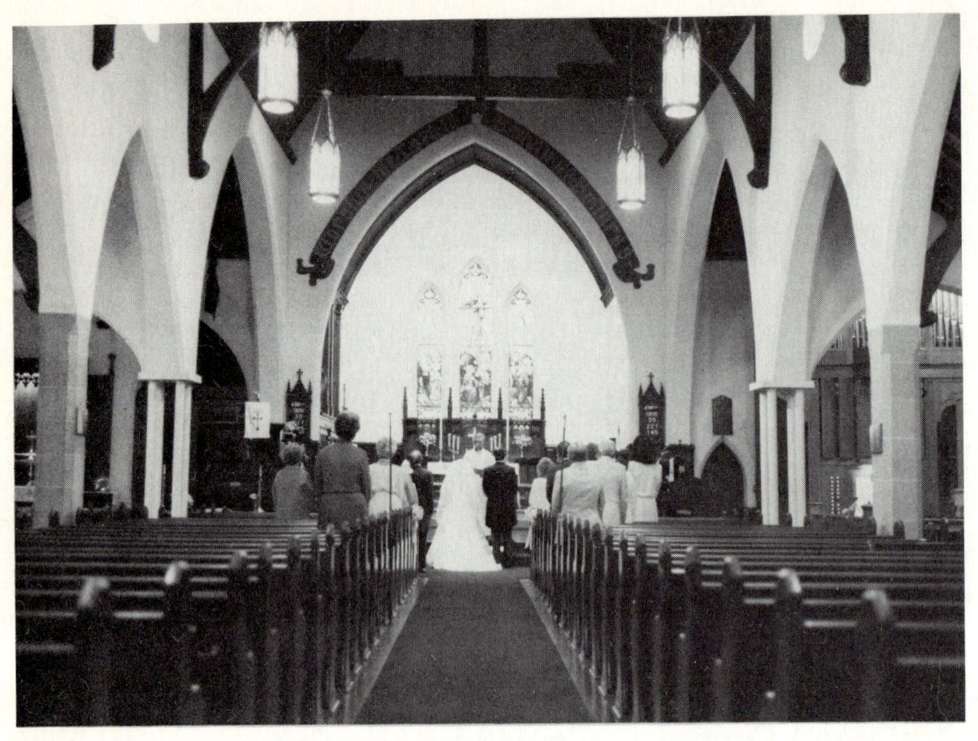

NEXT, I VISITED THE CHURCH, AND ASKED THE MINISTER WHERE I COULD SHOOT FROM DURING THE CEREMONY AND WHETHER I COULD PUT UP A LIGHT!

THE LIGHT, HE SAID, WOULD BE OUT OF THE QUESTION. FORTUNATELY, THERE APPEARS TO BE ENOUGH LIGHT COMING THROUGH THE WINDOWS TO SHOOT WITH. HE ALSO ASKED THAT I STAY AT THE BACK OF THE CHURCH ONCE THE CEREMONY BEGINS. THE BIGGEST PROBLEM FROM BACK THERE IS TO RE-CORD GOOD SOUND. A WIRELESS MIKE ON THE BRIDE OR GROOM WOULD BE ONE SOLUTION, BUT SINCE THE CHURCH HAS A PUBLIC ADDRESS SYSTEM, I'LL SIMPLY POSITION MY CAMERA NEAR ONE OF THE P.A. SPEAKERS!

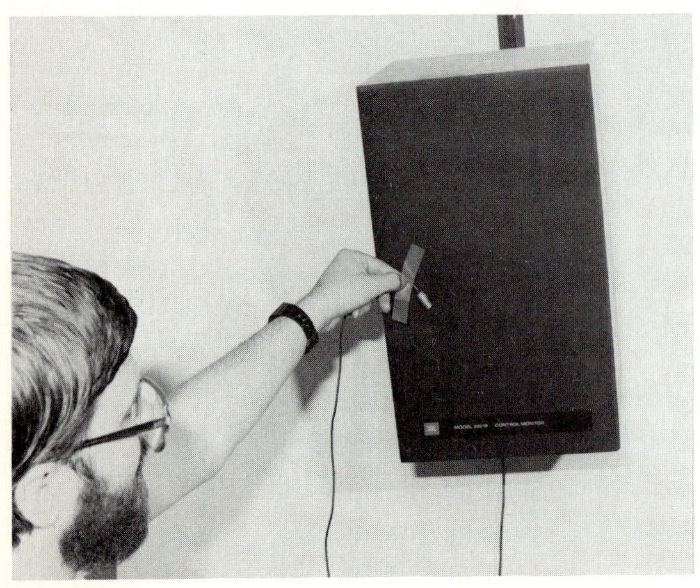

THEN I'LL TAPE A SMALL LAVALIER MICROPHONE RIGHT TO THE SPEAKER CABINET (ALWAYS POSITION YOUR MIKE CLOSEST TO THE **MIDRANGE** OR **TWEETER** .... THEY'RE THE SMALLER OPENINGS IN THE CABINET. DON'T PUT IT IN FRONT OF THE **WOOFER**... THE LARGEST OPENING. THE SOUND WILL BE BASSY AND DISTORTED IF YOU DO). SOME OF THE CLOSE-UPS I WANT, LIKE THE RING CEREMONY, WILL BE DIFFICULT TO SHOOT FROM THE BACK, SO I WILL RE-CREATE THEM AFTERWARD.

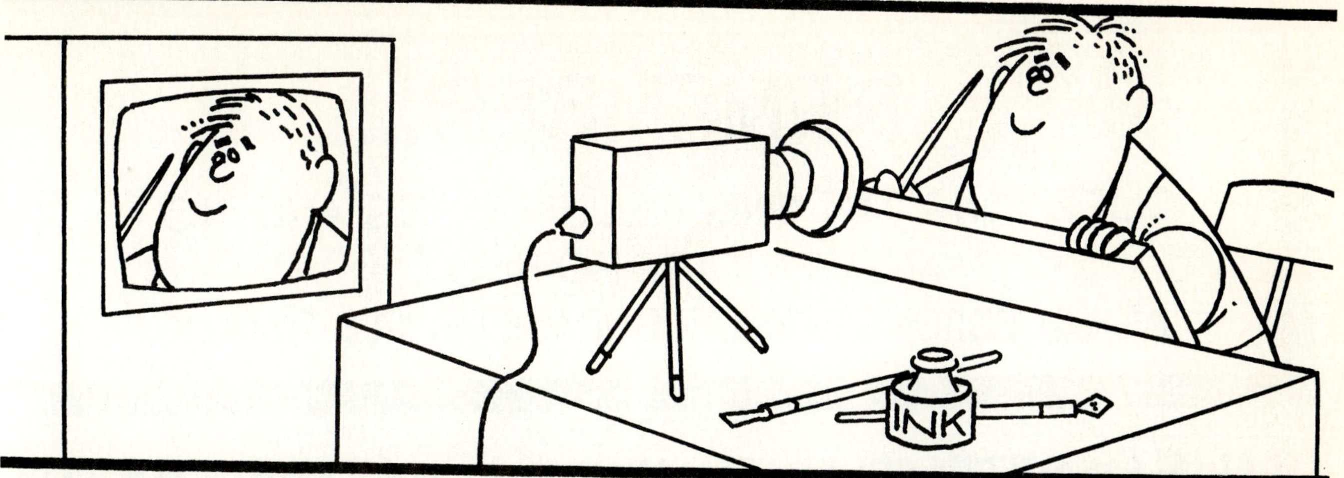

ANOTHER DIFFICULT SHOT TO GET FROM MY SHOOTING SPOT WILL BE THE SINGER AND ORGANIST. BECAUSE OF THIS, AND ALSO TO GET THE BEST POSSIBLE SOUND OF THEIR PERFORMANCE, I'LL PLAN ON ARRIVING ABOUT AN HOUR EARLIER ON THE WEDDING DAY SO THAT I CAN TAPE THEM REHEARSING!

ONE OF MY FAVORITE PASTIMES AT THE RECEPTION IS TO INTERVIEW SOME OF THE COUPLE'S FRIENDS AND RELATIVES ABOUT THEM. *SOME POSSIBLE QUESTIONS:*

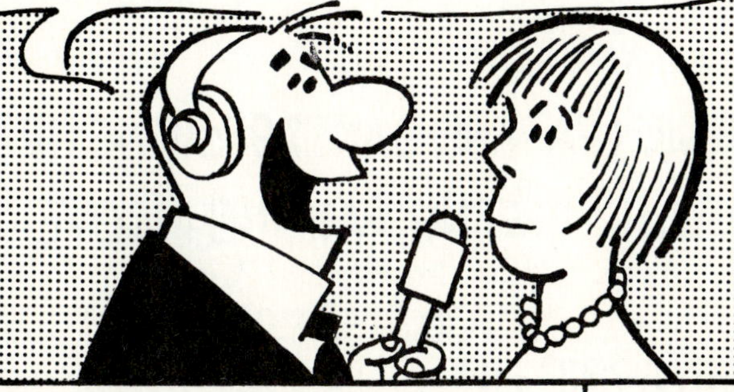

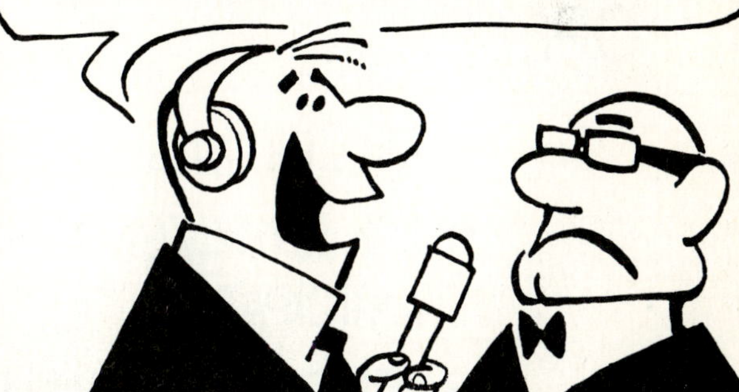

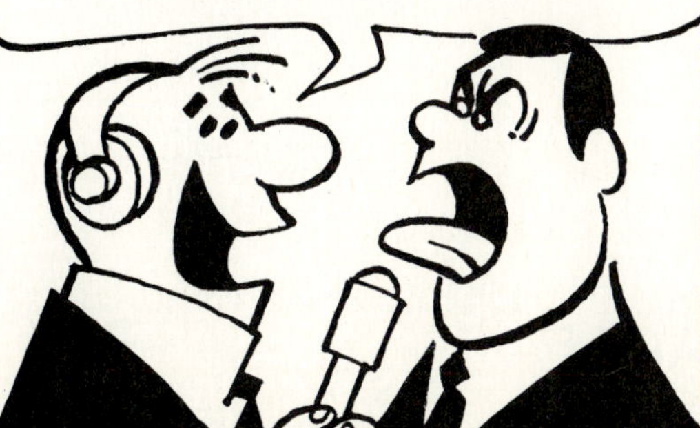

THE BEST QUESTIONS TO ASK ARE THE ONES THAT REQUIRE DETAILED RESPONSES. A POOR QUESTION WOULD BE:

REMEMBER....

QUESTIONS THAT ONLY REQUIRE "YES" AND "NO"
ANSWERS ARE BORING!
ASK QUESTIONS THAT ENCOURAGE PEOPLE TO TALK.

I'LL ALSO INTERVIEW PAT AND JANET BOTH BEFORE AND AFTER THE WEDDING. BEFORE, TO HEAR THEM TALK ABOUT THEIR ANTICIPATION, HOW THEY MET, AND HOW PAT PROPOSED. AFTER, TO TALK ABOUT THEIR PLANS AND THEIR FUTURE!

HERE'S MY FINISHED OUTLINE. AS I SHOOT THE VARIOUS ELEMENTS ON MY LIST, I WILL CHECK THEM OFF.

-OPEN

- STILL PICTURES WITH MUSIC (PAT AND JANET GROWING UP)
- ASK BRIDE/GROOM ABOUT MEETING, FALLING IN LOVE, ANTICIPATION.
- ASK PARENTS ABOUT GROWING UP
- TITLE GRAPHICS (PAT AND JANET'S WEDDING)

-CEREMONY

- SINGER, ORGAN PLAYER
- GUESTS ARRIVING
- BRIDE/GROOM COME UP AISLE

– MINISTER PERFORMS CEREMONY
– CLOSE-UP OF RINGS (STAGED AFTER CEREMONY)
– LEAVE CHURCH - RICE THROW - GET IN CAR

– RECEPTION

– RECEPTION LINE
– TOAST
– BRIDE / GROOM EAT
– INTERSPERSE INTERVIEWS WITH GUESTS
– BAND PLAYS
– BOUQUET THROW
– GARTER CEREMONY
– BRIDE / GROOM / PARENTS DANCE

– CLOSE

– ASK PAT / JANET ABOUT NEW LIFE
– MONTAGE OF PICTURES FROM WEDDING PHOTOGRAPHER
– SOFT PIANO MUSIC IN BACKGROUND
– END TITLE GRAPHIC (THE END)

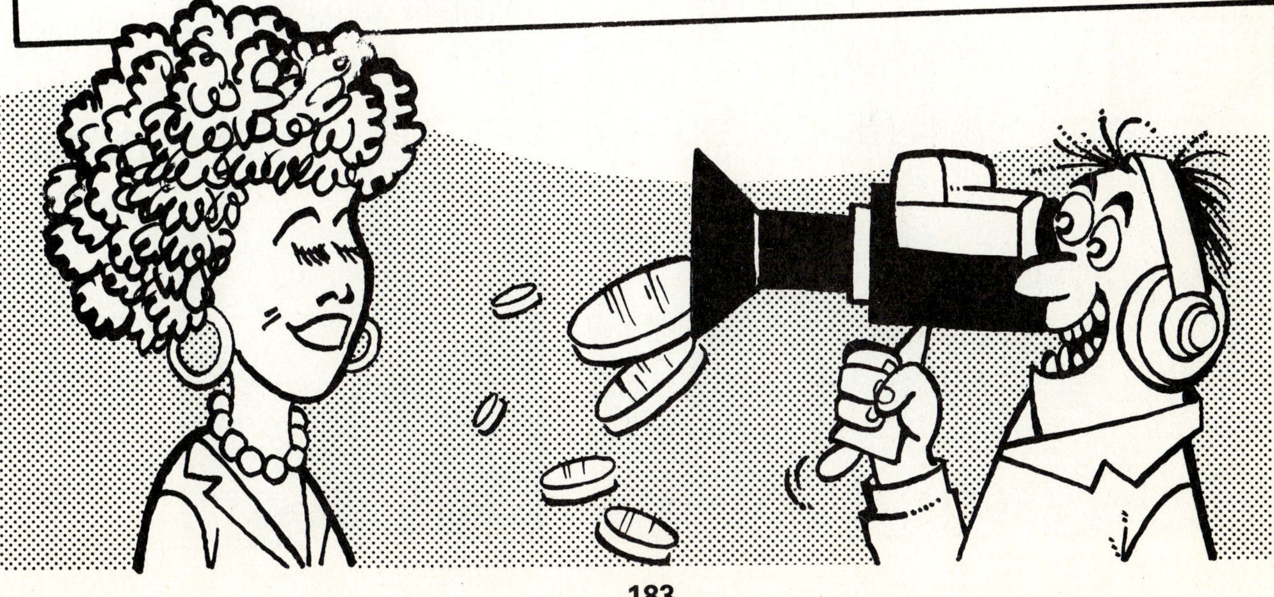

MUSIC VIDEO

FOR THOSE AMONG US WHO WATCH MUSIC VIDEOS, IT'S EASY TO APPRECIATE THEIR SOPHISTICATED PRODUCTION VALUES. THE LEVEL OF QUALITY ISN'T SURPRISING, CONSIDERING THE DAYS OR EVEN WEEKS OF SCRIPTING, SHOOTING AND EDITING THAT GO INTO MOST OF THEM. IS IT POSSIBLE TO PRODUCE A MUSIC VIDEO WITH HOME EQUIPMENT? OF COURSE IT IS... JUST DON'T PLAN ON ANY INCREDIBLE SPECIAL EFFECTS *(UNLESS YOU'VE GOT A FEW THOUSAND DOLLARS LYING AROUND)*.

IF YOU'VE GOT AN EDITING SYSTEM:

WITH THE LUXURY OF AN EDITING SYSTEM, MUSIC VIDEOS ARE LOADS OF FUN TO PUT TOGETHER. IF IT'S A LIVE GROUP I'M TAPING, I'LL HAVE THEM PERFORM THE SONG TWO OR THREE TIMES FOR ME (ALWAYS AT EXACTLY THE SAME TEMPO). THE FIRST TIME, I'LL SHOOT A *WIDE* SHOT WHERE THE WHOLE BAND CAN BE SEEN.

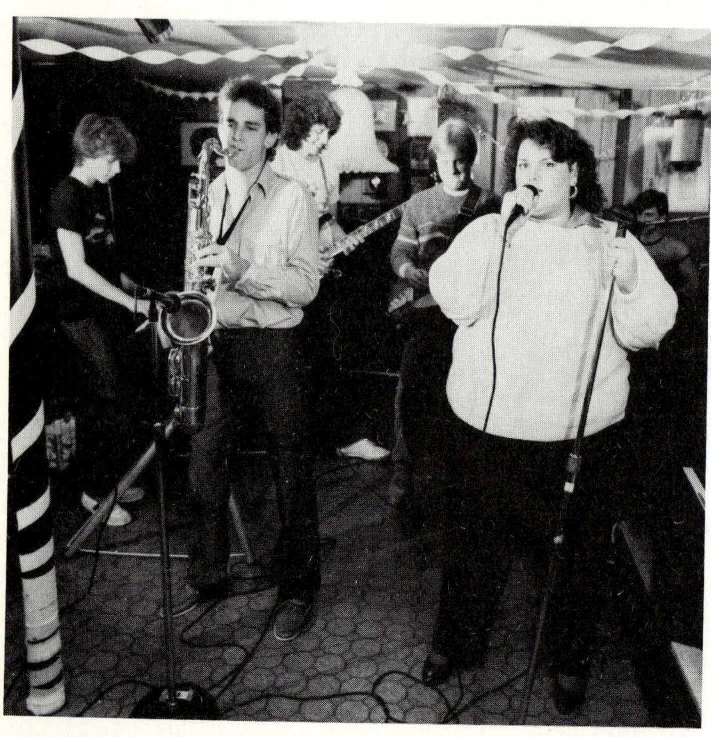

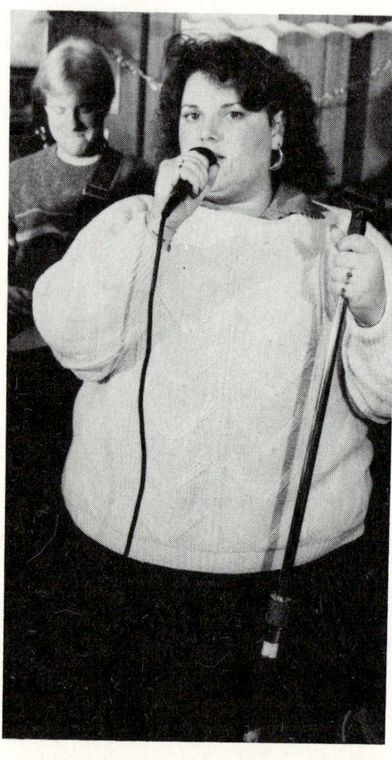

FOR THE SECOND TAPING, I'M ON A *CLOSE-UP* OF THE LEAD PERFORMER.

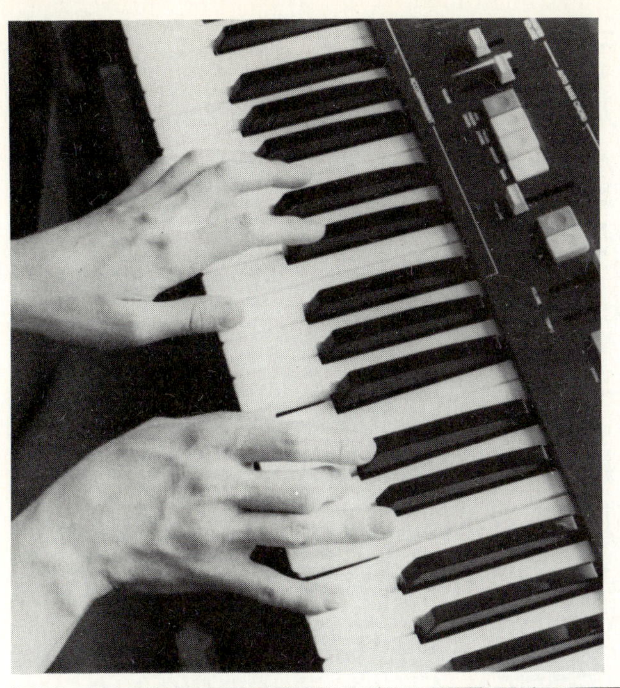

THE THIRD TIME I TAPE THE SONG, THE CAMERA IS ON MY SHOULDER, AND I'M LOOKING FOR INTERESTING INSERTS, LIKE CLOSE-UPS OF THE GUITAR PLAYER'S HANDS, OTHER GROUP MEMBERS' FACES, THE DRUMMER, AND SO FORTH.

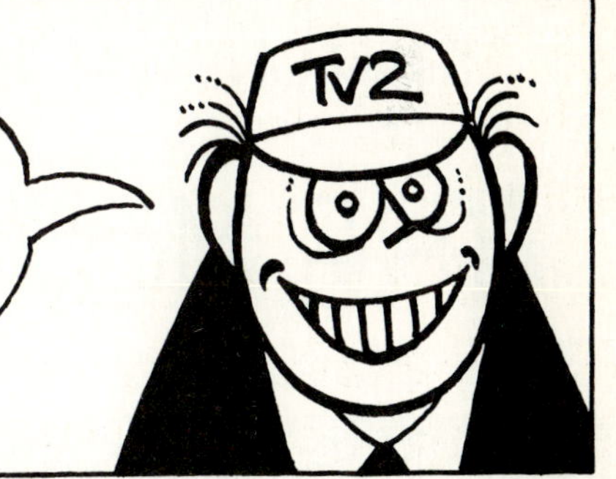

I EDIT IN TWO STEPS. FIRST, I'LL RECORD THE MUSIC AND MY *MASTER SHOT* ONTO THE RECORD TAPE. FOR MY MASTER SHOT, I'M USING THE CLOSE-UP OF THE LEAD SINGER, SINCE THIS IS WHAT I EXPECT TO USE THE MOST. THE SECOND STEP IS TO EDIT IN, USING VIDEO *INSERT* MODE (THAT IS, I WANT TO EDIT *VIDEO* WITHOUT DISTURBING THE SOUND I HAVE JUST RECORDED ON MY TAPE), SOME OF THE DIFFERENT ANGLES, COMPOSITIONS, AND INSERTS THAT I SHOT THE OTHER TWO TIMES THE BAND PERFORMED FOR ME.

THE FACT THAT I HAVE ALREADY RECORDED SOUND ON MY TAPE MAKES THIS EASIER, SINCE I HAVE ONLY TO MATCH THE TAPE I WANT TO EDIT FROM TO THE SAME PART OF THE SONG MY EDITED VERSION IS AT. THE IDEA IS TO CREATE THE ILLUSION THAT THE VIDEO WAS SHOT WITH 3 CAMERAS.

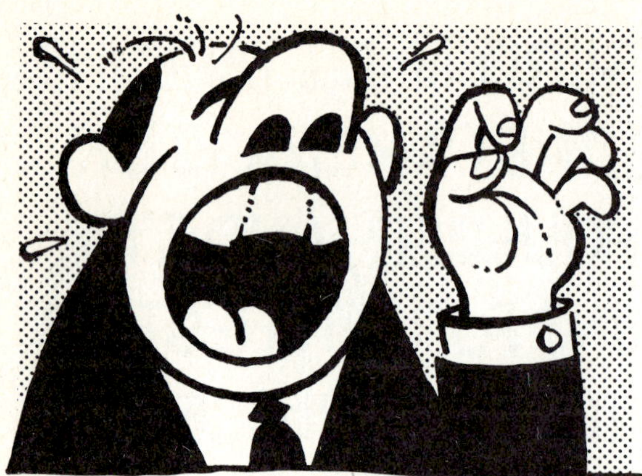

EDITING TOGETHER TWO OR MORE ANGLES OF THE SAME PIECE OF MUSIC CALLS FOR CAREFUL SYNCHRONIZATION OF YOUR TAPE MACHINES, OTHERWISE, THE MUSIC WON'T MATCH AT THE PLACES WHERE THE EDITS ARE MADE. AN ACCURATE EDIT CONTROLLER IS A NECESSITY FOR THIS SORT OF THING. FORTUNATELY, THERE'S MORE THAN ONE WAY TO MAKE A SHARP LOOKING MUSIC VIDEO.

THE MOVING-CAMERA VIDEO

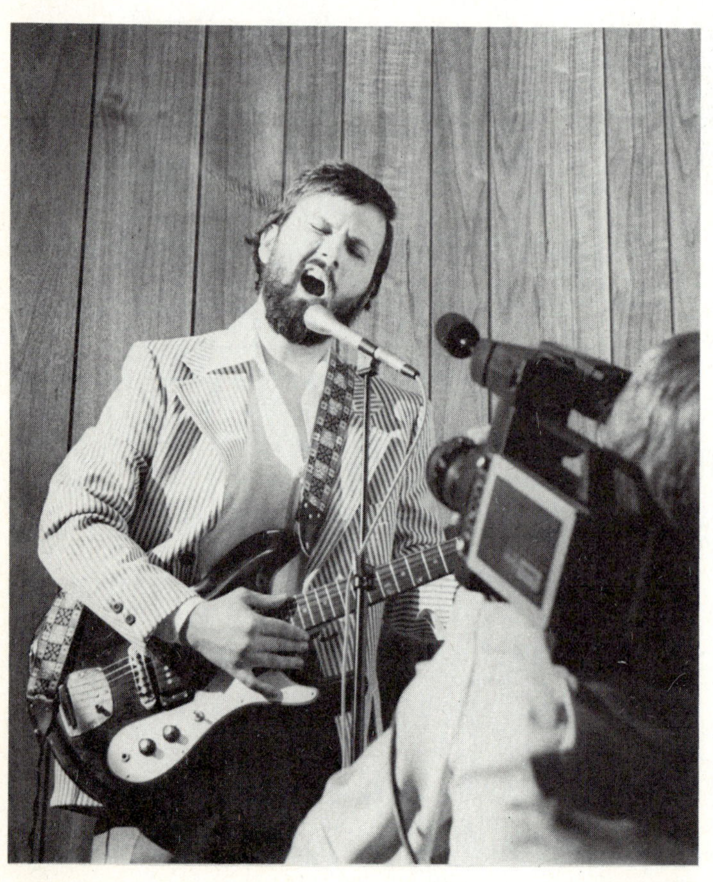

PROBABLY THE **WORST** WAY TO SHOOT A VIDEO (ESPECIALLY FOR QUICK-MOVING ROCK MUSIC) IS TO PUT THE CAMERA ON A TRIPOD AND NOT MOVE IT AN INCH. VARYING THE COMPOSITION (VIA THE ZOOM LENS) DURING THE SONG WILL MAKE THE TAPE MORE VISUALLY INTERESTING. BETTER YET, PUT THE CAMERA ON YOUR SHOULDER, SET THE ZOOM LENS TO **WIDE** (KEEP IT THERE) AND MOVE YOURSELF DURING THE SONG.

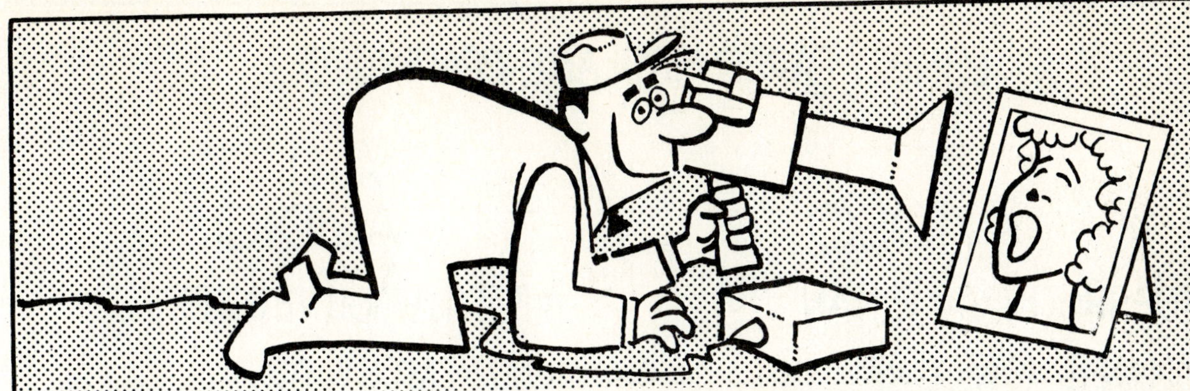

MAKE YOUR MOVES SLOW AND SMOOTH (REMEMBER, YOU WON'T EDIT THIS) AND STAY ON OR NEAR THE LEAD VOCAL MOST OF THE TIME. IF IT'S ROCK MUSIC, DON'T BE AFRAID TO EXPERIMENT WITH TILTED CAMERA ANGLES, EXTREME CLOSE-UPS (DON'T USE YOUR ZOOM WHEN THE CAMERA IS ON YOUR SHOULDER... *WALK* IN CLOSE INSTEAD) AND UNUSUAL COMPOSITIONS.

A STORY VIDEO

HERE'S A PROFESSIONAL-LOOKING MUSIC VIDEO PRODUCED WITH NO EDITING OR SPECIAL EQUIPMENT! THIS IS HOW I DID IT (YOU WILL NEED A RECORDER WITH AN *AUDIO DUB* FEATURE).

FIRST, I PREPARED A SCRIPT WITH THE LYRICS OF THE SONG IN MY *AUDIO* COLUMN, AND THE SHOTS I HAD IN MIND IN THE *VIDEO* COLUMN.

LONELY PAPER AIRPLANE

VIDEO	AUDIO
• MAN AT TABLE - PICKS UP PICTURE	: OH ELLEN, LOVE
• CLOSE-UP ON PICTURE OF WOMAN	: HOW COULD IT BE?
• SWISHPAN	: FEELINGS FLYING PAST.
• MEDIUM SHOT MAN EMBRACING WOMAN	: WE WANTED BOTH OF US,
	: TO SEE
	: OUR LOVE ENSHRINED AT LAST.

VIDEO | AUDIO

VIDEO	AUDIO
• WIDE SHOT OF SAME MAN	: BUT NOW YOU'VE GONE
• WOMAN IS NOW GONE	: NO REASON WHY…
• SWISH PAN	: ANOTHER MAN, YOU WROTE
• MAN BACK AT TABLE—	: AND ALL YOU'VE LEFT
• MEDIUM SHOT—PICKS UP NOTE	: TO SAY GOODBYE
• CLOSE-UP OF NOTE	: IS THIS STUPID PAPER NOTE
• CLOSE-UP OF MAN'S FACE	: THROUGH TEARY EYES
• TEAR ON CHEEK	: I'LL GIVE THE NOTE
• CU FOLDING IT INTO PLANE	: THE WINGS I THOUGHT WE HAD…
• WIDE SHOT OUTSIDE WINDOW	: OUT THE WINDOW
• PLANE FLYS OUT	: WITH OUR PLANS!
• MEDIUM SHOT MAN LOOKING OUT WINDOW	: HOW DID OUR LOVE GO BAD?
• CLOSE-UP PLANE-PAN WITH IT FLYING	: ON MY LONELY PAPER AIRPLANE,
• CLOSE-UP PHOTO OF LOVE	: I WILL WRITE MY DREAMS….
• MAN CLOSES WINDOW	: FOLDED, CREASED, AND AIRBORNE,
• PAPER PLANE CRASHES	: I'VE LOST MORE THAN IT SEEMS.

NEXT, I NEEDED A WAY TO TIME THE SHOTS TO FIT THE PACE OF THE SONG—MY METHOD:

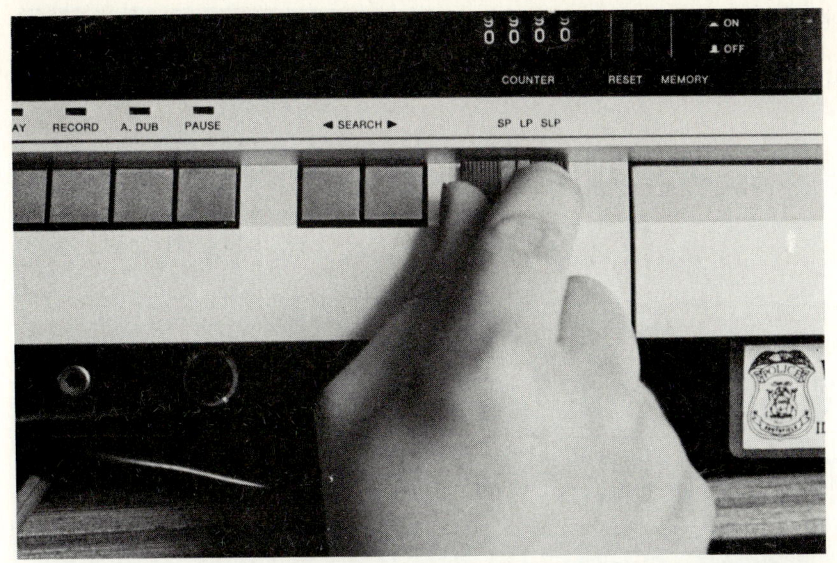
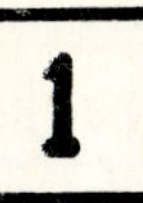

1

SET THE VCR TO ITS FAST-EST SPEED, AND START IT RECORDING. IT DOESN'T MATTER WHAT YOU TAPE BECAUSE YOU'LL SOON *ERASE IT.*

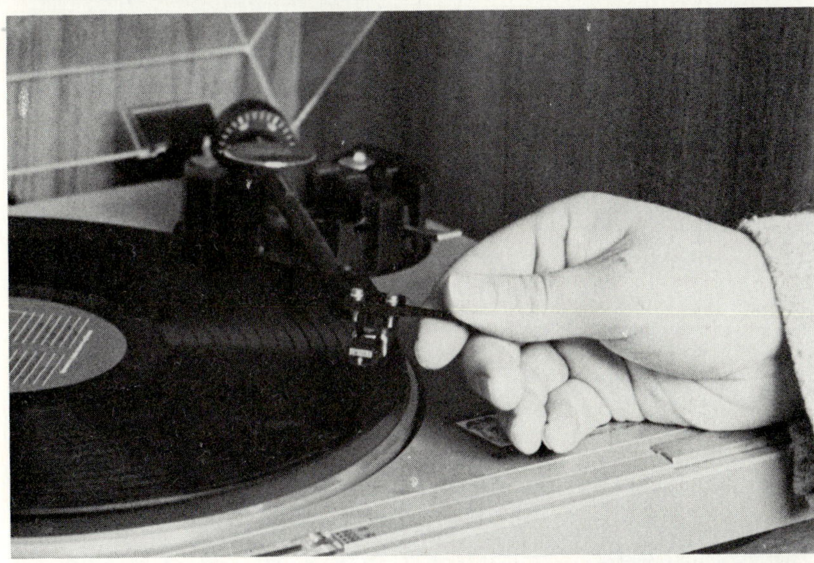

2

START PLAYING THE RECORD OR TAPE OF THE SONG. AT THE INSTANT THE MUSIC BEGINS, RESET THE TAPE COUNTER ON THE VCR *TO ZERO.*

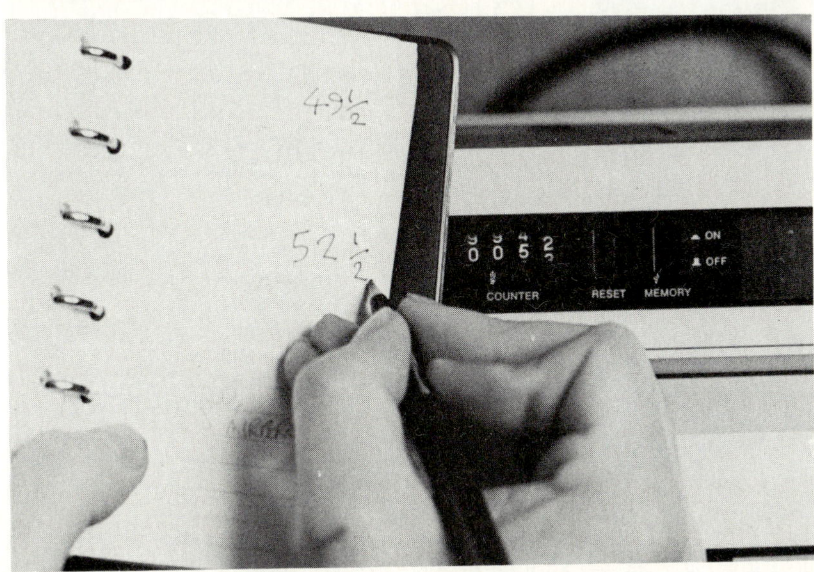

3

HAVE YOUR SCRIPT READY. AT EACH POINT IN THE SONG WHERE THE SHOT CHANGES, MARK DOWN WHAT THE TAPE COUNTER SAYS .... BE AS ACCURATE AS POSSIBLE*!* THESE NUMBERS WILL GUIDE YOU WHILE YOU SHOOT.

4 WHEN THE SONG IS DONE, REWIND THE TAPE TO JUST BEFORE ZERO. *THIS IS WHERE YOU'LL BEGIN TAPING!*

BEFORE PHOTOGRAPHING EACH SCENE, I WAS CAREFUL TO REHEARSE AND TIME IT SO THAT I KNEW IT WOULD FIT INTO ITS ALLOTTED SPACE. WHILE TAPING, I WATCHED THE TAPE COUNTER OUT OF THE CORNER OF MY EYE, STOPPING TAPE WHEN THE NUMBER FOR THE NEXT SCENE CAME UP (OR A FRIEND COULD WATCH THE NUMBERS FOR YOU).

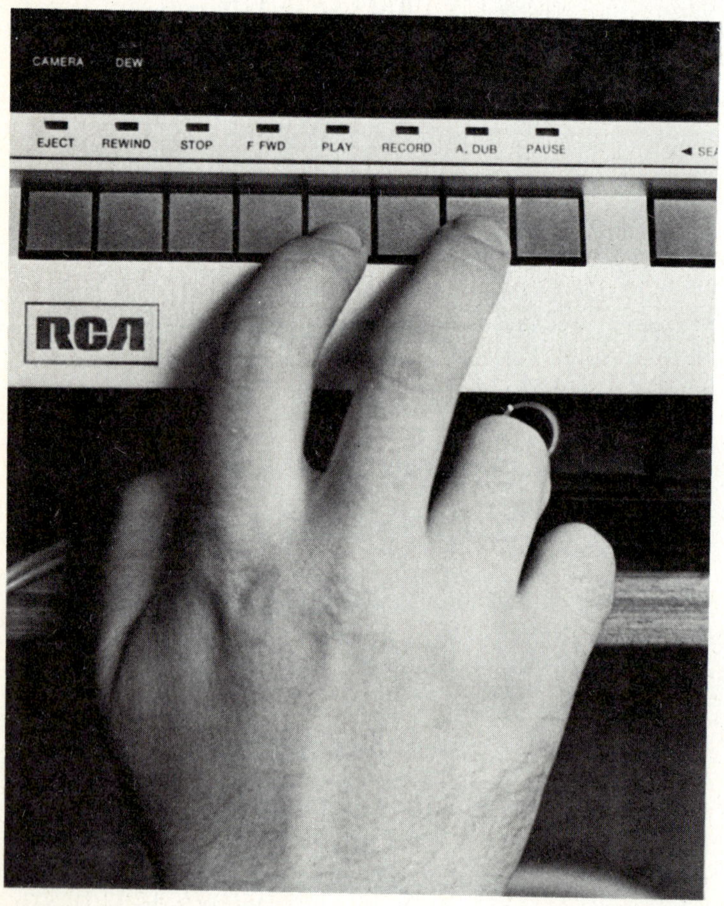

ONCE THE SHOOTING WAS FINISHED, I WOUND THE TAPE BACK TO ZERO AGAIN AND USED THE "AUDIO DUB" CONTROL TO RECORD THE SONG ON THE AUDIO TRACK.

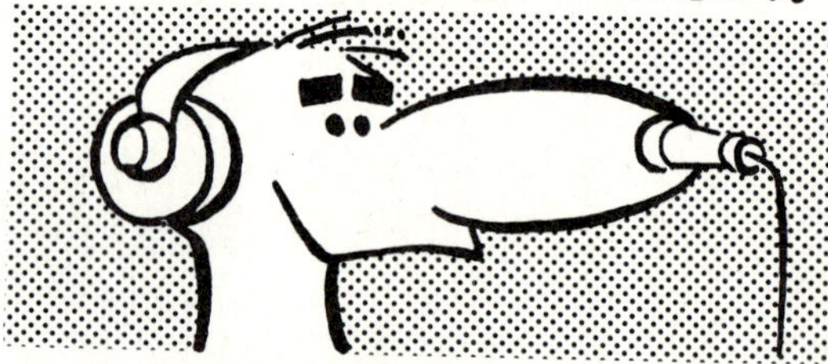

THE PICTURES MATCHED THE SONG PERFECTLY!

NEXT PAGES SHOW EXAMPLE "STORYBOARD" OF THE FINISHED VIDEO!

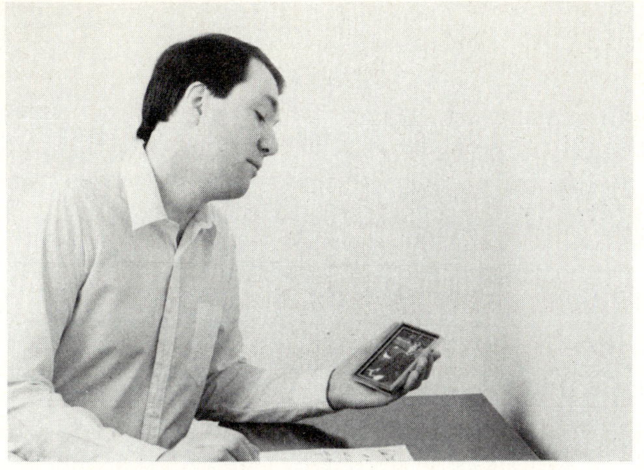

OH, ELLEN, LOVE, HOW COULD IT BE —

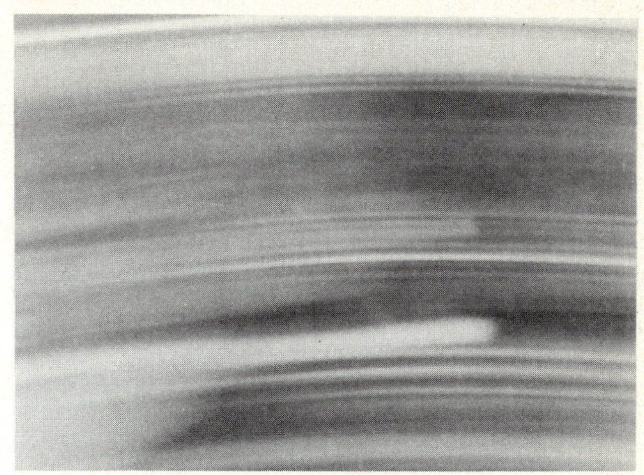

FEELINGS FLYING PAST.

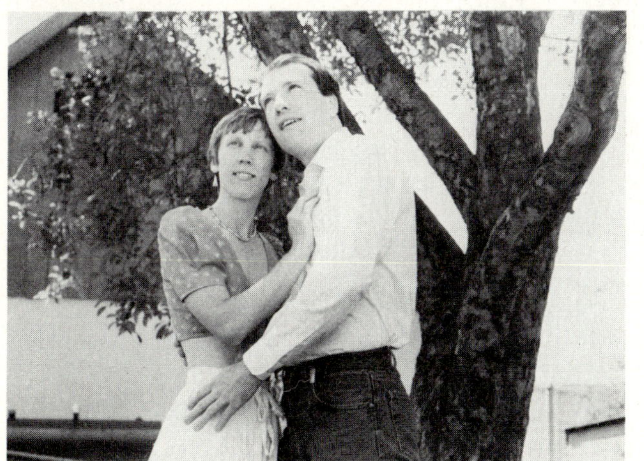

WE WANTED, BOTH OF US, TO SEE OUR LOVE
ENSHRINED AT LAST

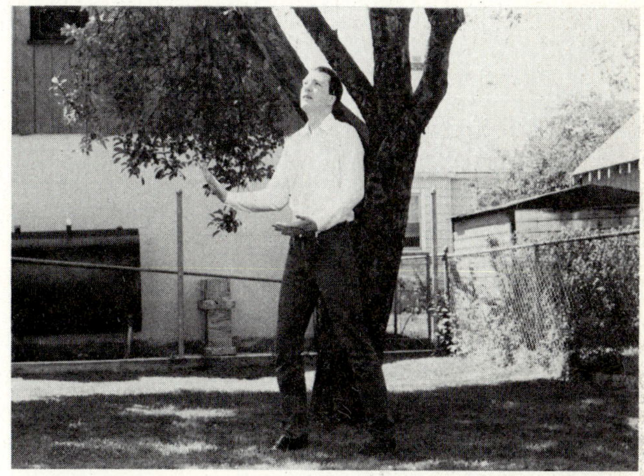

BUT NOW YOU'RE GONE NO REASON WHY—

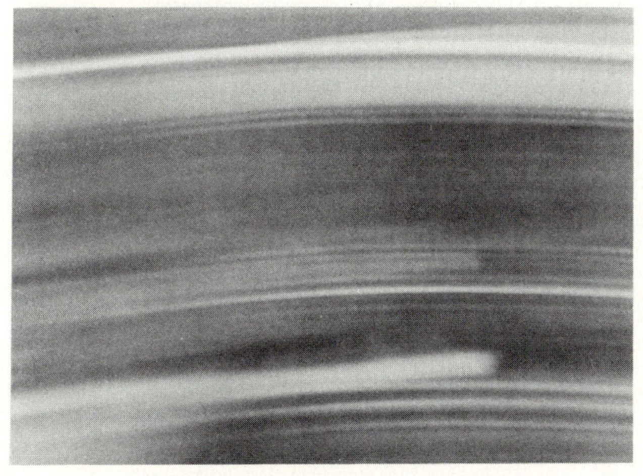

ANOTHER MAN, YOU WROTE.

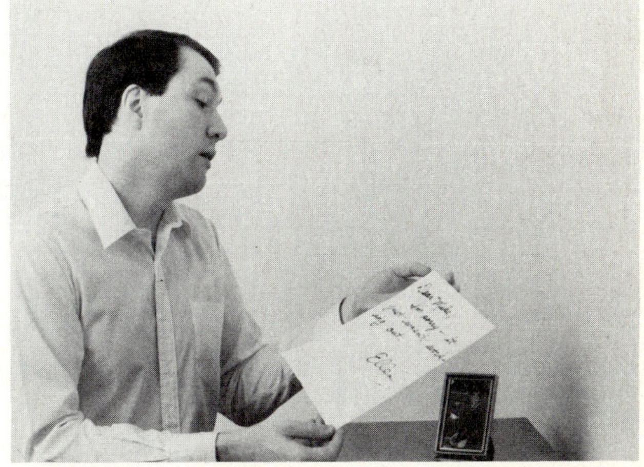

AND ALL YOU'VE LEFT TO SAY GOODBYE

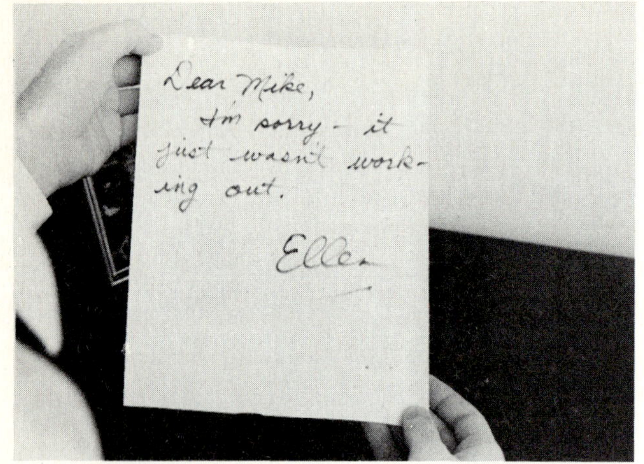

IS THIS STUPID PAPER NOTE

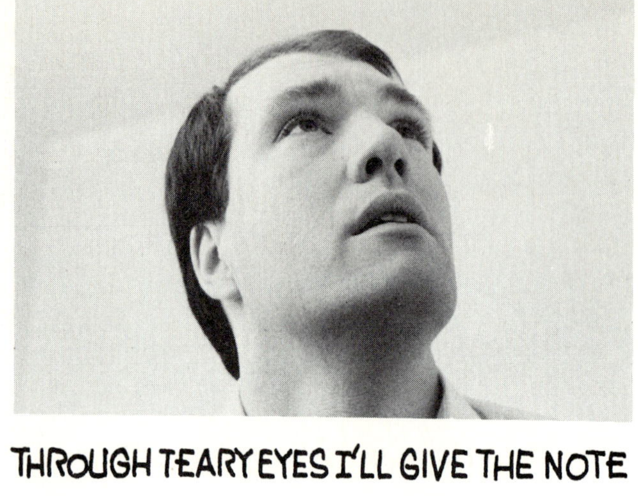

THROUGH TEARY EYES I'LL GIVE THE NOTE

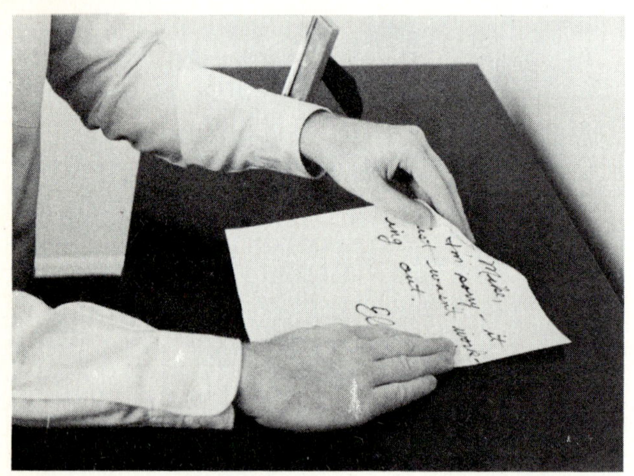

THE WINGS I THOUGHT WE HAD...

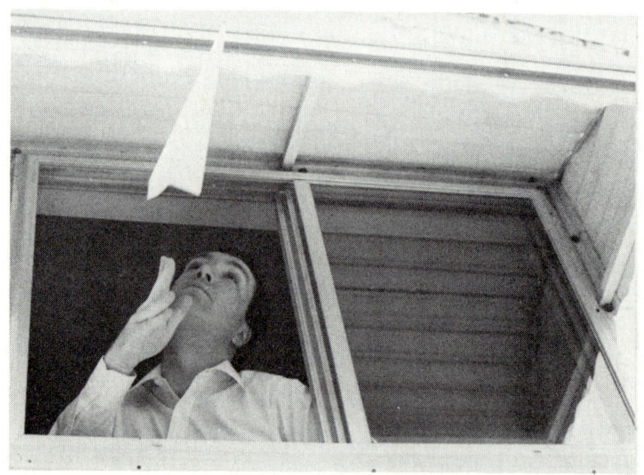

OUT THE WINDOW WITH OUR PLANS!

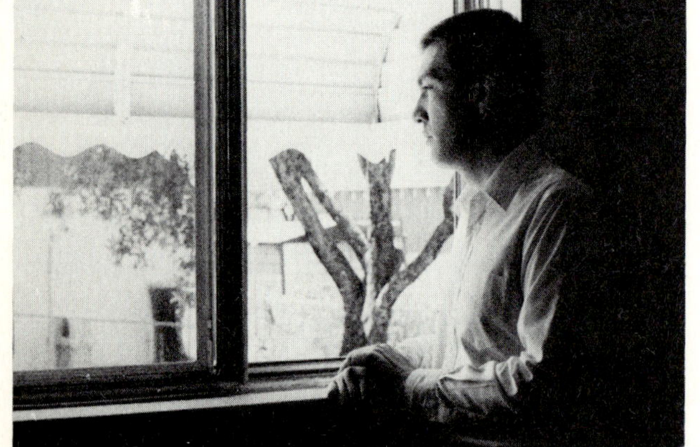

HOW COULD OUR LOVE GO BAD?

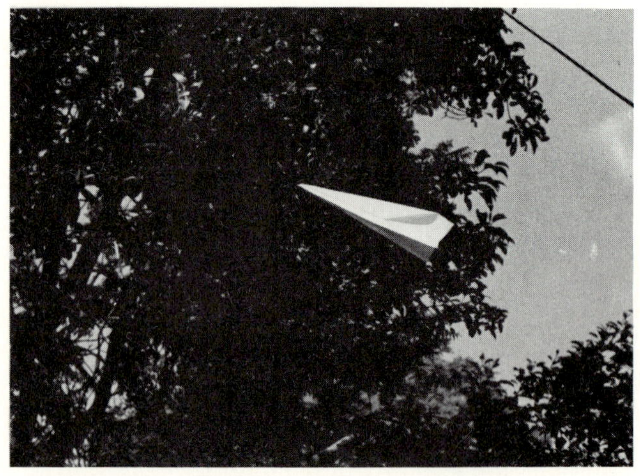

ON MY LONELY PAPER AIRPLANE,

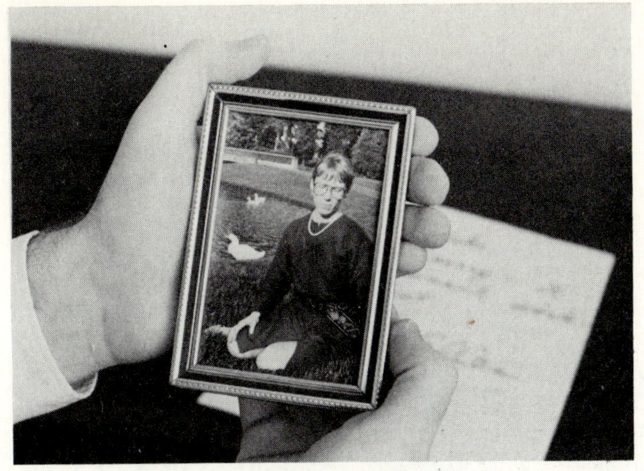

I WILL WRITE MY DREAMS.

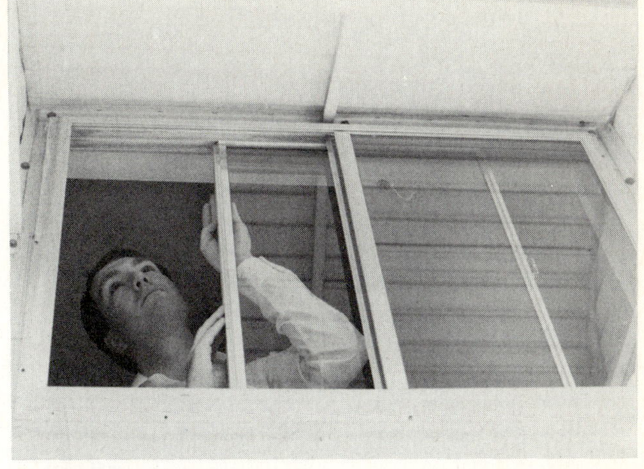

FOLDED, CREASED, THEN AIRBORNE –

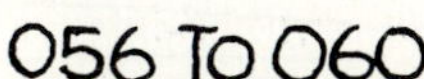

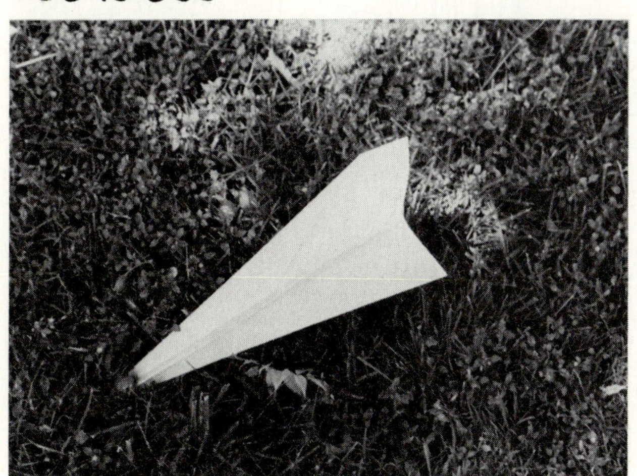

I'VE LOST MORE THAN IT SEEMS.

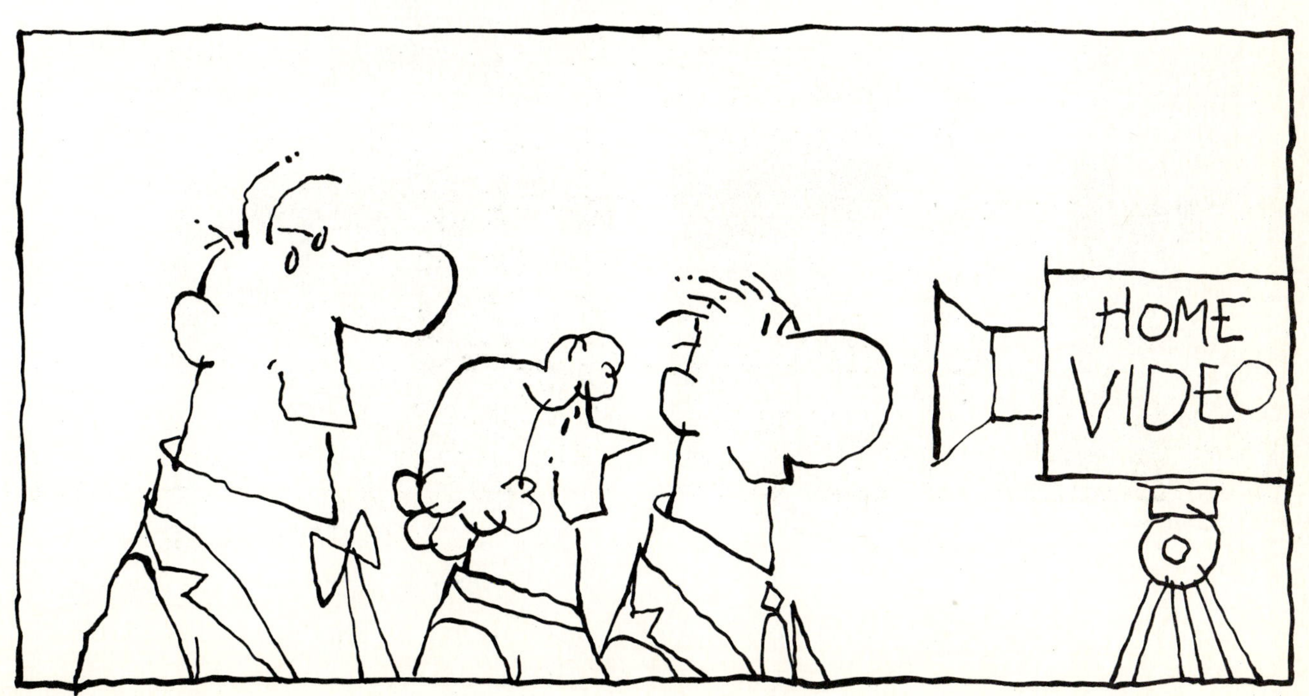

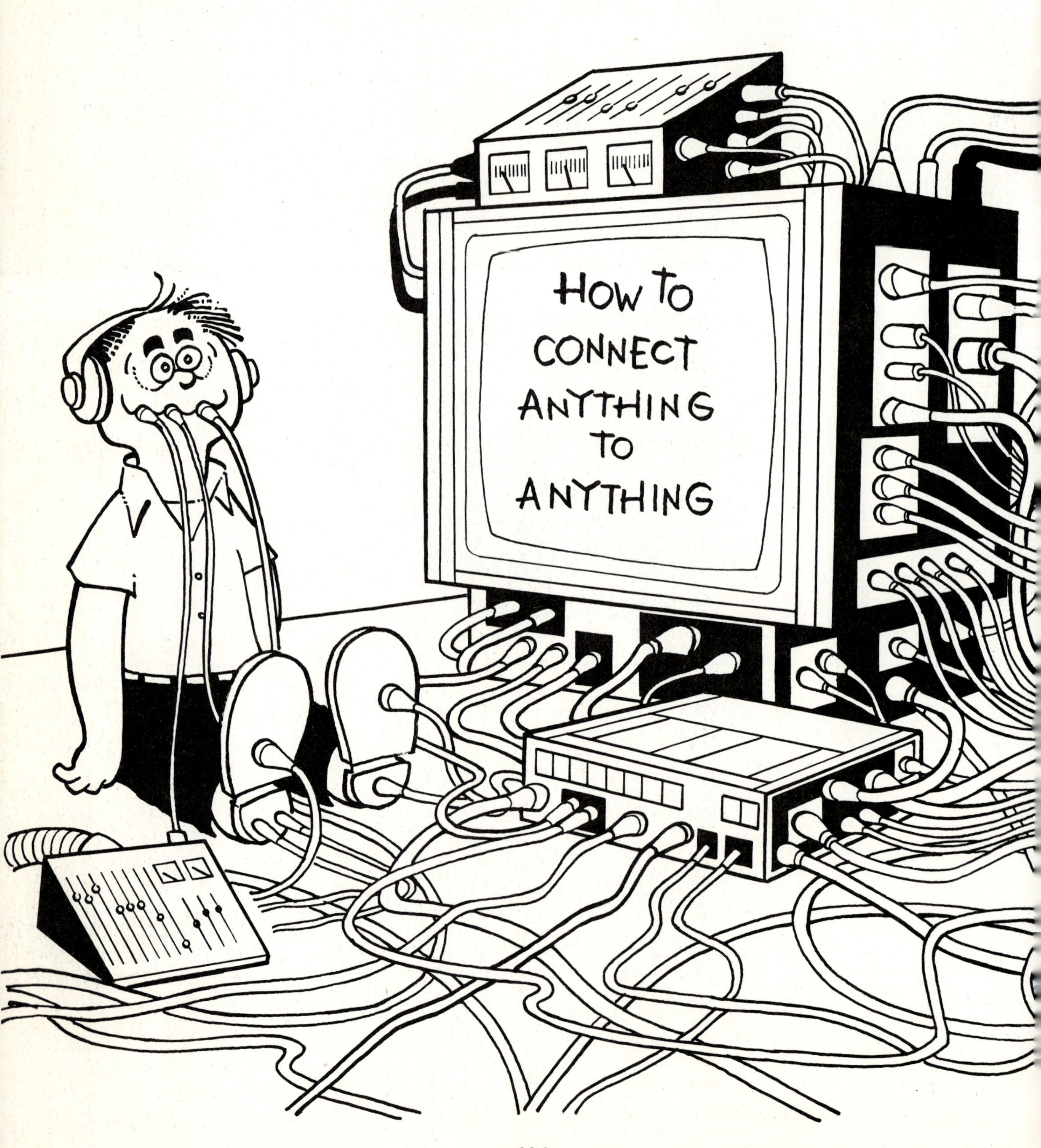

HOW TO CONNECT ANYTHING TO ANYTHING

THERE IS NO TASK MORE FRUSTRATING TO THE VIDEO ENTHUSIAST THAN TRYING TO MAKE SENSE OUT OF THE PROLIFERATION OF PLUGS AND CABLES THAT INTERCONNECT HIS EQUIPMENT. MANY VIDEOGRAPHERS CONSIDER THEMSELVES TO BE TECHNICAL NINCOMPOOPS AND MAY BE TERRIFIED AT THE PROSPECT OF DOING SOME HEAVY CONNECTING. IF YOU'RE HAVING AN ANXIETY ATTACK, I CAN'T DO MUCH EXCEPT TO REASSURE YOU THAT THERE ARE ONLY A HANDFUL OF FACTS TO REMEMBER FOR TROUBLE-FREE INTERCONNECTING. GRIT YOUR TEETH, THEN, AND READ THE FOLLOWING FOUR FACTS FOR FLAWLESS INTERFACING:

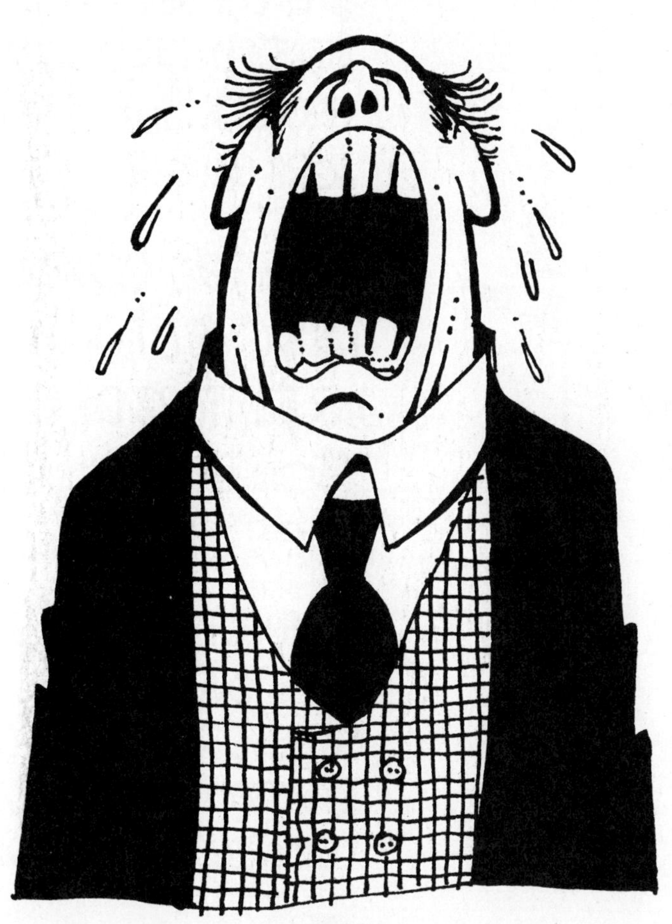

NUMBER ONE

A CONNECTOR EXISTS FOR ONE OF TWO REASONS. EITHER IT IS AN *INPUT* OR IT IS AN *OUTPUT*. OUTPUTS EMIT ELECTRICAL SIGNALS. *INPUTS* RECEIVE THOSE SIGNALS. WHEN TWO PIECES OF EQUIPMENT CONNECT TO EACH OTHER, *INPUTS* ALWAYS CONNECT TO *OUTPUTS!*

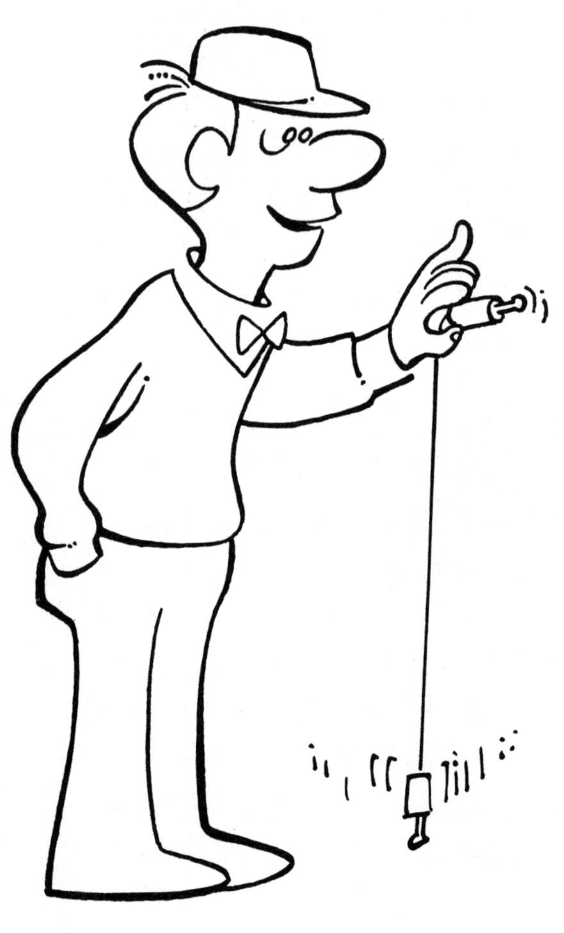

NUMBER TWO

CONNECTORS ON VIDEO EQUIPMENT MAY BE FURTHER CLASSIFIED INTO FOUR GENERAL CATEGORIES: **VIDEO, AUDIO, RF,** AND **CONTROL.** VIDEO CONNECTORS RECEIVE OR EMIT THE PICTURE INFORMATION. **AUDIO** INPUTS OR OUTPUTS PROCESS THE SOUND. THE **RF** CONNECTORS (RF STANDS FOR RADIO-FREQUENCY) EXIST SPECIFICALLY TO CONNECT TO A STANDARD TV SET.

AN **RF** SIGNAL HAS BOTH THE PICTURE AND SOUND IN A BROADCAST TYPE SIGNAL THAT A TV SET CAN UNDERSTAND. THIS CONNECTOR IS **NOT** RECOMMENDED FOR DUBBING OR EDITING BECAUSE THE **VIDEO/AUDIO** CONNECTORS CAN PROVIDE BETTER QUALITY.

CONTROL CONNECTORS ARE DESIGNED FOR REMOTE CONTROL OR EDITING DEVICES THAT CONTROL THE MECHANICAL OPERATION OF THE EQUIPMENT.

CONNECTORS IN ONE CATEGORY ONLY MATE TO A CONNECTOR IN THE *SAME* CATEGORY. *VIDEO* OUTPUTS CONNECT TO *VIDEO* INPUTS, *AUDIO* OUTPUTS CONNECT TO *AUDIO* INPUTS, AND SO FORTH.

NUMBER THREE

OUTPUTS OR INPUTS ARE DESIGNED TO EMIT OR ACCEPT ELECTRICAL SIGNALS. THE **LEVEL,** OR STRENGTH, OF THAT SIGNAL IS IMPORTANT. VIDEO SIGNALS ARE REASONABLY STANDARD, BUT AUDIO LEVELS CAN VARY QUITE A BIT DEPENDING ON WHAT IS BEING PLUGGED INTO WHATEVER ELSE.

AS A GENERAL RULE, AUDIO SIGNALS CAN BE CLASSIFIED AS EITHER **LINE LEVEL** OR **MIKE LEVEL.** AN AUDIO SIGNAL WILL FALL INTO ONE OR THE OTHER OF THESE TWO CATEGORIES! IF YOU WERE TO PLUG A **MIKE LEVEL** OUTPUT (LIKE A MICROPHONE) INTO A **LINE LEVEL** INPUT, NO AUDIO WOULD GET ACROSS. THE MICROPHONE DOESN'T PUT OUT ENOUGH SIGNAL TO DRIVE THE LINE LEVEL INPUT; CONVERSELY, A **LINE LEVEL** OUTPUT WOULD **OVERDRIVE** A **MIKE LEVEL** INPUT, CREATING DISTORTION IN THE SOUND.

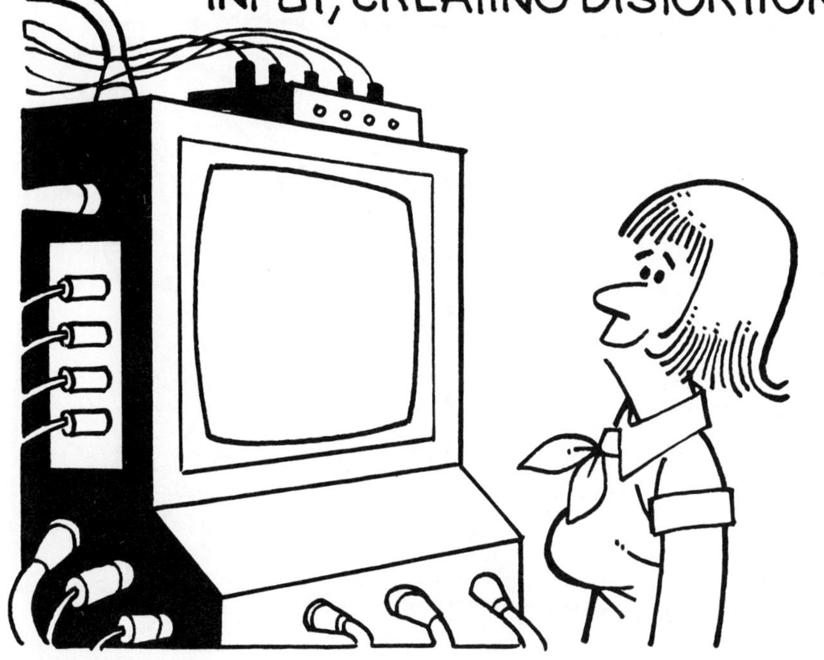

THERE WOULD BE TOO MUCH SIGNAL FOR THE INPUT TO HANDLE. TO CONNECT A LINE LEVEL OUTPUT TO A MIKE LEVEL INPUT, AN **ATTENUATOR,** WHICH REDUCES THE LEVEL OF THE SIGNAL, SHOULD BE USED. TO CONNECT A MIKE LEVEL OUTPUT TO A LINE LEVEL INPUT, A **PREAMPLIFIER,** WHICH BOOSTS THE SIGNAL LEVEL, CAN BE USED!

NUMBER FOUR

TO INTERCONNECT 2 PIECES OF EQUIPMENT, YOU'LL NEED A CABLE WITH AN APPROPRIATE CONNECTOR ON EACH END. PLUGS AND CONNECTORS COME IN DOZENS OF TYPES AND SIZES, AND IT'S NOT UNUSUAL TO RUN ACROSS A SITUATION WHERE TWO DIFFERENT TYPES OF CONNECTORS HAVE TO BE MATED. IF YOU'RE SERIOUS ABOUT BECOMING A "CONNECT ANYTHING TO ANYTHING" EXPERT, BUY YOURSELF A BOX OF CABLES, ADAPTORS, AND ATTENUATORS WITH AS MANY DIFFERENT PLUGS AS YOU CAN FIND.

ON THE FOLLOWING PAGES ARE SOME OF THE MOST COMMON TYPES OF PLUGS, CONNECTORS, INPUTS AND OUTPUTS FOUND ON HOME VIDEO EQUIPMENT!

SOME PLUGS AND CONNECTORS

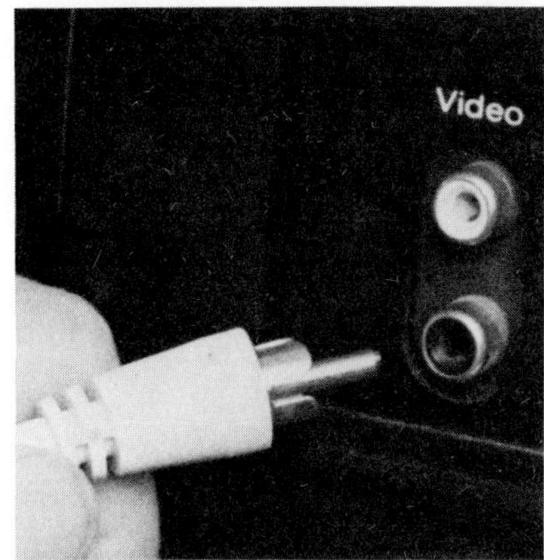

TYPE OF PLUG: "RCA" OR "PHONO" PLUG
TYPE OF SIGNAL: VIDEO
PURPOSE OF CONNECTOR: OUTPUT

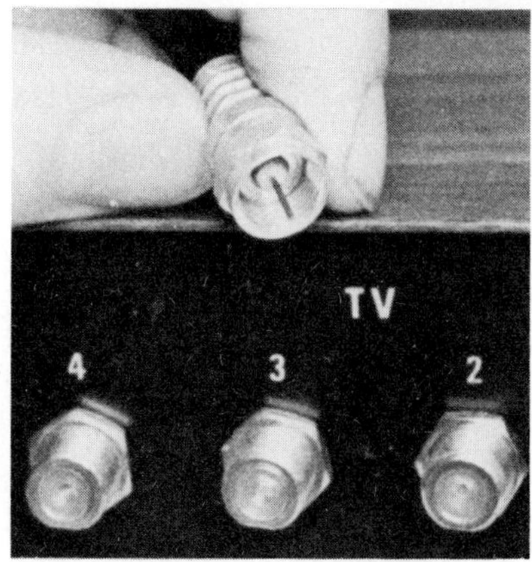

TYPE OF PLUG: "F" CONNECTOR
TYPE OF SIGNAL: RF
PURPOSE OF CONNECTOR: OUTPUT

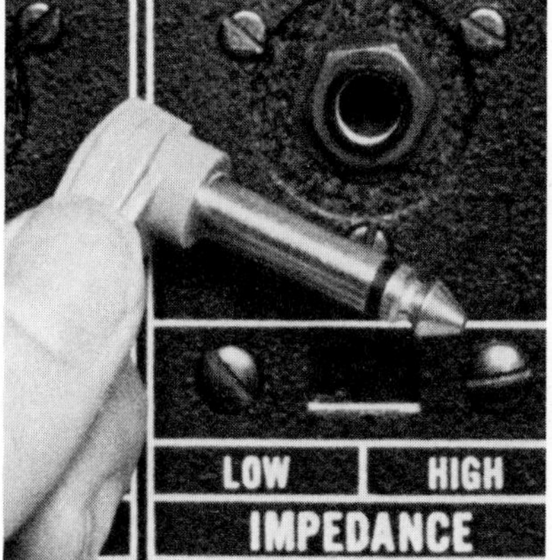

TYPE OF PLUG: "PHONE" PLUG
TYPE OF SIGNAL: AUDIO
PURPOSE OF CONNECTOR: INPUT

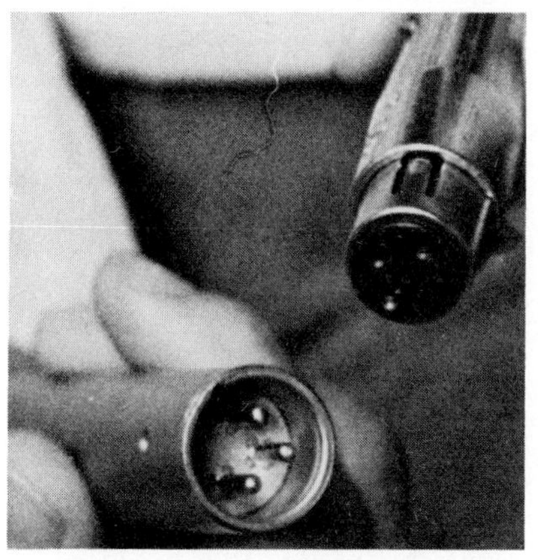

TYPE OF PLUG: "XLR" OR "CANON"
TYPE OF SIGNAL: AUDIO
PURPOSE OF CONNECTOR: OUTPUT

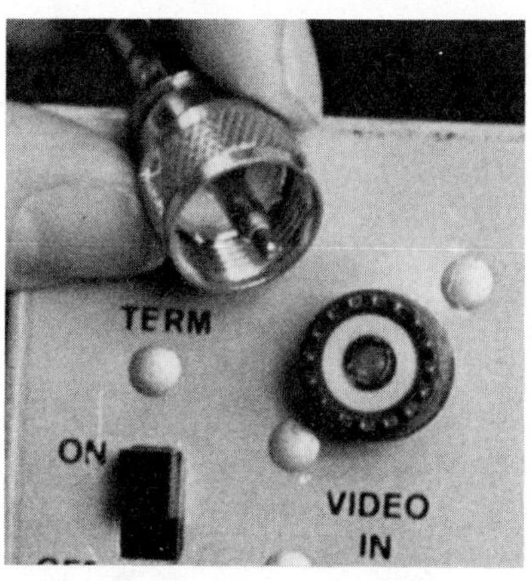

TYPE OF PLUG: "PL-259"
TYPE OF SIGNAL: VIDEO
PURPOSE OF CONNECTOR: INPUT

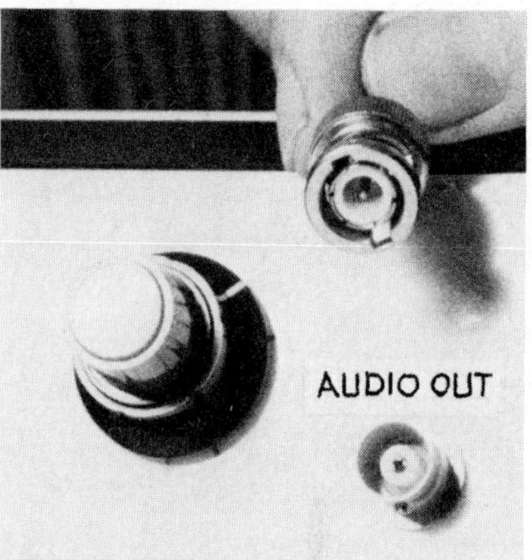

TYPE OF PLUG: "BNC"
TYPE OF SIGNAL: AUDIO
PURPOSE OF CONNECTOR: OUTPUT

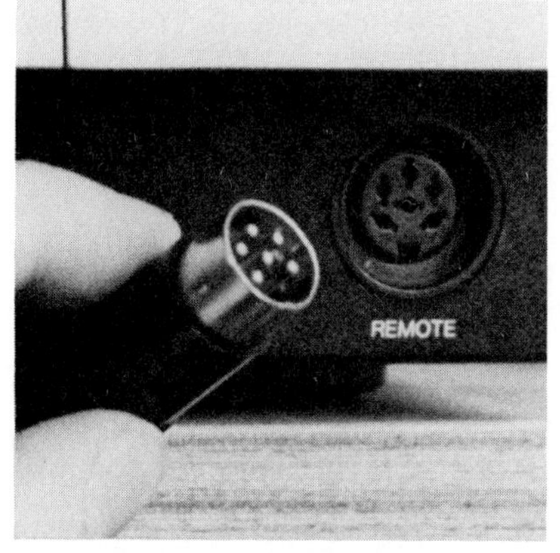

TYPE OF PLUG: "DIN"
TYPE OF SIGNAL: CONTROL
PURPOSE OF CONNECTOR: INPUT

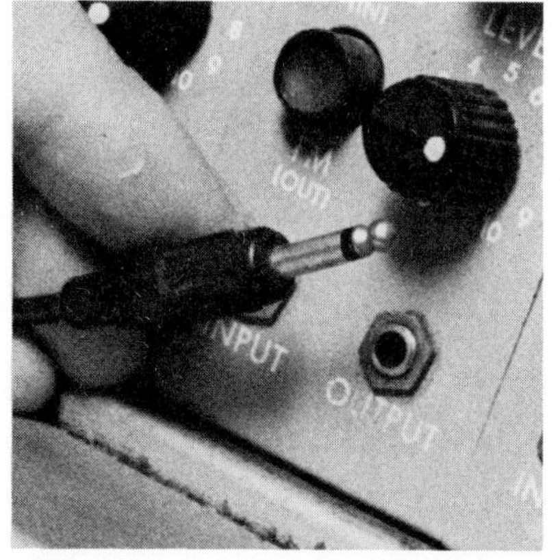

TYPE OF PLUG: "MINI PHONE" PLUG
TYPE OF SIGNAL: AUDIO
PURPOSE OF CONNECTOR: OUTPUT

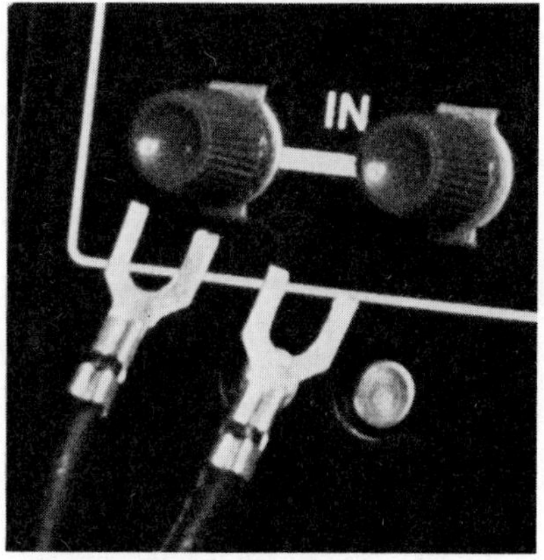

TYPE OF PLUG: "SPADE LUGS"
TYPE OF SIGNAL: RF
PURPOSE OF CONNECTOR: INPUT

CONNECTING A WIRELESS MICROPHONE

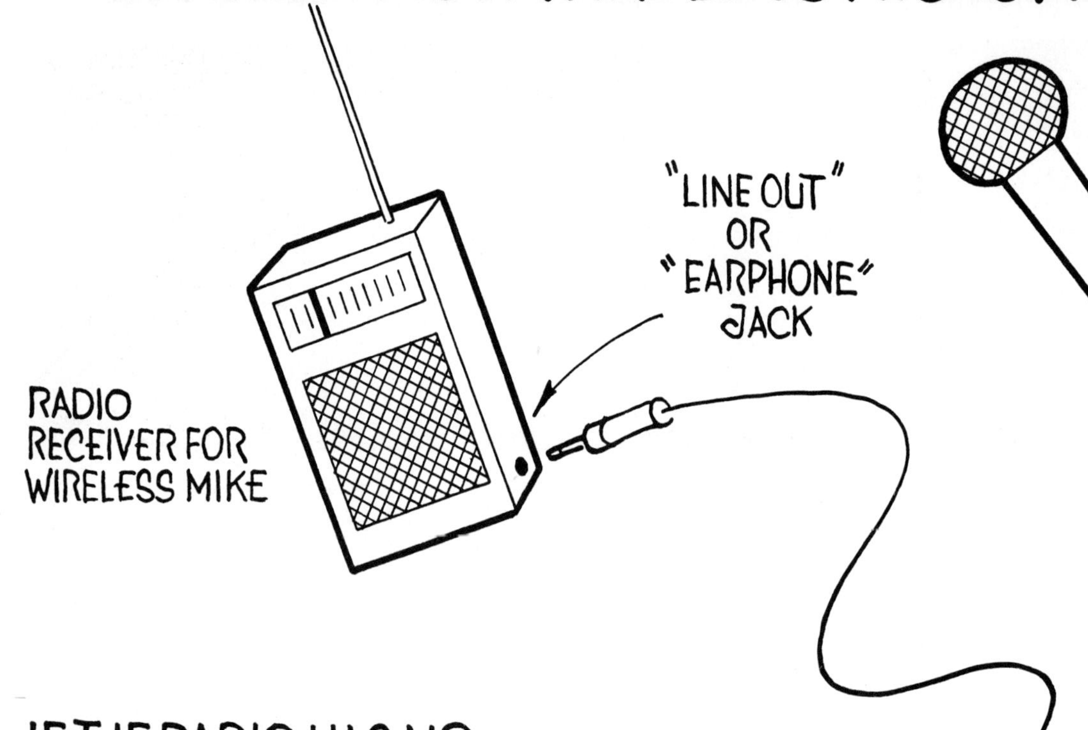

IF THE RADIO HAS NO "LINE OUT" JACK, YOU CAN CONNECT TO THE "EARPHONE" JACK, PROVIDED YOU ADJUST THE RADIO'S "VOLUME" CONTROL TO A LOW LEVEL.

IF YOUR RECORDER HAS NO "LINE IN" JACK, THE "MIKE" JACK CAN BE USED WITH THE ATTENUATOR.

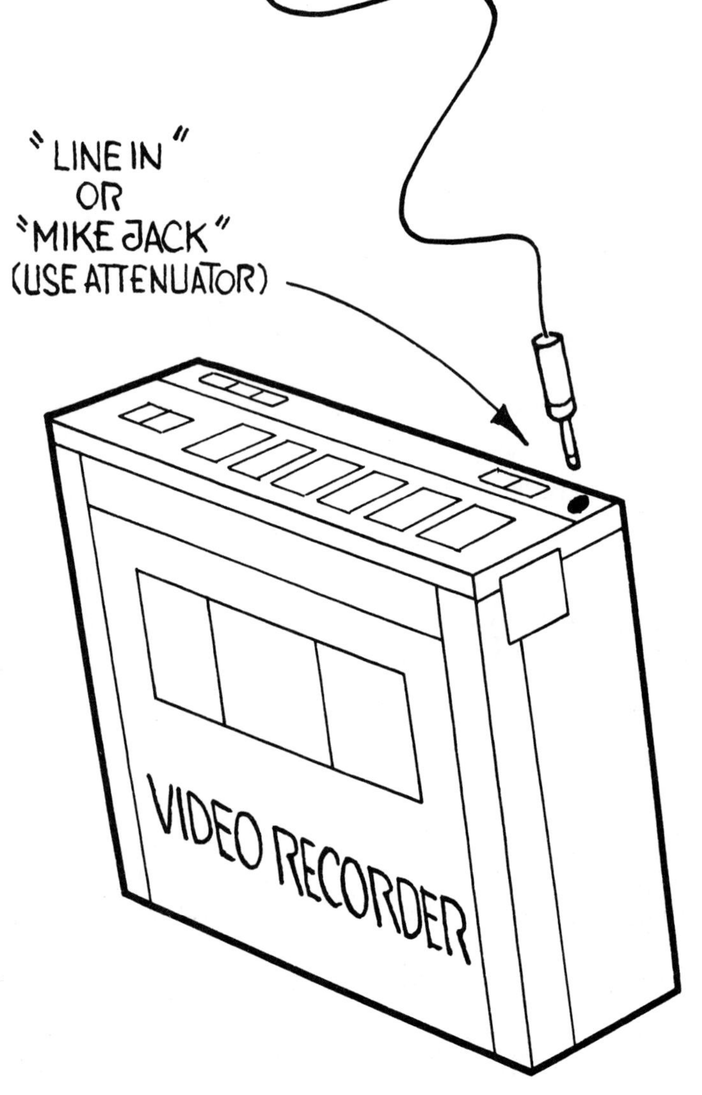

CONNECTING A HOME COMPUTER

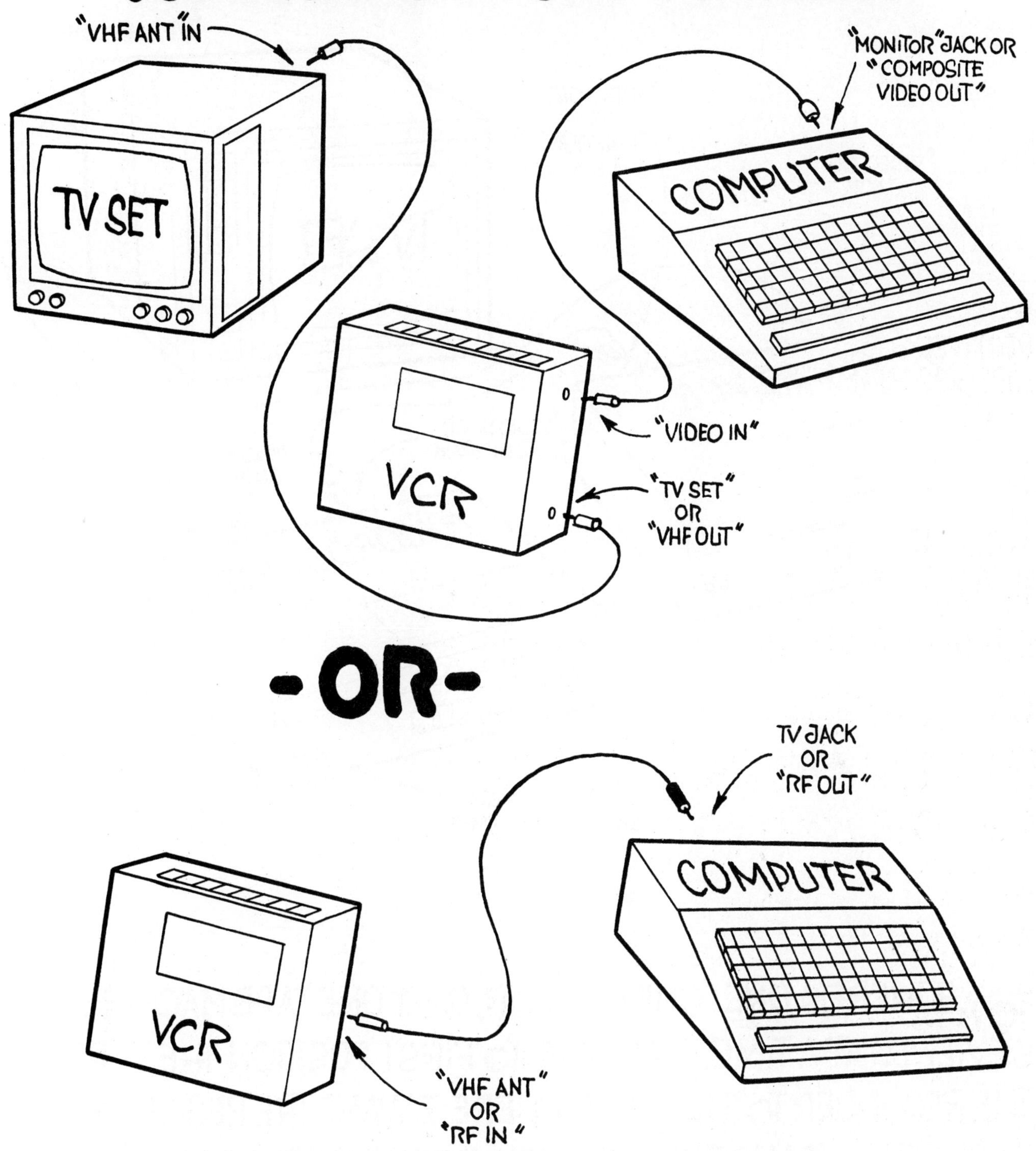

TO RECORD GRAPHICS FROM THE COMPUTER, THE VCR'S "TUNER/CAMERA" SWITCH SHOULD BE SET TO "CAMERA". MAKE SURE YOUR CAMERA IS NOT PLUGGED IN THE RECORDER.

COPYING TAPES OR SIMPLE EDITING

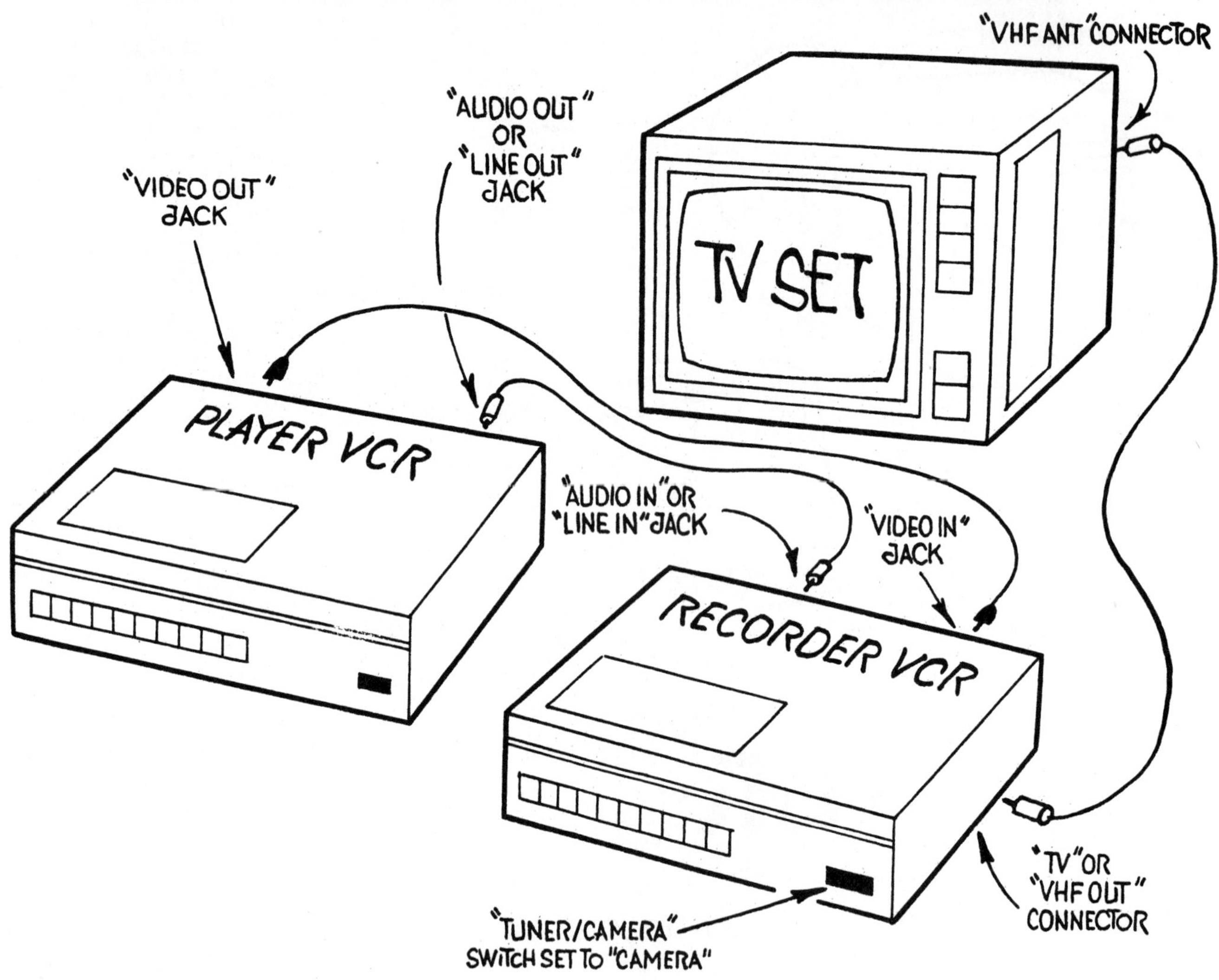

SINCE THERE'S ONLY ONE MONITOR, ONLY ONE TAPE MACHINE CAN BE VIEWED AT A TIME. I PREFER TO FIRST POSITION THE TAPE IN THE RECORDER TO THE PLACE WHERE I WANT THE RECORDING TO BEGIN, THEN **PAUSE** IT AND PUSH **RECORD/PLAY** (IT WON'T START RECORDING YET— IT'S STILL IN **PAUSE**). NOW I CAN SEE THE **PLAYER** ON THE MONITOR, AND CUE ITS TAPE TO THE RIGHT SPOT. FOR A SMOOTHER-LOOKING EDIT, **PLAY** THE PLAYER FIRST, THEN **UNPAUSE** THE RECORDER.

CONNECTING TO HOME STEREO

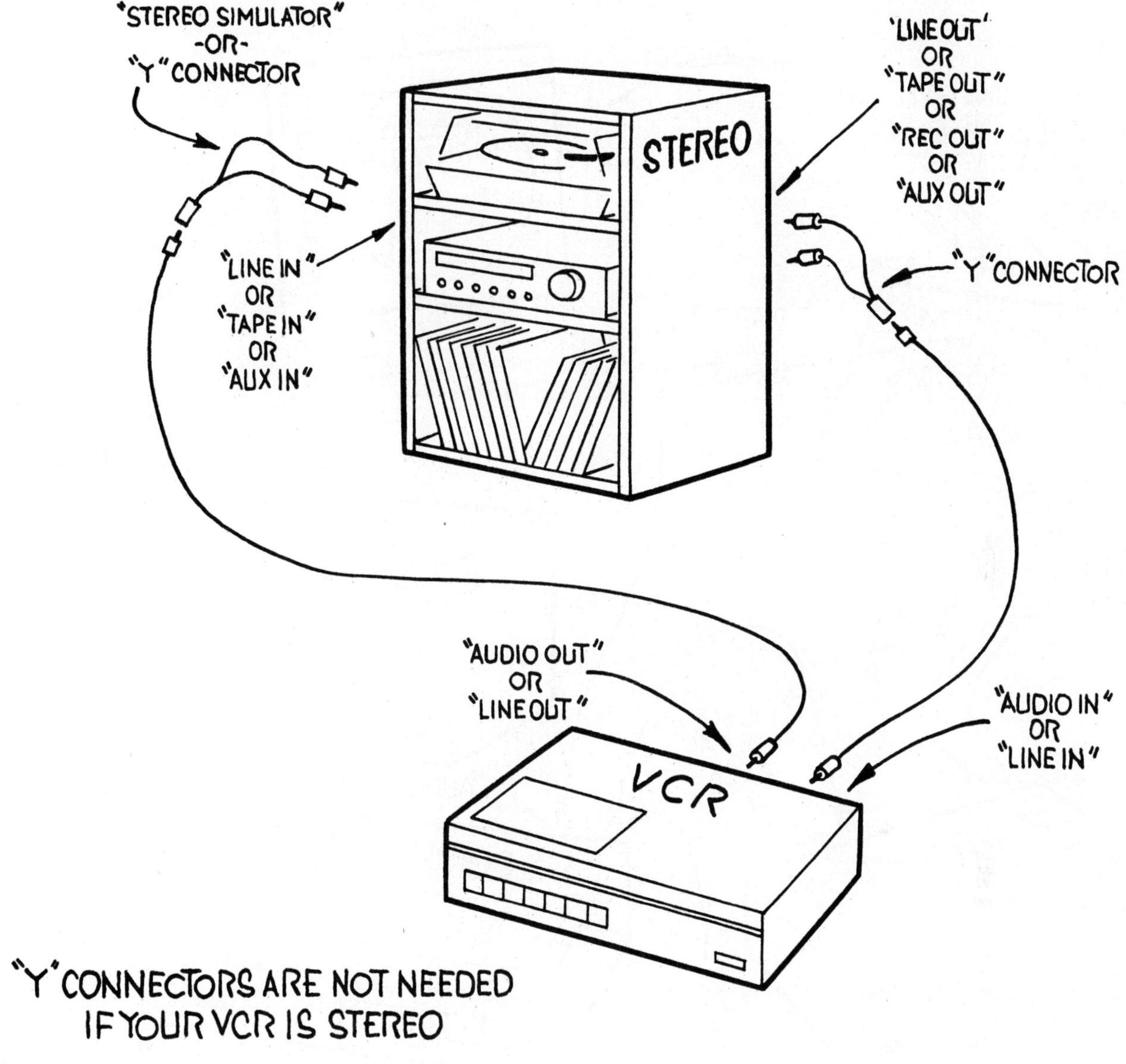

TO RECORD MUSIC FROM YOUR STEREO ONTO A VIDEO TAPE, SET THE TUNER/CAMERA SWITCH TO "CAMERA" AND USE THE "AUDIO DUB" BUTTON TO ADD MUSIC TO YOUR EXISTING VIDEO. TO PLAY BACK YOUR TAPES THROUGH YOUR STEREO, SELECT "TAPE" (OR WHATEVER INPUT YOU'VE CONNECTED IT TO) ON YOUR STEREO.

ADDING AN EXTRA TRACK OF SOUND WHILE MAKING A COPY!

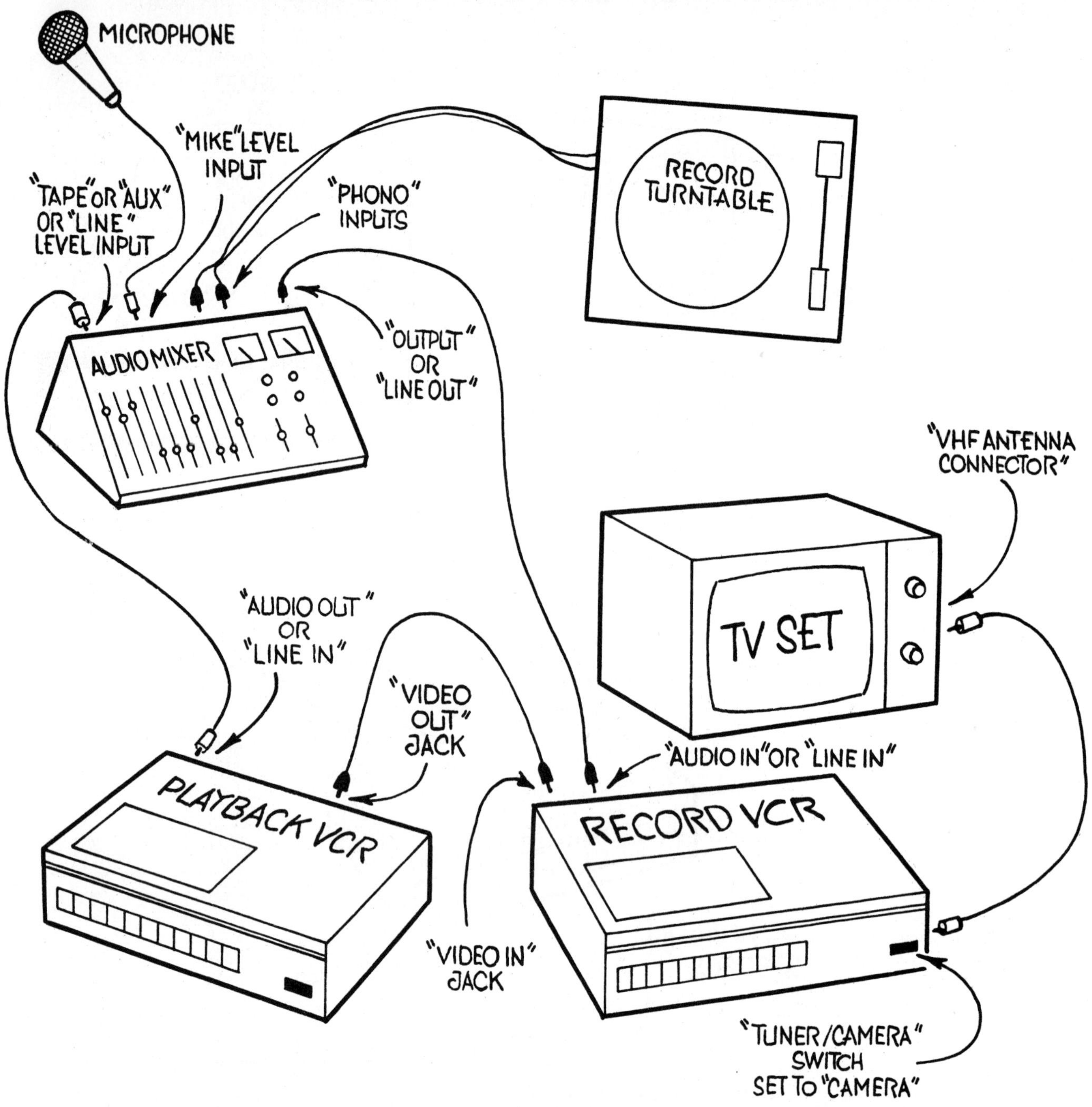

THE MIXER CAN CONTROL THE AUDIO LEVEL OF YOUR ORIGINAL SOUNDTRACK (IN THE "PLAYBACK" VCR) AND BALANCE IT AGAINST THE MUSIC FROM THE TURNTABLE OR NARRATION FROM THE MICROPHONE!

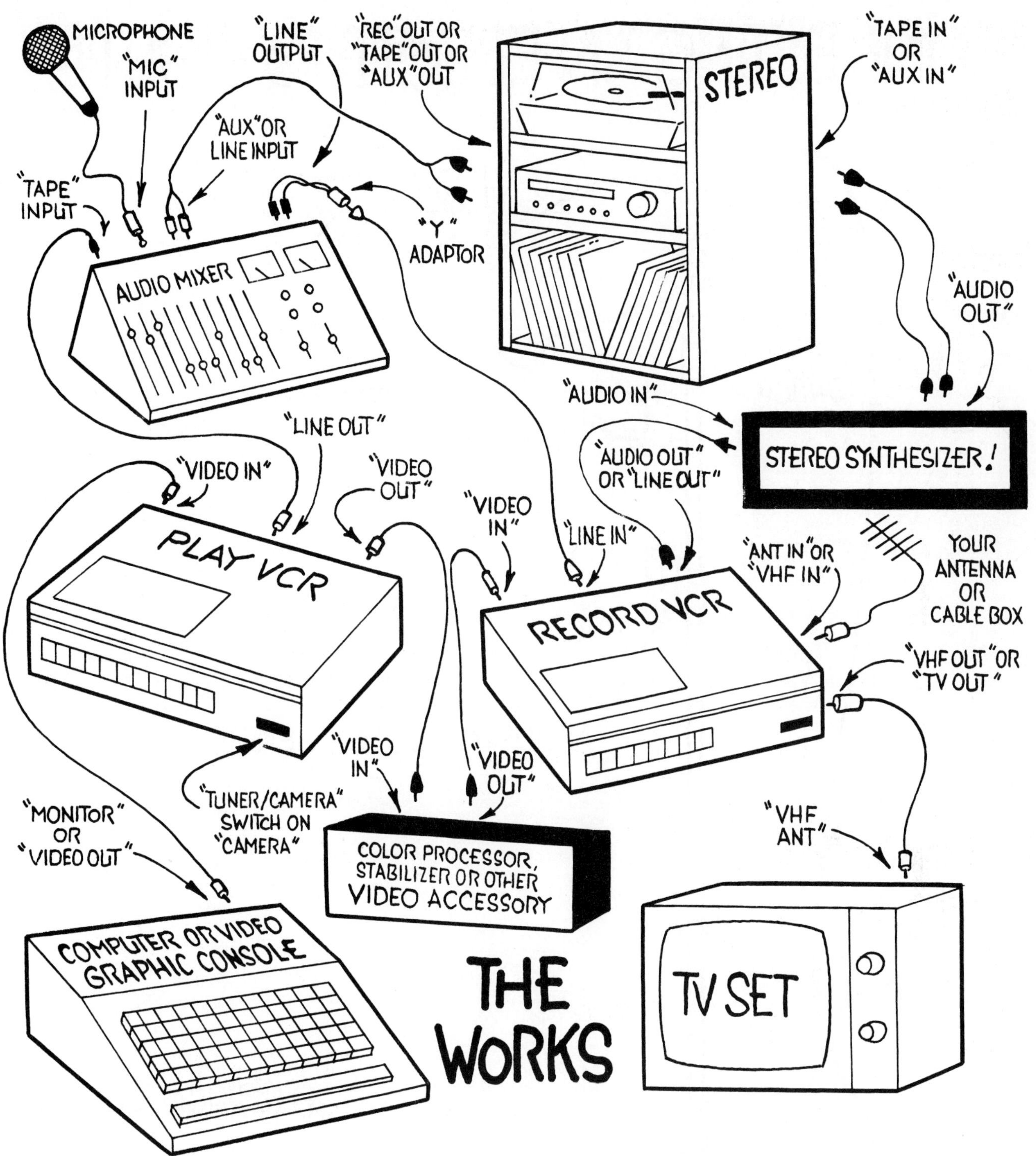

EVERYTHING PUT TOGETHER INTO ONE HECK OF A SYSTEM! SET THE RECORDER'S TUNER/CAMERA ON *CAMERA* TO EDIT OR DUB, AND ON *TUNER* TO WATCH OR *RECORD* TV SHOWS. YOU'LL BE ABLE TO VIEW OR RECORD THE COMPUTER'S OUTPUT WHEN NO TAPE IS IN THE PLAYBACK MACHINE.

CONNECTING AN ELECTRIC LIGHT

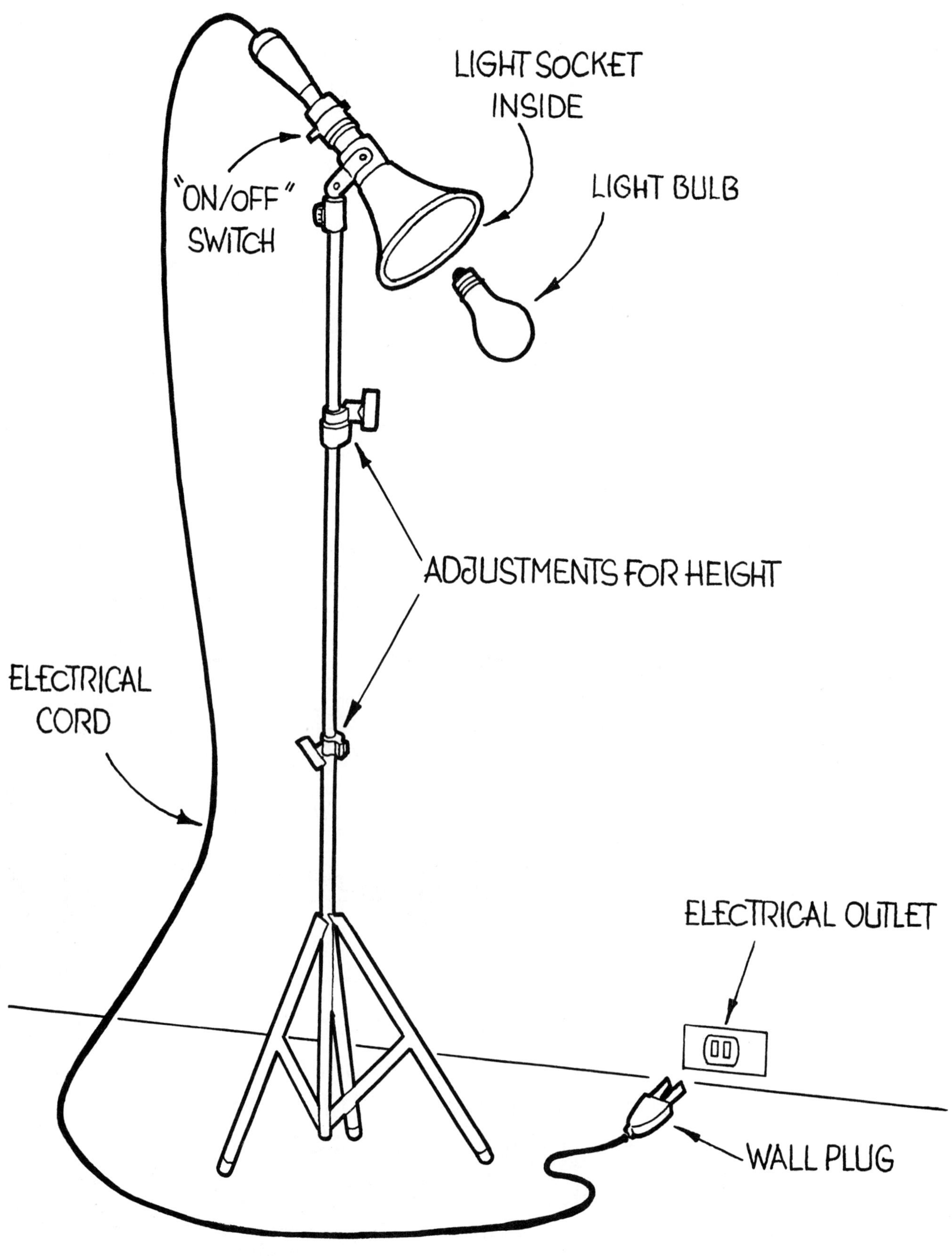

WHAT SHOULD I BUY?

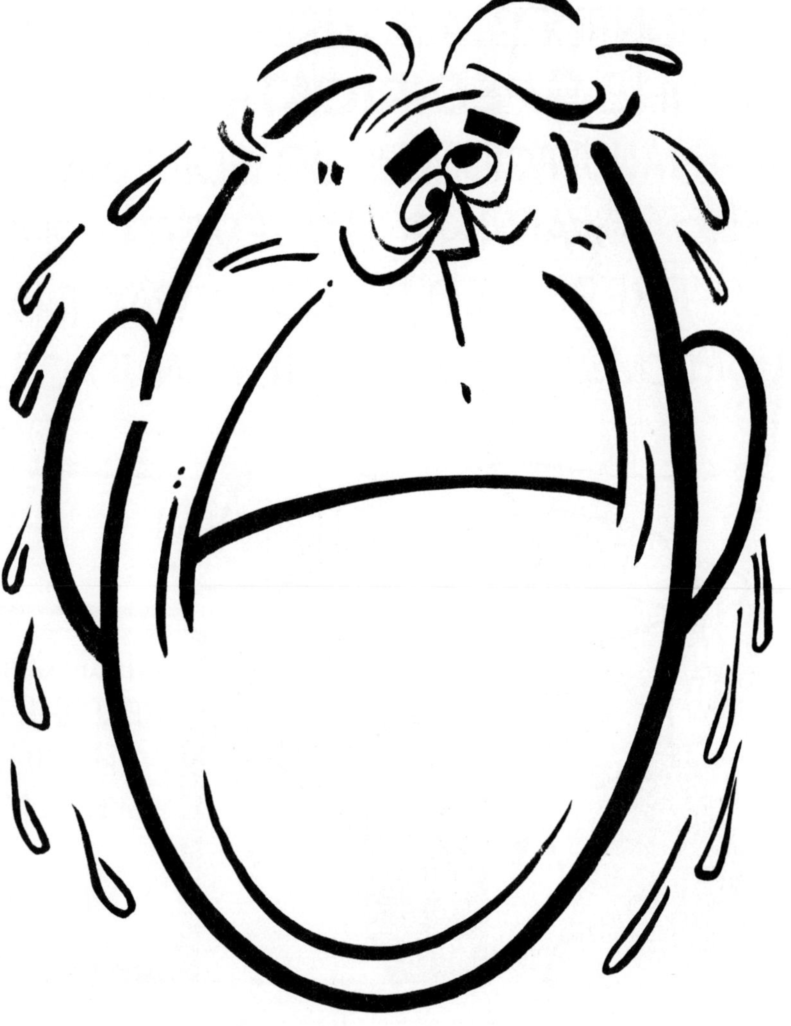

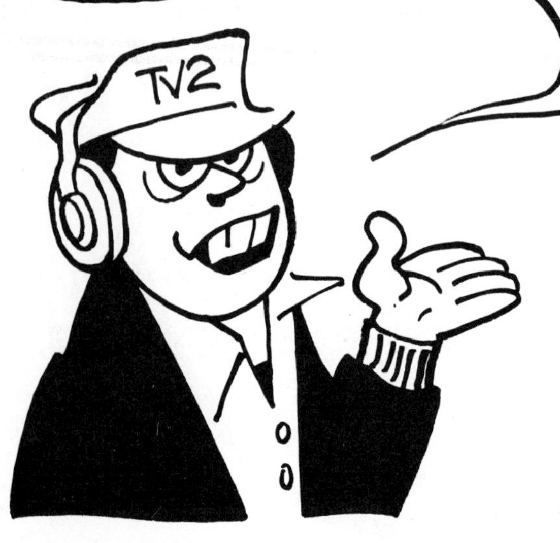

OF COURSE I CAN'T TELL YOU EXACTLY WHAT VIDEO EQUIPMENT YOU SHOULD BUY. IF YOU'RE INTERESTED IN MAKING INTELLIGENT DECISIONS, YOU'LL HAVE TO CONSIDER SEVERAL FACTORS AND WEIGH THEM AGAINST EACH OTHER. THERE MAY BE CERTAIN FEATURES THAT ARE IMPORTANT TO YOU, SUCH AS TAPE LENGTH, SPECIAL EFFECTS, OR HIGH FIDELITY SOUND. ON THE OTHER HAND, THE AVAILABILITY OF PRERECORDED FILMS OR COMPATIBILITY WITH YOUR FRIENDS' VIDEO FORMATS MIGHT BE PARAMOUNT TO YOU.

IF PURE TECHNICAL EXCELLENCE IS YOUR CUP OF TEA, THEN THE TEST CHARTS WE PROVIDE IN THIS BOOK CAN HELP YOU TO COMPARE CAMERAS, RECORDERS AND MONITORS. ALSO USEFUL IN COMPARISON SHOPPING ARE THE **SPECIFICATIONS** PROVIDED BY EQUIPMENT MANUFACTURERS OR VIDEO MAGAZINES. A WORD OF WARNING, HOWEVER: SPECIFICATIONS CAN BE PRESENTED IN SUCH A WAY THAT THEY WILL SEEM TO PROVE WHATEVER THE MANUFACTURER WANTS TO SHOW.

WHEN COMPARING SPECIFICATIONS, READ THE FINE PRINT TO ASCERTAIN THAT THE SAME MEASUREMENTS WERE MADE ON BOTH PIECES OF EQUIPMENT.... **UNDER IDENTICAL CONDITIONS!**

SPECIFICATIONS

APERTURE

A MEASURE OF THE **SPEED** OF THE LENS, OR ITS ABILITY TO ADMIT LIGHT. THE SMALLER THE NUMBER, THE GREATER THE AMOUNT OF LIGHT GATHERED BY THE LENS.

COLOR ACCURACY

THE DEGREE TO WHICH THE EQUIPMENT CAN DISPLAY THE ORIGINAL HUES OF THE COLORS PHOTOGRAPHED.

COLOR PURITY

THE DEGREE TO WHICH A TV, MONITOR, OR CAMERA CAN DISPLAY AN AREA OF COLOR UNCONTAMINATED BY OTHER UNWANTED COLORS

FLUTTER

RAPID VARIATIONS IN TAPE SPEED, IF LARGE ENOUGH, CAUSE A **WARBLING** EFFECT IN THE SOUND. THE GREATER THE AMOUNT OF FLUTTER, THE MORE NOTICEABLE THIS EFFECT WILL BE.

FOCAL LENGTH

THE FOCAL LENGTH OF THE LENS DETERMINES THE RELATIVE MAGNIFICATION OF THE IMAGE IT PROJECTS ON THE CAMERA TUBE. A WIDE-ANGLE LENS HAS A SHORT FOCAL LENGTH, WHILE A TELEPHOTO LENS HAS A LONG ONE. A ZOOM LENS LETS YOU VARY ITS FOCAL LENGTH OVER A SET RANGE.

FREQUENCY RESPONSE:
THE RANGE OF FREQUENCIES THAT A TAPE RECORDER CAN RECORD AND REPLAY IS KNOWN AS ITS FREQUENCY RESPONSE. THE HUMAN EAR HAS A FREQUENCY RESPONSE OF 20 TO 20,000 HERTZ. A TAPE MACHINE WITH A NARROW **AUDIO** FREQUENCY RESPONSE WOULD NOT BE ABLE TO RECORD ALL OF THE HIGH OR LOW FREQUENCY SOUNDS THAT THE EAR CAN HEAR. A RECORDER WITH POOR **VIDEO** FREQUENCY RESPONSE WOULD SUFFER FROM POOR **RESOLUTION**, OR SHARPNESS.

GREYSCALE TRACKING:
THE DEGREE TO WHICH THE CAMERA OR MONITOR CAN DISPLAY SHADES OF GREY WITH **LINEARITY** OR ACCURACY. IF THE EQUIPMENT CAN'T DISPLAY ALL SHADES OF GREY ACCURATELY, ITS GREYSCALE IS **NON-LINEAR.**

HORIZONTAL RESOLUTION

THE ABILITY TO DISPLAY FINE DETAIL IN A PICTURE IS DETERMINED BY THE **RESOLUTION** OF THE EQUIPMENT. EXPRESSED IN **LINES**, THE FIGURE FOR HORIZONTAL RESOLUTION REFERS TO THE MAXIMUM NUMBER OF VERTICAL LINES THE EQUIPMENT IS CAPABLE OF HANDLING **SIMULTANEOUSLY.**

IMPEDANCE:
THE DEGREE TO WHICH ELECTRICAL SIGNALS ARE AFFECTED BY RESISTANCE AND REACTANCE IN A CIRCUIT. WHEN CONNECTING EQUIPMENT TOGETHER, INPUT AND OUTPUT IMPEDANCES SHOULD MATCH AS NEARLY AS POSSIBLE FOR ACCURATE TRANSFER OF SIGNALS.

INSERTION LOSS

AN RF ACCESSORY CONNECTED BETWEEN A SIGNAL SOURCE AND AN INPUT MAY, BY ITS NATURE, CAUSE A REDUCTION IN SIGNAL LEVEL. AS LONG AS THE INSERTION LOSS IS SMALL, THE CORRESPONDING DECREASE IN THE **SIGNAL-TO-NOISE RATIO** WILL BE INSIGNIFICANT.

ISOLATION

WHEN TWO OR MORE SEPARATE ELECTRICAL SIGNALS ARE PROCESSED BY THE SAME PIECE OF EQUIPMENT, AN UNDESIRABLE MIXTURE OF THE SIGNALS MAY OCCUR. AS LONG AS THE **ISOLATION** IS HIGH, THE AMOUNT OF **CROSS TALK**, OR INTERFERENCE BETWEEN THE SIGNALS, WILL BE SMALL.

MINIMUM ILLUMINATION

EXPRESSED IN **LUX** OR **CANDLEPOWER**, THE **MINIMUM ILLUMINATION** SPECIFICATION REFERS TO THE LEAST AMOUNT OF LIGHT THE CAMERA CAN TOLERATE.

OUTPUT

THE LEVEL OF SIGNAL PRESENT AT THE OUTPUT CONNECTOR. THIS IS AN IMPORTANT CONSIDERATION WHEN CONNECTING EQUIPMENT TOGETHER.

SENSITIVITY:

THE LEVEL OF SIGNAL THAT REPRESENTS THE SMALLEST INPUT THAT A PIECE OF EQUIPMENT CAN WORK PROPERLY WITH.

S/N RATIO

THE **SIGNAL-TO-NOISE RATIO** OF A SIGNAL IS A MEASURE OF THE AMOUNT OF **NOISE** IN THE PICTURE OR SOUND (NOISE APPEARS AS SNOW OR GRANULARITY IN VIDEO, AND AS HISS IN AUDIO). EXPRESSED IN **DECIBELS** (db FOR SHORT), A HIGH RATIO (LARGE NUMBER) MEANS LESS NOISE.

THD (TOTAL HARMONIC DISTORTION):

INACCURACY IN THE SHAPE OF THE AUDIO SIGNAL THAT RESULTS FROM PROCESSING BY A PIECE OF EQUIPMENT IS REFERRED TO AS **DISTORTION.** SOME DISTORTION IS LIKELY, BUT LOWER FIGURES FOR DISTORTION MEAN CLEANER, SHARPER SOUND.

VERTICAL RESOLUTION

THE VERTICAL SHARPNESS OF THE PICTURE. EXPRESSED IN **LINES,** THE SPECIFICATION REFERS TO THE MAXIMUM NUMBER OF HORIZONTAL LINES THE EQUIPMENT IS CAPABLE OF DISPLAYING CLEARLY.

WHITE BALANCE:

WHEN THE CAMERA HAS BEEN WHITE-BALANCED, THE DEGREE TO WHICH THE COLOR **WHITE** AS PHOTOGRAPHED IS CONTAMINATED BY AN UNDESIRED COLOR TINT!

WOW

A SLOW VARIATION OF THE PLAYBACK SPEED OF A TAPE MACHINE THAT RESULTS IN GRADUAL AND UNDESIRABLE CHANGES IN THE PITCH OF THE SOUND.

ZOOM RATIO

A RATIO OF THE LONGEST FOCAL LENGTH OF A ZOOM LENS TO ITS SHORTEST FOCAL LENGTH. THE HIGHER THE FIGURE, THE MORE VERSATILE THE LENS IS, AS A GREATER NUMBER OF FOCAL LENGTHS ARE AVAILABLE FOR THE VIDEOGRAPHER TO CHOOSE FROM.

THE TEST PATTERNS

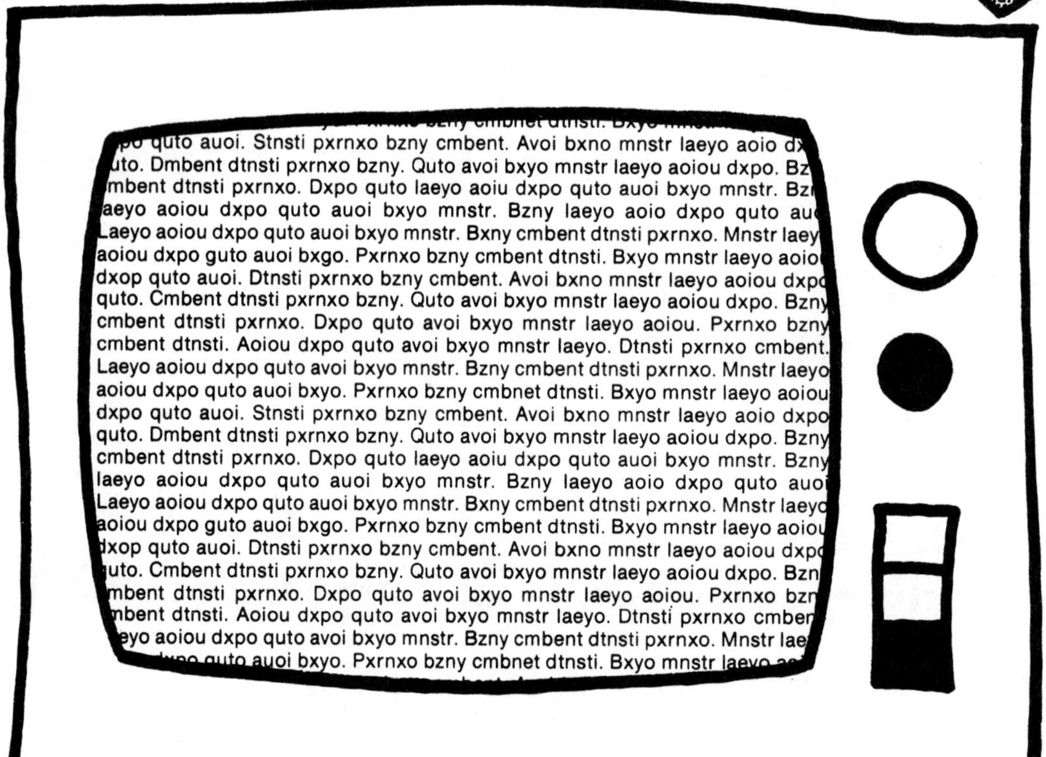

USING THE COLOR BARS

THE COLOR BAR TEST PATTERN IS WIDELY USED IN THE TELEVISION INDUSTRY TO CALIBRATE CAMERAS, RECORDERS, AND OTHER TECHNICAL EQUIPMENT FOR ACCURATE COLOR RENDITION. THE COLOR BARS REPRODUCED ON THE BACK OF THIS BOOK ARE NOT 100% ACCURATE TECHNICALLY, DUE TO THE LIMITS OF THE PRINTING PROCESS. THE PATTERN IS NONETHELESS PERFECTLY ADEQUATE FOR EVALUATING HOME VIDEO EQUIPMENT & RECORDINGS.

FOR OPTIMUM COLOR PLAYBACK OF YOUR WORK, POINT YOUR CAMERA AT THE COLOR BARS AND RECORD ABOUT A MINUTE'S WORTH AT THE BEGINNING OF EACH OF YOUR TAPES. WHEN YOU PLAY BACK ONE OF YOUR TAPES, YOU CAN COMPARE THE BARS ON THE SCREEN WITH THE ORIGINAL BARS ON THE BOOK. ADJUST YOUR TV SET OR MONITOR AS FOLLOWS:

1 FIRST, SET YOUR BRIGHTNESS TO A COMFORTABLE LEVEL, AND SET THE CONTRAST CONTROL TO THE POINT WHERE THE BLACK BAR HAS JUST THE SLIGHTEST AMOUNT OF BRIGHTNESS TO IT!

2 LOOK AT THE COLORS ON THE BOOK AND ADJUST YOUR TINT (OR HUE) CONTROL TO GET THE BARS ON THE SCREEN TO MATCH AS CLOSELY AS POSSIBLE.

3 FINALLY, SET YOUR COLOR (OR SATURATION) CONTROL TO MATCH THE INTENSITY OF THE COLORS TO THE BOOK'S COLORS.

IF THE COLORS REFUSE TO MATCH, IT'S POSSIBLE THE CAMERA DIDN'T COLOR BALANCE VERY WELL AT THE TIME THE BARS WERE PHOTOGRAPHED. WHEN THE **WHITE** BAR APPEARS COLORED, IT'S A SURE SIGN THAT THIS HAS HAPPENED. IF THE COLOR BARS **NEVER** APPEAR RIGHT, IT'S LIKELY THAT EITHER YOUR CAMERA OR YOUR TV NEEDS SOME SERVICE.

IF YOU'D LIKE TO USE THE TEST PATTERN TO EVALUATE DIFFERENT CAMERAS, MAKE SURE YOU SHOOT THE COLOR BARS UNDER THE SAME LIGHTING **(NOT FLUORESCENT LIGHT)**, AND VIEW THE CAMERA ON THE SAME TV SET EACH TIME. NOTE THE ACCURACY OF THE COLORS INTERPRETED BY EACH CAMERA, AND ALSO THE AMOUNT OF **NOISE** IN THE PICTURE. VIDEO "NOISE" WILL USUALLY SHOW UP IN THE COLOR RED FIRST, SO THE **RED** BAR IS A GOOD PLACE TO LOOK FOR A GRANULAR, SNOWY EFFECT.

USING THE RESOLUTION CHART!

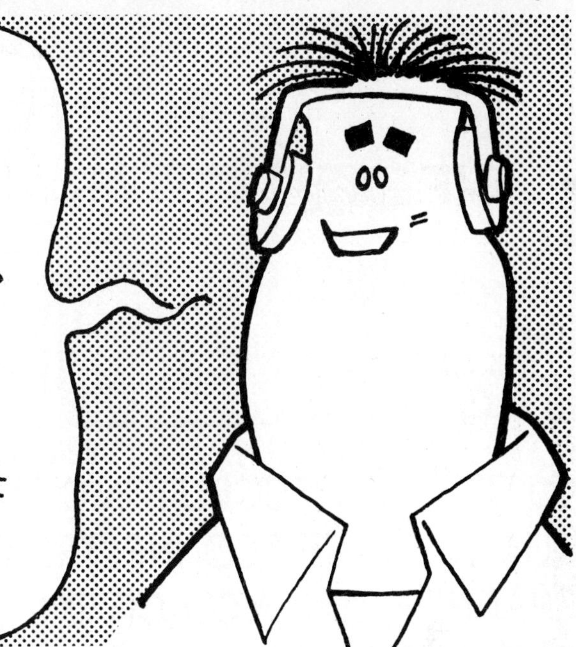

REMEMBER:
THE HIGHER THE NUMBER OF LINES RESOLVED, THE SHARPER THE PICTURE!

MOST HOME CAMERAS, RECORDERS, AND TV SETS HAVE RESOLUTION IN THE 200 TO 300 RANGE, MOST LIKELY RIGHT AROUND THE 250 MARK. SINCE THE VIDEO HAS TO PASS THROUGH CAMERA, RECORDER AND TV BEFORE YOU SEE IT, THE RESOLUTION OF THE WEAKEST PIECE OF EQUIPMENT WILL DETERMINE THE PERFORMANCE OF YOUR SYSTEM!

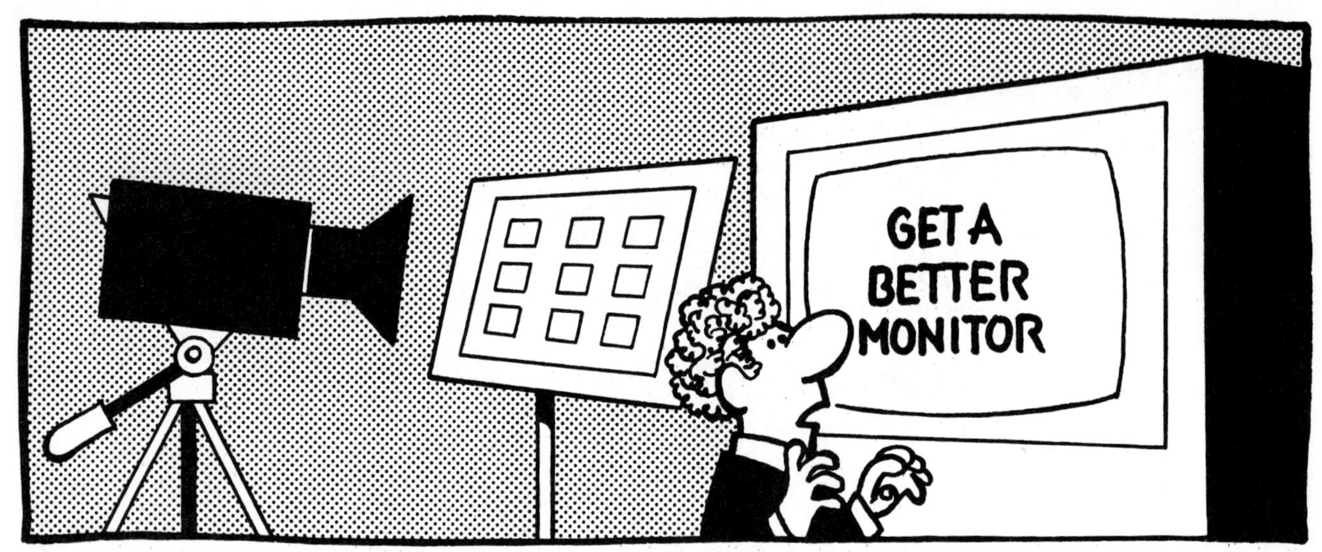

TO USE THE RESOLUTION CHART WITH YOUR CAMERA, HAVE A GOOD QUALITY TV SET CONNECTED (A BLACK AND WHITE SET MAY BE SHARPER THAN A COLOR ONE) OR USE A MONITOR IF YOU'VE GOT ONE. AIM YOUR CAMERA STRAIGHT AT THE CHART (DON'T SHOOT IT AT AN ANGLE) AND ZOOM IN ON THE SMALL BOX IN THE MIDDLE, MAKING SURE TO FOCUS AND CENTER YOUR CAMERA CAREFULLY. NOW, BEGIN TO ZOOM OUT SLOWLY, WHILE WATCHING YOUR MONITOR. AT SOME POINT, THE VERTICAL LINES ON THE TOP HALF OF THE CHART WILL BLUR TOGETHER. WHEN YOU CAN NO LONGER DISTINGUISH THE INDIVIDUAL LINES, WATCH THE TOP OF THE SCREEN. THE NEXT NUMBER THAT APPEARS THERE (AS YOU ZOOM OUT) IS YOUR ***HORIZONTAL RESOLUTION!***

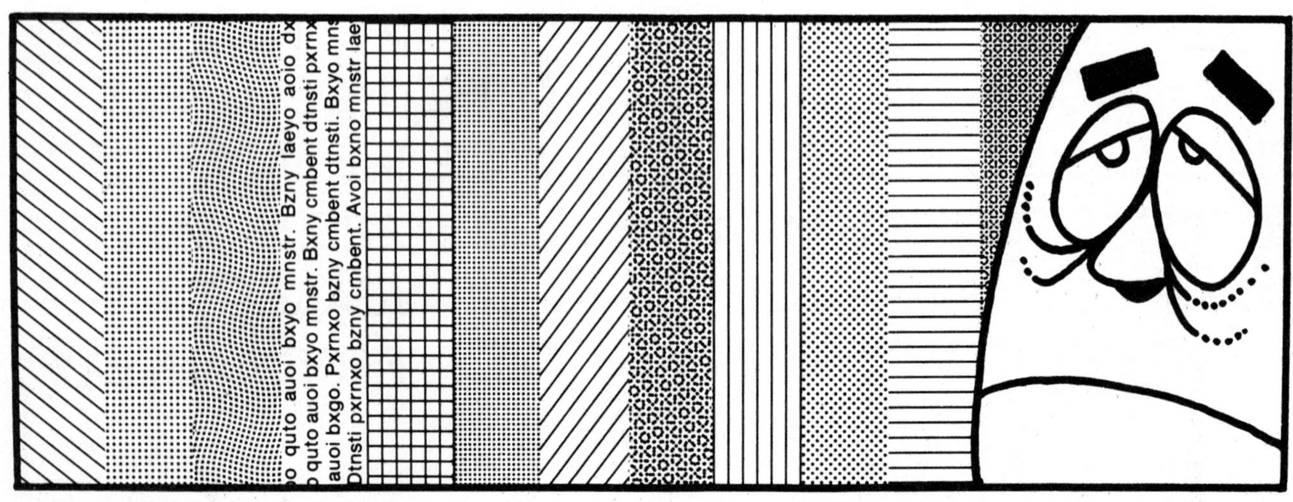

TRY RECORDING THE CHART ON YOUR VCR. IF THE NUMBER YOU GET IS LOWER, YOUR VCR'S RESOLUTION IS LOWER THAN YOUR CAMERA. IF IT'S THE **SAME** NUMBER, YOUR VCR HAS EQUAL OR GREATER RESOLUTION!

THE BOTTOM HALF OF THE CHART WILL MEASURE YOUR VERTICAL RESOLUTION. THIS TIME WATCH THE HORIZONTAL LINES AS YOU ZOOM OUT AND READ YOUR RESULT AT THE BOTTOM OF THE SCREEN!

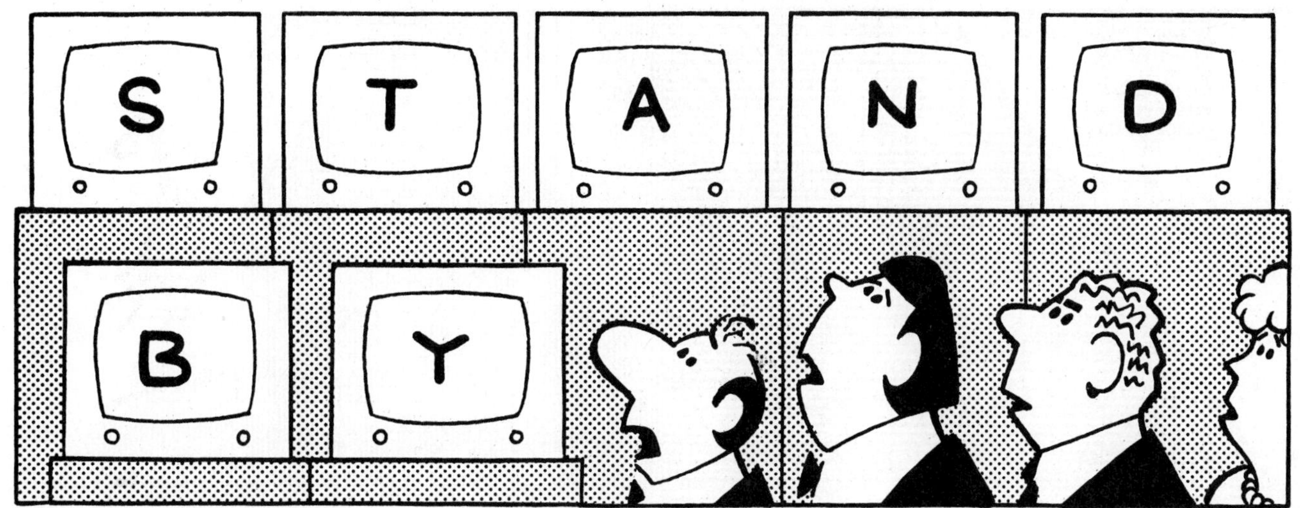

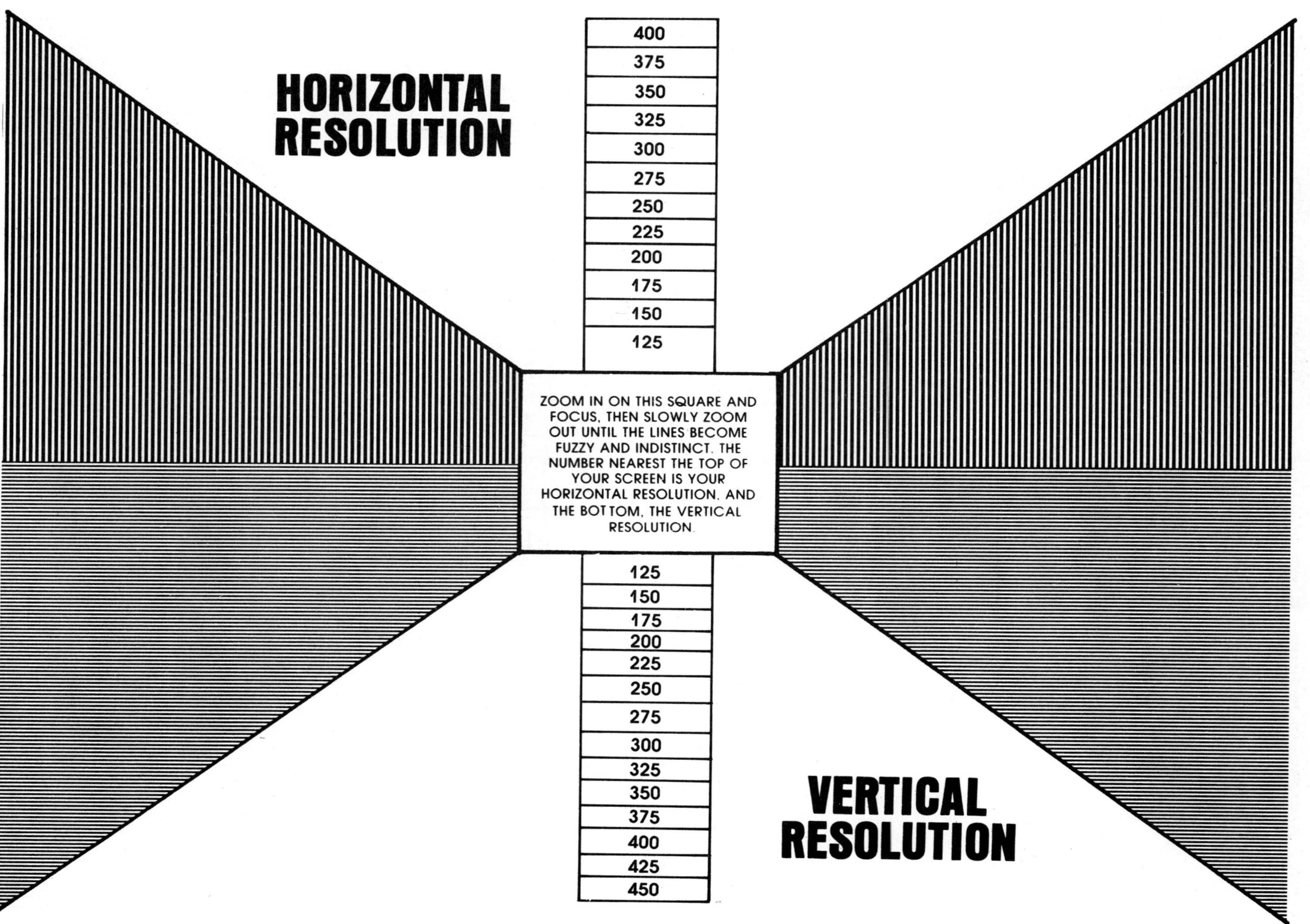

HORIZONTAL RESOLUTION
400
375
350
325
300
275
250
225
200
175
150
125
ZOOM IN ON THIS SQUARE AND FOCUS, THEN SLOWLY ZOOM OUT UNTIL THE LINES BECOME FUZZY AND INDISTINCT. THE NUMBER NEAREST THE TOP OF YOUR SCREEN IS YOUR HORIZONTAL RESOLUTION, AND THE BOTTOM, THE VERTICAL RESOLUTION.
125
150
175
200
225
250
275
300
325
350
375
400
425
450
VERTICAL RESOLUTION

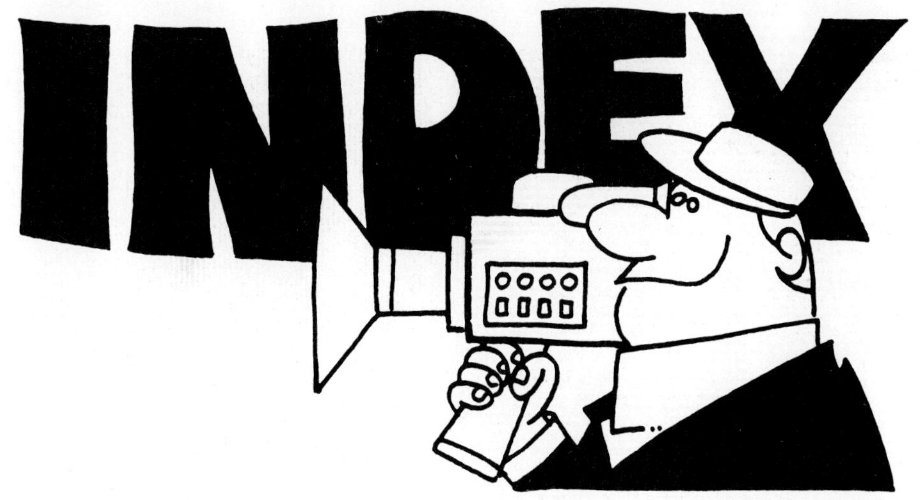

INDEX

A

Animation, 152
Aperture, 22, 209
  Depth of Field, 22
Aspect Ratio, 163
Attenuator, 99, 197, 200
Audio Adaptor, 68
Audio Distortion, 71
Audio Dub, 131, 140, 141, 143, 144, 190
Audio Level, 69, 197
Audio Mixer, 97, 143, 204, 205
Auto-Iris, 15
Automobile, 47

B

Background Noise, 74
Backlighting, 58
BNC Connector, 199
Boom, 40, 42, 44
Brightness Control, 215
Buying Equipment, 207

C

Camera, 6
  Dropping, 52
  Moisture, 51
  Movement, 37, 46-48
  Operating, 11
  On Shoulder, 38
Car Mount, 47
Close-Up, 27, 33, 122
  Attachment, 30
  Composition, 33

Extreme, 35
Color Accuracy, 209
Color Balance, 7, 13, 60, 64, 216
Color Bars, 215
Color Control, 216
Color Processor, 205
Color Purity, 209
Color Temperature, 60
Composition, 31
Computer Graphics, 164, 201, 205
Connecting, 194
Continuity, 129, 133
Contrast, 56
Contrast Control, 215
Contrast Range, 10
Control Signals, 196
Credits, 165
Cueing, 111
Cut-Aways, 132

D

Depth of Field, 21-22, 25-26
  Control, 25
  Focal Length, 22
Din Connector, 199
Disappearances, 151
Dissolves, 146
Distortion, 99, 212
Dolly, 41-44, 48
Dubbing, 196, 202, 205

E

Earphones, 71
Edit Controller, 116

221

SAFE AREA

Everything in this area will be broadcast

9½" x 7"